BORN TWICE

**Memoir of a Special Forces
SOG Warrior**

Praise for *Born Twice*

"Dale Hanson takes us from a northern Minnesota boyhood to the incredible stresses of U.S. special operations during the Vietnam War, the deadly world of MAC-V-SOG, the top-secret Special Forces project that conducted America's Secret War against the Communist forces on the Ho Chi Minh Trail. Shrouded in mystery and equipped with exotic weaponry, SOG operators suffered casualty rates in excess of 100% for three successive years.

Dale Hanson served with Recon Team Florida during one of the legendary missions of SOG, the killing of an enemy colonel who was carrying super-secret documents of enormous importance to the American war effort. After intense fighting, those documents were brought back by the team. Dale survived and went on to serve three tours with the legendary special operations group.

The American heartland can bring forth young men of great valor and commitment, and one such man wrote this book. To read it is to go along on a near-unbelievable story of deadly missions carried out by small Green Beret-led teams operating deep in enemy territory against all but impossible odds."

— **Michael P Buckland**, Special Forces SOG warrior

"At times light hearted and other times deadly serious, this recounting of Dale Hanson's formative upbringing and remarkable combat as a 'Green Beret' is exciting, fascinating reading. We both served as U.S. Army Special Forces recon volunteers, operating deep behind enemy lines on the Ho Chi Minh Trail in Laos, and infiltrating enemy sanctuaries in Cambodia. These were extremely dangerous, top secret operations, which tested Dale's mettle; the Christian values of his youth — integrity, placing others above himself, never shying from hard work and always demanding the very best of himself — shone brightly. Read this book and you'll agree with the Green Berets who knew him: Dale is one of the best."

— **Maj. John Plaster**, Ret. Special Forces, SOG author

"Each time I pick up a book or short story written by Dale Hanson, I know I'm about to read something unique and special. Dale is more than a writer, he is a wordsmith. *Born Twice* takes the reader from the bitterly cold Minnesota winters of his youth to leading a MACV-SOG recon team in the steaming jungles of Southeast Asia. If you want to know what it was like to run reconnaissance missions into denied areas during the Vietnam War, then *Born Twice* is a book you must read."

—**Dennis J. Cummings**, author of
The Men Behind the Trident: SEAL Team One in Vietnam

"Dale Hanson, an accomplished Alaskan novelist and poet, departs from his usual genre to take us on his journey from a young man coming of age in rural Minnesota to maturing as a Special Forces 'Green Beret.' Given the name Kam Baw Ya Chin, meaning 'eternal life, never die' by his Chinese mercenary counterparts in the secret Special Forces projects during the Viet Nam war, after reading some of his near death experiences, this name seems fitting. It may seem contradictory to be at once a committed Christian and a lethal Green Beret, but Dale was and is. Highly recommended."

—**Major John "Doc" Padget**, Special Forces Ret.

"Fifty years after the eight-year secret war ended in Vietnam, well-written non-fiction books by SOG recon men are surfacing. Add *Born Twice* by Dale Hanson — who served three tours of duty during the war — to the growing list of SOG books. Hanson's *Born Twice* is actually a story within a story. He brilliantly sets the stage for being hunted by communist soldiers on the ground in Laos in the dark of night, casually mentioning the damage his fingers sustained following face-to-face combat with three AK-47-firing enemy soldiers. Then he deftly shifts gears, taking you through his childhood in Ojibway country in northern Minnesota and his coming of age before joining the Army. Both aspects of this proud Green Beret's history make for a fascinating read. This isn't his first book and I hope it's not his last."

—**John Stryker Meyer**, author of *Across the Fence: The Secret War in Vietnam, On The Ground* and *SOG Chronicles: Volume One*

Other Titles by Dale Hanson

Haiku: Flowers in the Grass
The Great Catch
The Last White Seal Hunter

Contents

BORN TWICE

Memoir of a Special Forces SOG Warrior

DALE HANSON

Chapter One

That night in 1969 I lay on my belly in the total darkness of the jungle without moving, the detonators of four Claymore mines in my hands, and waited for the Communists to come for us. One of my hands was wrapped in a bloody bandage that had bled and coagulated repeatedly during the day and dried hard into a red cast with just my thumb and the tip of my little finger sticking out. The ends of my fingers were shot off, one knuckle was shot away and another finger hung inside the bandage by a thread of skin. To make up for the measured use of that hand I braced the plungers on a firmness of earth and positioned the heels of my hands on the triggers.

My fingers on my good hand were nervous. "One, two, three, four, one, two, three, four," they counted over and over as they passed across the detonators' plungers, keeping them side by side.

When the time came, I hoped that nothing would be living to my front after I pressed those detonators.

The enemy had a general idea where we might be — the direction of our running firefights, the signal shots of their trackers, and the baying of their dogs that chased us said that much. But we always changed the direction we moved, especially after an encounter, so they did not know

1

for certain where we holed up for the night. But throughout the day they massed large forces into the area to seal us off. We were effectively surrounded as they concentrated troops and ambushes into the area and constricted our movement. When the North Vietnamese could finally fix our location, they would sweep up our hill where it could be our final battle — unless my claymores cut a swath through the assault and we could fight our way through the cordon. We would evade, ambush, and move, over and over until we made it to "friendlies."

If we could not break out, we would fight in place until the end and hope that help could arrive with fire support from our aircraft.

The Communists were scouring every inch of ground, of that I was certain. The previous morning, we had ambushed and killed two North Vietnamese colonels and their escort after a fierce firefight. In our search of their bodies, we found and took a satchel case crammed full of money, top secret orders and documents. We would later learn that the colonels were the highest-ranking enemy ever killed behind enemy lines by a reconnaissance team. We also learned that the information in the satchel bags was the largest intelligence coup by any small unit in the Vietnam War. We were thirty miles behind enemy lines in Cambodia, deep into enemy-denied and controlled territory and we had kicked a hornet's nest. As a result, they martialed all their resources and Recon Team Florida became the focus of an intense manhunt involving thousands of enemy soldiers and trackers with bloodhounds.

I heard a thumping sound.

Was my heart beating so loudly that it could be heard? I held my breath to isolate the sound. I shut my eyes so I could focus only on my ears. I listened. My ears probed the blackness for any sound.

It was a still night and sound carried. Most nights behind the lines, if you listened for it, you could hear a sleeping monkey as it shifted its weight in a tree, or the sighing of brown grass when a barking-deer passed, or the knuckled legs of two bamboo stalks rubbing together as they gave up the moisture of the day. But this night was utterly still.

It seemed that nature held its breath where we were tucked in a grove of bamboo on the side of a hill. I heard a breaking sound like someone moving in the dense undergrowth, then realized that it came from a length of bamboo that popped with the temperature change of the night. Would the searching enemy think it came from us? A seasoned tribesman would have shushed the searching soldiers nearby and said, "No, no, bamboo pop. No soldier do."

When I could no longer hold my breath, I let it out as easily as I could and the passing air seemed loud to me. I shut my eyes again and listened. Dry grass rustled nearby, a long continuous shushing in the weeds. A snake was hunting for prey. Even a cobra was more welcome than an enemy point man closing in.

I continued to listen.

I heard the drone of an engine, faint and far away, and I hoped it was our spotter airplane coming to check on us before leaving for the night so we could advise him of our situation and perhaps get a gunship to circle nearby.

But the sound did not pass over us, instead the pitch of the engine changed like a burdened truck downshifting for a change in grade. From over the shoulder of a nearby ridge a faint glimmer of light, like a quarter moon shows long before it crests the horizon, indicated that a truck was coming toward the stand of bamboo where we hid.

Unbeknownst to us, a finger of the Ho Chi Minh Trail — that vital lifeline that the Communists built to carry their soldiers and supplies to the war in South Vietnam — lay below us from left to right. The intervening hills and thick vegetation muted the sound of the engines as they drove across our front.

I heard the thumping sound again. This time I knew that it was not my heartbeat. There were several muffled thumps across our front far down the slope. The engines stopped and many thumping sounds followed. They were very faint and far away, but they were there. At the end, I heard a dull clank of metal. Even from a distance I knew it was a tailgate.

I could imagine hundreds of soldiers in their yellow-green uniforms leaping from the truck beds and lining the ditches along the road, waiting for the command to sweep up the hillside.

I heard the muffled woof of a dog and I remembered the grey, long-legged ones we saw earlier in the day before we left powdered CS (tear gas) in our back trail for them to sniff up their noses and ruin them for a time.

Three of us Special Forces Green Berets and four Vietnamese that we trained made up our team and we readied ourselves for a fight of desperation. There was a light tap on my shoulder then a whole hand grasped my shoulder. We could not see each other in the dark so he placed his mouth at my ear.

"Han-Son, Han-Son. VC come. *Beaucoup* VC." Many enemy soldiers are coming.

I patted his arm twice in the darkness to let him know that I heard it too. I turned and tapped the Viet on the other side of me with the back of my wounded hand so it would not start to bleed again. I could feel him nod his head and he shifted his weight over his weapon.

I aligned the detonators side by side again and counted them, "One, two, three, four."

We listened and we heard nothing. Nothing at all.

None of us in our little recon team moved. Our people did not thrust their rifles farther forward to be ready to shoot. None of them piled grenades in front of them. We were frozen, listening, waiting people.

Not a sound.

Had the enemy changed its mind and decided to not sweep our hill? Were they waiting for us to come down in the morning where they sat in ambush?

Perhaps I expected a whistle to sound from below and muted commands and then the crashing of hundreds of feet through the undergrowth as they moved toward us. There was none.

Nothing.

A half hour. An hour. Nothing stirred to our front. I was prepared to let exhaustion have its way and doze with the plungers cradled in my hands.

I snapped awake. I heard a soft breaking of twigs in the distance to the right. Did I imagine it?

"It could be an animal," I thought. But as I listened there were other sounds across the front. Several creatures were moving on line with stealth toward us.

I remembered the tracking hounds they had used on us earlier. They would be among them. But for them, the Communists might sweep through without finding us.

I began to pray, "Lord plug the noses of those dogs."

My fingers began to count the plungers again: "One, two, three, four...."

Chapter Two

I was born on the old "war road" of the Red and Roseau rivers that the Sioux Indians used in their invasion of Ojibway country in northern Minnesota. The Sioux came in scores of war canoes and waged fierce battles to seize the wild rice fields of the shallow shores of Lake of the Woods for the victors' privilege of sliding canoes through the rice stalks and tapping their hulls full of rice.

The Sioux always came at harvest after the Ojibway had waited the full season and the rice was doubly precious — for its own worth and for the price of blood with which it was taken.

Northern Minnesota was fierce for its cold winters and for the fierceness of the Sioux who came in their seasons. Settler farmers who dared to homestead on the prairies faced both challenges. Some of the great Indian battles in North America were not just with the Apache, Comanche, Blackfeet or the Flathead Indians, and they were not fought only in Texas or Arizona, or at Custer's Little Big Horn. The Sioux Massacre was one great Indian war that wiped out scores of homesteads in Minnesota and into the Dakotas.

The armistice of that war was not scribed on parchment paper but written indelibly on a massive scaffold in which thirty-eight Sioux were hung en masse at Mankato, Minnesota.

Over time the wars ended and blood was no longer spilled for wild rice. Farmers settled the area and a small farm town with its own hospital was built on the site and war road became the town of Warroad.

It was in this place that I was born, on Sunday, Easter morning, 1947. At that time of year, the ice that remained on the lake then was not safe and the talk of the day might have been, "If you have not removed your fishing house off the lake, you best leave it." Patches of snow yet remained in the deep forest but the grass on the hospital lawn was becoming green and flowers were beginning to bloom.

The Roseau River, which was the "war road" of invasion, crested, overflowed its banks, and began to flood. In scattered fields tractors were stranded wheel deep in mud and soggy soil. That Easter morning, church bells pealed across the fields and streets of the little town, and the faithful went to church to celebrate the resurrection of Jesus Christ. Little girls wore new, frilly, white dresses, and boys wore bowties and their hair was slicked and combed with one unruly strand of hair rooster-tailed up the back.

It was then in the delivery room of Warroad Hospital that I met my mother. My father was Alfred Hanson, a tall, dark, Hollywood handsome Scandinavian, and it is said that the first words out of my father's mouth were, "I can't wait to take him hunting."

When we were discharged from the hospital my father brought us to our home twelve miles down the road near the tiny town of Roosevelt, Minnesota. It was a primitive affair. My dad must have reasoned, "It is good enough for now. It is all that one person could accomplish in the short time since the war." Only my dad would not have used a big word like "accomplish." It was livable because what little was on the tiny farm was functional.

Our place was not unlike Dad's own father's had been on the prairie. Grandpa was Sigurd Hanson and he began a family in a sod house in the Dakota Territory, married a Metis maiden (French-Indian) and began his family with no modern conveniences. As a boy, I remember listening to him talk of those hard times and the winter storms, and swelter of summer, and drought and snakes and how sand and dust constantly fell from the sod ceiling into their hair and food, and how smallpox came and took his wife and two children.

My dad told me that when Grandpa's family died out there on the prairie, he packed up and left it all. He loaded his wagon with his tinner-tools and he and his horse made their way east across the plains repairing pots and pans at the various homesteads until one day he saw Grandma and thought she looked mighty good and said, "This is a good place to stop."

They had eight children: a daughter and seven sons. Four of the sons were in World War Two, and two fought in Korea. One was in an all Norwegian-American ski regiment slated to jump into Norway and fight the Nazis but was plugged into the Battle of the Bulge to stop the hemorrhaging there and was horribly wounded. My mom lost a brother in that same battle.

My dad had spent the whole war in the Pacific against the "Japs," from the beginning before "Pearl," all the way to the very end. His army regiment was attached to the marines for the big battles, and his battle stars showed that he fought in Iwo Jima, Guadalcanal, Tinian and Kwajalein. Dad was a crack shot and they found out that he was color blind for blue and green. Rather than be a disqualifier, they discovered that he could see through camouflage. Dad relied on shapes, outlines, and straight lines; painting things green was to no avail in that. In effect he was a Pacific theater Special Forces soldier who worked far behind the lines and found the lurking enemy.

When his war ended, he went to "Ag" school and studied agriculture. He got a quarter section of land and began to carve out a farm by hand. There was no time for him to build a home in any finished sense — he built shelter, adequate for the time being.

He cleared the trees by digging deep below the ground and cutting the roots before toppling them over, root ball and all. What did not come out with the tree was set afire and the soil often smoldered in the ground for years where it contained peat. I remember seeing the smoke seeping through the snow in winter, the area around the place melted to the soil and the smell of burning peat drifting over the house.

To have it be a functioning homestead it required that everything be ready at once — a well, fences, a barn, chicken coops, garden, land cleared for use, and a place in which to live. He did it all with hand tools by himself. When he married my mother, it was adequate, "good enough for now."

Our house was a small single-story affair sheathed with black tarpaper, walls and roof, with strips of lath nailed over the tarpaper to keep wind from tearing it away. In those first four years of my life, we never had electricity, indoor plumbing or running water.

Our water came from a well that was dug near the gate of the fence. I remember with utter clarity, about the time I learned to walk, my dad taking me to its black mouth.

"Dale, I want you to know that this is our well and I don't want you to wander over here and fall in, not knowing that it is here. If you fell in, we would never get you out in time. This is where we get our water with that bucket. There are shelves along the side where we keep our milk and butter and cheese.

"Listen," he said as he showed me a large stone and dropped it into the blackness. It seemed a long time before the sound of the splash come back to us. "Never come here without us. Do you hear?"

He waited for me to say I would never venture near its open mouth, and he covered it with its lid.

God apparently gave me a good mind because I vividly recall things about those times that the experts say one cannot recall at so young an age. I remember when they got a crib so I would no longer be in my parents' bed. I was terrified of the dark and I remember holding on to those vertical side slats like a prisoner does in the bars of the big house and crying and crying.

I remember learning to eat with a spoon and how I placed the food on it correctly, but it always tipped before it got to my mouth. And how I finally learned to put a shirt on by myself.

My mom canned vegetables and deer meat and today I can still taste the flavor of that venison of long ago.

I had a toy tractor that I kept under the edge of the house out of the rain and played with it in the sand of the drive. I remember the charge of fear and electricity that shot through my nervous system as I reached for it one morning and a garden snake that was coiled on its warmth exploded in a flurry of movement. I gasped and recoiled in fear. In the mornings thereafter I would spank the area with a stick to chase away any lurking snakes and I would prove the area before I reached for my toy.

I remember pulling the coffee pot from the counter and scalding myself and shrieking in pain.

There were two other occurrences of those times that I recall only in the vaguest of detail.

Mom washed our clothes by hand in a large tub and washboard, scrubbing the items back and forth on the metal ribs. She had one luxury before she hung the clothes on the line: Dad had a motor that would spin a set of ringers to squeeze the water out of the clothes. They looked like two rolling pins, and she would place the clothes between those spinning wood pins. The pins would grab the clothing, which came out the other side, flat and damp.

Just as she was bending over to get another piece of laundry, I grabbed one and started it through — but my hand caught in the rollers and pulled my arm in all the way to the elbow where it could go no farther, and it ground into my flesh. Mom screamed and frantically pulled on my arm until the blood no longer gave her purchase. It was only then she thought to trip off the motor.

The other event of significance was that I wandered off from the homestead and was the subject of a manhunt for "the lost little Hanson boy." I recall pushing my metal tractor down the sandy furrow of the drive away from the clapboard house. Mom had turned her head for a moment and when she looked up, I was gone. My bare footprints were in the sand, but the paw prints of a bear followed in the same rut.

The word went out at Oseid's Grocery Store and the post office of the little town. Family and friends scoured the woods and area, shouting my name and moving on line. They searched all the way to the main road. When they found nothing, they returned to the house to begin again only to find me back at the steps playing with my toy.

My mom hated farm life, especially the harsh north country with no bustle or people. She was a country girl who left the farm after the mandatory eighth grade and went to Minneapolis, the big city, and from there spent the war working on the construction sites as they built the Alaska Highway. Her dislike for the loneliness and the poverty of the times won out in time, and I recall the day when Dad and Uncle Walt piled their two families in a 1930-era coupe automobile and headed for International Falls for work and a new life. My place among the bodies and luggage was to lay across the bench of the rear window for the hundred-mile trip.

"How long now, Dad?' I kept saying from my cramped place.

"Soon, Dale. Pretty soon," I heard over and over.

"The Falls," as the locals called our town, is the northernmost town of the continental United States and is the coldest town in the lower forty-eight states. If you look at a map of the United States and see where the lines of latitude cross our town, you will find that thirty percent of Canada is south of International Falls. Maine and Washington State are three hundred miles south of us.

Rainy River was the boundary that demarked Ontario, Canada from our part of Minnesota. On that river was the huge waterfall for which our town was named. It was the source of power for the community and for the paper and pulp mill that was the chief employer in the area. The waterfall was massive and violent and churned below where it fell on the rocks and then boiled into dangerous rapids below it. Logging and logging camps dotted the maps of our county.

Dad got work in the wood-room of the mill and got a mortgage on the house where my little brother and I grew up. We were in "the sticks" and just outside the town and lacked a few "town comforts." We had electricity but no running water or indoor plumbing for many years.

Clifford Pettis delivered water to us from his tanker truck for fifty cents a barrel. He was short with a large, round, solid-looking belly. He had black bushy eyebrows and his lower lip protruded and curled like the lid of a sardine can. He never smiled or spoke unless he had to, especially to us kids who watched the barrel fill up with his clear, clean water — watched it fill on tip toe with our fingers hooked on the rim. It would fill to the top, on the very edge of running over. I loved the smell of its freshness, and we watched the air bubbles float to the top and burst, releasing the smell of the "land of sky-blue waters."

"There, you can tell yer ma that I filled it to the very top. See?" he would say as he shut off the nozzle at the end of the hose.

I could visualize her checking to see that Clifford gave her the full fifty cents worth.

And, further, I could see Clifford Pettis in my mind chuckling to himself, imagining my mother trying to scoop out those first dippers full of water without spilling any over the rim. He would hover over the steering wheel with both hands at the top as he drove away — his cigarette hanging, stuck on his protruding lower lip, falling ash greying his dirty shirt.

Mom's other enemy and nemesis was Maston's field, across the road from us — a half section of empty field that Mr. Maston constantly plowed and disked but never planted a single time. Killdeer birds ran along the furrows for exposed bugs and worms, their whiteness contrasted to the black soil. Year after year the field was worked but no seed ever made its way through the dirt.

Mom swore that Maston waited for her to hang her wash on the clothesline and for the wind to be just right before he would start his tractor. Back and forth he passed, furrow after furrow and the black dust would rise behind the plow and drift over to our yard and her wet white sheets.

Our next-door neighbors were Osmer and Ada Pettis. How they ever had a son like Clifford I will never know. Osmer and Ada were the finest, nicest people I ever knew — especially Grandma Ada.

Osmer was a white man, huge with white hair under a grey brimmed hat. Every morning he stepped out on his back porch and made one very loud cough. "Aaah-haa!" It could be heard all over the neighborhood. It was only twenty feet from my mom's bedroom window that he would let out his sneeze and my mom always would say, "I hate that man."

Ada was a tiny thing. I think she was Sioux because Osmer told me that they got married where Sitting Bull was killed. Ada was always

Born Twice

"Grandma Pettis," and we loved her. She weighed about ninety pounds and always wore her coal-black hair up in a bun except at bedtime and prayer time when she let it cascade down her back.

My brother and I would charge over to their house in the morning just to be with them. Grandma Pettis would be ironing clothes for example. She had three irons heating on the wood stove. She would dip her finger in a glass of water, sprinkle it on the cloth, and she would iron until that one got cool and she would replace it on the stove and grab another that was hot. All the while she would smile and sing in her old lady voice:

> *My Jesus, I love Thee, I know Thou art mine,*
> *For Thee all the follies of sin I resign.*
> *My gracious Redeemer, my Savior art Thou*
> *If ever I loved Thee my Jesus 'tis now.*

Osmer would be sitting at their dining table with the red and white checkered tablecloth about to have breakfast as she ironed. It would be with ceremony that he placed a single boiled egg into a metal egg holder. He would bow his head in a prayer of thanks and then would tap the shell around it and carefully lift the eggshell from the white inside. With a spoon he slowly consumed the egg. Breakfast was a single egg, and we did not know that this household was one of poverty.

And Grandma Pettis would continue to iron her clothes and sing the next stanza in her tired voice that was full of love:

> *I love Thee because Thou has first loved me*
> *And purchased my pardon on Calvary's tree*
> *I love Thee for wearing the thorns on Thy brow*
> *If ever I loved Thee my Jesus 'tis now*

And Grandma would replace her cold iron with a new hot one from the stove, sprinkle the cloth, and iron the wrinkles of life from Osmer's work clothes.

> *I'll love Thee in life, and I will love Thee in death*
> *And praise Thee as long as Thou lendest me breath*
> *And say when the death dew lies cold on my brow*

If ever I loved Thee my Jesus 'tis now.

My brother and I would sit in chairs around her ironing board and watch her as she worked. "Who is Jesus?" one of us would ask. Her eyes seemed to mist over and with a voice that seemed on the very edge of weeping, she would smile so much her Indian cheeks nearly closed her eyes and tell us.

"Jesus is God, and he made the world and us, but man turned their backs on him and we became sinners and separated from him. But he loved us so much that he came to die on the cross for our sins."

She would look at us as we watched her and softly say. "I will teach you little by little."

Their place next to us was a tiny homestead out of the 1880s. It was a tiny log house whose logs were bleached as grey as the clouds and cement was chinked between the logs. It was one story and consisted of four rooms — a kitchen, living room and two small bedrooms.

Grandma had parakeets and canaries that were her company when Osmer did chores. She talked to them, and they cocked their heads and the canary sang with his chest out and throat full of notes. I never heard a bird sing so loudly. It seemed to sing just for them.

It was some years later that I read a poem about a man with a wooden leg and the bird in the poem reminded me of Grandma Pettis' bird.

> *There was a man lived quite near us;*
> *He had a wooden leg and a goldfinch in a green cage.*
> *His name was Farkey Anderson,*
> *And he'd been in a war to get his leg.*
> *We were very sad about him,*
> *Because he had such a beautiful smile*
> *And was such a big man to live in a very small house.*
> *When he walked on the road his leg did not matter*
> *So much.*
> *But when he walked in his little house*
> *It made an ugly noise.*
> *Little Brother said his goldfinch sang the loudest of*
> *All birds,*

So that he should not hear his poor leg
And feel too sorry about it.

Osmer had a small log barn just behind the house and two huge, black work horses. Osmer would curry them with his brush and talk to them as he worked. They were immense to me, and I could not fathom how a creature of such strength could be made to obey a weaker man. I lifted a harness from the wall. "What is this?" I asked.

"That goes over their backs and those strings keep the flies off them."

I held up another piece of tackle.

"That, Dale, is the bridle. This goes into their mouth and this loops over their neck so I can steer them."

"What is that part of the harness for?"

"Those are called blinders. It keeps the horse looking ahead for the work it needs to do. It does not get distracted looking side to side."

Mr. Pettis looked at me and continued. "It also keeps the horse from looking over at his mate to see if it is pulling its load. It is only important that the horse does its own duty."

I do not know if Mr. Pettis was trying to teach me a lesson in life or not, but my young mind filed it away and I never forgot it.

They had pigs and chickens and a mean rooster. One day I intruded into the fence and the rooster attacked me and I must have screamed because it attacked my face with its hind claws. Mr. Pettis came running with an axe and killed it on a stump on the spot.

"That'll teach you," he shouted as he tossed the dead rooster into the air and it cartwheeled in the air spinning, black and talon-yellow, and splattering red.

My brother and I often overnighted with them. Osmer would lay his hat on a chair and Ada would let her hair cascade down her back and they would be on their knees at the bedside, praying every night. They taught us to pray:

Now I lay me down to sleep,
I pray thee Lord my soul to keep.
If I should die before I wake,
I pray thee Lord my soul to take.

15

If I should live for other days,
I pray thee Lord to guide my ways.
Amen.

Sometimes when I would thus say my prayers I would add at the end, "Oh, and bless Mom and Dad too." It was with this postscript that I began to actually pray.

Osmer and Ada would then begin to pray, and it seemed to go on and on to us. When they had finished, we boys went to the living room and Osmer would slide two easy chairs, front to front for a bed with sides and we slept in peace before the Junger stove and sleeping birds.

We rushed over to their house one morning after breakfast as we always did. Mr. Pettis was about to eat his breakfast —a single slice of white bread on a plate. Grandma went over to him and poured some milk on the bread to soak it and Mr. Pettis prayed and ate that which was his meal.

There was a knock on the door and a small Indian lady came in crying with a black eye.

"Did so and so do that to you, Sally?"

She nodded her head as she sobbed and tried to tell Grandma what happened.

I don't know if the lady was a daughter or not. She was small and dark like Ada. Osmer and Ada were Salvation Army back in the days when they were about salvation and church, and feeding people was secondary. In those days Salvation Army bands played on the street corners with their drums and horns and accordions and the preacher preached under the streetlight. Someone was coming to Ada for help, and we had the sense to leave for home and give them privacy.

We were too young to read yet and could not read the Bible for ourselves, but we learned to respect it as the basis of truth. Grandma Pettis said it would be good for us to go to Sunday school and learn more about God. They always had to catch a ride from someone and wouldn't be able to always take us, but Mrs. Phakalides next door could. They were Baptist and their church was faithful to the Bible. So, my brother and I went to First Baptist from then on.

Chapter Three

Every Sunday morning my little brother and I dressed and combed our hair and walked down the gravel road to Mrs. Phakalides' house for our ride to church. Their place was the next house past Grandma Pettis, and it was everything that the little log house was not. It was a modern, spacious house of a sort one would expect the owners of "People's Café" to have. We would climb the six cement steps to the front door and knock and clean our shoes on the outside rug and sit in the deep chairs to wait for the taxi to arrive. The furnishings were expensive, and the wood and porcelain were dust-free and polished to a shine. They had a piano and there were white doilies with flowers in a vase on them. Beautiful rugs covered the oak floors and silenced the hard soles of our shoes when we charged into the living room.

They had a large radio with beautiful sound, the face of which was shaped like the stained glass window of our church. We must have taken our places in the soft chairs at the same time each week because the "Back to the Bible Broadcast" would begin its program on the air when we walked in and the theme music would play. "I love to tell the story of Jesus and his love, of Jesus and glory and Jesus and his love," and the announcer would cut in with the program of the day. I loved the music, and we would listen until the taxi honked outside and Mrs. Phakalides put on her coat and rushed us out like so many chicks.

Sunday school at the church always began in the auditorium with everyone there. We would sing a song and then be dismissed to our classes. The teachers would teach a lesson often acted out by figures or puppets or by following the pictures in a book. We did crafts that illustrated the lessons. My mind devoured the stories and I memorized verses and anecdotes without even trying to do so.

Like any child, I loved the stories of David, and Daniel in the lion's den, and the Three Hebrew Children in the fiery furnace, and Moses, and Abraham, and those about the life of Jesus. In each of them I learned truths by which to live. I imagined as we went home, what it must have been like to face Goliath as a young boy. I marveled at David's courage and considered what it was that gave him this confidence.

I learned about Jesus and salvation. I understood then, but only with my mind.

It was late spring. The snow berms were gone from our main street. For months they were piled so high in a long mound down the middle of the street that when I was in the back seat of Dad's car, I could not see over them to see the buildings on the other side of the street. It was late enough toward spring that when we left for church that morning, we did not need to burrow into winter clothes. During the service some ladies pulled their coats over their shoulders but in all, the biting cold of winter was gone but its lingering chill remained.

I could not read yet so I could not follow the words of the hymns, but I felt a part of the singing anyway. All around me people sang together. I heard Mr. Morris' deep voice behind me and Mrs. Carew's soprano off to the side. "Amazing grace, how sweet the sound, that saved a wretch like me. I once was lost but now am found, was blind but now I see."

The pastor's prayer seemed to go on and on. For a while I followed it all — "Bless Mrs. Martin in the hospital... traveling mercies for the Finsteads." I peeked and saw that all heads were bowed. "And be with our soldiers in Korea as they fight the enemy there and keep them safe."

I listened as attentively as I could. I was five years old.

Pastor Weins approached the pulpit slightly bent over as though burdened with a task before him. He held his Bible open with both hands as he walked to the stand and reverently placed it on the top and smoothed the pages down with his fingers.

I was on the aisle of a pew and could see him as he began. He did not look up at his congregation at first and I could see the top of his head. It was parted in the middle with hair cream and had a wave in it. He had thick glasses and wore a dark suit and white shirt and tie. I was close enough to him that I could see the faint pinstripe in the blue of his coat.

He announced his text with a somber voice and began to speak with a voice that sought out and entered every crevice in the church to ensure that every ear was listening. The voice was one of power and conviction. It might have belonged to Moses when he came down from Sinai and saw the golden calf and demanded, "What do you think you are doing?" Or it could have belonged to Nathan the prophet when he confronted King David as he pointed his crooked prophet finger at him and said, "Thou art the man."

The preacher had not been looking at his audience and at times seemed to shout at his papers. But though his eyes lacked contact with his people, he had contact with Heaven that morning.

He placed one finger on a single word in his text and the finger seemed to shake and it moved up his arm and body and finally out of his mouth. And he took that word and unfolded it for his people, and it was like an origami illustrating a concept to his flock.

I was very young but felt the earnestness with which he spoke, and I knew that what he said was a thing of great importance.

I was too young to start school but not too young to listen to that earnest man who seemed to pour out his heart. I listened intently and at the end of his message to his invitation to his people:

"Brothers and sisters you must stand today on the bridge of decision, and you peer down at the churning waters of sin and you dive off that bridge in faith and die to yourself and come up alive to newness of life."

I must have been stunned at what he said for I do not recall finding Mrs. Phakalides or the taxi ride home or the rest of the day.

I was five years old.

That week I wrestled with the message that Pastor Weins gave. Like being lost in a forest, I was lost among the beautiful metaphors and illustrations that were designed to show simple truths. I knew that I wanted to be a Christian but was more confused than ever. To be on the bridge of decision and gazing at the churning waters of sin below and diving off the bridge in faith and believing that I would live again was a concept that I took literally. My five-year-old mind did not separate the two.

I remembered a picture in Grandma Hanson's living room on the farm. It was a tall bridge scene from her village in Sweden. She kept it there to remind her of where she was raised and her family in the "old country" that she dearly missed. The picture was in black and white, and the scene was stark and death-like with its lack of real-life color. There were no green trees or colored flowers or blue eyes and pink faces — all was stark and dead like the white cold of winter which we had just endured.

I had a nightmare one night. I was standing on the bridge in the picture and the wind was cold and bitter against my face and I was shivering. For a time, I did not dare look down at the boiling water that slammed against the hard black rocks, but I could plainly hear them. I was on the railing. This was not a thing of suicide for the point was not death but life to me in my limited understanding. It was acting on that which I believed. Everything was up to me. Slowly I looked down, and I woke up.

Midweek, I played marbles in the driveway where the snow and ice had melted away. We played "chase" and our marble play sent my marble under the edge of snow at the ditch. I could hear the trickling of the melt below the snow, and it gathered momentum and loudness as it neared the ditch and the runoff. "Today is Thursday," I thought, "Three more days until Sunday."

Born Twice

Perhaps it was at the waterfall where we cross Rainy River into Canada where it would happen. I remembered stopping with my parents when we paused at Customs one time. I looked through the chain link fence at the enormity of it all, the long drop to the rocks below, the splash that carried the smell of the cold water all the way to our nostrils, my mom shouting over the roar of the falls, "Don't get too near the fence, Dale."

Perhaps it was here that they would take me after church, and it would happen.

The pastor's sermon was a blur to me. I hardly heard a word of it. He preached with the same earnestness of the week before — like a prophet of old. He looked at his people more that week — more like a shepherd counting his sheep, checking for lameness and wounds. He had black hair and dark eyes. He was not an old man — just older than my father and dignity was his mantle.

I tried to listen to his words but could only concentrate on the decision that I had made.

The pastor finished his sermon and walked around the pulpit to the front of the stage with a songbook in his hand. "And if you need help or have made a decision today, I invite you to come as we sing together.

The congregation sang and I could not see over the standing adults to the pastor.

Just as I am without one plea, but that Thy blood was shed
for me
And that Thou bid'st me come to Thee, O Lamb of God,
I come, I come.
Just as I am, though tossed about, with many a conflict,
many a doubt
Fighting and fears within without, O Lamb of God, I
come, I come.

I walked down the aisle to the preacher who seemed bewildered at this little boy who came at his invitation. He thought I was a child who had gotten away from his parents that morning. He looked down at me.

"Son, what can I do for you today?"

"Pastor, I am ready to have you throw me off the bridge."

He seemed bewildered as he looked at me. "I don't understand. What do you mean, son?"

"I'm ready to have you throw me off the bridge. What you said last week. I am ready. I want to be a Christian. I believe that I will die to myself and in faith come up alive."

The pastor got down on one knee to better see me. He put one arm over my shoulder.

"I wore my old clothes so we could do it today."

He pulled off his glasses and gazed into my own and then he smiled.

"I understand, son." And he called to his wife, "This young man would like to know how to be a Christian. Will you show him?"

His wife came to me and took me by the hand, and we walked to the nursery room where you could see the service through the window as the congregation sang the third verse:

> *Just as I am, and waiting not to rid my soul of one dark blot*
> *To thee whose blood can cleanse each spot, O Lamb of*
> *God, I come, I come.*

And the pastor's wife, a thin lady with yellow hair and glasses, sat beside me in one of those tiny red chairs that toddlers use, and explained the Bible plan of salvation. As Jesus said, "I came to him as a little child," and I asked Jesus to come into my heart and I became a Christian that morning. As Jesus said to Nicodemus, I was "born again."

That morning when I stepped down those stairs of the church to wait for Mrs. Phakalides and the taxi, I did not feel the steps beneath my feet. I felt like I was floating just above them. Something real had happened to me, and I knew in my soul I was Heaven bound. The rest of my life would be met on the basis that I was a Christian, and the values and principles of the Book would be the ultimate guide of my life. I discovered also that I would be prepared to risk all, even my life on that which I believed.

Chapter Four

I mentioned that Grandma Pettis' log home had four rooms, two of them being bedrooms. My brother Del and I really never saw the inside of the second bedroom. From the doorway we had the impression of a large bed in the dark interior and a few furnishings but that was the extent of our exploration.

It seemed that room was in readiness for someone, a refuge just waiting for a return and that all was just as they had left it before. Perhaps one of their children grew up there, studied their schoolbooks beside a soot covered lantern and slept in that space. It was like the prodigal's father in the gospels with the fatted calf and ring and robe in readiness, and the father constantly looking down the road for his return. It seemed that the room was prepared, the bed made, slippers set at the side. Only the covers needed to be turned down.

I think Grandma stored some things in the space close to the doorway because one morning she asked me if our Ma used the cloth from the flour sacks to make clothes. Meal and flour sacks were printed with many patterns on the cloth just for that. She went inside that bedroom where she kept her metal flour can and brought out several different folds of cloth.

"I am looking for more cloth of this pattern. It takes more than one sack to make a shirt. I haven't seen more of this one in the grocery store."

"I'll ask Mom," I said. "That is a nice pattern."

Ada pulled out several more folded squares of cloth and showed them to me. "I have these I can trade."

"I will find out, Grandma."

I went inside where Osmer was aiming his pump bee-bee gun through the living room window. "What are you doing, Grandpa?"

He squeezed off a round.

"There. See? I can hit a dandelion clean across the lawn."

He gave it a pump and faced me. "Dogs!" he said. "They keep doing it on my lawn."

"You're shooting holes in your window screen."

He looked for the first time at the hole the bee-bee made. "Bugs can't get through that," he said in excuse.

Osmer lowered his weight into his armchair and spat tobacco juice a dozen feet into his spittoon.

"I never see you miss, Grandpa. How far can you spit without missing the spittoon?"

"That one over there beside your chair but Ada doesn't like it when I spit far."

I heard someone come into the kitchen without knocking on the door and a woman about my mother's age waltzed into the living room. (My mom would have said that she waltzed.) She was skinny with yellow hair the color of corn that was dry and frizzed out like fine broom bristles. She chewed gum like a desperate act with her mouth open and she ignored me sitting there. She held a cigarette between her knuckles and squinted her eyes in the smoke. The woman wore a wide, shiny, silver belt over blue jeans. She did not look like any of us in the Falls.

This was a daughter, and she was from the big city. She came from Minneapolis to see the homefolks and even I at about age seven could not miss that she felt sophisticated as she returned to the little old cabin.

"That belt is beautiful," Ada said to her

"Yes," she said in a voice that was eager to claim that she was the source of the treasure. "This is made completely from gum wrappers. I save them. There is a certain way that they can be folded and joined together to make belts and things."

The woman removed the belt and began to show Ada her craftsmanship and how it was done.

I sensed that this was the someone for whom the empty bedroom waited. I waved goodbye to Grandpa Pettis, squeezed pass Grandma and the lady and crossed the lawn to our house.

Mom was in the kitchen canning dill pickles from the garden. It must have been her second batch because I could hear the popping of jars sealing in the corner. It seemed for days that when the neighbor ladies would talk, the first thing they would ask was, "How's your dill?"

The second question would always be, "Any asparagus this year?" Asparagus was always a challenge with our very cold winters and short summers. Dad planted them close to the side of the house where heat could reflect off the walls.

Dad was in the living room. He was in his jean pants and green work shirt and looked tired. He was on the night shift in the Wood Room of the Mill and spent his daylight hours cutting logs to sell to the mill. He smelled of pine pitch.

"Hi Dad."

He smiled his gentle, tired smile. "Your Uncle Laurence is here."

I turned and there he was. "Uncle!" I shouted and hugged him. All of Dad's brothers were a delight to me. They listened to me and treated me as if I were much older than I was.

"My but you are growing. Pretty soon you will be helping your dad in the woods."

I was careful to not bump his shoulder for he had been wounded twice in Korea. He was tall like dad, but he was blond whereas dad was a dark-haired Scandinavian. He was shy and quiet and seemed thin, and I attributed it to the hospital.

"Your uncle brought you a present," my dad said as he looked into my eyes. The look reminded me to show appreciation and that uncle did not have much money. Even then I fully expected a small toy, or a box of Cracker Jacks.

His hand appeared from behind his back and held it out to me. He seemed embarrassed that Dad may have made it out to be something more than it was. "Here," he said. "It isn't much."

I held it in my hands. It certainly was not a toy or Cracker Jacks. It was like a large book. It was Indian-red and there was a drawing of an Indian chief in full regalia on the cover. It said "Big Chief Tablet" on the cover and I just stared at it, not knowing what to think. I was disappointed. No caramel covered popcorn.

"Maybe there was something in it," I thought, and I flipped the pages with my thumb.

The tablet was just empty lined pages. I was not sure what to make of this gift.

"You can write anything you want in it," my dad offered.

Uncle Laurence saw my uncertainty. "Dale, you are very smart. You can do artwork in it. You can write a book," and he added as he looked in my eyes, "The pages are empty, but you can fill it with your wise thoughts."

I gazed at the big chief on the red cover and once again paged through the blank pages with my thumb. Page after empty white page was there waiting for my frail pencil of life to give them meaning. "It could take a lifetime to finish this," I thought.

Suddenly, my "Big Chief" took on great value. Its cost was what Uncle Laurence paid in the store. Its value would be what I would put into it.

And I smiled. I know my smile conveyed to my uncle my utter appreciation because he smiled.

For several days my pencil left no mark inside. My pencil lead would put nothing trite or banal in those pages. I would not diminish its value with just anything.

One night I lay on my back in bed and gazed at the ceiling. It was that time of day when dusk slips into the room and takes all the color, places it into her pail and departs leaving only the grey. I glanced at my Big Chief Tablet and thought, "In my life I will never save silver chewing gum liners to make a belt."

We were coming well into fall season. The dark brown cattails lifted their heads above the limp brown grass in the ditch along the road. The birch leaves were yellow, and the alders and maple splattered their orange and red among their foliage. Days became short and grey and bitter wind brought the cold surety of winter with it.

The gardens were in and canned, and only the plum trees near the railroad tracks lacked my brother's and my attention. There were four of the trees and we could see the plums from the road. The trees were on an empty lot but the Stavish brothers, who were several years older than us and much bigger, tried to claim them. As troublesome as the Stavishes were, the long thorns of the trees were certain to leave their marks on us when we climbed them for the red plums.

Saturday afternoon was blustery and biting-cold, and we were certain the Stavishes would not leave the comfort of their house by the railroad track to stop us. At first, we chomped on the plums while we were perched in the trees, visible to the world and even to the lazy Stavishes — who never one time ever picked a plum. We did not tempt our good luck with the neighborhood bullies, so we filled our pail, went home and set the pail in the sink.

When we were climbing down the trees with our pails, we had heard the first chug and escape of steam from the railroad siding and knew that a train would be coming our way and crossing the road near us. We ran up the dirt road to the crossing with our pockets full of nails and tape. We were making bows and arrows. We split the back ends of the shafts and tied in cardboard feathers. To make tips for the arrows, we taped nails and spikes to the railroad tracks and the passing train wheels flattened the spikes into sharp arrow tips.

We taped our nails to the tracks with friction tape as it was the same color as the tracks and hid our nails. Then we hid in the willow shrubs along the tracks until the train passed. We ducked down lest the engineer see us, stop the train and chase us down. As the caboose disappeared down the track, we retrieved our arrow tips always amazed at what the immense weight of the steel wheels could do.

It was evening. Mom and Dad were both working. We turned on the television set and looked over our arrowheads.

"I think I would like to make a spear. I mean a really good one. You know, the kind you could spear a bear with."

My brother looked at me as if to say, "You mean that YOU can spear a bear with."

"I think we could do it if we got a railroad spike. We might have to get it to run over it a couple of times."

"We might derail the train," he cautioned.

We thought on the problem.

Television was in its infancy back then and we did not have cable. For the first two years TV was mostly snow and was used more like a radio program; later, real television shows began to emerge from the snow. But our TV seemed to have an anomaly that no one has ever been able to explain to me. When the train would begin to chug at the switch station, head our way, gain speed and make the crossing a hundred yards up our road, it affected our TV. Each time the train chugged, the screen turned to snow for the length of time it took to chug. "Chug, snow, chug, snow."

We could hear it leave the switch siding. A slow chug and snow. Two seconds later, chug and snow. Then the chugging snow became closer and closer together until the screen was solid snow as the train got to top speed just before it crossed the road near our house.

This night the ritual changed. The chugging train did not continue down the line into the distance taking with it the snow. The chugging slowed down again. The screen was a whiteout of snow. In a few minutes we heard sirens.

We ran outside and down the road toward the tracks. It was dark outside, and we could not see well. Lights flashed on both sides of our road. We smelled rubber and engine oil and hot metal. People were shouting. I heard screams. An ambulance and firetruck arrived.

A car had tried to beat the train at the crossing.

I heard a muffled pronouncement from someone in the dark, "Everyone is dead. No one is alive."

We stopped in horror a couple dozen steps from the scene.

Here was a horrible crash right where we had retrieved our nails that had been crushed under those wheels. People were dead there somewhere in the dark. Perhaps their bodies were tossed into the very shrubs where we had hidden from the engineer.

This was violent death. We had only seen regular death in a casket before.

Cars began to stop at the sides of the road around us. Sightseers.

They were laughing.

From one car, high schoolers from our neighborhood ran to the scene. Both they and the victim car were out on this Saturday night. The victims were their classmates.

A teenage girl, a neighbor of ours, ran toward us. I saw her eyes — wide open like a doll — but not in horror, rather in excitement. Loudly she shouted to the boy who slid behind the wheel, "Did you see their heads?"

They did a bootlegger turn in the highway, for the road was blocked ahead, and passed us where we stood beside of the road. I heard laughing from their downturned windows.

November bitterness settled in with its frozen ground, and the fall leaves were buried under a crunch of snow. We were settled in from school. It was just after four when Dad came in from work. Mom had dinner ready.

"They are going to start a search for him. They are going to line up along the railroad tracks and cross all the way across Maston's field to the other road. They want you to bring flashlights or lanterns."

"I'll go over there and help," Dad said, and he rummaged in the cupboard for a flashlight and spare batteries.

"What's wrong? What's happening Mom?"

"A little boy is missing. They have been looking for him all afternoon. His name is Robert, and he is only four. He lives in the house just on the other side of the railroad tracks."

"Can I go help search too, Dad?"

"They only want adults to go that can keep up and not get lost too. You are still a little young."

My mother turned to me. "I am going to make sandwiches and coffee for the searchers. You can help me make sandwiches."

Soon I saw a line of lights along the tracks on the far side of Maston's field. Hundreds of them I thought. It must be that every dad in the Falls was on that line. In the distance I saw the beams of flashlights working left and right, the swaying of lanterns, and an occasional shout.

I put on my coat, crossed the road in front of our house and stood at the edge of the deep ditch. It was cold and crisp. The snow crunched and I could hear the steps of the men in the wide line of searchers. From time to time I heard them call his name, "Robert, Robert."

The line of men slowly passed in front of me on Maston's field from left to right, and the crunching of the snow crusts was loud. The steps were like the crunching of soldiers' marching boots in the newsreels.

The line of searchers was solemn. Other than someone calling, "Robert," from time to time, not one person spoke to the searcher next to him. As the line crossed directly in front of me, some lantern lights showed the forms of passing men. They were black against the lighter snow and the line of men crunched past and out of view. They seemed to be a dream passing before me.

They looked for tracks leading into the trees on the far side of Maston's and the men continued the vigil throughout the night. We took coffee and sandwiches to the collection area. Mom went to the store for more things to make sandwiches.

I thought of the cold and a four-year-old boy in the night. I thought of the anguish of Robert's parents too.

In the morning I went to school but could not concentrate, thinking of the missing boy and the crunching of feet in the dark in front of my house. At lunchtime the chewing sound of the raw carrots in my mouth was that of searcher's feet in the night.

When I came home after school, Mom was there. She was stirring something for dinner and did not talk.

"Anything, Mom?"

"They found him, Dale."

She kept stirring and didn't look at me. And I knew it was not good.

"They found his body in the septic tank. Somehow he fell in and drowned."

I could not imagine that horror. How could the parents cope with that?

I tried to erase the image from my mind, but another image took its place — that wreck at the railroad crossing when the insensitive teenagers laughed with their windows rolled down.

In one regard, those two events of death near our house prepared me for that aspect of life. Those deaths were down the road. They were across the field. But then one winter morning death came to our house and peered in through the window and left it fogged over. It came with a phone call and my dad answered.

He seemed to know what he would hear. Any day the cancer would take her. He stood at the cupboard where we kept the phone and took a breath and softly answered, "Hello?"

I watched him as he listened, and it seemed that each word that he heard took a degree of strength from him and left him at the end of the call with his arm hanging limply down with the phone in his hand. He dropped to a chair, and I saw my father weep as I never saw anyone cry before.

My aunt had died.

I remember the casket and the powdered body in it and its waxy appearance, and how the family kissed her form and wept and finally closed the lid for the last time.

She was buried in a country cemetery, and it was bitter cold and the wind moaned in the air above us and snow pellets seemed to flee across the field and dash into the grave. Our shadows shivered beside us, and like us, would not enter the black hole in the earth. I was freezing in my coat and my teeth chattered and my nose stung with the cold when they let the casket down with the ropes. The pastor was old and knew our family from the old homestead. He said the last prayer and tossed in the handful of earth with old-man's hands that were coursed with blue veins. "Dust to dust...."

No death ever left me with a callous on my heart.

I would read later that one of the tyrants of the world would say in effect that the killing of one person is murder, but the murder of a million is just a statistic. And the sentiment of the world seemed to agree with him.

A few years later, after Maston's field, I read Martin Gilbert's *History of the Second World War* and was so impressed with his treatment of the death of the individual. He wrote words to this effect: "On this day the two armies clashed in bitter fighting and twenty thousand soldiers died." Then in the next paragraph he would relate, "In the tiny village of ____, Mrs.____ and her six-year-old daughter clasping her cloth doll, were marched from their burning home, made to stand beneath the apple tree, and were shot."

I would never allow an individual to be a statistic.

Later still, I would find myself in Vietnam near Doc Smith's missionary clinic in Kontum and hear that she was trying to save a little boy's life. The Communists had driven chopsticks into his ears with hammers because he had heard the words of a missionary.

Late the next summer the countryside was hit with army worms — tent caterpillars. Everything was covered with them, covered in depth. There was no place out of doors where you could walk or sit. Lawns were lime green, and thick, inches thick. All the trees were covered. They hung on branches in masses, one stuck to the other hanging like clusters of green grapes.

We thought we would go to the farm. Perhaps it would not be so bad there. On the way we skidded around a corner, and it was only the gravel shoulder that kept us out of the ditch. The highway was thick with worms and their squished bodies were a slippery slime like water on ice in the winter.

A new car skidded on army worms and ended up in a ditch at the side of the road. The engine was running, and the windows were rolled up and the lady refused to leave her car and walk through the worms.

Tractor-trailers drove well below the posted speed. It is said the Canadian-Pacific train was stranded on a siding because the wheels could get no purchase to overcome the worms.

We stopped at Grandma Hanson's to visit.

Only the inside of homes were free from the infestation.

"We have 'em at Greenbush and Badger too," said an uncle.

"The government is thinking of importing a fly that burrows into the worm and lays its eggs and kills it, but then what will you do with all of the flies?"

Uncle Mel swept the front porch and steps without squishing any worms so we would have a place to talk outside. I was sitting there with Dad and some of the uncles and other relatives. Ole Ravendalen offered me some of his Copenhagen.

"Snuff, Sosh?"

He called me Sosh because when I was small and they had blueberry sauce for dessert I kept saying, "More sosh," so I became "Sosh" to him.

He pushed the open can to me. "Try it, Sosh."

I put a plug into my mouth and took my first and only chew in my life. After I could breathe again and my vision returned, I listened to the men talk. They all spoke of war, both World War Two and Korea. All of them had fought in some capacity. There was contempt for anyone who did not do his duty and fight. The thought of dying or being maimed was irrelevant.

Uncle Ray looked at the masses of army worms that filled the lawn. They had begun to crawl up the sides of the car and they inched up the porch posts toward us. "I never thought of it until now, but the army worms are the color of the Chinese uniforms. They came in masses like that too," and his voice trailed off as he became caught up in a memory of the war.

"They would just keep coming and coming and the dead just piled up. I guess they thought they had more men to die than we had bullets."

I thought of the army worms and remembered that they could jackknife a semi-truck or stop a train on the tracks, but it was a sacrificed worm that did so. I hoped that I would never have to fight an enemy that thought nothing of human life.

Chapter Five

I was in Woolworth's dime store drooling down the aisles thinking of all the things one could buy if that person had money. Woolworth's was not my usual haunt. Ronning's Army Surplus was where I usually spent my shopping time. I was a customer who agonized over a purchase and had to return to the store many times to select just the right item.

I was, however, an ideal customer in some regards because I would buy that which other discerning clients passed over. Another customer would say to Mr. Ronning, "That canteen has a dent in it and will not carry as much water as an undented one. I shouldn't have to pay the full price."

I, on the other hand, was a mark for Mr. Ronning. I might say to him, "That canteen has a dent and won't hold as much water, and the canteen cover is a little torn and muddy looking."

Mr. Ronning would look at me and say something like this: "Dale, I probably shouldn't tell you this and I don't want to make other customers jealous. They might not be as discerning as you are. This lot came from the Pacific Theater of the war. It is possible that this very canteen might have been on the belt of a soldier in Iwo Jima."

Here he would hold the canteen up to me to better see it. "I can

34

imagine the soldier taking cover from a sniper and falling into a trench and falling on the canteen."

"Yesss," I would say, utterly amazed at the discovery.

"And look at the cover. It could be the very soil from that awful battle." Here he would take his free hand and make to brush off the dried-up mud.

"No. Wait. I would like it as it is."

Ronning would run his hand back and forth through his thinning hair in thought. "I meant to put this in the four-dollar shelf, but since you found it in the two-dollar pile...."

It was in this manner I was able to add a web belt, a folding shovel and even a machete to my treasures. I was only able to add the machete to my trove because it was so dull that my mother did not mind me having it. Mr. Ronning thought it was probably dull because it had been used by a shipwrecked sailor to cut open the coconuts he lived on.

But back to Woolworth's.

Toward the front of the store, I chanced to see a series of hard cover books. The glossy covers bore scenes of great adventure, and the series was the great classics of modern literature. There was Tom Sawyer with the paintbrush, Huck Finn on the raft with Jim and their shelter as they drifted down the Mississippi, Long John Silver with his parrot and crutch, *Swiss Family Robinson*. The books cost forty-nine cents each.

Before I purchased a single book or turned a single page, I saw myself on that raft on the cover with Huckleberry Finn and could not wait to turn a page. I imagined letting my fishing hook trail behind in the current and a huge walleye with its opal eyes splashing at the side of the raft. How I thrilled for adventures fit to be placed in my Big Chief Tablet. I determined to buy those books and read them.

Tom Sawyer would be my first purchase. I set out to earn forty-nine cents.

I split some firewood for a hobo who had a shack by the railroad tracks and got fifteen cents. Then I walked down miles of ditches looking for tossed pop bottles. They gave two cents a bottle someone had said. I collected dozens and took my heavy trove to the closest gas station to collect. I found out that only certain brands gave a refund and got only twelve cents for my work. I was sticky hot from my effort, and I gave the man ten cents of my money for an orange crush from the pop machine that was so cold my head had a freeze.

One of Mr. Underdahl's neighbors had a coal bin that needed shoveling and I landed ten cents on that one.

The big adventure was the grain cars at the railroad siding. There was the draw of big money, but it came with danger.

There was always the possibility that the engine could slam into the string of cars just as I was getting in and knock me under the wheels. There was the possibility of the doors slamming shut while I was inside and the next daylight that I would see would be in California. People also warned me that Canadian-Pacific had the big railroad bulls who checked for people in the cars, and they would club them with their saps and toss them into the ditch.

Bums still worked the railroads. In the old days of the Depression, they were called hobos but now they were just referred to as tramps or bums. They might toss you off just for fun.

The goal of going to the grain cars was to gather the grain that was left over on the floor after the cars had been unloaded and sell it to folks in town who had rabbits or chickens. Sometimes when grain was loaded all the way to the very top, the space between the outer and inside walls filled with gallons of grain. You had but to loosen the bottom board for the treasure inside to flow out onto the floor.

That afternoon I earned enough to buy my first book and I sat in the shade beside the house and witnessed a murder and had Injun Joe toss a knife at me in a crowded courtroom and I even got lost in a cave with Becky Thatcher.

This began a love for books. Good literature. Sometimes I read by author, having found a great writer. On occasion I would read all but their last book, which I kept unread on my bookshelf. The writer was "kept alive" thereby on a walnut shelf.

When I was eleven, I got my first real job at People's Café at the end of the main street next to the train station. Some people would have called it a greasy spoon restaurant, but it did not deserve the pejorative.

Mr. Phakalides served hearty, hot, blue collar meals. People's Café was always busy. When you entered the door the warmth of the interior would pass over you and the aroma of the special of the day would make you stay.

When you came in and looked about for a place to sit, you would hear the clatter from the kitchen and the bumping of dinner plates and a waitress in an apron would point to you and say, "There's a place over here, darlin'."

I ate there once with my mom and was running my wandering fingers over the underside of the tables and wondered what the bumps were. A quick peek underneath revealed a thousand gobs of chewing gum that customers of the past stuck there before they ate.

Workers from the mill and the railroad came in at noon and sat on the barstools at the counter and talked to Mr. Phakalides. They were regulars and always familiar with him and called him by his first name, John.

Winos from second street were regulars too when they had money and it was cold outside. They sat in the booths with cold, red, runny noses and would crumble handfuls of oyster crackers into the soup they ordered and eat with both arms surrounding the bowl with their heads down.

People's Café had great hamburgers with buns slick with kitchen grease, honest fries and malts made with real ice cream. Next to Ronning's Army Surplus, this was my favorite place in town.

I got a job, seven days a week, from eleven at night until four in the morning for sixty cents an hour. Three dollars a night. Every morning I would hear the cab pull up to the door, the tires hissing in the wetness of the street, and Mr. Phakalides would come in with his half asleep face, go straight to the cash register and hand me three dollars.

My job was to scrub the floors and do a few basic things and when that was finished, I was the night watchman. I could make chocolate Sundays or malts and could get my meals free during the day if I wanted. I was proud and honored to work.

Mom taught me how to work. "Find something to do. Never stand around. You can always find a broom."

I bought a .22 rifle at Sears on credit and each afternoon walked to the store and put three dollars on my account.

The waitress at People's said that she never saw the café so clean.

One Saturday afternoon, still summer vacation, the rain beat down on the roof of our house on Old Highway Eleven. It was an unrelenting rain that would last the day if not the night. Even at my young age of twelve I could tell that this was not a passing thunderstorm to be accompanied with flashes of lightning in my window and the sudden crack of thunder that startled, then echoed from east to west over the top of our house.

My brother's and my bedroom was just under the roof and I could hear the full concert of rain drops. The thickness of the moisture-filled air left a closeness in our bedroom as if an invisible shawl were draped over my shoulders. This was a day to read or study.

I lay on the bed with my back against the headboard, a pillow on my lap as a desk, and propped up a book. It was one that I bought with money that I earned by stacking firewood for a neighbor and had saved for a day like this one. The name of the book was *The Last of the Mohicans*.

I had just finished reading the portion that said, "The North American Warrior caused the hair to be plucked from his whole body; a small tuft was left on the crown of his head, in order that his enemy might avail himself of it, in wrenching off the scalp in the event of his fall. The scalp was the only admissible trophy of victory."

I recalled skinning muskrats on the trap line and rolling the skin into a ball like a sock before putting it into my packsack. When I would arrive at home, I would unroll them and turn them inside out, wet, fatty, flesh side out, and I thought as I paused in my reading, "That must be what a scalp looks like." As I was caught up in trying to picture Cooper's description of a warrior, I heard my dad coming up the stairs. His footsteps were always slow and deliberate — tired steps — and I was always humbled that he made the effort to visit with us boys. Before I even saw him, I knew that he would be trudging up the steps in work pants and a button-down shirt.

He was tall, slim and handsome with his black hair combed straight back, his eyes blue and clear. He was a quiet man, never effusive with his emotions. His slim shoulders were already stooped with work and war although he was only about forty years old.

"Hi Dad."

He smiled.

"Well, you have the right idea of what to do on a day like this. What are you reading?"

"James Fenimore Cooper. It's *The Last of the Mohicans*."

Dad seemed surprised at this. "Can you understand him?"

I nodded. "He's pretty hard at the beginning but after a while I can follow how he talks."

He thought on this and nodded.

"Here's one that got my interest right off though." I rolled off the bed, went to the shelf and got *Treasure Island*.

I opened it to the first page. "This is written by Robert Louis Stevenson. Let me read to you how it begins.

"'I remember him as if it were yesterday, as he came plodding to the inn door, his sea-chest following behind him in a hand-barrow, a tall, strong, heavy, nut-brown man, his tarry pigtail falling over the shoulder of his soiled blue coat, his hands ragged and scarred, with black, broken nails, and the sabre cut across one cheek, a dirty, livid white.'"

I closed the book and looked up at him. "That was just one sentence. I can just see it, can't you, Dad?"

"I can," he said as he sat in the chair by the bed. "I'm glad you read. What kind of things do you like?"

"Good writing. I study things that interest me, and I read the Bible every day."

He tapped the arm of the chair three times with the tips of his fingers, which I learned by watching him over the years is what he did when he would say what he thought to be important.

"I am glad we have some brains in the family. You know, of all the people in our family and your mom's too — all the uncles and aunts and grandparents — none of us ever went past the eighth grade. They

39

were all smart people, but we all stayed in school as long as the law said that we had to and then we all went to work."

Dad pulled himself erect from the chair. "I remember reading that book too," he said, pointing to *Treasure Island*. "I really liked it. I was on the deck of a troop ship taking my turn in the fresh air and the seagulls kept dipping down on me thinking I had food. I remember thinking of the sand and the palm trees in *Treasure Island*. And then I thought of the sand beach and palm trees that we had just left after the guns and fighting erased it all and how beautiful it must have been before the war."

He turned to go but stopped and said, "I suppose the palm trees are all grown back by now and the islanders who lived through it all will have rebuilt their huts and have families. Some of them probably have sons your age."

Chapter Six

When I was thirteen years old, I got shot along the road that goes by Roosevelt, Minnesota. It happened where the dirt road crosses the railroad tracks and joins the main road, a couple of miles past the town and Oseid's Grocery Store and Charlie Cannon's Creamery.

It was November and cold, a still day, the kind that you can hear the dry snow soof across the toes of your boots when you walk, and hear dry twigs fall from branches that are loosed by thin chickadees' feet. The sky was clear of clouds and bore the image of twilight even though it was early in the day. The air itself seemed frozen in place and did not sift the dry snow from the drifts.

It was deer hunting season in farm country. The land was a patchwork made up of squares of fields and forest. My dad had a forty of open field across the road that led into a section of thick wood and brush. Dad was still driving to the farm from the Falls so it would be two of the uncles and we boys who would do this hunt. The uncles knew we would have no chance at all of sneaking up on a deer in the woods this silent day, so we decided to make a drive for deer.

The plan was for Uncle Walt and Uncle Melvin to make their way well around the wooded area to the far side and post where they could see anything coming from the thicket. My younger brother, my cousin and I would give them a half hour before we started. When it was time to begin our drive, we would station ourselves shoulder to shoulder, forty to fifty yards apart and make our way through the trees, driving the deer in it to the far side where our uncles waited.

We were warmly dressed for the hunt, and we stood at the edge of the field to wait for the time to begin the drive. I had a Winchester lever action 30-30, chambered and ready to fire should I see a deer.

We stood at the edge of the tree line and shuffled our feet to keep warm. Steam poured from our mouths as we talked. A half hour is a long time to stand still in winter in northern Minnesota. We started to get cold. We shivered. Our fingertips stung and we put them into our pockets.

I looked back at the cars. They were warm inside only a short time before.

"Let's go sit in the car," one of us said.

I opened the passenger door of Uncle Walt's car, opened the lever action on my Winchester and slid it across the front seat and ran to the other side and got in.

We piled in and shut the doors. The interior bore the faint memory of heat from when it was running.

"Hey, the keys are in the ignition. We could…."

"Let's go for a spin. We have lots of time," I said.

Del put his hands into his pockets and stepped back from the car. "I don't think so. I'm not going," He would have no part of us taking a joy ride in Uncle Walt's car.

I thought of a warm heater.

With a grin I turned on the key and pressed the starter button and the car leapt to life like a thoroughbred at the starting gate. Cousin Bruce slid into the passenger seat beside me and noticed the fully extended lever of my rifle and thought that I had forgotten to close it. He closed it. That single movement placed a bullet in the chamber with the hammer fully back and ready to fire. The barrel of the weapon was aimed at my hip.

I put the Ford into reverse and backed us over furrows left from last year's plow that were so frozen we bounced in the seat, I put us into drive and with the excitement of an adventure sped toward the main road on the bumpy frozen field.

The car bounced on the small frozen hillocks in the field, and I needed both hands on the wheel to steer the car. The car jolted on the big bumps at the edge of the field, but the Winchester did not go off. We thumped over the railroad ties and rails and onto the rough frozen edge of the old road and still the rifle did not fire.

But it was at the last, very hard, frozen line of crust left by snowplows that it finally happened. I had just aligned the car with my lane of traffic and was about to press the gas pedal. The ear-shattering explosion of the gun firing inside the car was intense.

The very second the rifle went off, Bruce burst from the car as if he were thrown by a blast and ran past my brother. Del, who had remained in the open field, thought the car had backfired and roared in laughter and pointed his finger at my cousin thinking he was such a chicken to run from a simple backfire. But as he passed, he shouted in terror, "Dale's been shot, Dale's been shot!"

The bullet entered my cheek and exited at my tailbone, one quarter inch from lifetime paralysis. Shock from the bullet thrust my leg out straight and hard as a board — right on the accelerator. All cars in those days could go a hundred miles an hour and any vehicle worth its salt would do one-twenty. My foot pressed the gas pedal full to the floor and the fast acceleration tossed my head back. The car picked up speed like a rocket down the country highway. Leafless trees became a grey blur along the road. I was wounded but knew that for the moment that was the least of my worries. Somehow, I had to keep the car on the road and get it stopped.

I tried to pry my leg off the gas pedal with both of my hands under my thigh. The shock of the passing bullet held it rigid and straight on the pedal. I could not budge my leg.

A glance out of the window demanded that steering was my first and major priority. I was approaching a speed on this country highway that neither the car nor I would soon be able to handle.

With my right hand I grabbed my pant leg and tore at my wounded leg to pull it off the gas pedal. I knew also I would soon pass out and no longer be in control of anything.

I was slouched behind the wheel trying to move my leg and could see the speedometer passing a hundred miles an hour. The slightest mistake on the steering wheel would be the end.

"God help me get my leg off the gas."

Perhaps in answer to that quick prayer, I felt the stiffness in my leg begin to lessen and grabbing my pants leg with a fist, jerked it off the gas pedal. I took the car out of gear as weakness began to flood over my body. I just wanted to sleep. I guided the car to the shoulder. I don't remember taking it out of gear.

Del and Bruce ran like a blur through the woods, shouting to the unseen uncles ahead, "Dale's been shot, Dale's been shot!"

At the far end of the stand of trees they found the uncles. They pointed toward the highway, "Dale's been shot."

The four of them dashed toward the road through the brush and snow and saw the car stopped at the shoulder of the road. I was slumped behind the wheel and the car seats were full of blood.

Uncles Mel and Walt, both of whom had been wounded in the war found me behind the wheel on the highway and did a preliminary first aid and slid me over to the passenger side of the car. Uncle Walt raced the car toward the hospital that I was born in at Warroad.

I recalled once or twice opening my turtle-heavy eyes and seeing the trees pass by in a blur. I asked him later, "How fast did you drive, Uncle Walt?"

He had to think a moment because his speed was the farthest thing from his mind, "We drove over one hundred twenty miles an hour the whole way."

I remember us pulling up at the hospital. Uncle Walt must have made a bootlegger turn to get us passenger side facing the building. Uncle Mel ran to the doors to tell them we were coming in with a gunshot wound.

Uncle Walt opened the door and was about to carry me and I remember weakly saying, "No. I want to walk. I need to walk."

He knew that I needed to do that so I would know that all my parts worked.

The hospital was set far from the road to make room for lawns and park benches, and I looked at the hospital door ahead and hobbled for it leaving a trail of blood on the sidewalk. My uncle walked beside me with both of his arms ready to catch me if I fell. Just as I stepped on the threshold all strength left me and I felt myself sink to the ground. Uncle Walt caught me and carried me like a small child into the emergency room.

Most of the next hours were a blur to me. I was in and out of consciousness, weak from blood loss. I remember them transferring me from a gurney to a hospital bed and being hooked up to IV bottles and tubes and nurses taking my pressure and the doctor talking to me.

My dad learned that I had been shot when he was in the grocery store. He had just driven from the Falls at the end of his night shift in the mill to join the rest of us on the hunt. When he arrived at Roosevelt, he stopped at Oseid's Grocery Store to buy something.

Mr. Oseid walked over to him with a look of great concern on his face. "How is your boy, Al?"

He did not know what he meant. "I have two boys. Which one?"

"The one who got shot this morning."

They say that my dad's face turned white. He was weak at the news. "What happened? How bad is he? Where is he?"

"Warroad Hospital, I think."

When the boys and the uncles ran from the woods toward the place where I finally stopped the car, they instructed the boys, "Run to Grandma's house and tell them what happened."

They boys were terrified at the event and the prospect of telling the grandparents the news. Shaking in fear they ran instead to the little barn on our homestead and hid inside.

Dad stopped at Grandma's as it was close and, on the way, to learn if they knew anything. It was the first they had heard of the accident as the boys were still hiding in the barn. There had been no news, and everyone was in shock when the boys overcame their fear and slunk into the house.

In time my bedside was surrounded by my family. I would walk. The wound missed all vital organs. I would recover.

It was probably the second night when the nurse came in to check on me that I asked her, "Am I supposed to slosh?"

"What?"

"Am I supposed to slosh? When I move, I can hear me sloshing. Listen," and I moved to the side and even she could hear it. I lifted the covers so she could see. I had rubber sheets below me so blood wouldn't ruin the mattress. I was lying in a puddle of blood as deep and thick as a puddle in a pothole.

The nurse dropped her blood pressure kit and ran from the room. I was bleeding out. It seemed to be just minutes and the doctor rushed in wearing street clothes and began transfusions and somehow stopped my bleeding.

I wouldn't use a bed pan and one night when I could no longer hold it, I slipped from the bed to the toilet. In the morning the head nurse admonished me like a schoolteacher with a ruler in her hand. "You left a river of blood all the way to the toilet and the seat is red with blood." She held up a shiny silver-colored bed pan. "You'll use this for me, won't you?"

My mom came to visit. Home was a hundred miles from Warroad, and she hated winter roads. She was always good when we were sick. "The hospital sent your clothes home and when I lifted up your bloody pants, hamburger fell out of the leg."

The day came that they thought I was stable enough to make the hundred-mile trip home from the hospital. Mom and Dad made a soft comfortable bed across the back seat with large soft pillows. Dad drove well under the limit so there would be no bumps to jostle me on the way. They made a bed on the downstairs couch so I could watch TV and not go up any stairs.

It must have been early or midweek when I came home, and when

Sunday came, I wanted to go to church.

"Are you sure? You can do this?"

"I want to go, Dad."

"If you are sure you want to go, I will take you."

I don't remember what I wore for a bottom over the layers of bandages, but I carried my Bible in my left hand and a large, soft pillow in the other. I could barely walk. Each step was a painful struggle. Dad watched me from the sidewalk to the front door — he wasn't a church going kind — and drove away only after the door shut behind me.

I forgot the dozen or more stair steps from the front door to the auditorium. I struggled slowly up and shuffled to the back row and adjusted myself on my pillow. I had no intention of making a spectacle of myself, but people stared at me not knowing what to say.

I thought I was on the mend — every day my body would be getting better all by itself. I was wrong. The healing regimen hurt nearly as bad as the bullet initially passing through me.

Every other day my mother brought me to the hospital where I lay face down on a gurney. "It will hurt more if I pull it slowly," the doctor would say every visit as if I had forgotten the previous visit with him and with one quick rip he would yank the tape off me, hair, scab and all. He would then take forceps with thin jaws about eight inches long and open the entrance of the wound and slide the jaws into the bullet hole as far at the tool would allow him. He then stuffed the channel that the bullet had made with gauze so the hole would not heal shut. It had to heal from the inside out. There was intense pain each time the tool broke the crusted opening of the hole on each side, and more as the jaws of the tool followed the path the bullet had made. There was no shock that accompanied the time I was shot to deaden the pain. Each visit, he would take out the old festering gauze and replace it with new and I would measure the amount of time it would take for the cavity to close completely by the length of the gauze that he had to pack into the hole.

"Only about two inches to go in today, Dale," he said one visit and I could anticipate a last visit down the line. Everyday pain was becoming less dull from the largeness of the wound but sharper and more intense to move and sit.

"One inch more, Dale. I think the next time will be our last visit." I looked up at him from my belly and smiled.

Dr. Crow was a retired army doctor, and we assumed my injury was a common thing to him. "You know, Dale, you were my first gunshot wound."

This would be the first of three times in my life when I would be shot by bullets.

Chapter Seven

I have been blessed with great mentors in every chapter of my life — people who guided me, steered me in the right way, taught me values and truth and most of all, saw qualities and potential in me that as of yet I did not see in myself.

Sometimes their influence was a subtle unspoken thing, a simple thing like conversing with me as if I were an adult and an equal. They seemed to listen to my words as if they had value.

I remember that summer after I had been shot, sitting at the breakfast table on the farm with Grandma Hanson and Uncle Mel. We had cornflakes and used milk from the barn from which the cream had not been separated. We talked together and exchanged ideas and conversed about things we had considered. Our hands were across from each other on the table as were our minds. We talked of values, of life, theology, and philosophy — what life was all about.

Uncle Mel stayed on the farm with Grandma and Grandpa because his wounds from the Battle of the Bulge had been very serious and he had never fully recovered. As I ate my corn flakes, he dipped sugar cookies that Grandma made into his coffee and asked me questions. He would ask, it seemed, as one who was asking news from someone who had just returned from the old country and waited for a reply. He would listen and ponder my answers and value them.

I remember watching Grandma Hanson smile in delight when we talked, and I considered later that her delight was not in the answers and concepts that I presented as much as that they came from her young grandson who sat across the checkered tablecloth in the tiny town of Roosevelt, Minnesota.

The pastor of our Baptist church in the Falls also took time to guide my life. I read the Bible every day and devoured the truths in it and he was there always to answer my questions. I gave the message in church a few times and even spoke on his radio program.

His father was a famous preacher and the president of a bible seminary. He knew the great thinkers and writers and evangelists of the old tent days when preachers spoke to ten thousand listeners in giant tents without microphones. I was privileged to hear those famous, learned men as they came to our little church. I sponged in their words and read their books.

I think I tended to bounce my ideas and findings off others. Harold — one of the guys in our church youth group — and I were pedaling our bikes to the lake to fish. Harold was several inches taller than me, and he wore thick glasses and had big round knees like softballs, and he had big hands like the green hands of Frankenstein's monster. He had one of those large Adam's apples that constantly moved up and down — when he breathed, when he talked, and when he was thinking. He thought with his mouth open, and his thick glasses seemed to fog over as he did so. Harold was always pensive and paused before he spoke. When he spoke, it seemed his voice came from deep down in a well. He was too big for his small bicycle and his knees pumped up and down as we peddled.

"So, here's what I have been thinking," I said to him as he pedaled beside me along the road. "I have been reading in the book of Isaiah in the Bible and right at the beginning I came across this verse. It says, 'Come now and let us reason together, though your sins be as scarlet they shall be as white as snow.' Do you see?"

"No," he said as he looked my way, the handlebars following his eyes.

"Oh, watch your rod. I almost got a daredevil in my eye."

He glanced at the wayward rod and steered back to his side of the road.

"No. I don't see," he said as we stopped at the bridge beside the bay and rolled our bikes under it so no one would see them while we fished.

"Just this: God says that we could take the Bible and find the answers to life if we used sound reasoning," I said as I pointed my rod tip behind me and ducked under a tree limb and followed the shore.

Before I could finish the thought, he said, "If that is the case then, everyone should come up with the same answer. And they don't."

I put a small crocodile lure on the end of my line and cast to where a log angled into the water.

"Exactly. There are plenty of people with brains who come up with the dumbest answers. Hey look, Harold. Something broke the water by the lily pads."

He cast at the spot, but his lure hung up on the pads. He tried to tug it off without breaking his line.

"The problem is that people don't know how to be logical and think clearly. The second half of the verse is — remember God is talking — 'reason together.' Sound reason has to be based on sound premises. I think that if you had a room full of people and they used sound principles and reasoned correctly, they would all have the same answer."

Harold's lure hopped off the pad and plopped into the water a couple of feet away and a big northern pike grabbed it with a huge splash. We saw its grey-green side with its spots break the surface and Harold held his rod with both hands, the butt of the rod snug against his belly with the line playing out with a squeal.

I knew that he wouldn't hear a word until he either played-in that northern or his line broke, so I waited. It took ten minutes for him to play the energy out of the fish and work it to the shore. At the water's edge — the very last yard of water, he hefted the flopping pike out of the water and as it hung in the air the line broke, and it lay flopping on the rocky edge. We both ran and grabbed it with our hands on its quill-less back and tossed it higher up in the grass. He looked at me and let out a long breath and grinned. A line of water from the fish's splash rolled down one frame of his glasses.

"So, what were you talking about now?"

"We forgot to bet on the first fish," I reminded him. "I have been reading books on logic and what they call critical thinking. You know — how to think and reason."

I waited for him to comment on that, but he did not.

"So, Harold, I am going to read and study all I can find about sound reasoning. That seems basic to me, don't you think?"

Harold busied himself casting his daredevil lure into the water by my log.

"I found a textbook on logic in the library. I'm going to order it so I can underline in it."

Harold must have seen movement under my submerged log because his mouth was open, and he was focused on the spot and his Adam's apple went up and down like a bobber. I gave up.

"A dollar on the next fish," I said.

I had another friend in our church youth group named Leroy and I could tell even then from how he was while we were both young that he would be a very good man later on. He was short and strong and of a sweet disposition. His hair was brown, and he had stooped shoulders like someone who did heavy chores before school every day.

Leroy was not slow, but he did have a mannerism I had to get used to.

When I talked with him, he studied me as if my words came out in visible letters and he was reading them. I would speak and he would say, "Yuh, Yuh," and I knew he was following my thoughts. If I paused to be sure he was listening he would say, "Yuh!" and I would go on.

He lived at the very end of the farthest county road from my house in an old unpainted house and outbuildings with his parents and two older sisters. His dad had gotten out of prison some time before and his face was pale like Swiss cheese. He could not have been forty or fifty, but his hair was the color of a weathered grey barn and his eyebrows were thick and black. He was built like Leroy and was quiet and sad looking.

I had a trap line that started at Leroy's house and went three miles down the railroad tracks to where a ditch that was almost as wide as a small river crossed it. Every Saturday I would heft my pack and .22 rifle and walk down the tracks on the railroad ties. Railroads are built on a grade above the water table and in winter the wind would blow the snow off the tracks into the ditches, so I did not have to trudge in deep snow. En route to the very wide cross-ditch I nailed a wood rat trap to every other telephone pole to catch weasels. Ditches lined both sides of the tracks and where open water ran under the snow crusts I set for mink and muskrat.

The cross-ditch that was nearly a small river in the distance was my nemesis. I set for mink as I walked on the ice, placing traps and scent in the hollow logs and on the dead trees that leaned over the ice.

Bank beaver lived in the stream and their activity was invisible under the ice. In places the ice was paper-thin, and every Saturday I managed to find one of those places and fall through the ice.

Winter water in Minnesota will elicit real pain. It is so cold as to be instantly numbing and life threatening. As I would break through, the shock of the freezing water would suck all the warm air out of my lungs, and it felt like death ran its boney hands down my back. Somehow, I would arrest my descent into the blackness — hands extended straight out on the top of the ice. I would grab something and work my upper body from the hole in the ice and lay on my chest. Then I would inch myself away from the fissure, crawling or grabbing at anything protruding through the ice.

Once out, the frigid cold outside turned my clothes into frozen armor. My fingers ached. My ears would freeze and with each step they felt heavy and dead and floppy.

I would stumble those three miles like a stick figure, shivering and feeling pain along my backbone and fingertips. As it always happened every Saturday on my trap line, I would find myself knocking on Leroy's family home. In minutes I would be huddled under a blanket beside the wood stove with a cup of hot chocolate in my hands.

Leroy's sisters would thaw my cauliflower ears.

"I think your ears will be okay," a sister would say as she gently rubbed them.

And Leroy would say, "Yuh, Yuh."

I was putting on my wool socks that had dried under their stove and thinking of the kindness of Leroy's family as I was waiting for my dad to pick me up with his car.

"Leroy, I have been thinking a lot lately about a verse I read."

"Yuh?"

"I'm still memorizing it, but it goes something like this — 'And Jesus grew and increased in wisdom and stature and favour with God and man.' It's from Luke in the Bible."

He sat across from me on a chunk of stove wood with his hands on his knees and waited.

"Remember, we're all supposed to be like Jesus, and he was perfect." Leroy said.

"Well, I think the verse tells us all the areas in which he was perfect. Listen."

Leroy leaned forward and waited for the words to appear from my mouth.

"I think the verse says he was perfect physically, mentally, spiritually, and socially. It's all there. Do you see that?"

"I'll get my Bible," he said, and he returned with his big King James Bible from his room, and he turned to the Gospel of Luke.

"It is the end of the second chapter," I said.

"Found it. Yuh."

"See, he is God and becomes also human by being born in Bethlehem as a baby and grows into a boy like us and he grows as he gets older. He increases. See that?"

"Yuh."

He read the verses and I watched his head move left to right as he read. He started to nod his head and began to smile. "Yuh. They are all there, Dale."

"Leroy, I am going to take those four things and start to be the

54

best I can be in all four of those areas. You watch. Maybe we both can, Leroy."

Leroy's sister came over to us. "Your dad's here. Put this over your ears. She started to put the wool cap on my head, but she stepped back and smiled. "Your ears are swollen and look like Dopey's of the seven dwarfs. But cute."

Monday morning found me at my desk in history class. Mr. Hendy was the teacher. He was very tall and thin and when he moved it seemed that his bones were all stiff and he moved slowly and with deliberation. His hair was short and brown, and I loved to hear him teach.

We were on the American Civil War and Mr. Hendy had just fought a battle in front of his desk — I mean fought it! He had a pair of authentic swords from that war, one from the North and one from the South. He ran one of the swords through a felt hat and held it over his head. Mr. Hendy's eyes were wide, and his eyebrows raised and he looked at us in the class as if we were the soldiers in his army. He described a Confederate general who waved his hat in the air and shouted, "Follow me — for Virginia."

He had piles of buckles and canteens and pouches and crumpled, yellow letters from the war on his desk and at certain parts of his narrative he would pull a musket from the pile and point to the wall to our right side and shout, "BANG!"

And anyone who had taken a notion to slumber or were already doing so would bolt upright in their chairs as though they themselves had been shot.

He would then talk about Pickett's Charge at Little Round Top, and point the union smooth bore at the other wall and shout again, "BANG!"

Then he would talk about the North trying to preserve the union and end slavery, and then it would be the South fighting for states' rights. "Forget slavery for a moment. What side would you join but for that?"

When his animated enactment of the battle was over, we set ourselves to a task of writing answers to questions from the text.

I must have forgotten my commitment to the intellectual aspect of being like Jesus in every area, for I found myself looking out of the window and daydreaming — me in a white canvas tent of a Philip R. Goodwin painting. I caught myself and went back to the task at hand.

Several minutes later as I worked on the assignment, I heard the rustle of cloth and Mr. Hendy was standing beside me. He smiled as if I were the one person in class that deserved his attention.

He slowly slid the current issue of "Time" magazine on my desktop. He placed his finger on an article and held the magazine flat with his finger. "Read this, Dale."

I read it. It was written by a respected historian on the battle we had just studied in class. It was relevant and exciting to read.

When I finished, I looked up at him and he could tell I liked the piece. Mr. Hendy smiled in appreciation.

Then he cast his eyes back down at the article and tapped it three times with his forefinger. When he saw that I was looking back down at the article, he slowly slid his finger down and revealed the name of the writer: Fred Hendy.

Mr. Hendy wanted me to know that he was worth listening to. I also felt that he considered me someone worth investing his time in.

I talked with Mr. Hendy in the hall one day and told him about my verse in Luke in the Bible and my determination to be what I could be in those areas.

"I just don't see the relevance of some of the classes to real education. Mr. Hendy, do you realize that there is no such class as, 'how to think and reason?' You would think that would be basic, wouldn't you?"

Mr. Hendy stopped his stiff walk down the hall and looked at me. "I never thought of that. You're right."

Mr. Hendy looked up toward the ceiling and stroked his chin with one hand. "How could we miss that?"

I went on. "It's like you can't do algebra and geometry until you can do math."

"What class are you going to Mr. Hanson? I'll walk with you."

"Some classes are against all that I believe. Take biology. Right at the beginning they show you the biological tree of life with all those branches. Everything living is a branch on that tree. You can trace every branch to that one root — the trunk of the tree. That assumes evolution. If, like the Bible says, everything reproduces after its kind there should be a forest of trees."

Mr. Hendy stopped and laughed out loud — as if he were a general who had just discovered the battle plan of his opposing force.

"Let me challenge you this way," he said. "You study, and whenever you see a conflict, you do your own research and come up with truth. It seems to me that you have to hear the other side of an issue first to know what the issue is. Every time you challenge something in your own mind and come up with truth that you can verify, you will become stronger for the effort.

"The bell is about to ring. You don't want to be late. Let my urge you to go as far as you can in math and science and take a language. You need to relate to people to act out your Christianity. You cannot do that if you are ignorant."

I was not sure how to answer yet. "Thank you, sir."

The class bell rang.

One of the coaches stopped me as I cut across the parking lot on my way to work at the grocery store.

"Dale, I saw your name on the honor roll."

I was B+, about the best I could do since I was doing all the advanced math and science classes, and was working until ten every night at the store, plus I read the Bible every night before homework.

"You can do much better than that. You should have all A's."

This was not the person who coached me in sports, and I did not think that he even knew that I existed. Somehow, he thought I was capable of doing good work. Within his gentle scold was a compliment, but more, it opened my eyes to my own potential.

"Yes, sir. I'll try."

I was convinced that there were fundamental issues that were the core truths of life and I needed to say them out loud to someone. I was talking to my friend Harold who sat in the passenger seat of my

1948 Chevy Fleet line car. It was pouring rain and the vacuum wipers could barely hold their own as we drove over the hills by the lake. He watched me through his thick, foggy glasses with his mouth open and his Adam's apple swallowing up and down.

"So, I know my own existence. That's a sure thing. Everyone can get that far," I said as I double clutched the transmission and put it into lower gear. "But it seems that there are foundational questions everyone needs to answer to know what life is all about."

"And?"

"The questions of life are: Who am I? Where did I come from? What am I doing here, and where am I going?" I looked over at him and he was listening.

"That is what philosophy tries to answer — those four questions."

Harold was talking but I couldn't hear above the roar of the rain. The wipers couldn't clear the windows quickly enough to see the road and the windows were fogging up.

Harold leaned toward my ear. "We must be near City Beach. Let's get under one of the shelters."

I drove as close as I could to one of them, shut off the engine and we dashed inside as quickly as we could but got soaked anyway. The downpour roared on the roof, but we could at least hear each other.

Harold was wiping his glasses as he spoke. "Philosophy. You were saying about philosophy."

"Yes. I have been reading the philosophers and they are all trying to find those basic answers and each of them disagrees with the other philosophers. They present us with their conclusions first and then they try to show, step by step, how they arrived at them."

A breeze from off the lake started to blow the rain into the shelter and we moved to the far side. The streetlight reflected off Harold's glasses.

"What I did was — I took their reasoning and conclusions and thought to myself, 'What is that based on?' And I kept following their reasoning point by point to what had to be the very first premise that could possibly be their starting point. There wasn't one. Their reasoning was only based on a theory."

"I know where you are heading," Harold said with his deep voice. "Christianity."

"Exactly! We have every answer. Who am I, what am I doing here, what is my purpose, where am I going? All there in the Bible. I am created by God, his child, with a purpose in life, and I will go to Heaven when I die. All there. I have the answers and meaning in my life."

Harold leaned back against the table with his long legs straight out before him. "Cool," he said. He placed his hands behind his neck and tilted his head up toward the ceiling and said again with satisfaction in his voice, "Cool."

"And there was only one aspect left to consider. The answers are there to read. But is the Bible, my own starting point reliable and provable?"

Harold leaned forward and rested his hands on his knees. "Yes, you can prove that it is true. You can look at science in the Bible, fulfilled prophecy, lots of things."

"Right," I said, "We know what we believe and why we believe it, but the PHD can only hope that his theory is true."

Our young brains were tired of thinking, and we sat back and listened to the deluge around us.

The rain continued to blow into the shelter from the open side and pool on the concrete floor. We sat on top of the picnic table with our feet on the bench seat and listened to the storm. From time to time, lightning flashed over the lake and we counted the seconds to the crack of thunder.

"Six seconds. A mile and a half away."

A long-haired dog entered the shelter and shook off the wetness from its fur, the tags of his collar sounding metallic in the room. It found a dry place at our feet and lay there as if we were old friends.

Late that spring, an old, wrinkled, used-up cowboy taught me an exercise that I added to my workout. This is how it happened:

I padded the hard bench seat of Mr. Pettis' hay wagon with an armful of yellow straw and his two huge work horses pulled us down our road. It was a pleasant day, and the only sound was the hollow clopping of hooves on the pavement. Mr. Pettis gave me the reins to hold.

"Here, you drive. Dan is the one on the left and Bess is the other'n."

I wasn't a child anymore, but I sensed a shyness in me for when I held the reins, I saw a bow in the line. I had rendered no instructions with the reins and the horses plodded along with the last command given to them yet in their brains. Mr. Pettis told me how and I turned us down a side road to his field. The side road was not much more than two parallel clay ruts just wide enough for the wagon wheels that led to a large open area. This was where Ada and Osmer Pettis grew their vegetables for the year.

I looked over to Mr. Pettis and said, "My Uncle Bruno asked me if a horse pushes or pulls a wagon."

Mr. Pettis could see his giant horses in front of us as we made our way. He looked over at me and smiled. "And what did your Uncle Bruno say?"

I know I must have had glee in my face when I answered. "He says they push the wagon. They push against the harness and the harness pulls the wagon."

"Your uncle is pretty smart."

There was a water-filled ditch along the path, and I saw a red winged blackbird on a cattail stock that had survived the winter. It made its call and another one answered from a place we could not see.

It was late spring — late enough that the standing water from the melted snow of winter had disappeared and left the meadow dry and ready for the plow to turn the soil.

On the far side of the field, nearly unseen for its smallness, was a tiny shack. It could not have been more than ten by fourteen feet square, if that. There was no hard siding on the structure, only the squares of insulite that the mill produced. We locals would buy insulite siding that had broken corners and the mill couldn't sell to customers. They were cheap to buy, and we would side our hunting shacks with them. Jesse's house was sheathed with them.

Mr. Pettis stopped his wagon and pointed at the place with the wagon reins that he now held in his hand.

"I want you to meet that man. He is a very poor man, but you will be richer for your time with him."

Mr. Pettis began to walk across the field with long, strong strides. I had never seen him walk with vigor before. In his little log house next to ours he shuffled about, but then, his house was small and there was no room to stride. Out here in the open fields and fresh air, a briskness lengthened his steps. Today in his blue bib overalls and his grey hat with tufts of white hair sticking out under the brim, he seemed a younger man.

Mr. Pettis gazed down at me. "Jesse is his name, and he is an old man — lives alone out here with no electricity or water. Was a cowboy in the old days — the real thing. Lost both his legs in a blizzard. He'll tell you about it once you get to know him."

As we approached the shack, I saw large holes that led under the shack. They looked like burrows.

Osmer saw me looking. "Rats," said Mr. Pettis. "Says that they keep him company. Now that is real loneliness. I try to stop in from time to time."

As we neared, a nearly bald man swung out of his front door on a pair of crutches with a pink plastic leg held high under each armpit and plopped into a chair on the porch. He was pale with a round face and a fuzz of hair on his jaw and the top of his head. He was busy strapping his plastic legs with attached shoes to the ends of his stumps when he noticed us in his yard.

"Osmer!" he yelled. "I didn't see you coming or I'd've had these on sooner."

"Mornin' Jesse."

Jesse placed his hands on the armrests and pushed himself upright from the chair, stomped his legs on the planks as if to set them firmly to his stumps, and then adjusted his suspenders to his shoulders.

"And who is this young man?"

"This young man is Dale Hanson. He lives across the field and down the road next to me and Ada."

Jesse hobbled over to me and took my hand. "Pleased to meet you, Dale Hanson. If Osmer brings you here, you must be a good'un."

He was shaky when he took the step over to me and he stooped and readjusted the problem leg. He looked up at me and said, "One thing sure. When you lose both legs you can at least decide how tall you want to be."

He smiled at me, and I saw eyes that were old and bullet grey.

Mr. Pettis smiled at him. "Too bad you didn't freeze your brain then. You could have decided how smart you wanted to be."

Jesse cackled.

"Ada made you a loaf of bread. I have it in the wagon. I'll drop it off before I go. Meanwhile you fill this young man with some of your wisdom. I have a garden to plow."

Jesse and I talked in the sun — he from his chair next to the outside door as I sat on the planks of the deck and leaned against a rail. Over the next two hours the sun rose from the shoulder of the sky to straight above. From time to time I could hear scurrying in the burrows close by. Crows cawed from the budding trees along the field.

"My legs were frozen black," he said. "I was mending fences when the blizzard hit, and it was Montana cold. It was a white-out and I couldn't see anything to make my way back to camp, so I started to follow the fences. I became too cold to think. My brain just shut down. I came to a gate with a signpost, and I rubbed the snow off the sign and found out I had been going in the wrong direction."

Jesse paused as if he were reliving the ordeal.

"I was so very, very tired pushing all that way through the snow drifts to get where I was, and to think I would have to go back just to start all over again... I just sat down in the snow. I was too tired...to weary... too cold to..."

"Next thing I knew they had me in the bunkhouse and the foreman was sharpening a butcher knife. He had his back to me, but I could hear the sweeping of the sharpener back and forth.

"They were giving me whiskey to put me out, but I wouldn't go under.

"The foreman looked over his shoulder at me to see if I had passed out but when he saw me looking at him, he turned away and continued with his sharpening. His back was to me, and I could not see the knife, but the shuuh, shuuh, shuuh, of the blade being sharpened told me everything.

"There were several silent men in the room all huddled around me where I lay on the bunkhouse table, their eyes frozen on the foreman as they waited. I glanced over just as he nodded to them. His back was still turned to me, so he looked over his shoulder again and nodded one time and raised his eyes. I saw the wrinkles on his forehead deepen just as they all grabbed my arms and legs. I saw the foreman with his sad eyes when he approached me and I started to scream — before the knife ever touched me, I started to scream.

"Someone was petting my hair and talking to me and telling me it would be over soon. I think that I had no shame. I was weeping and pleading with them when they cut through the flesh. When they got to the bone, they went at me with a saw, and I started to puke. I felt every tooth of the saw as it made its way through the bone. Once when I stopped screaming long enough to take a breath, I heard the cutting of the saw just like in the woodshed, and I could smell my own blood and the bone.

"When the foreman got through the first leg, the guy at that leg didn't have anything to hold me down with. He tossed my leg to the side and ran to the stove and got a red-hot iron. He wrapped his hands thick with rags against the heat and came to me at the table. The iron sizzled when he cauterized my stub. They wouldn't let me see down there but I could see the steam rise from the place. With the sounds and smell and pain I banged my head over and over on the tabletop."

"They saved my fingers anyway. Got them." He wiggled them in the air for me to see.

I glanced across the field and saw the blue overalls and flour-sack shirt under them passing up and down the rows of his garden. He told me before that it was a one-person job and that I should just visit with his friend. But even so I felt that I should be there helping.

"There's water in the barrel. The dipper is hanging off the lid if you want some."

I walked over to it. The dipper was filthy, and I was ashamed to think that I had studied what hand he used for things. The dipper hung on the right side of the lid, so I held it in my other hand and drank from that side of the dipper. I replaced it on the former side and then remembered Jesse's legs.

"Can I bring you some?"

"Yes sir."

I brought it to him.

"It smells good, like Clifford Pettis' water."

"It is that. He brings me the small barrel. Two bits a barrel. Won't bring t'other. 'fraid I might fall into the big'un with'in my legs."

I considered making my leave to help Mr. Pettis but Jesse halted my departure.

"Let me tell you about snakes."

I sat down where I was before.

"Montana has its share. It's the rattlers I hate."

"We only have the garter snakes here. You can pick them up. I only have seen the other in pictures. They look wicked."

Jesse looked across the field to the place where the sky and grass met, as if a memory had been tucked into the space.

"I fell off my horse. Don't know how I did it, but it happened, and I slid into a gully. No sooner than I stopped rolling at the bottom there was a big diamondback rattler buzzing at me about to strike. I didn't have to tell myself to freeze — I was skairt-froze. When I could think I eased back and pulled out my pistol and shot it. Took its head clean off and it lay in a heap.

"I started to back away and there was another. The way a cowboy shoots a snake is you point the barrel at its head as close as you dare, and you make little circles around it. Pretty soon you can see the snake's head following the muzzle. That is when you squeeze the trigger.

"A snake strikes at heat, and it takes a bite at the hot lead bullet that comes for it. Head shot every time.

"I started to move and climb out of the gully and there was another snake, and then another, and another. Snakes everywhere. I shot six or eight getting out of the pit.

"When I got to the top and looked down. The gully was crawling with them. Must have been a mass of them coming to mate.

"We came back with dynamite and blasted it. The area stunk for days with dead snakes."

"Wow!" I said. "Jesse, I shoot all the time. I buy .22 shells by the case, and I sure don't shoot like in the movies."

"Cowboys have a way of shooting. None of us could afford lots of ammunition. We put our finger in the trigger guard to the second knuckle. We would just point the knuckle at what we wanted to hit."

"I'll try it," I said.

I saw Mr. Pettis coming toward us with a loaf of bread under his arm.

"One more thing to tell you, young Mr. Hanson. "About holding a pistol."

"Cowboys worked hard, and you would think we would not need to get more muscle to hold that heavy pistol, but here is what we did. We would tie a piece of cord to the middle of a thick stick, and we would tie the other end of it to a weight — maybe a half dozen horseshoes. We put our hands on the ends of the stick and would hold our arms straight out in front of us. We would roll that weight up to the top of the stick and then slowly unroll it to the ground. Do that up and down a few times and holding a gun is easy."

Mr. Pettis came to us with his shirt and hat brim discolored by the sweat of the day.

"Here is that loaf of bread. Ada put in some wild strawberry jam too."

Jesse's face beamed in appreciation. "Tell the Missus, 'Thank you.'"

Mr. Pettis looked over at me. "Did he fill your head with his stories?"

I recalled his stories. "When I shut my eyes tonight, I am going to see amputated legs piled in a corner and my room full of poisonous snakes. I think I will sleep with my light on."

I determined to make my workouts practical. I got a chunk of an old axe handle and tied off one end of a piece of cord to it and a gallon of paint to the other end. I stood and held my arms straight out like Jesse said and rolled the paint can to the top of the wood, then slowly unrolled it to the floor. I rolled it up to the top and back down again three times to make it one set. I did three sets to a workout — nine times up and down. My forearms burned and got to where I could not rotate it another time.

A few weeks later found me standing on a chair doing my nine reps. I was getting forearms like Popeye. By the end of summer, I was standing at the top of the stairs rolling the paint can from the basement to the first floor. I had a strong grip and could certainly hold a gun.

My dad taught me an element of practicality also. I told him that they had us doing chin-ups in gym class. Dad thought back to his army days and said, "There is no practical use for a chin-up. There is nothing that you can do with one. He took me to a fence. "Climb over that wall using your hands like you do for a chin up."

It didn't take a second to see the point. My hands had to face away from me to pull myself over. From then on, I would only do pull-ups. They were much harder to do than chin ups but by high school, my personal workout included three sets of thirty-five pull-ups.

Push-ups. My dad said, "They tell you to do them wide apart. That will give you a wide chest, but it will not help you in real life. Watch," he said. "I am going to come at you, and I want you to stop me, but freeze when I say so."

Dad came toward me fast and I put up my arms to stop him.

"Stop! Where are your hands?"

I looked. They were at his shoulders.

"See they are shoulder width — not wide apart or narrow. Now shove me away from you."

I did.

"You just did a push-up. You were standing up, but the motion was a push-up. Most exercises are for a use, and they are practical."

They say that dips are three times as hard to do as push-ups, so I rigged up two shovel handles across the stairs to the basement to do dips — three set of seventy for a workout. We made a rudimentary set of weights and a bench. I did martial arts, and ran, and had a philosophy of exercise which was, "It is the one that you cannot do that helps you." I never stopped working out the rest of my life.

Chapter Eight

There was a stretch of time in my maturation that I am not proud of. Alcohol was the chief culprit, but the condemnation was that it was incongruous and did not reflect who I was.

For an unknown reason I wanted to know what it was like to be under the influence, intoxicated. Maybe I simply thought that I could not very well speak against that of which I knew nothing. Whatever my rationalization, my first taste of booze was done in a controlled manner.

I got a school friend and told him what I was going to do. I got a bottle of what they called "hundred horse vodka" and brought it home. It was winter and my dad was asleep. I called my friend over to our house and essentially stole my dad's car. I drove out to the lake and took a side road that ended at a couple of farms. I cracked the bottle and started to drink. Before we got to the end of the road my head started to spin, I got dizzy, and I got drunk.

I had planned for the friend to take over when the time came. It came.

"Zhoo zrive," I said. He was more than ready to get me away from behind the wheel.

The friend turned us around and we headed back to town and our house. I rolled the window down, hung my head into the freezing night air, and puked the ten miles all the way back.

At the house he laughed at my drunkenness and watched me stumble and stagger into the house.

In my bedroom, everything was swimming around. I was dizzy and very drunk. Had I not heaved for ten miles in the twenty below zero air I probably would have heaved in the bed. "In all," I thought to myself, "That episode is over. I sure am glad I did not get caught."

Morning came. My dad called to me to get up. My mouth was dry and stuck together. I pulled myself together and came down the stairs as if nothing had occurred the previous night. The night before was my secret.

Dad looked at me and said, "I want to show you something outside."

I was clueless, but when we stepped into the driveway and walked to the passenger side of his car — the evidence of my escapade was clear. There was hard evidence.

From the passenger window and along the entire side of the car was the vomit of ten miles frozen to the side. That morning I stood in the driveway in the cold with a straw broom and multiple buckets of hot water and cleaned with the faint Bible verse whispering into my ear, "Be sure your sin will find you out."

There was a girl who melted my heart and turned me into putty. Her name was Molly, and she lived across the river in our sister town in Canada. She was pretty and always cheerful, and I tried to be with her whenever I was not in school or working. To get to her house in Canada I had to cross the bridge and go through Customs but the officers at the border crossing had a working agreement with our local police that any juvenile with alcohol on his breath would be arrested. The fine was automatic — one hundred dollars.

This beautiful girl was a candle flame, and I was the moth drawn to that flame, but I did not dare to walk across the bridge with alcohol on my breath. The only solution for me was to cross Rainy River with its strong current by walking on the logs that were contained by a log boom where they waited to be hauled into the mill. When I could see that the logs spanned the whole width of the river, I walked them like the loggers of the old days.

Twice I fell off the logs and into the river and the current. I determined before ever starting the crossings that if I ever fell, I would never try to get back on the logs along their sides. I knew my body would spread the logs apart when I went under, but the logs would close over me, and I would not have the purchase to spread them apart again. I held my breath and felt my way to the end of a log and pulled myself up from there. Once in the dominion of Canada, Molly would find me soaked and wet and knocking at her door.

I had a 1953 Cadillac with a 1958 Chrysler engine in it that effortlessly went 120 miles an hour. I could drive at speed, and never did it feel like I was driving fast. My dad said that I could pass anything on the highway except a gas station.

Some of us went for a drive in my car. I thought how much I enjoyed that automobile. The engine purred with raw power. It was spacious and comfortable. This had all the new inventions: power steering and power brakes, unlike my old Chevy that I had to double clutch to get into most gears.

We were heading toward the lake country when a friend said from the passenger seat, "My dad says the smelt are in."

The passenger's name was Eddie. I couldn't tell you his last name for my life. He was an Eddie, one of a dozen Eddies in our school. Every class has a bunch of Eddies. They all look the same: average height, tending toward slim, not athletic. They were never in sports and there was nothing to recall them to mind years after a class graduated and dispersed into the world. Eddies do not have buck teeth, nervous twitches or unusual mannerisms to set them apart. Eddie would be the perfect spy. The enemy spy cameras could pan the crowd and never notice Eddie.

This Eddie had brown hair in the normal close-cut and looked forward as he spoke. He never was one to invigorate a conversation with his insight. But there was always an Eddie to sit in the passenger seat so you were not alone.

"My dad says that the smelt are in," Eddie said a second time.

We all looked at him. This was useful information.

Smelt are small fish, not much more than six inches long. At our house my mother dipped them in flour and deep-fried them like French fries. They were a delicacy at our table as our town was far from the source of the fish, and it was rare we ever had any. They did not taste fishy and when deep-fried, were eaten bones, fins, and all. When we could get them, I did most of the cleaning.

When I had buckets of smelt to clean, it took about ten seconds to clean one. The magic tool was a scissor. One snip took off the head, then I ran one of the two blades down the stomach and snipped again. Without setting the scissor down I ran my thumb down the stomach cavity and pulled out the entrails. Time me — ten seconds max.

They are slender and swim in large schools and spawn in the streams that feed into the Great Lakes; Lake Superior in our case. The nearest spawning stream out of Superior was two hundred miles from our town. Perfect for a 1953 Cadillac with a hot 1958 Chrysler engine in it and soft comfortable seats.

"They are in! We got some at our house, so I know that it is true," said a voice from the back seat. He was another Eddie.

I think that we all got the idea at the same time. None of us had ever caught a smelt. Our fathers were always working and too practical to drive all the way to Lake Superior just to catch a fish that did not look all that different than the minnows they used for bait.

"Let's do it," I loudly said. I had heard how it was done. I imagined us wading in the tributaries of that great body of water with our swaying lanterns and dip nets scooping the precious prey into our tubs. It was an irresistible adventure.

"I'll rig up the dip nets with garden hose around the metal, so we don't tear the mesh off on the rocks," said my brother Del.

"I'll get the beer!" announced the other Eddie from the back seat.

"We all need to get hip waders and lanterns," I said.

"My mom works at People's Café. I bet she could get us some food to take," said Eddie from the front seat.

Eddie was showing promise.

"I'll get the beer," second Eddie repeated.

Before we knew it, we had skipped school on Friday for an early start. We also made an early start on Second Eddie's beer stash.

We found a fast-moving stream that flowed into Lake Superior that we could wade and started to dip in the pools for smelt. The rocks were slippery to walk on with water slime on them and Eddie's beer in our systems, but we were catching smelt and living a dream.

Darkness fell on us and added to our adventure. The night was chill, and the stream was cold against our waders.

"Have another beer," said Eddie Two.

I kept thinking to myself, "I really do not need beer to make this trip a pleasant memory."

I slipped on a wet, mossy rock and went in over my waders. The icy shock froze me in place. My waders were full of water. I decided to exit the stream, sit on a boulder and empty my boots.

I was tugging on them by the heels and trying to remove what in its wetness clung to my pants. The rubber of the boots squeaked against my wet socks. "You know guys," I said into the darkness, "They say that smelt are salt water. If that is true it means they came all the way from the Atlantic Ocean and they had to swim all five of the Great Lakes just to get to the extreme west end of the journey so we could catch them. Think of it!" No one answered from the night.

"Well, anyway, I'm going to put these smelt into the trunk and see what we have."

The tub in my trunk was immense. It was one of those square wash tubs from the farm that held at least fifty gallons. It was half full.

"We are making headway on filling this," I announced into the dark. When I didn't get an answer again, I went back and checked on the guys. Both Eddies were crumpled up in balls and sleeping along the bank. I found a place nearby and sat down and dozed. It seemed but a moment and morning came with greyness and a local fog rose from the water. I let the guys sleep and shut my eyes again.

We dipped for smelt all day Saturday and Saturday night and most of Sunday. For the most part we had filled the tub to the brim with fish and the extra buckets beside them. I thought to myself, "Except for the beer I would not have changed anything of the trip."

"We better head back. As it is we will be driving all night to get to class in the morning."

The two Eddies tipped the last of the beer and shuffled like zombies into the car. I headed down the highway for the seven-hour trip back home as the automatic streetlights began to light along the highway. I was a little dizzy and my eyes were dry and scratchy.

I drove for several hours, at times nearly sleeping at the wheel, but the occasional deer along the road with their headlamp eyes forced me awake. I caught myself nodding at the wheel and it came to the time I knew that I would be fully asleep at the wheel.

"Hey, can one of you guys drive? I am getting dangerous."

Front seat Eddie spoke. "I can do it." He sounded like Wyatt Earp — "Meet me at the O.K. Corral."

I stopped the car and he sauntered around and slid behind the wheel of my thoroughbred Cadillac. I got into the back passenger seat next to my brother and was instantly asleep.

Sleep was easy as I sat there in the back. We had gone on for the last two and a half days with almost no sleep, were constantly dipping our nets in the cold stream, and of course nipping at Eddie Number Two's libations. The car was warm, and the purring of the engine was soporific.

I had gotten to that place in slumber when most senses sign off, but something lurched me awake. The world around us in my car was utterly silent — no conversation, no shuffling around, no indication that anyone — anyone including driver Eddie, was awake. For the first time also, I had the impression that we were traveling at speed.

With a gasp I leaned far enough over the back seat to see the speedometer beyond the one hundred twenty miles per hour mark, and Eddie's eyes closed and his chin resting firmly on his chest.

"Eddie!" I shouted at him but at that instant the Cadillac left the highway and was completely airborne for twenty feet. We hit a steel culvert and embankment nose first to the sound of crashing metal and breaking glass.

I never passed out. I recall every microsecond in detail. I remember flying over the back seat and my head hitting the windshield with a dull thud. My knee smashed into the dashboard as I was whipped across and flew over it. My elbow smashed on top of the hood of the car, and I recall bouncing on the hood then flying through the air and into the night and landing in a field.

The moment I landed in the weeds I sprang to my feet and ran to the car. Everyone was still inside.

"Is everyone okay? Anyone hurt?"

I ran to the car and yanked open the doors. "Are you okay?" then to the next door, "Are you okay?"

None of us was hurt. Steam poured from the engine. The sounds of broken, settling metal parts popped in the night. My car was crinkled and smashed like one of the beer cans that Eddie Two smashed under his boot.

I had a hundred small cuts on my face, none of them deep. I had no broken bones, nothing sprained. I did not limp or hobble. A glance at the crumpled heap that was now embedded into the embankment and it left me amazed at our escape from injury.

We walked around the car considering our predicament and finally concluded, "There is nothing that we can do here. We just have to get back to town and figure it all out tomorrow."

I looked around. There were no lights of houses where we could borrow a phone to call for a ride. There was no glow on the horizon indicating a town within walking distance.

"We will have to hitchhike a ride to the Falls," I said, and I walked to the side of the road and waited for a car to flag down.

A fast-moving tractor-trailer came by at speed. As the truck approached, I stepped to the shoulder with my thumb out. In its headlights I noticed a sparkling on the highway. My trunk lid had been torn off with the impact and the tub with ten thousand smelt littered the highway. The truck had no intention of stopping in a remote area with a man with a bloody face beside the road.

The truck drove over the first of the smelt and began to slide and swerve on the pavement. I saw the brake lights come on and as the driver regained control of his rig he put on the gas and sped away down the road.

Truck after truck passed us by, never stopping or slowing, but all skidding and sliding along the blacktop on a layer of slippery smelt.

"Maybe if we could put some light on the car crash, they would know that we were in trouble. We found a couple of unbroken flashlights to shine on the car and the next tractor slowed with his window down.

"Trouble?"

"Yes sir. We fell asleep at the wheel. It's pretty smashed up. Can you give us a ride?"

"Hop in son. I'll get you home."

The next day we went to school, tired and as lifeless as scarecrows. I had many cuts on my face, but the others did not have a mark on them. Del and I never saw the two Eddies again. They never called or asked about the car or asked if they could do anything.

When I got home from school, I found that my dad had hired a wrecker to haul my car home. I did not know the exact place on the highway to mark the place for them, but they had no difficulty finding it. Miles before they saw the wreck, they saw the circling cloud of gulls and ravens in the sky that were feeding on our smelt.

My car was so smashed and embedded into the concrete and steel that when the wrecker pulled it from the culvert, it came out in two pieces. Dad left it in the yard where I would see it every day and ponder my narrow escape.

I did ponder the accident. I squeezed through the crumpled door and sat behind the wheel one last time. To my right I saw the place where I was ejected through the windshield, and I could see hairs from my head still stuck to the edges. The driver of the wrecker left the back half of my car directly behind the front half and I sat in the back seat also and wondered how it was possible for me to be ejected from there and fly through that windshield and land in a pasture and not be hurt.

I sat on the back steps of the house and studied the wreck. "Dale, it is as if God Himself had thrust me out of that vehicle and said, 'Young man, I guess you haven't been listening to me, so I did this to get your attention.'"

I don't know how long I sat there, but the evening mosquitos were in my hair and ears, and I said to myself, "That is not who you are. The drinking and parties are for someone else, but not for you."

I determined that my life would never center around alcohol or a party again. I swatted the mosquitos off my face and went to my car and pulled off a couple of the nobs from the dash to remember it.

Those heavy round knobs sat on my dresser for years as a reminder, long after the car had been hauled away and forgotten.

Chapter Nine

The first Monday morning after high school graduation I filled out my application to work at the mill. It was early when I walked up those outside stairs to the personnel office, well before the day shift began. The night fog still hung over the river that bounded the mill and lay like a shawl over the shoulders of the drunks that were passed out on the bank. As I walked across the parking lot, a man with a black metal lunch pail slammed it on the hood of his car, jerked the back door open and shouted at a wino who had crawled inside and passed out in the back seat.

I had dressed neatly for the interview but was also prepared to work a shift had one been available. I held the door for a secretary who carried a cup of steaming coffee with both hands.

"Are you here to see Mr. Strain?"

"Yes ma'am."

"He should be here in a minute. He always comes in early before shift."

"Are they hiring now?"

"Mr. Strain will have to tell you that. I'll give him your application."

I took a chair and waited to be called. I chose the one closest to his door so anyone coming into the office would know that I was next. The secretary called my name.

"You can go in now, Mr. Hanson."

Jack Strain was in his thirties, a blond pleasant man with a firm handshake.

"You have a grip, Mr. Hanson, and callouses. That's a good sign. I read your application and it looks good. Why do you want to work for us and why do you think that we should hire you?"

"College, sir. No one ever told me about grants, and I want to pay my own way. I won't burden my parents with tuition. And," I continued, "I actually like physical work. My parents taught me a good work ethic and you can check with the people I have worked for."

He smiled at me. "We try to help our college kids, so when we can, we will put them on. We don't have any openings right now, but we will call you."

"Do they come up sometimes during the day?"

"Sometimes they do, Mr. Hanson."

"Good, I will wait in the waiting room."

I stood and shook his hand and thanked him and when the door closed behind us, I took a seat outside of his office. The secretary looked at me with a puzzled expression. I remained there until it was well into the shift, and I was certain that they would not need anyone that day.

Just before seven the next morning I returned to the office. The mill parking lot looked full, so I parked next to the lot on Second Street, just outside the Busy Bee Bar. The door was open and a man with a black eye was sweeping spilled beer into the street. The bar was dark inside with just enough light to reveal the outlines of the metal barstool legs. Spilled beer of the night before reeked its sour smell into the morning.

Two Indians stumbled from a door next to the bar and into the street. One of them was a solid looking man with a deep red-brown face and I wondered if he had been one of those who had slept, face up into the sun on the river bank the day before. The other Indian was a woman, much younger, who walked on rubber legs and all but stumbled into him. She wore a heavy dress, black shoes and white anklets and complained in a loud drunken voice. "I da wan' go there, I wan' go...."

The Indian man never uttered a word. His mouth was a thin line across his face. His eyes were as black as stone arrowheads.

I checked in with the secretary and took a seat in the waiting room. This time I brought a large book, Herman Melville, and settled in to wait. With the book, they knew that I was prepared to be there the whole day.

Wednesday was a drizzly day tending toward rain when I arrived, and I wondered where the derelicts went on days like this.

I held the door for the secretary again, but this time she had two coffees in her hands. "I got one for you too."

Mr. Strain opened his office door and smiled at me. "I suppose that you will sit in my office until you get a job, won't you?"

Before I could answer, he continued, "Well we can't pass up on a good man like you, can we?

His secretary smiled at me and winked.

"How about tonight on the midnight shift in the wood room?"

Unlike those hundreds of workers who zombied through the mill gate with their lunch pails, I liked the place. The smell of the wood room was the odor of forests and trees and bark and sap and water and fresh air blowing off the river. The wood room was the first stop of the logs on their way to become paper to make *Reader's Digest* and numerous other periodicals, and containers and siding for houses.

"Got your steel toed boots on?" the foreman asked. "I have the perfect job for a young man with your muscles," and we walked to the outside of the huge building where a railroad track sided it. Several railroad flat cars, which were essentially boxcars with no sides, lined the place, filled to overflowing with eight-foot logs.

He handed me a pick. A pick is the length of an axe, but instead of a blade, it comes to a point with a slight hook on the end, the shape of a very thin beak of an eagle.

"See that conveyer belt between the tracks and the building? Your job is to unload these logs from the railroad cars onto the conveyor belt where they go to that man up there," and he pointed to a man in a small shelter with an open side facing the flat cars. The man waved at me with a hand that held a small pick. "He is called a sawyer. They run a saw that will cut these logs into four-foot lengths. From there they go to a very large bark drummer where the logs tumble until all the bark comes off."

He looked at me to be sure I was following the procedure.

"You only need to unload logs when the conveyor belt is moving. Follow me," and we climbed up the end of the cars to the top of the pile.

"You hold the pick like this and stick the hook-end into the end of a log and slide it off the car on to the belt… like this." The foreman slid a few logs on to the belt.

"You try."

I began to slide logs onto the conveyor. The motion was similar to cutting grain with an old-time scythe.

"There are a few tricks you will learn to make it easier, and the sawyer will certainly have something to say about how he would like the logs arranged, but this is good for now. I see that the belt has started. It's all yours."

The foreman let me stay on the night shift most of the summer. I loved the physical labor and the smell of the building. Some nights I worked the river and pulled logs from the booms to a conveyor belt with a long pike pole. I learned to start a log and then use the river current to guide the rest to the belt.

I worked three jobs at once that summer. Because I worked the night shift at the mill, my days were free to keep working at the grocery store. Mr. Samuelson, for whom I had worked the previous three years, let me go to full time at the store and adjusted my hours so I could work both places.

"Anything that I can do to help. You have been a very good employee for us."

The third job was to work in the woods with my dad. Dad still worked full time at the mill in the wood room, but he moonlighted by logging. He secured a special contract that no one else wanted — for logs that had to be peeled in place. Imagine having to manually peel the bark from every log. During the week when there were open days from the other two places of employment, I peeled logs for a company that made fence posts.

Eight feet was the standard length of a log for the mills. That was the width of both truck trailers and railroad cars. We felled the trees, limbed them and cut them to length. Then dad came along with his chainsaw and scored a groove the depth of the bark along the length of each log.

A large part of that work in the summer of 1965 involved peeling the bark off every log. Two conditions were necessary to do the work. The first was that the tree needed to be peeled right away while the wet slippery moisture was still between the bark and the wood. The second necessity was a good tool.

The tools did not exist anywhere, so Dad designed and made them from leaf springs from a car. They were flat, slightly beveled inventions shaped like large rib bones, the ends of which were about two or three inches wide. We improved our tools the first hours that we used them. I found that the sharpness of the tool dug into the wood instead of sliding between the bark and the fibers and the square corners needed to be rounded for the same reason. After a few hours of peeling, we found that the square edges of the tool blistered our hands, so we beveled the corners and taped them. Ultimately the most effective tool for the task was a simple one.

To peel the logs, we got on our knees and placed our tools into the grove made with the chainsaw and worked it between the bark and the wood, loosening the bark all the way around the log the full length, like a casing. When we finished peeling a log, it lay there on the forest floor, a bare log glistening like moist flesh, and beside it lay a single piece of bark like that of the shed, hollow skin of a snake.

That summer was very hot, Midwest hot, and humid. Hunkered over the logs on my knees, sweat slithered down my face and into my eyes. I clawed my fingers through my hair, but my head still felt sticky and crawly. Sweat coursing through my hair and onto my face made my head feel like bugs were crawling there. I felt sticky. Mosquitoes buzzed around me and were caught in the hairs of my ears, and buzzed there until I dug them out. Horse flies and the deer flies stung like the plagues in the Book of Revelation, and always where they could not be swatted. It seemed that a deer fly would make a diversionary attack somewhere and then a horse fly would strike at the unguarded place. They must have read Sun Tzu.

My knees hurt from supporting my weight on twigs and I began to carry a large chunk of moss with me to put under them as I moved along. My back ached from being bent over for hours and I relieved the pain by stacking peeled logs to give it relief. At the end of the day, we could barely stand and walked like old men. Dad, from his many years in the woods hunting and trapping, knew of a flowing artesian spring nearby and we tasted water that seemed to flow from Heaven.

It was July 28, a full month before I would leave to go to college. My back ached from being hunkered over my batch of just fallen logs and I stretched my back. I had gone most of the summer on just a few hours' sleep each night. A very slight breeze passed over the site, just enough to keep the flies and mosquitoes from us and dry the sweat from our faces. The relief was luxuriant.

I looked around. There was moss in various colors around me. Sun beams entered the clearing, having twisted their shoulders to get around the poplars and branches and lay exhausted, like me, among the shadows. For the first time I saw that I had been peeling in a good patch of blueberries and I began to eat some of them.

I heard Dad's chainsaw stop nearby.

"Hey, Dad. Lots of blueberries here."

"Be right there. I need a break."

Dad looked as tired as I felt, and he sat down heavily and leaned against a tree.

We had a transistor radio with us. Sometimes we listened to a baseball game on it when we went fishing. I turned it on.

The radio had just cut into the President's press conference speech on Vietnam. We ate blueberries as we listened and sat in moss as thick as a cushion.

Why must young Americans, born into a land exultant with hope and with golden promise, toil and suffer and sometimes die in such a remote and distant place?

The answer, like the war itself, is not an easy one, but it echoes clearly from the painful lessons of half a century. Three times in my lifetime, in two World Wars and in Korea, Americans have gone to far lands to fight for freedom. We have learned at a terrible and brutal cost that retreat does not bring safety and weakness does not bring peace.

It is this lesson that has brought us to Vietnam. This is a different kind of war. There are no marching armies or solemn declarations....

Dad reached into his pack and pulled a mason jar of Kool Aid and handed it to me. I took several swallows, wiped my mouth, and handed it back to him.

Most of the non-Communist nations of Asia cannot, by themselves alone, resist growing might and the grasping ambition of Asian Communism. Our power, therefore, is a very vital shield. If we are driven from the field in Vietnam, then no nation can ever again have the same confidence in American promise or in American protection.

In each land the forces of independence would be considerably weakened, and an Asia so threatened by Communist domination would certainly imperil the security of the United States itself.

We did not choose to be the guardians at the gate, but there is no one else.

"Let's call it a day, son. I'm all in. I bet you are too."

"I have to work tonight. I could use a couple more hours of sleep."

Dad put the chainsaw and gas can under a tarp behind a log while I gathered our packs. I handed him the Kool Aid as we walked.

"The President is sending fifty thousand more troops. Maybe I should enlist and go too but I've been so focused on college I haven't paid it enough attention."

Dad had his head down in thought as we walked out of the woods. Perhaps he was remembering that he enlisted when his war was just starting up.

"You will need to do what your conscience tells you to do. For now, just go to school. If this is a quick war and you enlist it will be over before you are trained enough to go, and you will have been able to do neither. If this is a big war you will have plenty of time to go."

"I think you are right, Dad."

The summer of sixty-five passed in a blur of work and sleep. Summer flowers dropped their leaves. Blueberries darkened to blue-black and began to fall from their stems. Partridges drummed in the woods and twice I even saw them sitting on our felled logs, their tail feathers spread as they drummed with their wings. Although it was early for me to expect a sky full of duck and geese, I heard swans fly high overhead as I slept in my bed — or did I dream it?

Before I had adjusted to the thought, it was time to go to school. I had been accepted at Bob Jones University, a Christian school of very high moral and scholastic standards, and I looked forward to it like a mason jar of Kool Aid at the end of a hot day.

Dad gave me his car. It was a nine-year-old Ford that ran well and never had problems. He put tires on it, had a tune up done, changed the oil and filled the tank.

"Yours," he said. "You shouldn't have any problems with it, even driving all the way to South Carolina."

Bruce, my friend from church and youth group, enrolled at Bob Jones also, in part for its very high scholastic standards and reputation, but also because the university had the largest gallery of famous religious paintings in the world. The great masters were all represented on the walls: Rubens, van Dyck and many of the other old masters of religious art; Flemish, Italian, Spanish, renaissance, baroque, and a few contemporary artists to include Salman's *Head of Christ* and *Christ Knocking at the Heart's Door*. Bruce was a talented artist and enrolled as an art major.

Bruce was a handsome, blond young man who was always ready to smile and for an adventure. From where we grew up in northern Minnesota, neither of us had seen much of the world. We had never seen a Black person. I met only one Jewish person in my life. His name was Irving Shear, a short, dark-haired man who always wore black who never forgot my name. We decided that we would see more of the world as we traveled to South Carolina stopping at every state on the way and visiting every capitol city.

We went west, far out of our direct route to school, passing through all those states and capitols and when we came to the Atlantic, made our way south. We were passing through New Jersey and turning on the radio, heard Carl McIntire on his program. His voice was heard on six hundred radio stations, and he was exposing Communism and the fifth columnists in America. He blasted the liberal left who wanted to give Communism a free hand in Asia and marched in American cities to oppose our entry into the war.

McIntire was saying into the microphone, "Freedom is everybody's business — your business, my business, the church's business — and a man who will not use his freedom to defend his freedom does not deserve his freedom."

For the next half hour as we traveled over one of the small states, we heard him unmask those in congress and the colleges who sided with our enemies.

"Bruce," I said when the program was over, "I am almost certain that I will be involved in fighting Communism. I know that I am supposed to go to college and study for the ministry, but I think the world is in great danger."

I looked over at Bruce. Bruce always had a way of listening that suggested he was hearing what was said for the first time.

"I have been thinking of Communism and how it is growing, and I think that I can put it in a real context. Tell me what you think of this…"

He studied my face as I went on.

"You know how we Christians have been zealous in spreading the gospel? It's the Great Commission of Christ and every Christian is to be involved."

He nodded his head.

"Jesus initially gave the Commission to twelve men and the gospel spread from there. That commission was given about two thousand years ago. Starting with twelve men and proceeding for two thousand years — how many people, living and dead, total, do you think have heard the gospel? Not been converted — just heard it?"

Bruce tried to imagine the centuries and revivals and printed Bibles and books.

"Millions! Maybe, hundreds of millions."

"I read somewhere that they think that one billion people, living and dead combined have heard the basic message of salvation."

Bruce knew that I had more to add to what I had just said. So far it was only a factoid, a statistic.

"Listen to this, Bruce. Karl Marx published *The Communist Manifesto* with Friedrich Engels in 1848, and in 1918, Communism really began to spread from the work of just a handful of men. The famous ones that we have read about were there. This is 1965, less than fifty years after, call it fifty." I looked at him from my driving. "How many people living today have become Communists? Not just heard the message but are waving the little red book of Mao around or flying the hammer and sickle in Russia and Vietnam?"

Bruce's eyes sparkled and he seemed enthralled at my proposition. "Ahh, I don't know. Millions," and he thought of China's huge population. "Many millions."

"I looked at him carefully. "Bruce, they say that two billion people are converted Communists."

I let it sink in, but I was not sure that he caught the import of what I was getting at.

"Bruce, both started out with a dozen men, but in fifty years they have reached twice as many people as all of Christianity has in two thousand years."

I waited a minute for him to digest what I had said.

"That is why I think that Communism has to be stopped at all costs, now."

I felt myself nodding my head at my own conclusions.

"Bruce, you cannot imagine how hard this is going to be for me to sit in a classroom when there is a war on."

Bruce's face took on a serious expression, but it was clear that he himself would not be involved. We were coming into our nation's capitol, heading toward the Capitol Building. "Do you think those people who are protesting just like to riot? Are they stupid?" he asked.

I know I sighed out loud, for I was saddened by my own words. "No. I think that they believe in Communism, and they are helping the Viet Cong."

Blocks from the parts of the city that we wanted to see, we noticed the previews of the disappointment that lay before us. We wanted to see cherry blossoms (even though it was the wrong time of year) and pristine white buildings and reflecting pools. Instead, the smell of tear gas stung our eyes blocks from our goal. Debris littered the night-washed streets, and long-haired hippies, and hairy-legged misanthropes struck the hood of my car with their signs, "Out of Vietnam Now."

***

They called Bob Jones University "The Buckle in the Bible Belt." It was the epicenter of fundamental, Biblical Christianity. In that the school believed that they represented the Lord, the school took great care that nothing would ever damage the reputation of the institution. Everything about the college was done with quality. There was not a shoddy aspect to be found on the grounds.

Students were ladies and gentlemen. Girls wore dresses and the boys wore ties before noon. Chapel was mandatory as was church, either on campus or at a Bible-believing church in town. Students did not party, they studied. Regardless of one's major, the school insisted on a well-rounded education and that included concerts, and plays. Bob Jones Jr. had a brilliant mind with absolute recall and could recite all of Shakespeare's plays by heart.

I took on an eighteen-hour load and worked full time at Buy-Low Super Market in the meat department. I worked after class and did a twelve hour shift every Saturday. Waiting on customers at the meat counter was my first experience with southern "Black folk." They would come to where I worked behind the glass and order something, and I would have them repeat what they wanted until I discerned English in their speech. "Ah wanna ha' pawn mull," for example. The last syllable of a sentence was lifted in tone and always sounded like a question instead of a statement.

I would ask them to repeat it until I discovered what they wanted — in this case, a half-pound of mullet fish. I would smile at them when I understood, and I suspected that they always came to my end of the counter just to hear that "Yankee" talk.

I majored in theology and minored in Koine Greek, the common Greek of two thousand years ago in which the New Testament was written. That Greek is the most exacting language in the world so a direct translation of it into English is exactly what God wanted to say.

Other classes included exegesis, theology, philosophy, logic and homiletics. I finished my black belt in judo and excelled in gymnastics.

On Sunday some of us preached in the Carolinas and Georgia, mostly in the prison work farms and jails. Prisoners wore the striped jump suits and ball and chain and broke rocks until the boss man brought them back as he rode upon his tall horse with his shotgun cradled over his lap.

It was late in my junior year, and I had started a ministry in a couple of prisons and was driving back one day with a few other students in the car. My car's gas was on empty, and I silently prayed that we would make it back. I know that I was "called" to go to college and prepare for the ministry, but I was also convinced that I needed to do my part in the war against Communism.

I philosophically believed in the war. I was a Christian and prepared to die — the draftee might not be. I wanted to do my part.

Someone in the car was talking about the domino theory. "People in the news and the protesters are mocking the domino theory."

"How can they mock it?" I protested. "It's right there before their eyes. Now you have North Vietnam, then it was Laos, then it was Cambodia, now it's South Vietnam. They are toppling one after the other. Thailand is next."

"Maybe it isn't our concern," the voice said.

"Let me tell you something about how long the United States and Thailand have been friends," I said over my shoulder. "When we were fighting the American Civil War, the king of Thailand (then it was called Siam) offered Abraham Lincoln troops and elephants to help win the civil war."

The next few miles passed in silence with only the wind outside our windows and the sound of our rubber tires on the pavement as we were all deep in our own thoughts.

"I have decided that I am going to enlist. But if I am going to quit college and do that, I am going to be the best. I am going to try for the Green Berets."

"Do you believe in the war that much?" the voice asked again from the back seat.

"Some people are dodging the draft but as for me, if they wouldn't send me to Vietnam, I would write my congressman. If I had to, I would pay my own way to get there."

At the end of that semester, I closed my Greek lexicon and my book of Strong's Theology and placed them with the rest of my books on the shelf in the room where I grew up. Next to those books were the round knobs from the crumpled dash of my Cadillac and a small cardboard box that my Uncle Herb had sent home just days before he was killed in the Battle of the Bulge. Inside that box were pieces of shrapnel and several bullets that he had picked up from the battlefield. Dozens of them were bullets with bullet holes through them — from a conflict so severe, the gunfire so intense, the very air so thick with flying rounds that bullets collided in the air.

I remembered as a young boy rolling those bullets in my fingers and considering such a battlefield whose very air was a downpour of death. If I survived the war I would finish my studies, but for now I had a duty to perform. I quit college and enlisted in the army.

Chapter Ten

The sergeant sat behind his desk with his hands folded and patiently waited for what I had to say. Behind him on the wall was a large poster of a soldier who was standing erect with his bayonetted rifle in his hands amid a battle filled with destruction. The colors of the scene were as dark as a thunderstorm, black and deep purple, and the fire and flashing explosions were in stark contrast against that darkness. The soldier in the painting looked to the side over one shoulder and the artist skillfully placed duty, courage, and sacrifice into his eyes. The caption of the poster said, "Courage and gallantry in action…Infantry, United States Army."

To the right of the recruiter, on his desk, was a bronze statue of a Minuteman, whose base was squared and even with the edges of the table. To his left was a cup filled with olive drab pens, his name plaque, and a stack of brochures in a neat pile.

I wanted it in writing. No one enlists to be a Green Beret, I knew that, but I wanted a guarantee that I could try out for it. Only a few could make it. "One hundred men will test today, but only three win the Green Beret." Isn't that what the song said?

I was physically fit — I could not imagine how I could be more so. My scores in the intelligence and aptitude tests were extremely high and I did not want to be syphoned off to an area the military deemed more needful.

"I want it in writing," I told the sergeant. Perhaps this is the only time in a military career when someone can demand something of a superior.

"Right here," he said, turning the paper toward me so I could read it. "Right here."

He put the eraser end of his pencil on the words. "Airborne, Application to Special Forces guaranteed."

I held his pen in my hand, black ink only on a government document, and looked at the sergeant. I looked into his eyes for truth before I signed. It was February 14, 1968 when I penned my name and began perhaps the greatest adventure of my life.

Basic training was at Fort Campbell, Kentucky. Prior to leaving I memorized the long passage in First Peter One, which ended with "if ye do these things, ye shall never fail." I enjoyed the training and admired how the military could take two hundred independent minds and turn them into a single unit with one will. I studied the traits of those who trained us — what I disliked and what I admired in the character of those sergeants and sifted them for the traits I would one day wish to see in myself.

Sometime around the fifth or sixth week we earned the privilege of going to the canteen after the end of a training day. Two of us were leaving the company area and proceeding down the sidewalk toward it when a loud voice of command halted us.

"Halt! You two. Halt!"

We stopped in our tracks and looked toward the voice.

"Attention!"

It was one of the sergeants.

"Who is in charge of this formation?"

I was bewildered. "What formation?" I thought. There were just two of us just walking off to the store.

"Who is in charge?" the voice repeated.

"We are just walking to the Canteen, Sergeant."

"There are two of you. That is a formation. Who is in charge?"

"I don't know," I admitted.

"Someone is always in charge. Which one of you? Who has the most rank?"

"We are both privates, Sergeant."

"Then who has the date of rank?"

We looked at each other. "We joined the same day."

"Then whose name is first in the alphabet?"

I thought, "I'm Hanson, he is Baker."

"He is Sergeant."

"Then call your formation to order. Someone is always in charge in the army. Is that clear?"

And as we marched in step to the canteen, I pondered his words. There was a subtle wisdom in what he had chosen to impart to two privates that evening. They were not wasted on me. I would not assume that the duty to act belonged to someone else. The crisis of any minute could fall on me. I would be ready.

A couple of weeks later our company graduated basic training and three of us were the honor graduates of the class and promoted. Baker and I were in that group, and I wondered if that sergeant thought to himself, "Those two soldiers will be leaders some day and they need an extra lesson in military life."

The trucks met us at spotless and manicured Fort Gordon, Georgia, and whisked us, "the unwashed," off in deuce-and-a-half trucks with the white star on the side and olive drab canvas tops, and we proceeded to our destination: Camp Crocket. Our boots never touched the dusted sidewalks of the main post. Our camp would be where we spent the next eight weeks of advanced infantry training. We sat on the plank benches of the truck bed with our duffel bags piled in the middle and watched the red cloud of road dust billow behind us.

Someone had a transistor radio and I listened to the lyrics of a popular song of the day.

A rainy night in Georgia

91

A rainy night in Georgia
Lord, I believe it's rainin' all over the world
I feel like it's rainin' all over the world

The trucks went for miles away from the main post and signs of civilization along the red gravel road. From time to time we turned off and drove on smaller roads, deeper into the forest with only the music and the sound of the road keeping us company.

"Quick, turn the music off. I think we're here."

We pulled into a central area and were met by a middle-aged master sergeant with a large belly and permanent scowl on his face. Next to him were several young sergeants and a few staff sergeants.

Training began immediately. It was intense and unrelenting. The cadre tried to break us physically and emotionally. There was little sleep. For the next eight weeks none of us walked anywhere — we ran. In the mess hall when we ate hot food, we were allowed three minutes to eat it and leave. There was one shower for the entire camp, and it was a mile down the gravel road. We would be grimy and sticky with sweat with the training and as walking was not allowed, we ran the mile to the shower. The water was a relief in the heat and dirt of the day, but when it was over, we had to jog back to the camp, and we became sweaty again.

Camp Crocket was a semi-secret place tucked ten miles in the woods outside of Fort Gordon. We were trained with an intensity that was outside the protocols of any other advanced infantry training. Someone said that even Congress did not know of Crocket's existence and that it was a secret training camp funded with "excess government funds." Camp Crocket's mission was to train and prepare soldiers to be commandos and paratroopers. Each of the men in the battalion were motivated to that end.

The top ten percent of us were specialized in mortars and direct fire weapons whereas the rest concentrated on infantry tactics. I was trained in mortars. One of my classmates became a lifelong friend that lasted through training and my tours in Vietnam and civilian life.

As I was in very good shape, I made five and ten mile runs along the road after the training day and practiced my judo skills in the sawdust pit. I have always loved knives and had three Pro Throw knives and I practiced throwing them to relax in the evening.

As I walked to my place in the woods and my tree where I practiced with my knives, I noticed drug use for the first time in my life. I was ignorant of drugs, but I could not escape the numerous discarded stockings and round cans of Kiwi boot polish that I often saw tossed into the shrubs. The user stuffed the opened cans of polish into the toes of their socks and put the open ends over their noses and sniffed until they got high.

One day the cadre had the battalion sit on long tables under a huge tent and six hundreds of us took the qualification text to go to Special Forces Training. Of the six hundred, three of us passed. When we three completed parachute school, our next assignment would be Fort Bragg for Special Forces training.

Graduation found us on the parade field — a bunch of meat eaters — no, raw meat eaters, young men in green uniforms who no longer spoke, but growled and drooled, ready for war. A small percentage of us were promoted. I was fortunate to be promoted again. What would I ever do with sixty-eight dollars a month?

The cadre of sergeants who were over us and marched us to training, were all graduates of the non-commissioned officer's school. Graduates of that school were promoted to sergeant and the honor graduates became staff sergeants and were sent to Camp Crocket as their first assignment before going to Vietnam. After graduating us, those sergeants were sent to the 173rd Airborne and intense fighting in Vietnam. All were killed before our Camp Crocket bunch even finished parachute school.

> *I want to be an airborne ranger*
> *Live a life of guts and danger*
> *Here we go, All the way, Everyday*
> *Up the hill, down the hill,*
> *All the Way*
> *Airborne! Airborne!*

We were the largest class of airborne troopers to ever graduate from jump school in history. The demand for more paratroopers in Vietnam was but a small explanation for our large class. The larger reason was that the Governor of Texas decided that all his National Guard would be airborne qualified. No soldier would be marking time in his state. There were more than twelve hundred in our class.

The instructors, or "black hats," were professional in every regard. There was the right amount of stress and pressure to weed out any weakness in the ranks. Jump School took in raw materials, like a machine of industry, and produced a finished product — the paratrooper, conformed to the standards of industry. That product, the airborne soldier, left with a sense of accomplishment and pride and he was aware that his silver wings set him apart from all other soldiers.

I do not know where the Texas National Guard spent their time when the formal eight to five training was not occurring, but I know where officers went, and I know were the rest of us were. We, the enlisted, were in the hands of a cadre that was nearly sadistic in their treatment of the regular army guys. We were up at three in the morning to screeching and harassment and petty details that Pharaoh would have been loath to assign his Hebrew slaves.

Placing the enlisted under pressure and reasoned training was expected, but we were essentially on our bellies crawling across a parade field hour after hour, turning over the stones so they would be able to dry in the sun on both sides. We would have five hours of harassment before we were finally marched to the parade field to begin instruction. We would stand in formation there and wait for air-conditioned buses to arrive at the curb so the officers in their clean uniforms could step off and join our formation.

Clearly, they had gotten up around seven, had a breakfast and put on their clean uniforms and joined us — minus harassment. They all claimed that they removed their rank from their uniforms so they would not get special treatment, but just be of the regular men. In the end, we all received our silver wings, and they would claim that they went through the same school that we did.

When class ended at five, we marched back for "chow" and were then harassed until eleven every night.

"Jump week" arrived and it was time to jump from real airplanes. There had been the jumps from trucks and mock airplanes, and the leaps from the towers, and now the real thing was here. We all had our personal butterflies and degrees of nervousness. Some wondered if they could actually jump from an airplane. Some would not. They would freeze at the door and no amount of shouting at them, shoving them, pushing them or threatening them would get them past the door into the howling wind outside.

We woke to a bright sun and a hearty breakfast. Some of the soldiers perhaps thought of the Last Supper. The atmosphere of the day was completely different. There was no harassment. This was the first of a series of parachute jumps that qualified the soldier to wear those silver wings.

On loudspeakers, heard over the whole compound, were the airborne songs of jump day. The first to greet the day went to the tune of *The Battle Hymn of the Republic.*

> *There was blood upon the risers, there were brains upon*
> *   the chute,*
> *Intestines were a dangling from his paratrooper boot*
> *He was a mess, they picked him up and poured him from*
> *   his boot*
> *And he ain't gonna jump no more*
> *Gorey, gorey, what an awful way to die*
> *Gorey, gorey, what an awful way to die*
> *Gorey, gorey what an awful way to die*
> *And he ain't gonna jump no more.*

"Get your steel pots on and get on the trucks," a sergeant ordered, and we clambered onto the bed of a line of deuce-and-a-halves. The drivers double clutched the trucks and a cloud of black poorly burned diesel smoke poured into the bed.

The jumpmaster of the day gave his briefing, and we were issued our main parachute and reserve. We hoisted on our chutes and the jumper next to us handed us our straps from behind. "Right leg strap!" he shouted. We answered, "Right leg strap," and snapped it into place.

I swallowed. It was happening.

"Left leg strap!" the man next to me shouted. He might have handed me a snake for all that mattered, and in my nervousness, I would have hooked it up by its fangs.

The jumpmaster checked us out and cinched our straps tight enough to bow us together and we snapped our reserve chutes to the front and shuffled aboard our assigned C-130 airplane that hissed and growled on the tarmac. The plane lumbered down the field to the runway where we lined up behind other planes. The engines revved to the max RPMs as the pilot held on the brakes.

I looked to the side and saw the other jumpers, some of them with their eyes clinched shut; on others, fingers nervously twitched and drummed the handles of their reserve chutes.

The brakes were released, and we accelerated down the runway and lifted off into a bumpy sky. The jumpmaster stood and screamed, "Six minutes" and held up six fingers.

He slid the door open and sunlight flashed inside, and the wind shrieked by and I saw the earth far below. "One minute," he shouted, but we could only see his lips move in the noise.

He started the jump commands. "Get ready," he shouted at us, and his eyes communicated terror rather than readiness to us. We all slapped our knees and stomped our feet one time on the deck of the plane.

"Stand up!" We stood and tried to turn toward the open door, our chutes bumping those of the soldiers beside us.

"Hook up!" I made certain to hear my hook snap in place and I ran the safety wire through the hole. The jumpmaster continued the commands and he pointed to the opening. "Stand in the door."

The hands of the first man standing in the door were clinched at the sides, white and veined.

"Go!" and the masters at both doors screamed, "Go, go, go, go," as they gathered the hook ends and all but pushed the jumpers out of the plane.

There was the thrill and the terror of falling from so high, and the silence, and the jerk of the opening. I saw the drop zone below and the green smoke blowing across the field, and the ambulance parked near the trucks. The landing. The roll. The gathering of the chute by its apex and with it in its kit bag, walking exultantly toward the trucks with a smile of satisfaction.

FORT BRAGG, NORTH CAROLINA — THE HOME OF THE GREEN BERET

The movies always have it wrong — dead wrong. Some captain comes in with a mission to save the world and gets assigned a dozen or so undisciplined, half-drunk expendables just rescued from the county jail, with personal problems, and he has to mold them into a unit capable of fulfilling a mission against all odds and with the clock ticking. Only Captain Wonderful can make it happen.

The truth of the matter is that should a team be needed to perform a mission, the Group Commander would say something on the order of, "I have three operational teams available — take any one of them that you like. All of them are qualified to do your mission."

The men of the Green Berets are the finest, most intelligent and highly trained soldiers of any army, of any country, and of any time. There are no privates in Special Forces. Everyone is an expert in several fields. They are first and foremost professionals and a team. None of them need to be questioned regarding his ability to do a mission. The beret on their heads is the proof that they have met every test.

Training Group at Fort Bragg, the home of the Green Berets, was there to weed out and prepare selected soldiers to be those professionals.

We arrived for training that day and stood before a modern barracks with squad-sized rooms, our duffle bags before our feet, and listened to a briefing from the first sergeant. He did not scream or berate or demean us when he spoke. The soldiers who stood before him were those who had been weeded out from basic, and Crocket, and jump school, and a battery of various tests. Phase One, which we would shortly begin would be the last great indicator of our caliber and would further diminish our numbers.

We had a few days before our training began and the time was ours except for formations and work assignments. My friend Mike found me in the squad room.

"Hey, they have a jump manifest on the bulletin board. They are always making parachute jumps and have empty slots for straphangers. I put our names on the manifest."

I can't remember what I told him, but I was ready to go. My heart was in my throat. I was always nervous about jumping. I had well over a hundred and twenty jumps on active duty and I was nervous on every one of them.

We caught a truck to the airfield with a few other members of our class. It was a blustery, cold day for North Carolina, with an overcast sky that matched my heart. Most of the airplane was filled with senior NCOs who were trying to get enough jumps for their senior and master jump wings.

The jumpmaster gave his instructions to us. "There are occasional wind gusts, but I think they are within our parameters. I will be watching for smoke on the drop zone. That is all. Let's chute up."

We put on our chutes and reserves and the master checked us out and we shuffled aboard the groaning airplane. The C-130 lumbered down the runway and lifted off into immediate turbulence. The jumpmaster stood to give the command of "Six minutes," and wrapped his hand around the steel cable above him to steady himself.

He slid the door open I saw only greyness instead of cheery sunlight. We bounced in the sky as he screamed out, "One minute!"

I was the second man in the door, a tall senior sergeant with straw colored hair showing at the back of his helmet was first.

"Go."

We all ran out the door, Special Forces fashion, and the back blast threw me into the sky. I felt seconds of falling, then the jolt of the chute opening, and I saw the plane disappearing in the distance with a line of white chutes opening under it, like swimming jellyfish.

I looked down to locate the landing zone and the place on it toward which to steer. There, near the trucks and ambulance, was the large pot that held the signal smoke. Red. Don't jump red. Apparently the wind picked up as the jumpmaster give the command to jump. The smoke did not rise into the sky but sped horizontally like a dense flock of desperate, escaping, red birds.

I pulled the correct risers and turned my chute toward the field, but the wind kept blowing me backwards — fast. The place I would land was a stretch of hard sand and when the toes of my boots touched the ground, I did the parachute landing fall but the wind drug me across the field at the speed of the wind. I tried to unclick the quick release that would unhook one side of my chute and collapse it, but the pressure on the release was so much it would not budge. I dug my heels into the ground to slow myself and they dug two furrows into the dirt a hundred yards. It seemed that I was heading in the direction of Georgia when the wind lessened and I gathered up my chute, glad to still be at Fort Bragg.

As I headed toward the trucks, I came across the heel marks of the senior sergeant and saw him gathering his chute. From his expression, I concluded that he did not want to talk.

On every occasion, Mike and I put our names on every manifest for extra jumps.

Phase One began. In addition to the professionalism of the instruction, there was also a sense of urgency in all that we did. The overarching word that comes to mind is "mission." Our instructors were masters in their fields, legends in Special Forces, of whom any number of books could be written, who made it their work and duty to produce soldiers worthy of wearing a Green Beret.

SF is unique of all other units in the military. We are called "force multipliers." The best way to explain it is to say that if you were to take a battalion of six hundred paratroopers, or Rangers, or Marines into a denied area for six months and at the end pull them out of danger and find that they had no casualties you would have six hundred of them left. On the other hand, if you inserted an A Team of twelve Green Berets behind enemy lines for six months, you would discover that they had secured the area, built a base camp, and trained an independent army of six hundred indigenous soldiers to continue to fight.

Every sergeant in SF becomes in effect a unit commander as well as functioning in his own area of expertise. Every Green Beret chooses to be a sergeant in Special Forces rather than an officer anywhere else.

Fieldwork and classroom work were given at a level to create extreme pressure day and night until it culminated in the practical application of it all at Camp McCall.

The final exercise involved a night parachute jump with full equipment and weapons. The cadre thoroughly searched our packs, even disassembling the hollow metal frames of the rucksacks looking for hidden food. Even a bouillon cube was enough to expel the offender. Everything was laid out on the ground for inspection before we repacked it all for the mission.

We chuted up at the airbase and with our rucksacks snapped below our reserve chutes, could barely stand. We sat on the tarmac at the edge of the runway leaning back on our chutes and waited as the airplane hissed toward our ramp.

"On your feet!" was the command, and it was only possible if you rolled to one side and pushed yourself up with your hands. Once up I helped the soldier next to me by taking his hand and pulling him up. We staggered aboard and made our way forward and dropped heavily into a seat under the dim red overhead light.

We all sat back with our thoughts. Not a person smiled, talked or looked around. I saw the jumpmaster standing at the door as he stared at the light and waited. I had my hand on my static line hook and worked it on and off its loop. My fear was of not having it handy and able to hook up in time and having the shove of shuffling bodies push me out of the door unhooked.

We started to move. The jumpmaster took a step to the side to regain his balance. The big airplane maneuvered left and right to the active runway where the engines of the C-130 shrieked before we rumbled down the active runway, accelerating as we went and lifted off into the night.

The jumpmaster touched his headphones tighter to his ears, stood and held out his splayed hands twice and shouted into the recesses of the plane, "Twenty minutes."

The airplane made a couple more turns and slowed to an airspeed that was safe for us to jump.

He held out his fingers and screamed over the engine noise, "Six minutes."

The jumpmaster got on his belly and looked out of the open door in the direction of flight searching for the jump zone and the smoke.

He stood and faced us with wide eyes and shouted, "One minute."

"Get ready," and he began the jump commands.

I couldn't wait for him to shout, "Hook up," for it was my one fear that night and I would be certain that it was done.

"Hook up."

I hooked on the cable with the open end facing the inside of the craft and tugged until I felt it click and threaded the safety wire through the hole.

We were sounding off for "equipment check," and I knew that we were so packed together that none of us could do so, but we all sounded off for equipment check as if we had.

Moments later we stumbled to the door and the blackness outside and as we approached the opening the wind grabbed our packs in front of us and thrust us out of the plane.

The ground was as black as the sky. I could not discern field or tree or the presence of a drop zone at all, but a small light blinked at a place and I made for it. Other chutes drifted toward me, and it appeared that we would collide in the air. I pulled on my risers and just as we separated, we touched on the ground and gathered up our chutes and made for the light of the "friendly forces."

Over the next several days we put our skills into practice. We linked up with our "friendly guerrilla force" and taught them classes and conducted raids. Most nights we trained all night, maneuvering to target areas as we evaded the numerous forces that attempted to find us.

We had one meal the whole exercise — a goat that we killed by slitting its throat and we slept but four hours on one occasion.

We had a class in a safe area. We were in a bleacher and the instructor explained waterboarding. He stated that it was the practice that each of us would go through it. A cloth would be placed over our mouth and nose, and water would be poured on the cloth. There was no torture involved and one minute after it was concluded the person would be completely normal with no ill effects. Due to time constraints only two or three were able to undergo the boarding.

Our people came up gasping at the effectiveness of the questioning and they wiped the water from their hair and said, "Wow."

"We have another little exercise that you might like but we will not be doing it either because of time constraints. We have this pit over here and we put you in it with this big snake," and he held up a huge black snake holding it firmly just behind the head. "This is Otto. Otto does not like water."

Here the sergeant lowered the snake into a basket and thrust its head down with his forefinger and slammed the lid closed.

"We put you in this pit with Otto and then we run this garden hose into the pit and fill it with water — all the way to your neck. Where do you think Otto goes?"

It had been days, it seemed, since we stopped in some thicket to rest longer than was necessary to plan for the next exercise. We had a light rain all afternoon and we shivered anytime we stopped and waited for our patrols to return and report. I was glad about the drizzle because it softened the dry leaves and twigs and let us move more quietly and with more stealth to the next target.

We were weary and sleep deprived but carried out our missions, some of which involved navigating long distances most of the night to a target. Some of the men tied their rifles to themselves lest they walk off and leave them somewhere. We were moving to a target and the soldier in front of me slept as he walked. His feet clopped heavily to the ground in front of him and from time to time he stopped mid step with his head down. He would wake just before I came to him and then begin again as though just wakened. He trudged ahead with his shoulders slumped and as I watched him, his rifle slipped from his fingers. It dragged behind him in the twigs and leaves until it caught crosswise between two trees and jerked him to a stop. He was in a daze and moved like he did not know what was happening to him.

I ran up and picked up his rifle and gave it to him. "Just keep on.

Don't quit. Keep going."

The soldier was so weary that he did not recognize that what I gave him was a rifle or why I was giving it to him. I waved my hand in front of his eyes. He seemed not to see them.

"I'll get in front of you. You just follow me, okay?"

He did not respond. He had a green cravat around his neck, and I tied one end of it through a button hole of his shirt. Holding the other end in my hand I led him as he stumbled in the pine forest.

"Last mission, gentlemen," said the sergeant, "is this cross-country to a target."

He looked at the weary men in front of him.

"You will route march quickly to a location and when you arrive you will be told what you are to do."

None of us knew how long it was to the target. It was sunset, just getting dark when we proceeded at a fast pace. The sergeant did not tell us how far we would be walking. We walked along fields, ditches, old roads, through stands of forest — mile after mile. We never stopped.

When are we going to get there? Won't we ever take a rest stop?

We walked hour after hour. I was in great shape, but I was weary with the walk. The pace never slowed. Soon I could make out faintness in the sky and the tree line began to show in black silhouette. We had walked all night.

We began to see lights, the edge of something. These were side streets of an abandoned complex, rows of empty barracks from a former war, and only the silent commands of old ghosts told of soldiers who once lived there.

Daylight.

We walked.

Things began to look familiar. This was Fort Bragg. This was Smoke Bomb Hill! We rounded one more bend in the road and we found ourselves at our own barracks.

A sergeant stopped alongside us. "Gentlemen the exercise is over. Take a shower and get some sleep. Morning formation is cancelled."

Our Phase One class was in formation on the parade field with our new berets, minus the flash which would indicate that we had completed the full training to be a Green Beret. We were at parade rest and a major with a full flash on his beret addressed us.

"Gentlemen from Phase One, which you have all completed now, you will proceed to your primary MOS training — your military operational specialty in SF. As you know, there are five of them and most of you have stated your preference. Some of you will train to be Special Forces medics. Some of you will specialize in weapons or demolitions or communications. The fifth specialty is normally reserved for senior noncommissioned officers with several years in Special Forces.

"That MOS is called 'Operations and Intelligence,' and goes by the numerical of 11F. It is from this schooling that we get the team sergeants and intelligence sergeants. This is the first time in my memory that we are offering the training for SF soldiers under Sergeant First Class.

"If you are interested in applying for this school, here is the criteria: You must have an IQ of 130 or higher and make a full commitment to complete the training. Upon completion of Operations and Intelligence training you will be immediately assigned to a certain highly secret project."

The major passed his eyes over the group before him before he continued.

"You will agree to a tour of one year in this classified mission. This is a top secret project and suffers very high casualties. Eighty five percent of you will be dead in three months."

He let the statistic sink in.

"If you are interested be at building ___ at sixteen hundred."

He turned to the sergeant in charge. "Take charge," and he saluted. "Dismissed."

I figured it out. If eighty-five percent of us die in three months and a tour is a year, what number do I have to start with to end up with me at the end of a tour? About four thousand. I am not suicidal, and the odds were daunting, but when you are young, you think that you are immortal. When Mike and I arrived at the building there were thirty-seven of us. All of us finished the training and went to SOG. Only a few of us came home.

Born Twice

It was at the far side of the main parade field — where presidents and congressmen and generals sometimes sat in bleachers for significant events — that we had class for the operations portion of our training. The building was nondescript, a barracks-like structure whose only signage was the building number. It was there that we learned all aspects of running a Special Forces team. The team sergeant of an A Team does it all. He does all the planning, coordinating and training of the team. Should the team be committed behind enemy lines to set up a guerrilla army, the team sergeant sets up a training schedule for the recruits, basic training, gives patrol orders and assigns missions to accomplish. That was the subject matter of those first weeks.

We walked to class on a flower-edged sidewalk and took our seats for instruction at the appropriate hour and sponged in all the ingredients to organize, train and equip a guerilla force in war.

There came a time part way through our training when class was moved to a large brick building in the center of a field for the highly classified intelligence portion of our training. The compound was contoured by concertina wire and armed military police patrolled the perimeter. Various antennae and screens rotated on the roof to prevent electronic eavesdropping. We showed our identification to the MP at the gate and that got us as far as the lobby. There we presented our identification to the sergeant, who checked our names from the roster, and we signed the logbook each time we entered the building. We were searched coming in and leaving and were not allowed to take notes.

Instruction covered subjects such as intelligence gathering and spy craft. We learned how to run agents behind enemy lines, counterintelligence, safe cracking, codes, reading fingerprints of persons passing through our lines, and the use of cut-outs and dead-drops.

Our cadre of instructors were without peer. They were sharp, professional, and experts in their fields. I remember Worley. He was brilliant, wealthy and a world class martial artist. He was recovering from serious wounds, one of which required a metal plate in his head.

One day a sergeant who was new to us taught class. Unlike the other instructors who wore laundry-pressed uniforms and gave perfect, polished units of instruction, this sergeant seemed to not fit in starched fatigues. His uniform was baggy, and he appeared to have emerged from the rain and hung out to dry but was still damp. The Sergeant First Class had a scar that cut a gully just under one eye next to his temple and furrowed to the corner of his jaw. Most of his fingernails were missing and only stubs of a few remained on one hand. He was average height, his hair was thin to a stubble on his head, and in age he appeared to be in his late forties.

"My name is Novey. Dis is my third army, dis Special Forces. I vas in Europe and fought against da Nazi. Den de Communists defeated da Nazi and took their turn brutalizing my country, so I fought against dem. I joined de Americans because my country was destroyed, and my family, dey all perished. I joined the Green Berets to fight de Communists."

"The vorld has plenty of Communists to fight. I vas in Korea on the east side of the Chosin Reservoir when da marines refused to help us regular army. Then I vas in Central America and da Cubans."

The sergeant moved to the podium and the light there set his deep wrinkles and scars into shadow.

"I cannot remember how many times dat I swam de Rhine on intelligence missions into Eastern Europe... Von time I got captured. Twice I vas shot — vonce in de river and almost did not make it back across."

He took a deep breath — as though he was deciding if he should go on.

"Most of vat you have learned you vill use in Europe, urban situations. I vant to tell you something you need to know in Vietnam and da rest of Southeast Asia."

"Anyone see da James Bond movies and the Communist group called SMERSH? Dat isn't just Hollywood. SMERSH is real. It exists. De name has changed, call it KGB if you vant. SMERSH is Russian and means, 'death to spies.' You think, 'Dat is Europe, but I am going to Asia.'

"Da Russians use cut-out countries for deniability. You studied dat already. Von of those countries dat dey use is my own country. There are two thousand people in von place in Czechoslovakia just studying de art of torture. Did you hear me? Dat is all that dey do. They practice on political prisoners and dey sometimes get American prisoners. Castro sends some of his Cubans to torture American prisoners for practice. Dey do not care so much about information that da prisoners possess, dey just enjoy torturing Americans."

The sergeant bowed his head and sighed as he ran the forefingers of one hand over the scars on his face. He spoke quietly and paused after each phrase of his sentences.

I leaned forward.

"I vant to tell you von more thing… Ve actually know where most of our American prisoners of war are… Ve know their names… Ve know if dey are in a bamboo cage half sunk in mud and where in de jungle dey are… Most Americans who are captured are in base areas in Vietnam… Some are kept in de tunnels under da country… Some prisoners are taken into Laos or Cambodia or even farther to visit our Cuban tormentors.

"Most of you people who go to SOG who get captured vill be captured in Laos or Cambodia or North Vietnam. It is there dat your journey vill begin. You are very valuable to dem. A soldier who captures you can get a reward of enough money to live on for five years. Dey have a medal minted just for anyone who kills or captures someone from SOG. It is like our Bronze Star or Silver Star only it is just for those who kill or capture one of us… And when they capture you, our government vill deny dat they know you."

His eyes scanned us, pausing at us individually, looking into our eyes.

"Our government has files on all our soldiers who have been captured. Ve have our assets on da ground and our spies in da skies. Ve know," he said, hitting the podium with his fist.

"On some of the files, written in small letters on the top right-hand corner, are de initials, 'MB.' It means, 'Moscow Bound.' Dey go to Czechoslovakia. You must prepare for this."

He stood there with his head bowed with both of his fingers outstretched on the top of the stand and drummed the surface with his fingertips, but there was no tapping sound to penetrate the depths of the room. The soft velvet thumping of his nail-less fingertips were thunderclaps in the room.

"Von more thing and I am through. I have seen dis in too many wars. Someday, ven ve defeat them and demand our prisoners back, a dignitary in a suit vill have a list of all our prisoners dat de Communists have, and we know that dey have dem. Dey vill call out de name of the prisoner and dey vill check his name from da list. At the end there will be many names dat have no checks beside their names. Names of prisoners that ve know dat dey have.

"The man from the government will not ask for those men. He vill just fold up da paper with dignity, and place it into his breast pocket, and walk away."

With a loud sigh and without looking up at any of us, he slowly left the room.

I thought of that sergeant in his broken body as a sack of treasure, with his sorrow and sacrifice, and wisdom, and tears inside his rumpled uniform, drawn up and cinched at the wrinkles of his neck.

It was Saturday and we had the weekend off. Some of us got on the manifest for a jump from a C-130 with "JATO" (jet assist take off). I was nervous as always. The C-130 was a four-engine plane and its jets seemed to scream and shriek at the edge of the runway just before we were all but catapulted into the air. There were four rows of seats in the plane filled with paratroopers who were going to jump en masse at one of the large drop zones.

I looked up and across from where I sat was the sergeant in charge of our training area. The First Sergeant's name was DeLuca. He was about five seven, slim and wiry with black hair and Italian features. He was a professional soldier through and through. He had a knack of cussing out his troops and shouting at them — but he never failed to communicate his love and concern for his men.

He caught my eye and shouted, "You have never jumped this plane before, have you?"

I shook my head. My chin strap was tight under my jaw.

"Thought so. Just don't do a full jump out the door. Just get your toe out and do a hop. They say if you jump out too far the jets can burn off your chute."

"Thanks a bunch, First Sergeant."

Monday marked the first day of the last week of our training. The instructor was teaching the methods the Communists were using in the United States to accomplish their ends.

"Let me talk to you about the Communists' use of the fifth column. A fifth column refers to the efforts of any group of people to undermine a larger group from within. They might be likened to termites working inside a tree. On the outside the tree looks healthy and strong but the inside is rotten and ready to fall. The fifth column will use anything from music to marching against the war. Their activities might seem harmless and have merit on the outside, but they have a goal in mind. They want the destruction of America and to remake it into a Communist State."

For the next four hours the instructor exposed Communist Front Organizations at work in America.

"Take for instance, music. Pretty innocent stuff it would seem. But you take a hypnotic beat and their lyrics, and get them into drugs and sex and you have termites eating at the soul of the country."

The sergeant began to recite the findings of The House Committee on Un-American Activities regarding various record companies and musicians and their stated goals.

I had read the books years before and what he said was confirmation to me. I read, *Rhythm, Riots, and Revolution*, and *A Nation of Sheep*, and *The Ugly American*, and Orwell's, *Animal Farm*, and dozens more books. I read the books of David Noebel, and Hargis and Schwarz regarding the Russian Pavlov's mind warfare and hypnotic music.

"The Communists will use any movement to weaken the country and drive a wedge through us."

He began to pass out some photographs. "Take the race riots that are going on. Just as we are at war over there, the fifth column is orchestrating anti-war marches and riots, and race riots. This is no coincidence.

"About a year ago, a certain civil rights leader was shot. They have made him out to be a national hero. They tell the story that he spent his life energy for racial equality. Actually, he had another purpose in his activities. This man's life energy was spent on creating a fifth column for the Communist party.

"Gentlemen, before you is a photograph taken at a Communist training school at Monteagle, Tennessee. You will notice the gentleman in the white short-sleeve shirt and black tie is that civil rights leader. Next to him is the head of the Central Committee of the Communist Party, next to him is the head of the Southern conference of the Communist party, and next to him is the head of the Folk School for Communist Training."

The instructor held up several black and white photographs. "We have many photos from several sources and meetings. We have the eyewitness reports of our undercover agents.

"The FBI states that this person was a member of sixty Communist front organizations-more than any other person in America."

The instructor tossed his photograph to a corner of his lectern. "These are not doctored pictures; you can see that. Technology has not gotten to such a level. This man was a Communist who used race to further the division of our country. He was a womanizer and an alcoholic, but you will never see any of these things anywhere, because his record has been sealed to make him a hero. No one is allowed to see his file — if it even exists anymore. You will only hear the panegyric — only the good things.

"The point of all of this is to tell you that there is an active fifth column always at work. And you will see that in Vietnam also. We have had some of our reconnaissance teams wiped out by infiltrators even in their own teams."

It was cold when we jumped into a small valley somewhere in North Carolina for the final phase of our training. It was a night combat equipment jump, which meant that we leaped from the C-141 airplane with fully packed rucksacks and rifles at night from about five hundred feet above the ground. The reserve parachute which was hooked just above our packs was useless in that if we had problems with our main chute, there would not have been enough time for the reserve to open before we landed on the drop zone.

The jumpmaster screamed the commands, but his words were torn from his lips by the JATO, the four engines and the wind that shrieked by the open door beside him. We studied the gestures of his hands for instructions. When it was time to stand, we could barely pull ourselves from the canvas seats. We could not walk. We waddled and stumbled to the door. I was the second man to go out the door and I waited just behind number one who waited for the signal. I noticed the jumpmaster's face when he rose from his last look out the door, as the red dome light above him highlighted his features and shadowed his eye sockets like a skull.

"Go!"

The jumper before me seemed sucked out of the plane. I only got one toe to the edge of the door before the relative wind grabbed my protruding rucksack, sucked me out of the airplane, and threw me into space.

I heard myself gasp, "Uuugh!" when the chute opened and felt my legs swing up just as I reached for the risers. Frost and pale moonlight revealed the zone and I steered for a single small blinking light that marked the location of our "friendly forces."

We were met on that drop zone by the chief of the friendly forces, turned in our chutes and did a tactical march to a safe area. For the next ten days our class of SF troops, with all our MOS skills represented, conducted training which simulated training and leading friendly forces behind enemy lines.

It was winter and cold, and the layer of snow made the security of our base area a priority. Hundreds of people searched for us where we hid, and our tracks were a problem.

I was on a reconnaissance away from the base area when I heard a shout and I saw several aggressors looking in my direction.

"Hey, stop!" they shouted as they ran to capture me.

I sprinted away from them in the opposite direction of the camp, determined not to be caught. I ran in desperation through the trees and brush, jumping over logs and a small creek, and nearly a mile later left them panting behind me. There were three of them and they were bent over with exertion with large plumes of steam pouring from their mouths. Thinking that I was clear of them, I slackened my own pace and tried to catch my breath, when more, fresh aggressors emerged from the tree line and took up the chase.

I had enough lead that by the time they began to close the gap, they too ran out of breath. I glanced over my shoulder and saw my nearest pursuer bent over with both of his hands on his thighs gasping for breath and I could hear him gasping across the frozen ground.

A third group of aggressors emerged from a depression made from a frozen creek bed and shouted for me to stop.

For a third time I ran, determined that I would not give up, for to do so was to be expelled from the class. I ran as fast as I could and sought out areas that were free of snow and hid my tracks. I was willing to charge directly through dense thickets when they were not. I leaped across a half-frozen pond whereas they ran around it. When I thought that I could not run another step, I looked behind me and my back trail was empty of pursuers. I studied the forest and thickets and saw no movement. I got my own breathing under control and listened and heard no sound. Ten minutes — and there was no sign of pursuit. I knew that I could not go back in the direction of our base area so I looked for a place to hide until dark when I could make it back to my people.

I found a farmer's brush pile and squeezed inside, ever deeper into its recesses until I knew that I was concealed. I found a small aperture from which to see and settled in to wait. Other than the small area from which I had entered the pile, several inches of snow covered the trees and fields around me.

I remained in place for hours. My toes were numb, and my fingers ached and could no longer feel my rifle. My back hurt deep into my bones. I shivered and a thin twig moved with my shaking.

"I will not leave this place and be caught."

I listened for movement and watched for any activity in the area.

No deer ventured across my view. I did not see a bird, not even in the sky. Dusk slipped into my hideaway and the horizon greyed, shade by shade until finally darkness erased the meadow and shrubs around me. I squeezed out of my sanctuary and made my way in the dark to my base camp.

For ten days we conducted guerilla operations "behind enemy lines" and evaded and maneuvered without getting caught even though many hundreds of military and civilian forces tried to catch us.

Final graduation arrived and this time when we dawned berets, they had the full flash. We had but to wait for our orders. We put our Fifth Special Forces Group flash on our berets and waited, and waited.

For two weeks we waited. We put our names on every jump manifest and became experts at evading work details. One weekend Mike and I hitchhiked to Greenville, South Carolina and visited Bob Jones University, but we were anxious to go to our assignment and were just filling up time.

Before DeLuca left for his next assignment, he told me, "Now you get into trouble getting orders, you contact, 'A' in the Pentagon."

"A?" I asked.

"Ya, you know in the James Bond movies, they have 'M' and they have 'Q' who designs all the gismos. Well, we have 'B' in Special Forces. 'B' is Mr. Baker. They have 'M' for Miss Moneypenny, well, we have 'A' for Mrs. Alexander. She is our person who does all our assignments. Just tell her DeLuca told you to call."

I thought of an old whitehaired lady at an old roll top desk with a picture of her cat on top and eight sided glasses on her nose.

"Old lady?" I asked.

DeLuca laughed. "No. Blond and a real looker."

I thought of Rebecca in the Bible, "Well-formed and comely."

"Here is her number." DeLuca wrote it on a napkin and slid it across the table to me in a manner that Long John Silver might have slid a piece of the treasure map over to Jim Hawkins.

I would like to say that I entered her office in the Pentagon without knocking, glanced about the room, and tossed my beret to the hat rack where it made a perfect ringer with my Fifth flash landing outward, and that Mrs. A saw me and cried out in delight, "Dale!" But it didn't happen that way.

Monday morning, I just called the number on the napkin. She answered her phone on the second ring and was pleasant and polite. I introduced myself and said that I was waiting for my Special Forces orders for Vietnam.

"So, you want to go, is that it?" she asked.

"Yes ma'am."

"Well, I try to give priority to the ones who want to go. Just you?"

"Actually, my whole class."

"I will get on it."

Wednesday, I called again, and Friday. The following Monday Mrs. Alexander recognized my voice and said, "Your orders are on the way." It was as simple as that. It is amazing what a napkin will do.

Chapter Eleven

VIETNAM

April 1969 — Our SOG-bound class of Special Forces soldiers flew by commercial airline to Vietnam and like most soldiers who came into the country at that time, touched down at a place called Cam Ranh Bay. The view through my porthole was an arid scene; dry, hot, dusty with light-brown sand. As we slowed at the end of the runway and began our turn to an off-ramp, the wind vortex from our wings sent clouds of dust swirling past the window. We taxied down the ramp and I saw the landing lights of the next airliner as it descended on the runway that we had just left a minute before.

We were herded from the plane to waiting army buses and proceeded on a dusty gravel road between sand dunes toward a distant military complex which was comprised of row after row of army barracks. The windows of the bus were all covered with dusty hardware cloth, "To keep Charlie from throwing grenades into the buses," said the driver. He seemed to expect an enemy at every bend in the road, for his forehead was rolled up in wrinkles as he kept looking to the top of the sand berms which hid the road from above. As we drove, I wondered where an enemy could possibly hide in that empty piece of land.

The barracks were dingy and hot, and the in-processing seemed interminable as we waited for our paperwork and the flight that would take us to our base camp. The air was heavy and humid, and steam curled up from the corrugated roofs as we read from pocket books with pages that were tacky and stuck together. Just for a change we took brief walks along the company road between the long rows of barracks buildings, all of which looked exactly like the one that we had just left, with soldiers sitting on the landings and stair steps, who talked and smoked and read from soggy books and waited.

As it turned out, we Special Forces people were not in a general pool from which they filled the requirements of other units, but even then, someone told me that if they ever tried to commandeer me for another unit, I was to go AWOL and find my way to the nearby A Team and they would ensure that I got to our own people.

It was midafternoon when a buck sergeant with a clipboard in his hand shouted into the barracks announcing that our transport had arrived, and we passed by him as he read out our names. Our bus driver this time wore a uniform that was as dusty as his bus and he took us to a waiting C-130 airplane and within the hour it circled the beautiful coastal town of Nha Trang, the home of the Green Berets in Vietnam.

This time the view through the porthole showed no swirling dust, but rather, the beautiful South China Sea. Offshore, the sunlight sparkled off tiny rivulets of waves, and the sea nearer the coast was the color of blue-green Chinese jade, and as it shallowed to the beach, it became translucent yellow where the white sand beneath it shone through. We banked to final approach over tree-lined streets and villas with red tiled roofs and touched down on the runway, the tires making one short squeak on the hot pavement.

A trio of three-quarter-ton trucks met us. We held our berets in our hands so the wind would not blow them from our heads and felt the sun on our foreheads as we rode in the back. The ancient and the modern met on the road to our base. At the side of the road a farmer made his way astride a grey water buffalo. Young men passed us on sputtering motorcycles and wove in and out of traffic, their mufflers spitting black smoke. Our senses only began to take in our surroundings when we pulled into the compound and began to in-process.

This was the headquarters for Fifth Special Forces Group. All Green Berets in Vietnam passed through those doors — the men of the A Teams, the "Mike Forces," special projects and advisors. A tour of duty began here and we in-processed and waited for an aircraft to take us to our place of duty.

At this time, SOG was referred to as Command and Control, or C and C. Those of us assigned to CCC (Command and Control Center) had a day to wait. The rest of our class that were assigned to CCN (North) and CCS (South) had already left so we used the time to explore.

We wandered down the streets of Nha Trang in the afternoon and took our pictures next to the huge Buddha statue in the city center. A skinny Vietnamese man with grey whiskers and teeth that were black from betel nut sold us Chinese noodle soup with a boiled duck egg and shrimp that was caught "just this day" in Nha Trang. Displayed in the shop windows were the wares of the East, and the smell of sandalwood incense drew us into the dim interiors and smiling vendors. "Genuine Rolex watch just for you."

Back in our own compound we strolled along the bunkers and watched the rice farmers work their paddies beyond our perimeter. They worked quietly in knee-deep mud, planting under the shade of their conical hats. The fecund odor of their fertile fields drifted past our guards and machine guns to our nostrils on the other side.

Artillery sounded from time to time and the passing rounds overhead broke the sound barrier and in my newness to war, I did not know if I should dive for cover. The ripping sound of automatic weapons in the hills where a Special Forces A Team was located followed the artillery barrage. A prop-driven airplane dropped its ordinance along the hill, and there was a white flash and the area became silent. I listened for more exchange of gunfire in the hills but only heard the nearby sucking sound of the water buffalo as they pulled their hooves from the mud.

Some of our group, Mike Buckland, Terry Spoon, Dennis Bingham, Randy Rhea and I ate at Francois that evening — it was a popular restaurant owned by a Frenchman who stayed on after the French Indochina War. The restaurant rested on pilings and overlooked the South China Sea, and as we sat at a candle-lit table, I heard the rhythmic lapping of waves below. We ate lobster removed from the shell, chopped and cooked with spices, cheese and onion and replaced into the shell.

Early the next day, Mike and I were making up our cots, neither of us talking, both deep in our thoughts. In a few hours we would land at Kontum. We would be in CCC, a project so hush, even other Green Berets would whisper the name. It was not talked about because of its secrecy and danger. When an SF man heard that you were assigned there, he would look at you as if it would be the last time you would ever be seen again, like someone leaving the death bed of a dying friend.

We knew the risks, but the reality did not hit us until Kirschbaum.

His appearance was as if all the dire statistics and our apprehensions were written on paper, then those words squirmed and struggled off the page and slipped into a uniform when Kirschbaum walked into our barracks. He sifted into the room like drifting sand; unheard, unnoticed, and then he was there. His uniform was bleached pale green from numerous washings and days in the sun. He was tall, pale and slim with longish hair the color of old sandals, and his mustache covered both lips. He seemed to not notice us as he went by, indeed he seemed not to be aware of himself. Without expression or sound, he laid his belongings on the cot as we observed him.

We might have not looked at him twice except that both Mike and I saw a faded red patch with a white skull wearing a green beret sewed to his left pocket. This man Kirschbaum was from SOG. He was someone assigned to CCC, had been there and was still living. It was the awe that we felt upon looking at this simple soldier that articulated what we were in for.

And it would be, several weeks later, that Mike would find himself on Recon Team Maine — Kirschbaum's team.

A C-130 flew us to Kontum the next day. Our approach was no nonsense — there was no gentle entry into a downwind traffic pattern to alert the enemy in the hills of our coming. There was no gentle bank into a crosswind leg, just a straight-in descent into final. Our descent took us through a layer of turbulence that reminded me of flak in the bombing runs in the World War Two movies. As the airspeed decreased to maneuvering speed the pilot put on flaps and it felt like brakes. There was the hissing and growl of landing gear and then the bump and the rumble of tires on the asphalt. They lowered the tailgate as we taxied, and heat and sunlight flashed into the cabin and my eyes watered with the brightness. Hanging on to a red cargo strap, the crew chief peered out the back then turned to us and shouted over the noise.

"Gentlemen. Sorry to ask you to leave by the back ramp as quickly as possible. It seems that if we tarry too long on the ground it gives Charlie a chance to lob in a few rockets. We don't want to lose another plane."

We nodded and made our way down the ramp with our packs and before we even got to the enclosure, we felt the prop blast press our fatigue shirts to our backs as our plane turned and made its way for takeoff.

A staff sergeant met us with a three-quarter-ton truck. "I'll give you gentlemen a ride to the FOB," he said, spelling the word, "F-O-B."

When he saw the puzzled look on our faces he said, "Stands for forward operation base. We used to be referred to as FOB2. CCN was FOB1 and so forth. They change our name from time to time. Most of our people refer to us as FOB or CCC."

I was sitting next to him as we drove from the airport. "That compound on the right is the Mike Force for II Corps. About sixteen Green Berets and three companies of 'little people.' They do some hellacious fighting."

We passed several wrecks of airplanes covered with vines and tall grass. "Some of those wrecks are French from the Indochina war — shot down or destroyed by rockets that hit the airfield."

We passed a graveyard with large headstones. In places, Vietnamese emerged from behind some of them in their conical hats and baggy clothing.

"Were they hiding? What were they doing?" Mike asked from

behind the driver.

"They were taking a dump. They don't have a great love for the French."

Just after the graveyard was a large empty field, perhaps reserved for more French, and then a large white building which may have belonged to a plantation owner in the past. The sergeant slowed and pointed at it with an index finger which protruded from a white bandage on his hand. "That is a place you never want to enter," he said. "Most locals who are brought there never leave again. That is the National Police Station. They are known by us as 'The White Mice.' People get 'questioned' there."

A thin Vietnamese man with slicked-down hair and a white shirt stepped out of the dark interior holding a cigarette and leaned against a porch column. He inhaled deeply and slowly and glanced up at us on the road like a voyeur watches a passing girl. Our sergeant accelerated slightly and looked away without making eye contact.

He lowered his voice. "They use some of our information and the CIA works with them."

The sergeant looked at me and whispered, "They get rid of the fifth column — the Viet Cong that seem to be untouchable. They disappear."

We drove through the pleasant tree-lined business district of Kontum City and our tires bounced over the cobblestoned street and then we passed through the brothels and shanties at the edge of our destination.

Highway 14 had two paved lanes and passed through the center of the CCC compound. Armed, helmeted Chinese guards waved us through the gate.

"I'll drop you here at the S-1 so you can sign in and get oriented. See you around camp gentlemen."

"I was hoping for recon," I told the captain at S-1.

He looked up at me. "I think they have a team for you. I'll walk you to the door."

The captain pointed across the center of the compound to a modest single-story building. "Just go over there and see Sergeant Howard. He will get you squared away."

I threw my kit bag over my shoulder, crossed the courtyard and stopped in front of the indicated building. The sign above the door simply said "RECON," but above that was the clear outline where it seemed a horseshoe had once been nailed but later removed leaving its unbleached image on the wood. A sergeant appeared beside me and glanced where I had been looking.

"I never noticed that before," he said. "Someone must have put a horseshoe up for good luck. Don't know why they took it down."

I looked over at him and I smiled. "I minored in Greek in college. That is also the Greek letter omega. Was there ever a project here called Omega?"

He looked at me in surprise. "I better have that painted," he said. "I'm the First Sergeant of Recon Company. S-1 said you were coming by. Let's go inside."

First Sergeant Robert Howard was a solid looking man about six feet tall with the stature of an athlete. His face was square and tan, with a fresh scar on his right cheek. For the next twenty minutes he spoke quietly and without smiling, explaining the mission and history of C and C.

"We have a hundred percent casualty rate in SOG. It is almost certain that you will be either killed or wounded during the year. When the commanding general of Vietnam was here, he said our missions were so dangerous that our people should get a silver star just for getting on the helicopter to go."

Bob Howard paused to let it sink in.

"Why do you want to be on a recon team? Why did you enlist?"

"I am very anti-Communist and I believe they must be stopped. I believe in this war so I will be here until we win."

He listened without interrupting me.

"As a Christian I am ready to die if I have to. I am physically and mentally prepared for this."

Robert Howard nodded his head when I said that. "My wife teaches Sunday School in our Baptist church in Alabama. I understand that."

"I have one opening on a recon team and I will give it to you if the One Zero approves you. The man who runs the team is called a One Zero. That position on a team is based on experience, not rank. In this case he is Master Sergeant Norman Doney. He is very experienced, and he has a good team. He has Team Florida."

He stood up. "I will walk you over and introduce you."

We stopped at the door. "Why aren't you a sergeant?'

"My rank has been frozen nearly a year because of training. I have to have a parent group to promote me."

Bob Howard looked at me. "Well, I think you are out of uniform. We have a small tailor shop next to the gate. Next time I see you I want those sergeant stripes on. I will make sure the paperwork gets through today."

We started across the parade field. "Oh. There he is now."

He had been walking across the parade field toward us, an older soldier around forty years old wearing a black "boonie" hat. He had master sergeant stripes on his shirt, master jump wings, CIB (combat infantry badge), and the red SOG patch sewed to his pocket. He was a serious looking man nearing six feet.

"Sergeant Doney, I think I have found the soldier for you to round out your team. This is… Sergeant… Hanson."

"Sergeant Hanson," he said formally, and he seemed to size me up by looking directly into my eyes. "So, you think that you want to run recon."

"Yes Sergeant, I do."

His smile was one of pleasure and amusement. "Well let's talk about it and I will tell you about the team and what I want to do. I'll help you with your gear and get you to the team room."

"Team Florida is mostly Chinese Nungs with a few Vietnamese," he said as we crossed the field to the recon side of the camp. "I want Florida to specialize in prisoner snatches. My Chinese are very good. They were with Sergeant Howard when he was put in for the Medal of Honor the first time."

Doney stopped and faced me. "You probably didn't realize that Sergeant Howard, who you just met, is probably the most decorated soldier of all time. He is just waiting to go to the White House to receive his Medal of Honor. This is the third time he has been nominated. They won't let him go to the field anymore, so they put him in charge of Recon Company."

We entered a long barracks that was sectioned off into team rooms and stopped at the third door and entered.

"This is the team room for the Americans on Florida. The rest of our people have their own team room in the next barracks. You can take that bunk," he said, pointing into the dimness of the room. "The one over there belongs to Ken Worthley who is on extended leave and will probably take over the one zero slot when he comes back. The bunk there belongs to Joe Morris, and he has only a few months left on his tour. My billet is in the next building.

"Let's walk and I'll show you the layout of the compound and tell you about the team."

We canvased the entire camp — mess hall, dispensary, officers club, Security Company, the B company strike force, Tactical Operations Center (TOC), Vietnamese section and supply building, and all the while we talked.

We stopped behind the motor pool and maintenance building beside a large, sandbagged bunker. The guard was in silhouette inside leaning against a machine gun. Heatwaves rose visibly above the corrugated tin roof. "You will get fully up to speed with the team in the next few days. I will introduce you to the team tomorrow. Remember — they have been fighting for years already. They work for us, but we never treat them like privates.

"First thing, we will get your web gear, rucksack and weapons prepared so you can be ready to train in the morning. We will spend this week at the range shooting, doing magazine drills, and immediate action drills. We will do one in-country mission and then I want us ready for missions over the fence."

We were at the edge of our perimeter overlooking the nearby Montagnard village of longhouses that were elevated from the ground on poles. "How would you like to see yourself down the road?" Doney asked as we watched a pig root under one of the houses.

I just blurted out, "In six months I want your job. I want to be the One Zero of a recon team."

He seemed amused when he looked at me and he gave me one of his Doney smiles that I became so used to over the years.

"Then from now on I will teach you more than to be a member of this team. I will be teaching you to replace me when I leave."

Apparently deciding that I was someone worth investing his time, Master Sergeant Doney became not only my team leader, but my teacher and mentor, a father figure, and a friend until the day of his death. He was my tutor in every regard. Doney analyzed every activity in the field always looking for lessons to learn. Compliments were rare from him because doing a thing correctly and flawlessly was the norm to be expected.

I remember one evening after a long day was over, Doney and I were sitting on the sandbags that lined a mortar pit and going over the things of the day. Florida's training that day was precise and sharp like a commando dagger — but there on the sandbags Master Sergeant Doney expanded on the training and honed it to razor-sharpness. I recalled teaching martial arts and how precise I was on the smallest detail — that was Doney.

I lay on my bunk that night and recalled some lines of Stanton Davis Kirkham that I had imperfectly memorized while in high school that fit my time with Doney:

"You may be keeping accounts, and presently you shall walk out of the door that for so long has seemed to you the barrier of your ideals, and shall find yourself before an audience — the pen still behind your ear, the ink-stains on your fingers — and then and there shall pour out the torrent of your inspiration. You may be driving sheep, and you shall wander to the city, innocent and open-mouthed; and shall wander under the bold guidance of the spirit into the studio of the master, and after a time he shall say, 'I have nothing more to teach you.' And now you have become the master, who did so recently dream of great things while driving sheep. You lay down your staff and take upon you the regeneration of the world."

When Doney became the Command Sergeant Major of Fifth

Group in Nha Trang and I had need to go there, he would say, "You will have dinner with me at my table and then we will go to the movie that is showing, and you will have real ice cream, and you can tell me all that you have been doing." When Doney retired to his hometown in Oregon there was always a spare bedroom for me, and he and his wife Patti would treat me to a steak dinner. At our SOG reunions Doney always reserved a place at his table, and he would introduce me to the legends of SF and made me feel that I was a member of that fraternity.

One day we were walking to the mess hall and Doney said, "My wife mailed me this. I just got it in the mail today."

What he handed me was the March issue of *Men's Magazine*. The cover bore a blurry picture of Norm Doney with the caption, "Sergeant Doney's Six Man Mission Impossible Team — Drive Out and Kill 200 VC."

He smiled. "That was from my last tour when I was in Project Delta. We were doing a recon deep into a VC sanctuary and I caught 200 VC on a river delta doing their morning exercise. I managed to call in artillery and aircraft at just the right time."

Doney and I went over to Supply with my laundry list of needs and gave them to the supply sergeant. The list was extensive from bedding to field gear — compass, signal flares and panel, smoke, grenades, extraction rope, the dozens of items needed to be fully equipped. The supply sergeant gave the list to a Chinese man who began to assemble everything in as routine a manner as a grocery list.

"We will need to choose some weapons," Doney told the man across the counter.

Doney told me that which I already knew — "All of our missions 'over the fence' into Laos and Cambodia are sterile. We take nothing that indicates our country of origin. If we were ever caught or killed and our bodies were left behind, our country would deny ever knowing us. We go in with no identification, not even a laundry mark on our clothes — nothing American.

"That parameter includes the weapons we carry. I hope it changes, but for now the M-16 and CAR-15 are considered unique to America and we can't take them over the fence."

The SOG supply building of our camp was the candy store of weapons. "Pick what you want." I studied the arsenal, tried out several choices and narrowed it down to the Swedish K. The weight of the suppressor eliminated all movement of the muzzle — you could write your name with bullets, and the only sound was the bolt as it seated the next round. Although the cyclic rate was only half that of the AK-47, the magazine held more rounds. This was my choice of carry "over the fence."

It took two trips for us to carry everything to my "hootch" and Doney got me started on configuring my web gear.

My other teammate was Joe Morris, a skinny red-haired soldier who looked like a teenager. Joe was friendly and open and though he had more combat experience than I did, I thought of him as a younger brother. He sat on the end of my bunk as I was configuring my web belt to accommodate Swedish K magazines.

"Look at my hands," he said. "My nerves are shot. Every mission I think that I am going to get killed. I keep saying that this is the last one that I will do but then I do the next one."

He sighed and looked at the floor.

"Doney told me that we will be in the field in a week," I told him. "But I think it will be an in-country one."

Joe looked at me with his brown eyes as he talked. "We call those 'training missions' because they are still inside Vietnam, but Doney says we have to remember that fifty thousand Americans have been killed in those training missions."

"Bob Howard said that Doney is a great team leader and our Indig (the indigenous people who worked for SOG) are very good," I said, trying to encourage him.

Joe put his hands in his pocket so I couldn't see them shake. "They are good. But everyone gets killed or wounded in a year. I haven't been touched one time… yet."

"Joe, you know how hairy the missions are, yet you keep going. That is real courage."

Joe looked at me with his big brown eyes. "These missions are like walking in the rain thinking one of the drops won't hit you. We just barely make it back from these missions and it's getting to me."

He was pressing rounds into magazines as he talked. "You know Dan Ster. They call him Shakey Ster. He gets off the choppers from a mission and he shakes so you can see it and his face is white through the camouflage and he shouts, 'I will never do it again.' But the next mission comes, and he gets back on the chopper and does it again. I just don't know how he does it."

Joe sighed and slapped the magazine against his leg to seat the rounds and tossed it to the empty bunk. "I'm going to bed."

We were coming from the range after practicing with our foreign weapons and John Plaster saw me with my Swedish K.

"Dale, I used the Swedish K on a mission, and it didn't penetrate the foliage or have knockdown power. I talked with the Colonel, and he said that we can take our CAR-15s now. I guess that SOG HQ thinks that enough of our M-16s have been captured by the enemy that they don't betray our nationality anymore. I wonder if Doney knows."

I looked down at my K and its green gunmetal finish. "I would certainly be for that. The M-16 has twice the rate of fire than this. I will tell him."

I spent the rest of the day reconfiguring my gear. I was able to draw a CAR-15 and all our Indig on the team would carry one except for three of our Chinese. Two of my Chinese carried M-79 grenade launchers, and Chin, the Chinese point man, carried an AK-47 and wore a CHICOM hat with the red star of the Communist Chinese army on it. Chin was the first man in front, and we felt that an enemy seeing him would take a second to decide if he was friend or foe and that would be just the advantage he would need.

I removed the linings of six canteen covers and attached them to my belt. Anything that I needed quickly I placed toward the front in easy reach. One canteen cover held eight grenades and I fit twenty-four M-16 magazines in three of the other covers by laying two magazines flat on the bottom and the rest upright with the bullets facing down and away from my body. I carried one canteen of water toward the rear and my RT survival radio to the rear on the other side. A coiled rope for extraction was snap linked to the belt.

It became easy in time to know just how a soldier functioned in the field by how he arranged his gear.

Doney's rule was that web gear is never taken off in the field, even to sleep. That meant that nothing was attached to the back of the belt.

A harness went over my shoulders and attached to my belt to support the weight, and field dressings, smoke grenades and my knife hung from it. My compass was always clipped between the buttons of my shirt and secured by thin cord that went around my neck. A lanyard went through the hole in my signal mirror and tied off through my pocket buttonhole. A signal panel and pen flares were in a side pocket.

Doney did not allow frag grenades to be attached in the open to the harness — especially phosphorous grenades — to prevent a bullet or shrapnel from setting them off. Only smoke grenades would be carried attached to the harness.

I did magazine drills over and over, hundreds of times, placing two rounds in each magazine and engaging a target. When the two rounds were spent, I exchanged magazines from the canteen cover and fired at the target again. Hundreds of times — until I could change magazines in about two seconds and never take my eyes from the target. I was never satisfied. The rounds had to be on target. I must be able to exchange magazines in at most two seconds. And I must never need to look at what my hands were doing.

We practiced immediate action drills hour after hour — first drawn out on paper with circles to represent each of us, then we acted it out on a table using pistol rounds to represent each of the men on the team. After that we walked through the motions on the bare shooting range of the Yard Camp, then in tall grass, then thick jungle. We simulated attacks from the front, either side, the rear and we watched for the hand signals from Doney — "break contact, get on line and attack, stay in place and fight."

We were at a break in the foliage and in the distance, barely seen, were the remains of an old French road. It was half overgrown with grass and segments of gravel faintly appeared between the trees and banana leaves, seventy yards away.

"Nhoc," Doney said to one of our Chinese people, "Could you hit that road with the M-79 from here if there were enemy on it?"

Nhoc smiled at him. The M-79 works like a single-shot shotgun — you fire the round, and the weapon breaks open like a shotgun and you insert the next round into the breach, close it, aim and fire. Nhoc began to quickly fire the explosive grenade rounds toward the road. In seconds, he had fired four rounds from the weapon and all of them were in the air before the first one landed on the ground. The rounds all impacted on the road one after the other, all along the road turning it into a wall of shrapnel. Nhoc cradled his 79 over his arm and smiled, one of his rare Chinese smiles.

It would have been impossible to imagine the closeness of our team. We were brothers. We were a team and cared for each other and called each other by our first names. We visited each others' homes, were honored to be at each others' weddings, and attended the births of each others' children.

On Saturday, Norm Doney and I built ladders. He gave the team the weekend off. In a few days we would draw supplies and insert for an in-country mission, but today, in the small empty space behind the motor pool, we built the "Doney Ladder."

"C and C has never used these before, but we used them in Delta," he said as we laid out three parallel lengths of wire cable. "Remember how hard it is to climb up a rope ladder into a chopper? It is hard when you are in the best of shape. On a mission we have to do it with full gear and a rucksack. Add to that the possibility of being wounded or weak from being chased... almost impossible."

We cut off a couple dozen six-foot lengths of aluminum tube and attached them to the three wire cables for rungs.

"Here's how they work: The ladder is rolled up like thread on a spool. That end is attached to the 'O' rings on the floor of the helicopter by those snap links. The chopper hovers over us and they kick off the roll and the ladder unspools to us in the jungle. We don't need to use an LZ that the enemy might be watching.

"For now, we are going to hook it to the water tower so the team can practice climbing it."

We hooked our Doney Ladder to the supports of the water tower, and he placed one hand on the edge of the ladder as he explained its value. "We start to climb. You have been on the run or have been wounded and can't go any higher up the rungs. Wherever you happen to be on the ladder, you just snap off with the link on your harness where the rung is joined to the cable. Really wounded? They can just roll up the ladder under you like a stretcher. This is what we can use if the LZ is too small for the chopper to land."

That afternoon Doney had the team practice on the ladder and Bob Howard had all his recon team leaders present to observe. The Kingbee pilots listened as Doney explained its use and how to rig them, and they spoke at length with their crew chiefs, who would be the ones to rig them and throw them down to the team.

"This is just another way to get in and out of a target," Doney told them. "Sometimes there is so much fire on the LZ the choppers can't land without being destroyed. So, we find a small opening and we get pulled out on strings and we dangle under the helicopter by a rope and hope that we don't get dragged through the trees and pulled apart or that a bullet doesn't cut the rope and you fall a thousand feet. At least with the ladder you have three metal cables that have to break before you fall out of the sky."

Colonel Abt, the commander of CCC quietly watched and listened. "The enemy is relentless to stop our missions. I have heard that they are committing watchers at every opening in the jungle capable of landing a helicopter. We should have any tool available if we need it. Good work Sergeant Doney."

Chapter Twelve

IN-COUNTRY MISSION

"Take two salt tablets and drive on," was the ubiquitous sign on every table in the mess hall. It said without saying it that Special Forces brooked no whining or excuses for anything. "You say you have a broken arm? Well, you have two arms, don't you? Take two salt tablets and drive on." We had just finished a breakfast of bacon and eggs and French toast, and the morning was already hot. I swallowed two pills with the last of my water.

"Take your malaria pill too," Doney told me in a tone that said, "You should know better."

Joe Morris smiled at me like a brother whose parent had just chided his sibling.

I took it.

The three of us left the mess hall and as the screen door swung back on its spring, a staff sergeant from S-3 joined us as we walked. "This is your warning order, Norm. You have an in-country mission. Your briefing is at ten."

A charge of electricity, a moment of vertigo when it seems one's body is lifted from the ground, one's mouth is dry, and a moment of dread came over me, which I would experience for a few moments at the announcement of every mission. Then it passed. It was time for business.

At ten we were seated in the briefing room of the TOC in folding chairs. There was a lectern at the front and a wall of maps covered with an opaque sheet with the words "TOP SECRET" printed on it. Representatives of Operations, Intelligence and Communications were in the briefing room as well as Bob Howard from Recon Company, and Col. Abt, the commander of the base.

"This is the briefing for Team Florida," the captain began. "As you know, the missions of this camp are all cross-border in Laos, Cambodia and North Vietnam. Your mission, however, will be an in-country one. Our cross-border missions receive first priority of our assets and from time to time support may be committed there and you may be asked to hold in place. Though your mission is in-country that is not to say that it will not be a dangerous target."

The captain turned around and lifted the sheet from one of the maps. It was a larger scale map which depicted Dak To and Kontum in the center and the Special Forces camp of Ben Het a few miles to the Northwest. "As you know, tens of thousands of enemy infiltrate into South Vietnam in our area of the tri-border. The area to the west of us is saturated with enemy. We have been finding a huge increase in troop movements from the Ho Chi Minh Trail massing west of us. Ben Het is under siege as we speak. We are not certain what other targets they have in mind."

"Your mission will be to insert in this area," he placed his pointer at an area west of Kontum and South of Ben Het, "and find and monitor any infiltration routes, storage areas, truck parks or base camps of the enemy. Should you find an opportunity to catch a prisoner it will be appreciated.

"You will be inserted by Kingbee helicopter at a site to be selected by you in this vicinity, where you will accomplish the elements of your mission."

As we took notes, the captain gave us the details of our support and logistics. A staff sergeant with a pronounced limp received the pointer from the captain and presented his intelligence portion of the briefing.

"As you are aware, Ben Het has been under siege for several weeks. Their siege began when the 66th NVA regiment attacked with ten Soviet PT-76 tanks and about 650 rounds of artillery followed by a large ground attack. It is believed that thousands of NVA have joined the attack. There are signs that the enemy are tunneling under the perimeter and may have progressed beyond all three lines of the defense perimeter. They have been announcing to the defenders by loudspeaker that this will be a Dien Bien Phu and they will all be killed. Needless to say, there is concern that some of the little people might defect or desert the post."

The commo people gave us one-time pad code books, frequencies, and call signs, and we left the TOC and prepared for our local training mission.

The metal helipad was cold and wet from the night air as we sat on it and leaned back against our rucksacks and waited for our helicopters. The Kingbees, when parked overnight on our own helipad, were too tempting a target for the enemy gunners on the hill. When the choppers tarried, we could expect rocket fire aimed at the helipad, so our choppers based for the night at Pleiku under sheltered revetments on the other side of the hills. The rocket fire, when it did come, was sporadic and was not accurate, and the very lack of accuracy made it a general concern for all of us in camp. It was as likely to hit a barracks or the mess hall as a sitting helicopter.

Modern technology of war can interpret the trajectory of an incoming round and send accurate return fire capable of destroying the launch pad and crew. But despite Kontum's return fire, the incoming fire continued. It was the primitive nature of the incoming rockets which made eliminating them difficult; the Communists used lengths of hollow bamboo with the segments carved away for their launchers. They aimed the rockets at our base with a compass and set the angle by estimate and used timers to set them off. When the rockets struck, the gunner was far away. Our sophisticated return fire merely turned lengths of bamboo to shards, as "peasants" in black sat on a hillside with binoculars and measured the success of their efforts.

Our aircraft arrived just as we began to shiver, and the fog lifted, and we could make out pale sky through the passes. There were three heavy-looking H-34 helicopters. We saw them first as small dots in the pass, and we heard the hum of far-off engines. The hum became a rumble of rotor blades as they neared. In moments it seemed, the dots took on the shape of themselves, and color and clearly defined decals. They made an aerobatic approach and landed with the flair and speed of mallards landing on a pond. We placed our hands on our flop-hats to keep them from blowing away and bent our necks toward the ground and closed our eyes from the dust. The cowboys had arrived.

They came ready to go without pep talk or preamble. The Kingbee pilots were Vietnamese in black jump suits and Hollywood sunglasses. I glanced over at Joe Morris. He had his head down, caught up in his own thoughts and was scratching the dirt with a twig. Our Indig were passive and waited without expression. I looked toward Doney and waited for a signal to rise and go. He was at the edge of the ramp showing the chief pilot the location on the map where he wanted them to drop us. I couldn't hear over the engine noise, but I could see the pilot shaking his head with his finger on the map. Doney put his hand on the pilot's shoulder and shouted into his ear and the pilot nodded in affirmation.

When the two of them were agreed, Doney pointed to Ba, our tail gunner, giving the thumbs up. We helped each other off the ground and, bent under our rucksacks, hobbled aboard the nearest chopper, last to first. There is only one door on the H-34 and the door gunner sat behind his 30-cal. eating an apple as we lifted off. Clouds of dust sprayed in all directions as we left the helipad and banked left over the Dak Bla River and the city of Kontum and sped to the west.

I tried to follow the route we were traveling from what I had memorized on the map — as much as was possible in the near windowless Kingbee. About twenty minutes out, the door gunner braced his legs and grabbed his machine gun with both hands and leaned far forward. My heart began to thump. I was not sure if it was fear or exhilaration. It was like the moments when I was standing in the door and waiting for the green light and for the jumpmaster to shout, "Go!"

Another Kingbee flashed past our open door in the opposite direction. We were not moving together, and in the frenzy of movement and my ignorance, I did not know if we were evading enemy fire from the ground, or if he was prepping the landing zone (LZ) with his machine gun or trying to draw fire. Was this a hot LZ or a peaceful meadow? All my care to follow our route to the target was lost in those seconds for the pilot banked hard-over and spiraled down so tightly its G-force made me dizzy. I smelled engine fumes. The G-force pressed me into my seat. We were into the third spiral down and I swallowed to keep from puking, when the maelstrom abruptly ended, and we plunked down into a hover a few feet off the ground.

Doney tapped Chin on his shoulder, "Go, Go, Go!"

In seconds we were on the ground and using the noise of the Kingbees to hide the sound of our rushing feet, ran for the nearby tree line. We barely made it to cover before the aircraft were out of sight and dropping into the next valley making a fake insertion. I realized the choppers had gone, and the noise with them, when I heard my boot break brittle twigs on the ground. Everything around us was deathly quiet and still. My heart beat with adrenaline. We froze in place. Would enemy soldiers rush to our LZ after hearing the descent of the Kingbees? Would a watcher signal our presence with his rifle? I closed my eyes to isolate my sense of sound. When I was certain there was no sound of enemy, I studied the horizon around me moving only my eyes. I examined every leaf, every branch, every shadow.

Ten minutes. Doney softly clicked his tongue and nodded to Chin. We rose and slowly moved north. We maneuvered for several hours, stopping often to listen as we looked for signs of the enemy. Near an area of thick bamboo where we made a security stop and waited in a defensive perimeter, we were startled by voices. They sounded near us, even among us — loud and heedless of our presence. The voices hung in the air, floating like a fog. They were clear voices, but their location was elusive. We listened, trying to get a fix on their location.

Doney looked back at Noi, who crouched next to him with his CAR -15. He cupped his own ear with a free hand, pointed in a direction and raised his eyebrows. The signing said, "Are the voices coming from there?"

Noi nodded his affirmation.

Doney pointed the direction he wanted Chin to lead, and I saw the red star on the crown of his Chinese hat nod in affirmation. He crouched forward and crept in the direction of the voices, the barrel of his AK-47 parting the shrubs. Carefully, for the next two hours, we searched for the source of the voice but, like a mirage in a desert, the human that made them could not be found.

It was hot and muggy and sweat beaded on the side of a blade of elephant grass and rolled down its length like a moving round bug. My hair was sticky with sweat and itched. It was late afternoon toward the end of the day, and we paused to eat. We never ate or transmitted from where we would overnight lest an enemy smell our food or follow our radio beam to our remain overnight (RON). Joe Morris transmitted our final report of the day to the FOB, whispering with his head under a tarp, and as day gave up its brightness, we moved into our RON.

We were in a tight circle with Ba, our tail gunner, slightly to the rear watching our back trail. We laid out Claymore mines and memorized the horizon before us in the fading light. In the dusk we heard voices that floated in the air again, snatches of sentences, tendrils, voices whose location could not be fixed.

"*Bac Viet*," Ba whispered to me, "North Vietnam. They have accent. They no VC, they soldier from north."

I was the second from the last in our column next to Ba. He had the second worse position in the column next to the point man, who was the first to be in a firefight. Ba had to watch for enemy following us on our back trail and he also had to cover our tracks. Ba spent much of our reconnaissance walking backwards. I placed a claymore mine behind a tree facing our back trail. I had the detonator with me and wanted to be near him if trackers followed us into our RON.

"I don't think VC know that we are here, or they would not talk so loudly," I whispered in his ear.

"*Toi khong biet*," I don't know he said, but he stared almost without breathing at our back trail.

I listened, trying to ascertain if the voices were static; someone in place, or if they were from soldiers passing by on a trail, but the voices stopped and I heard them no more. I listened for movement in the undergrowth — a snapping twig, a startled animal, fabric rubbing against a blade of grass.

Someone was chopping wood below the ridge where we had holed up for the night in a bamboo thicket. At the beginning there was one woodcutter, then he was joined by others with axes. There were voices again, this time fixed in the valley below our ridge. Ba whispered to me again that they were not local loggers but, "*Bac Viet*," North Vietnamese. "Number ten — very bad."

I heard trucks, their engines laboring below us. My map study showed no roads in the area, and I wondered if the enemy was making roads. I wished that I could ask Doney about that, but he was on the other side of the circle.

Sometime after midnight I heard rain tapping the leaves like a sudden shower. I had a very thin square of tarp and drew it over my shoulders mostly to protect my rifle from the rain. The sound continued for several minutes before I realized that no raindrops were falling on me. There was the sound of rain but no shower.

All around us was the sound of the tapping on vegetation. Something was clearly moving through shrubs and elephant grass. All of us were alert and tense. I know my eyes must have been huge as I sat there, barely breathing. I listened for twigs breaking, a cough, metal touching metal, voices. But I heard only the tapping, and leaves being brushed aside.

The sound continued for a half hour and seemed to brush past our location in our RON. As if on a command, the sounds ended — like Zulu warriors who had just come into position, and then there was utter silence. My mouth was dry. I did not notice it before, but I had not moved during that time and my mouth was open.

Around two or three in the morning the sounds passed by us again. This time they seemed to move past us to our west perhaps fifty yards away, first the sound of tapping rain, then the soft brushing of ferns and long grass. "Locusts," I thought, "The sound reminds me of locusts passing through."

The tapping ended as abruptly as it began, and the jungle became dead quiet. I became conscious of the slightest sound among us — the fabric of my clothing moving against itself, the shift of my body on the ground. In time I dozed, counting on my senses to alert me to danger.

Morning is a time of peril for a recon team in the field. If the enemy has fixed its location, he has had the whole night to set up an ambush when the team leaves the RON.

Chin and Doney left the rest of us in the RON to probe for signs of ambush. They drifted from us like silent shadows, nearly invisible, and I watched as they crawled to the west until the undergrowth swallowed them from view. We lay on our bellies and waited. Slivers of morning sun filtered through the leaves exposing insects flying in the beams. Moisture evaporated from the forest floor and rose where I watched for their return. Then I watched a patch of grass part and Chin emerged, followed by Doney. He signed us to rise, and Florida patrolled to the west.

We had been moving west and north in the direction of the tapping sounds and voices that we heard in the night. A troop of monkeys passed over us in the trees and we took advantage of their noise to move more quickly through the brush. We had moved faster than we should have, for we all but stumbled on a high-speed trail. As we neared its edge our senses screamed in alarm. We were on the edge of the trail not yet seeing it and we sank to our knees. A certain danger lay on the other side of the bushes which we could sense but not define in words.

My hands were sweaty and slippery on my rifle, and I wiped them cautiously on my pant leg. I realized what alarmed me: It was a smell like fresh-mowed summer lawns. I remembered as a boy cutting through a thicket of nettles with a machete that I bought at Rawling's Surplus Store. I smelled that odor now and ten feet ahead of our column was the source.

Doney and Chin crept forward and found the trail. It was truck-wide through tall grass that had been mowed down by passage in the night. We lined up along it in ambush formation. Doney pointed at Chin and Noi, touched his eyes and pointed up trail. They faced in that direction with their weapons ready. He then pointed at Ba and Nhoc, touched his eyes and pointed down trail and they stood at the ready in that direction. Joe and I stepped onto the trail with Doney. I felt fully exposed, like a bug crawling across a bullseye. We were in a place of peril.

The trail was hard-packed and new, and all vegetation had been trampled into the dirt. One muddy rut bore the clear imprint of a boot in the clay. Pond water was slowly running into it and the mark was not yet full of water. The maker of the print had just passed. I looked to the edge of the trail and saw that blades of grass that had been bent over were unfolding and beginning to stand upright. Hundreds of soldiers had just passed by. My mouth was dry. Perhaps the next company of enemy would be upon us as we were so exposed. With nervous fingers, I took out my camera and took a picture of the boot and sandal prints still filling with water.

Perhaps a battalion of soldiers had passed this way. Doney took pictures and a compass heading of the orientation of the path.

This was not the place for a recon team to tarry, nor a place for us to capture a solitary soldier. We all walked backwards off the trail until we could maneuver from the area. Florida set up a perimeter far enough away that Joe could make a secure contact with the FOB.

"There were loads of bicycle tracks on my end. It looks like the NVA (North Vietnamese Army) are moving in force," Doney told us. "This is one of their big infiltration routes into the South anyway, so we won't know if this is routine or something big." Doney paused as he just thought of it. "They are heading in the direction of Ben Het. They might be part of the siege."

The passing units were far too large to try a prisoner snatch and the terrain did not lend itself for an ambush to get one. We waited for instructions from the FOB. I felt adrenaline tense up my body. I wondered what the FOB would tell us to do. "Find out if they have base areas or supply points, and then call air strikes or artillery on them," I thought.

We faced the direction of the trail and waited. Some of our people leaned back on their rucksacks with their weapons ready, their eyes piercing the jungle like an eagle's. Two of my Chinese placed their rucksacks in front of them like a shield and lay behind them with their rifles propped on top of them. Ba watched our back trail on his knees, with one shoulder against a tree.

Joe listened for radio traffic from the FOB. The handset was tight over his ear to mute the sound. He made a quick movement as he listened, then cupped his hand over the mouthpiece and whispered to Doney.

"They have a team in trouble, so all the air support is tied up. 'Do not engage,' they say."

We sat in place holding plastic bags containing our meals with one hand and our weapons in the other and squeezed rice and anchovies into our mouths. Our eyes never left the foliage before us. It was hot and my skin was sticky and itched and I would not scratch. A leech made its way down my arm flipping end over end as it went. Twice more I sensed movement along the trail; the soft padding of feet on the hard path and brushing of cloth against the foliage, and the rhythmic paddling of bicycles. The sounds came from the west and spoke of mass movements of troops and were a grave concern to our very small team.

Although we were only taking a break, I held up a Claymore mine and looked at Doney with my forehead furrowed up in question. He gave me his "Doney-smile" and nodded, and I rolled out my mine to the front toward the sound of movement. Doney motioned for Noi to do the same.

We knew that our intelligence people would want to know everything about those passing down the trail — uniforms, preparedness, weapons, numbers — the whole lot. To know that we would have to get close and monitor the trail. But the last radio traffic said, "Air assets committed."

"Chin and I are going down there and watch. If we get in trouble, Joe you have the radio and you know what to do. Dale, we will try get back to you. You need to decide to wait for us, or come and help, or if it looks like we didn't make it, lead the team to the east."

For two hours we remained in place in our defensive perimeter expecting the sounds of a firefight to break the silence and shouts of men in desperation or pain. We were prepared to interpret the battle by the caliber of rifles fired and the thumping of grenades and the direction the battle was moving. I was prepared to assault in the direction of the firefight, scooping up my Claymore as I passed. And we waited, listening and watching for the slightest disturbed blade of grass to indicate that Chin and Doney were returning.

Slowly turning my head, I glanced at my people. They were unmoving and pale — like ivory Buddhas where they waited. I saw twigs moving to the front, and in the sights of my rifle saw a few blades of grass part and the red star on Chin's hat, then his dark eyes and smiling face as he entered our perimeter.

We made an RON on the side of a hill away from a stand of bamboo. In the heat of the day and cool of the night bamboo snapped and popped of itself and we wanted to hear without its interference.

With darkness and the jungle birds nodding to sleep, we prepared for the night. I laid out my Claymore and placed a CS grenade in front of it. Any soldier who survived the blast would have to make it through the tear gas with running eyes and snot streaming from his nose.

During the night we again heard the passing of companies of soldiers down the trails. They passed in their units with the tapping of the blades of grass and scraping of boots and sandals on the path. Their passing reminded me that as a boy I would hear the geese passing overhead in the night, unseen in the darkness outside of my bedroom window. A rendezvous, all going in the same direction, passing flock after flock after flock.

"Company after company," I thought.

For the first time, it seemed that the enemy knew of our presence. I heard signal shots when we stopped and when we began again. Although we did not transmit or eat in our RON there was a single shot, just as I laid out my Claymore mine. Twice I heard bamboo sticks tapping together. Morning would be very dangerous.

Very early in the morning — before the first grey slips in and exposes the faint outline of hills — I heard movement to our north and to the east. It wasn't loud and careless, like movement passing on a trail to a destination, but it was a slow, exploring, seeking movement. I listened and willed the sounds to pass by us as if on a trail, but it stopped off to our flank. I prayed that it was monkeys that I heard.

Dawn, with her thin fingers, spread the leaves of the canopy above us and showed a small skin of sky that was pale yellow — oriental yellow. The sky said, "This day will be very hot."

"At least it is not overcast and rainy, preventing air support if we need it today," I thought.

We squeezed tubes of breakfast and readied for what would happen. Joe made contact with his radio.

"They want us to come out," he said.

A signal shot was fired less than a hundred yards to our flank followed by bamboo sticks tapping each other.

"Tell FOB that they will need to come right away. They are going to try to drive us into an ambush. Tell them our coordinates — the enemy knows where we are anyway."

Doney made a circle in the air with a finger that told us to get ready to move out. I gathered my Claymore and two of our people did the same.

It seemed obvious to me that they would be driving us to an ambush somewhere below. I thought, "Surely, they must know that we are smarter than a tiger that the British Raj drove from the backs of their elephants. They must know that we will try to evade to the side somewhere."

Doney signaled for me to come to him.

He pointed to his map for me to see. "We are here." He put his finger on the spot and dirt from his touch marked the place. "They are along this little ridge. We can hear their signaling. They will try to push us down to this area where they can ambush us. If we evade to the side, they know that we will get to the first LZ and try to get pulled out there. It will be certain that the NVA will be waiting for us there. We will not do that. We are going east until we get to the smallest opening in the trees — just big enough for those ladders."

He signaled to Joe. "Tell FOB this : 'Have Sgt. Howard rig up what we just built.' Use those words. Howard will know what I mean."

Nhoc crept forward and placed a Claymore on the enemy side of a large tree and hid it with a few shrubs. He glanced toward me and when I nodded "Yes," he started a ten-minute fuse. He crawled back to us like a crab whose rock had just been turned over, his eyes and weapon never leaving the advancing enemy. Snapping twigs told of their nearness. Our people were bent over and crouched, expecting an immediate, deadly firefight.

Doney gave the signal and Chin led the way. We went quickly to the southeast not trying to hide our trail, then we changed direction and moved to the northeast, moving now with stealth. As I covered him, Ba walked backward and erased evidence of our passage.

Our Claymore went off with a thunderous boom, followed by dozens of rifles firing on full-automatic. The shots made popping sounds and were clearly from AK-47s, the standard weapon of the PAVN — People's Army of North Vietnam. Grenades exploded, their "krump" sound muffled in the distance, and I knew that they were near where our mine went off, thinking they were under attack and shooting into the bushes.

It was a ten-minute fuse. They were ten minutes behind us.

To our front was an opening in the canopy where the sun shone through revealing a meadow that was large enough for a helicopter to land. We began to skirt it as we suspected that it would be surrounded by soldiers. I interpreted every blade of grass to be but camouflage. At a place, Chin froze and Doney gave us the closed fist symbol. We froze in place. He gave the palms down signal, and we sank to the earth and studied the foliage.

The sunlight entered the edge of the meadow and highlighted pale faces and pith helmets. Some of them swayed back and forth like upright cobras as they peered into the foliage and looked for us.

The NVA in the meadow heard our Claymore and the perceived firefight, for two of them pointed toward the sound and shouted. A dozen soldiers in their yellow-green uniforms trotted up to the officers with their rifles slung over their shoulders. One of officers pointed to a place in our direction and they ran to an appointed task. Another group of soldiers were sent to the side of the opening near us, and they bent over and crept in our direction.

I continued to study the opening. Sunlight shone on a short horizontal object. I studied it. Something had to be there; then it became clear. The shine was the barrel of a machine gun, and I was able then to make out the outlines of the gun crew where they were in hiding.

We needed to maneuver away from the field.

Doney nodded in the direction he wanted Chin to lead, and we crawled away to the east. At intervals, we stopped to listen. Ba and I set up on our back trail and waited for the enemy to pursue.

There was a single shot followed by another to the west. Trackers were on our trail. Another shout, muted in the jungle, answered the first. Another shot was fired a hundred yards from the first. They were closing on us.

A hand signal made its way down the line to our tail gunner, "Cover our trail."

Doney had us move in a radically different direction. I covered for Ba as he removed the traces of our passage. The pace of our escape was now the speed that our tail gunner could erase our trail.

Joe was on the radio. "The Kingbees have just left Pleiku — ten more minutes out. They will still have to rig the ladders."

Joe's face was white, and he looked at the ground and shook his head. His expression said, "They won't get here in time."

Although he whispered, I clearly heard Doney ask him, "Do we have any other air support?"

Joe spoke quietly into the set. He swallowed before he answered. "All of the assets are committed with a team in trouble. FOB is trying to get someone to break free."

Doney remained calm. I read his thoughts — we would make for the first suitable opening in the trees, then dig in for a fight.

Shouts came from several areas to our west. I imagined the enemy in their pith helmets and yellow-green uniforms, AKs slung over their shoulders as they clacked bamboo sticks together — "More, so they could stay on line, as they moved against us, than to drive us ahead," I thought.

They were getting closer. If the helicopters did not arrive soon, we would have to make a stand wherever we were.

Ba had his rifle slung so he could hide our passage with both of his hands. I extended my rifle over his crouched form as we moved.

The NVA began to fire rocket propelled grenades (RPGs) into the trees and the shrapnel rained onto the ground as they burst. The impact was off, and I was reassured that they did not know exactly where we were, but I did hear them in the brush and I knew that they were closing on us.

Doney had us moving faster and I knew that Ba could no longer completely hide our trail. He was leading us to a place where we could set up for the last fight. We found a small break in the trees just large enough for our ladders and too far for the NVA to quickly get to. We made a defensive perimeter, and I was about to lay out my Claymores when we heard the distant rumble of the Kingbees.

"I hear you at one two zero," Joe said over the radio, and the helicopters adjusted.

The NVA began to fire their weapons into the brush. They fired RPG rounds into the trees hoping to learn our exact position.

I knew it would take time for all of us to climb the ladders. I held up my mine so Doney could see it and the five fingers of my other hand.

The three of us placed them in front of us and I put a five-minute time fuse in each one. We had five minutes until they went off toward the enemy.

"You are fifty meters out. I am shooting a pen flare in front of you," Doney shouted, as Joe gave him the handset. He wanted the Kingbees to know our exact location and that they were not taking tracer fire from the NVA.

Doney popped the flare and it streaked skyward in front of the lead helicopter. It had the loudness of a pistol and as soon as it went off,

I heard shouting and the brush breaking as the enemy, now knowing exactly where we were, began to rush us.

Our Chinese shot round after M-79 round toward the advancing enemy.

The pilot banked once and dove to our location and my flop hat blew from my head, and I staggered as I was shoved by the rotor blast that laid the tall grass flat to the ground. I looked up and saw the metal belly of the Kingbee as it dropped to a treetop hover over us. The door-gunner leaned back and placed both feet on the rolled up Doney Ladder, shoved it out of the door and returned to his machine gun. The ladder unrolled before us and our people began to climb, two at a time on either side of the ladder.

I could no longer hear the shooting or explosions over the helicopter engines. I glanced back and saw the flailing of the underbrush and vast movement in the shrubs and elephant grass, and I imagined the angry shouting and cursing at us. I saw the shuddering of the brush and leaves as the NVA charged through it and I watched the explosions of the M-79 rounds that shredded those leaves.

Ba and I were crouched facing the approaching enemy to hold them off while others made their way up the ladder. We sensed that it was our turn to climb, and we slung our rifles and grabbed the cables of the ladder and climbed on the outside of the rungs. Our feet were heavy as concrete, and we used the heels of our boots for purchase on the rungs. Our legs were like rubber and when we climbed, our feet pushed the rungs away from us. The weight of our rucksacks pulled us backward from the ladder, but we hung on and climbed. Any bullet, any wound, a simple cramp in our legs would end our climb to the safety of the helicopter.

We were exhausted at the top and grasped the metal rings that were anchored to the floor and dragged ourselves aboard.

On the floor we collapsed and screamed for breath, but there were those behind us still climbing who needed our help. Gasping, we lay on our bellies and crawled to the door and reached for the hand that grasped the lip of the floor.

Doney and Chin were the last up the ladder and at the top, as they pulled themselves inside, looked down just as our Claymores sent their lethal charges into the jungle. Chin smiled and pulled his feet into the chopper. We made a steep bank to the east and the FOB — and the mess hall.

Chapter Thirteen

STAND DOWN

The Communists had gotten grenade-close. They were a deadly yellow-green cobra in mid-strike, and we were its quarry, just snatched away. We saw the black disks in its yellow eyes and felt the tip of its black tongue, but in the end, it was without its prey, wounded, and left to slither off into the weeds. Doney was still hanging outside and clawing to get into the chopper when the pilot began to fly from our small opening in the jungle. I was worried as I grabbed the back of his belt and hefted him aboard that the pilot would forget that he had a length of ladder hanging below us and tangle it in the trees and pull the helicopter down. I lay on my belly with my head out of the door and watched as the lower rungs of the ladder clipped the treetops. The ladder straightened behind us as thin limbs wrapped around the rungs and I watched as it tore itself free of the branches. I closed my eyes and sighed in relief.

I lay back against the wall on the far side and set my rifle across my knees. My eyes were dry and itched from the debris lifted up by the rotor blades and I closed them for relief. I took in one long breath of air, filling my lungs, and slowly let it out and I knew I could be asleep before the next breath if I let my weariness have its way. When I opened my eyes, I saw empty shell casings all around the mounted machine gun bouncing and shivering on the floor like tortured things.

I looked around. We were all collapsed on the floor of the Kingbee with our backs propped against our rucksacks. Adrenaline had left her seat in our bodies and weariness sat in her vacant chair.

Some of our people lay back with their eyes closed in sleep or private thought. Doney gazed about, reading the faces of each of his people. Chin, our muscular point man with his AK-47, was awake and seemed ready for another round. He caught my eyes and smiled. He took off his CHICOM hat with the red star, a relic that the Communist Chinese wore in Korea, which he always wore while on point. If the enemy saw him first, they would have to wonder, "Friend or foe," but where we fought, everyone we met was a foe. That second was crucial. As they wondered, he shot. He carefully folded the soft cap and slipped it inside his padded shirt. His smile was broad and narrowed his eyes to horizontal slits. He turned and stared out of the side door of the Kingbee as we descended over Kontum City and the FOB on the far side.

Kingbee pilots do not arrive, hover, and settle down elevator-style like the Americans do with their Hueys. They dive to the tarmac like an airliner, and before the rotor blades fully stop, they hop out of the pilot seat with a yawn, their sunglasses in place and their cigarettes lit. The more dangerous the mission, the more affected their boredom. Salem cigarettes were their favorites. They called them "Sah-LEM," with the accent on the "lem."

Bob Howard met us on the tarmac with a three-quarter-ton truck. In its bed was a huge tub of ice water and cans of beer and soft drinks. I pulled out a Coke and blew the ice from the rim and gasped from its coldness.

"Welcome back," he said as he shook our hands. He called many of our little people by name as they had been with him one of the times he was put in for the Medal of Honor. "You can put your gear in the back of the truck. We will get it to your team room."

He studied Doney's eyes as he greeted him and I read in that look, "Was it close?"

He looked at Howard with his Doney smile and the smile said, "It was."

The staff sergeant from intelligence met us too. "I know that you boys are tired and have things to do, but I need to debrief you as soon as we can while the intelligence you got is still usable."

I admit that the priority in my mind was not on a debriefing. I had been thinking of something cold on my dry throat, a hot meal, a shower, and the care for our little people — a dozen things. But the staff sergeant's words reminded me of the reason we went in the first place.

"We will be there."

"An hour then?" said the sergeant.

"Give us two."

Leaders see to their people first. Always. When all the needs of your men are met, then, and only then, do you look to yourself.

"Everyone okay? Anybody need to see *Bac Si* doctor?"

The team shook their heads to say that they did not need to go to the dispensary.

"Nhoc, you have blood coming down your arm."

He lifted his arm and said, "Thorns do. No number ten. Okay."

Joe Morris had gone to the Sioux mess hall to be sure it was still open for them. "Sioux" was one of the terms we called our people, after the Indian tribe. It came from the technical term for our people — Special Commando Unit, or SCU, pronounced with a silent "C."

"After you eat, take a shower and clean your weapons and we will see you then," Doney told them.

We made it in time to our own mess hall, but we were still in our grimy fatigues with maps and notes in our side pockets and our compasses still around our necks and clipped between our top two buttons. The camouflage on our faces was thinned and smeared by sweat and insect repellant to a wet clay that clogged our pores.

We ate slowly and I got a brain freeze from the Kool Aid. We were tired and quiet, and I heard utensils tapping a Morse code of approval of the meal and the low murmur of voices in the room. Several of the guys stopped by the table to say how glad they were that we were back.

I slid the malaria dispenser across the table to Doney and he gave me his Doney smile.

"Dale, you come with me to debriefing. Joe, see to the team. When their gear is in order give them the rest of the day off. We will see about some leave time tomorrow."

A SOG debriefing is a lengthy, tedious interview between the Special Forces recon soldier who has just returned from his mission and an intelligence sergeant who tries to extract every item of useful information gained during the mission. The returning recon man may be injured. He may have been running on adrenaline and no sleep for days. He may be physically exhausted — my own web belt with grenades, ammunition, radio and canteen weighed fifty-five pounds. Another forty or fifty pounds would be in my rucksack. The soldier may have been in multiple firefights and may have been on the run just hours before the interview.

We arrived at the debriefing room, took our places on one side of a folding table, and retrieved our maps, cameras and notebooks from our side pockets.

"I have coffee and soda if you want some," the sergeant said as he took his seat.

"Coke," I said.

"Same."

When we were ready, he said, "Let's start with your insertion. Where did you land?"

Doney looked at his map and cross-referenced with his notebook, then gave the coordinates.

"What time did you insert?"

Doney gave it in military time.

"Describe the LZ."

"Fifty yards across. Waist-high elephant grass. Some dead trees."

"Were there signs of enemy activity on the LZ?"

"No."

"Where did you go from there?"

"Into the tree line fifty meters to the northwest."

"What kind of trees?"

"Deciduous hardwood."

"What kind of canopy?"

"Triple."

"Visibility?"

"Forty meters. Lots of shrubs and undergrowth."

"Any sign of enemy?"

"No."

"Where did you go from there?"

Doney consulted his notebook and his map and gave the coordinates.

"What occurred at that place?"

"We crossed a stream."

Doney anticipated the next questions and filled in the details.

"The stream was dry with a gravel bottom. It seemed to run only during the rainy season. It was oriented northwest to southeast. The sides were a cut bank about two feet deep and lined with tall grass."

The questions continued dot to dot on a map with each dot paragraphed with information.

"Another Coke?"

"And what happened there?" the voice droned on.

"We heard voices."

"Male or female?"

"Male. Some of them sounded young. My interpreter said they had the accent of the north, perhaps Hanoi. Some of them sounded chatty, certainly unaware that we were nearby."

The questions continued another hour.

"Tell me about the trails you saw."

"Fresh. Hundreds of soldiers had used them only minutes before we came. The trails were wide enough for a truck or soldiers to pass four abreast. We have pictures for the photo lab."

"Orientation?"

"They came from the direction of the sanctuary in Cambodia

coming off the Ho Chi Minh Trail. They then veered to the north in the direction of Ben Het or some other sanctuary on the Viet side of the border."

"Tell me about the enemy you encountered prior to your extraction. Were they disciplined? Did they have a military order? Did they seem to have good leadership? How did they signal? What kind of weapons did they have?"

Doney filled the sergeant in on all the details he could remember, and I filled in a few of the gaps.

"The soldiers you encountered. Describe the uniforms. Were they the black of the VC or the yellow-green of the NVA? Were they all dressed the same or were their uniforms mixed? Did they wear web gear? What kind of weapons did the regular soldier carry? Did you hear any commands given?"

My Coke was flat and made me thirstier and my mouth felt furry.

We relived the mission as we tried to give accurate information.

The sergeant set down his pencil before he went on. "Would you like water?"

It seemed a fresh mountain stream had moistened my mouth and I know that I smiled as I drank it.

He picked up his pencil and began again.

"When I ask these next questions some of the new recon men who have never been debriefed before will think I am nuts. Here goes:

"When you were in those last firefights, did the enemy soldiers have haircuts? Were they well-groomed or did they look shaggy like they had been on the march for days or weeks? Were their uniforms in good repair or did they look worn and torn and dirty? Did they look well fed or were they thin and without energy? Did they wear boots or sandals? Did each soldier have a rifle or did they share one?"

These were details I had not anticipated and did not notice when we evaded the pursuing enemy.

"When you first saw the enemy, did he carry his weapon at the port, ready for action, or were they slung over their shoulders? Specifically, what weapons did they have? Did they have a point element ahead of their larger units or did they seem to move in a mass?"

It was two hours before we completed the debriefing and left the S-2 building. The bright daylight stung my eyes, and I pulled my floppy hat with its brim from my pocket and put it on.

"You know, Sergeant Doney, I have to admit that when they were shooting at us, I didn't look to see if he had a haircut."

Doney smiled and spoke to me like a father to a son. "James Bond would but he wasn't with us on this one. That's why we keep a detailed notebook in the field, Sergeant Hanson. We remember the big picture of a stressful moment and the details are not that important at the time. We just see blurry enemy uniforms and flashes of explosions, and sometimes tracers coming at us. Then we get to an intel sergeant like him, and he will try to get us to relive that snapshot in time, and pull out details that we did not know that we even remembered."

"I remember when I was in 11F School," I told him, "one of our teams brought in a captured AK-47 and a uniform taken from a dead enemy soldier. They examined the stock of the rifle — it was the first time they weren't using wood on the stocks — and they traced the material and learned that it was made in Czechoslovakia. They examined the cloth of the uniforms, and they could tell exactly where the cotton was grown in the world and where the uniform was made. From the blood and stomach fluids on the uniform, they knew what he had been eating and that he was anemic."

We stopped at the flagpole and sat on the concrete rim.

Doney started to say something but remembered that we were in the open parade field and soldiers do not normally sit during the day especially at a headquarters. "Let's go over to the bunkers and sit there."

As we walked in that direction he said, "The information that we got will be important to someone of course and our people will faithfully send it up the line to them. But what we learned these last few days will be just one paragraph on a single piece of white paper mixed in with other reports. You would hope that the clerk in that General's office would realize the cost of those few sentences. Maybe our people who helped to hold the pencil should end our sentences with exclamation points for our people who were captured and tortured or mutilated or sent home under a flag."

Doney pointed to a bunker and we sat on the sandbags and could see across to a very small hamlet next to our perimeter. I could smell the charcoal maker's shop next to the road.

Doney held his hands out in front of him as if he were holding an invisible bottle, one hand at the bottom and the other at the side. His eyes focused on a place where a label would be in modern times, or where the sunlight would reflect on the colored glass.

"If we loved perfect vintage wine and we found a bottle of it that was a hundred years old and we paid a thousand dollars for it, we might think, as we pulled the cork on some special occasion and saw the spray escape the top, of its rarity and preciousness and cost. We might ponder its survival all those years and the care that was given to it in those secret cellars. We would open it with ceremony and slowly, and appreciatively, almost reverently, sip its redness."

I could see the image my team leader was sharing with me.

"Dale, why can't our intelligence people and government unfold our reports like something precious, information that we had to get at our peril and with our blood and see the truth they hold in their hands?"

"Yes," is all that I could answer.

We saw Joe Morris farther down the perimeter and I waved him over. Doney's voice was quiet, and I strained to hear him. He uttered that which festered in his mind — his frustration with the people in clean white shirts behind the mahogany tables who received SOG's after-action reports. I was certain that what he would say, he would never mention again.

"Sergeant Hanson, it seems that the Country Team — the ambassadors and military brass, and intelligence people, and politicians — will accept any intelligence we give them about troop movements, and trails and staging areas, but they will not believe anything we tell them that does not fit what they want to hear.

"We told them that the Communists had tanks. 'Oh no,' they tell us, 'You are mistaken. They are a guerrilla army and they do not have tanks. What you are hearing and seeing is tractors to make roads.'"

"They must have great hearing in Washington to be able to correct the hearing of our people who were on the scene," I said.

Doney continued, "So we send them pictures and they still do not believe. 'Kinda blurry,' they say, 'Could you have gotten closer?'"

Joe wiped dirt off a sandbag and sat near us.

"And then, those enemy tanks that they didn't believe we saw stormed out of the jungle and overran our camp at Lang Vei.

"A month ago, we told them about tanks the NVA had stashed in the jungle around Ben Het. Well, they are under siege now and it all began with an attack with ten of those tanks that they didn't believe we saw.

"We told them about the enemy having those black helicopters and about the MIG jets. Skeptical was what they were about that one. At least until one of our pilots had a dogfight with one of them."

Joe added, "Oh, and don't forget about the Black deserter who is working with the NVA against us. The recon team was in a firefight all day and toward evening when they were surrounded there comes this voice across the bushes, 'Hey boys. Y'all be dead by mornin', y'hear?' But Saigon says, 'There is no record of such a person.'"

"I'm going to take a shower," Doney said, "but I'll tell you one more and I will be done with it.

"My friend Dennison was running recon and they were certain there were Russian advisors on the ground with the NVA. A couple of times they saw them: tall, blond men clearly speaking Russian. He kept reporting it and the higher ups kept telling the teams how mistaken they were. Seems that the government did not want that kind of information. So, Dennison and his team set up an ambush and they killed a couple of them.

"Dennison cuts off their heads and puts them in a sandbag that he brought for that purpose. When he gets in from the mission, he hops the first plane heading for Saigon, and he storms into the regular meeting of the Country Team. The ambassador, CIA and the generals are all there around the long table. Dennison marches up to the table and rolls the heads out on the table. He grabs one by the hair and drags it over to the ambassador and pries the lips apart and spreads the jaws wide. 'See those teeth? See those fillings! Those are Russian fillings.

These guys are Russian.' And he storms from the meeting leaving the heads on the table as the next item of business. My friend Dennison hops the next plane back to the FOB and waits for the next mission."

Doney's movements were measured and deliberate as he stood. "Well, we are soldiers, and we just do our duty, don't we? I need to get out of these grubbies and take a shower. See you at dinner."

It was midafternoon. A yellow arm of sunlight reached through our window and inched its fingers across my bunk where I cleaned my rifle. The Fourth Infantry from the firebase at Marylou was firing artillery rounds over our camp at a target on the ridgeline. I felt the change in air pressure as the rounds passed overhead and was no longer startled when they cracked the sound barrier. I had my transistor radio on and imagined the gun crew around the field piece. They would be shirtless in the heat with cigarette butts jammed in their ears as one man pulled the lanyard. I set my rifle in its place as I listened to the song.

> *I am so afraid of dying*
> *Before I dry the tears she's crying*
> *Before I watch*
> *Your sea birds flying in the sun*
>
> *At Galveston*
> *At Galveston.*

I overhauled my web gear and propped it on the chair with the straps out so I could put it on in the dark. After a long cold shower that removed the camouflage grease from my face and hands, I luxuriated in clean fatigues and strolled across the compound. Maids in their black silk bottoms and white tops were gathering the laundry they had draped on the concertina wire to dry. I smelled the freshness of the soap and the clean air that dried them.

"*Chao ong,*" said a girl as she folded a shirt.

"*Chao Co dep long,*" I answered. Hello pretty girl.

I passed a team room where they were preparing for a mission, filling magazines and seating the bullets. AFVN radio blared from a transistor radio on the window ledge, and they were all singing the

157

lyrics, "War! Huh, yeah. What is it good for? Absolutely nuthin'. Say it again y'all! War, huh…" And though it was an anti-war song, the music sounded like a call to fight. The Americans' heads were down facing their work and they bobbed to the rhythm and they shouted with the song, "War, huh…!" One of the men was adding red peppers to the dry ingredients in his PIRs, officially referred to as Personal Indigenous Rations.

At the edge of the camp were the latrines. Each morning, Viet workers lifted the back doors and pulled the tubs of excrement from below the seats and burned them with gasoline. When they burned, the smoke was thick and black and heavy and did not rise far into the air. Now the burning was over, and the tubs were cool. The men worked the tubs back into place and I saw the leading edge of one dig into the gravel and the workers grasped the rim and walked it side to side into the space. The brown tub waddled like a huge, fat brown man.

"Han-Son, Han-Son," someone called. I turned and saw Chin and Nhoc coming toward me. They were in civilian clothes and town-ready. Chin was powerfully built and stocky and always smiled. Nhoc was taller, slender and serious. Nhoc had the face of an Asian scholar with round cheekbones and dark tired eyes. His face narrowed below his cheekbones and his skin was tight around his teeth. His teeth were off-white, the color of rice, for he did not smoke or chew betel nut. His hair was black and parted carefully and combed.

"Han-Son," Chin said as he felt my bicep through my sleeve, "You strong man like me. Very strong. We make you Chinese now. We adopt you. Your name, Han-Son, is same-same Chinese now. We see old Chinese man in Kontum. He will say most auspicious way to write your name."

"He will tell us best way to write, 'Han' and best way to write 'Son.'"

"I am honored, Chin. Thank you, Nhoc." And I patted Chin on his back as they left the gate and turned toward the city.

I watched as they disappeared into the haze of the hot day and the exhaust of motor scooters and pedicabs and a line of deuce-and-a-half trucks that was filled with troops. As I stood there, a sound caused me to look to the side of the road. An old Vietnamese man with a thin white chin beard was tapping the hollow bamboo bars of a birdcage with his long fingernails. The old man looked at me with jaundiced whites in his eyes and his own eyes seemed bird-like. Inside the tiny cage of sticks was a sparrow and the bamboo slats pressed its wings to its sides. The misery of the creature was plain. I considered buying the bird so I could let it fly.

There was a voice at my shoulder. It was measured and soft.

"If you buy that bird the old man will catch another and be at the gate again tomorrow."

"You are reading my mind Sergeant Doney."

"Walk with me to Supply. Are you any good with a pistol?"

"I think so. I grew up with guns."

"I want to get you a High Standard .22 pistol with a silencer. I want you to get very good with it. I want you to hit a small moving target and never miss."

I nodded. I was glad to be away from the old man and the bird.

"We will use it for our prisoner snatches."

Supply was next to the gate of our camp and Doney paused at the door. "Most of the prisoner snatch teams like to shoot them in the leg so they can't run away. I prefer to shoot in the shoulder or upper arm. If we pop 'em in the leg, we might have to carry them and that will slow us up. I like to see what side he holds his rifle and shoot him in his gun hand side. I think that if we are close enough to shoot him in his shoulder, we are close enough to run him down."

The American supply sergeant met us just inside the door with both of his hands flat on the countertop and waited for our requests. He had two "rockers" under his sergeant stripes. He was middle aged and balding, and a red burn-mark coursed down one cheek and disappeared into the collar of his shirt. Nothing that we would ask for would surprise him. When Doney told him what he wanted he just nodded to his Viet clerk, and he disappeared into the darkness of the interior and in minutes retrieved our High Standard pistol complete with untraceable serial numbers and silencers.

"What else, Norm?"

"We'll need several bricks of ammo for practice and missions."

He nodded to a Chinese clerk and simply said, "Chin," and he scurried away for it.

"Holster?"

"Yes," I said. "I'm left-handed and I think the only place that I can carry it is on the front straps of my rucksack. There is no room on my web belt, and it will take too long to get to in my rucksack.

He nodded his understanding, for he recalled his own web gear from his time in the field. "We have a left-hand holster, but you will have to modify it yourself. I can get you a second one so you can wear it on your belt to practice at the range."

Supply had everything except a penny gumball machine at the door. We gathered our things and thanked him. He placed his hands flat on the counter as before and spoke to our backs in a quiet voice, "Careful."

That first evening back from the field settled into the routine of night camp sounds. Small bats chased moths around the light at the gate, their soft leather wings flapping as soundlessly as their shadows under them. Only the soft chirping of their sonar revealed their presence. At the far side of the camp a tribesman kicked a half-full beer can which rolled into the perimeter wire and caught fast. He mumbled and his boot crunched gravel as he stumbled toward his barracks. Pots and pans were shelved in the mess hall as the night crew cleaned on the other side of the camp. A door shut with finality in the village and a muffled voice inside the hut drifted to us through our perimeter wire. A flare went up at a nearby camp with the familiar "fffftt" sound but I did not see its glow.

I did my private workout outside in the dark. We had no indoor gym, but there was a high bar behind the club, and I began there with three sets of thirty-five pull-ups. The bar was next to the perimeter, and I felt ill at ease during my sets. I was an easy target hanging there in the dark with both hands on the bar, so I checked for anyone lurking in the area before I began and during each set listened for the rustle of clothing or feet moving on the ground. It was cloudless, moonless and very dark. Like the Bible said, "It was a darkness that could be felt." I was part way through a set on the bar when our people sent up a mortar flare. The rocking, descending flare created shadows that crawled around me and crept toward my legs. Again, I looked for enemy hiding in the area.

I smelled cigarette smoke and eased my way toward the perimeter. A faint red glow showed from a main bunker, and I watched the glow move in an arc toward an unseen mouth and brighten when the guard puffed. The glow lit up his fingers and I wondered if an enemy could sight on them with his B-40 rocket. I coughed to let the soldier know of my presence then made my way inside.

"*Chao um*,"

"*Chao um Trung Si*," he said. Hello Sergeant.

"Dark!" I said.

I looked toward our wire and trip flares and minefields.

"How can you see tonight?"

"No can do, Han–Son. Sometimes flare come, and I look see. Other time I watch with my ears. One time I think VC come, then flare do, and I see mouse."

It was completely dark, but I knew that he turned toward me and was smiling at his little story.

I looked toward the west. The utter blackness had erased the horizon, then a very faint light flickered on the other side of the ridges. Rapid dim flashes, dozens per second, revealed the contour of the hills. It was like heat lightning in the Midwest with the expectation of thunder but no sound.

"See that?" I asked.

"Yes. Think maybe B-52."

"What's over there?"

"Think maybe Ben Het," he said as he stomped out his cigarette stub.

The flickering lasted for several minutes, and I watched the sky until it was over. If it was indeed an Arc Light strike (the codename for B-52 bombing missions), it was a massive one involving many bombers. I stood in the darkness next to the tribesman and strained to hear the explosions. Perhaps I imagined the low rumble of the bombs that fell in that distant and desperate battlefield. The flickering on the other side of the hills ended and the sky returned to utter darkness. A dog barked somewhere in the village and as I turned to go, I was not sure that I heard the bombs at all.

I had not slept since our in-country mission, and I dropped into bed. My custom was to read a passage of the Scripture every day and I propped my pillows under my head and read the Old Testament Passage where the Philistines had defeated the Hebrews and disarmed the country. Only the king and his son had a weapon. Jonathan, the king's son, and his armor bearer decided it was time to fight back and the two of them made a commando raid behind enemy lines. With a confidence in God, courage, and just one sword they conducted the raid that inspired the people and ultimately freed the country. It was at the place where Jonathan climbed the cliff on his hands and knees to attack the Philistine outpost that I fell asleep.

I had been dreaming. It was the first of a recurring nightmare that would visit me in my sleep the rest of my life. The dreams came in varied forms, but the theme would always be the same. Sometimes they would slither into the room where I lay — a deadly snake with eyes the color of yellow-green uniforms. It would slither through a slit in the window screen and stretch itself along the sill and wait there as still as wood until it located me in the darkness. I could see the shadow of its head as it swayed left and right with its black tongue flicking in and out. It would drop from the window ledge to the floor with a soft muffled thud then slither to my bedside. I could hear its scales grasp for purchase on the wood like long dry fingernails. The serpent would crawl up the post and I would lay there paralyzed holding my breath. My dreams were about being hunted and chased and sometimes I would be caught. The adversary was always ubiquitous and beyond my ability to destroy.

Sometimes I would squeeze my gun's trigger and nothing would happen. Sometimes I would crawl into the root system of a tree and cover myself with leaves and determine that I could stay there perhaps for months until the searching enemy was gone forever. I would be captured and as they were about to thrust a molten needle into my eye, I would twist my face away and burst upright in the bed with a gasp. When the nightmares came, which was a rare thing then in the war, I felt guilty because I had not been chased enough behind the lines to earn them.

In this dream we were being chased by the Communists. Somehow, I had been separated from the rest of the team and I had dug in and covered myself with sticks and leaves and waited until I had to shoot. There was a rustling of dried leaves to my side as they came toward me, but I dared not turn my head. The rustling was closer, and I heard them laughing for they thought they knew where I hid.

"Come out, come out, GI." They taunted.

I could see them — grinning serpents with wide mouths and mucus dripping from their fangs.

Then in my dream an enemy placed his mouth at my ear and said, "Shush, shush," like to a baby, "Shush, shush."

With my heart thumping in my ears like approaching footsteps, I came awake but did not move. I heard the shushing sound again, but this time it was not in my dream but in my room. I opened my eyes and looked in the direction of the sound. A large moth-like insect with stiff dry wings was caught at the window. "Shush, shush," it frenzied against the screen.

I was ashamed of myself for having the dream. I rolled out of bed and dressed, and I never told anyone about the moth.

We were on stand-down, and I took advantage of the time. I worked out with the karate class. Many of our people were from the First Special Forces Group that was based in Okinawa, so we learned Okinawan karate, the most martial of the karate styles. Years later, Skip Ettinger from our class became the grand master of the style.

I went to the carpenter shop and paid the Viet to make me a few nunchakus. We used heavy mahogany and countersunk bolts into the ends for greater effect. The wood was dense and hard and clinked when the two halves tapped together.

The Dak Bla River at the edge of Kontum was a mile from the

FOB, and during the day when the road was safe I did a speed run of the two miles there and back. I was never a fast runner but always tried to do it in under twelve minutes.

The days were pre-monsoon sunny and as much as can be in a unit such as ours, they were halcyon days. We received no incoming from the enemy and none of our teams in the field were in trouble. Kontum took one hit from a rocket our first day of stand-down and there were no casualties. It slammed into a corrugated tin roof of a warehouse left over from the days of the French. The slam of the impact was loud and unforgettable, and the roof was twisted into knots, but otherwise our days of stand-down were of no event. One of the men in the companies thought things were too quiet. "Ominous!" he said, like a farmer looking to the sky above his grain fields.

Doney introduced me to the old hands, the legends of SOG.

"Hey," he would say, "Remember in Robin Moore's book, *The Green Berets*, when one Green Beret comes out of the jungle alone and crosses the river? Well, this is the guy that Moore was writing about."

Our compound was filled with legends and heroes. "This is the man who started the OSS," Doney would tell me. "This is the man who was the model for Ian Fleming's James Bond." Norm Doney introduced me as if I were of their group. I reveled in their stories, and they tutored me with their experience and wisdom.

On Thursday, Mike Buckland and I checked out the recon jeep and drove into Kontum. The main street was cobblestoned with red brick. Huge trees with red blossoms reached their boughs across to the other side of the street and shaded the sidewalk. The scent of ginger, spices and sandalwood wandered from the open doors and sat on the benches on the walkway. A charcoal artist had just finished a sketch of a young Vietnamese girl holding a pair of dog tags next to her cheek. Her eyes were tight in anguish and the tears in the drawing seemed to roll from the canvas.

I purchased incense in a soapstone container that had hand-carved elephants marching around the rim. With its trunk, each elephant held the tail of the one in front until the last held the tail of the first. I wondered if the artist was making a statement about blindly following the one in front as they walked around the vessel. While Mike talked with the charcoal artist, I stepped outside to keep an eye on our jeep and watched a rickshaw driver pedal by. He had long, skinny legs with enormous knees and as he puffed by, his mouth was a huge open cavern that was either black with betel nut or contained no teeth at all. The skinny chest that housed his heart resembled the fragile sticks of a cage with the panting bird ready to fly away.

We left the charming business district of Kontum and drove to the far side of town, past white mice headquarters, the French cemetery and the airport, to the B Company Mike Force compound. This compound was home to a company of warriors — a dozen Green Berets and a battalion of Montagnard tribesmen. These "Yards," as we called them, were fearless and loyal to Special Forces. It is said that half of the male Montagnard population of Southeast Asia served in SF units and died side by side with their Green Beret leaders.

The Mike Force — or "Reaction Company," or "Strike teams" as they were often called — were fighters. They would be called upon to exploit a target discovered by a recon team, or block the entire movement of the Ho Chi Minh Trail for days at a time, or rescue a team in trouble, or fill in the decimated ranks of a compound about to be overrun. Mike and I wanted to meet some of our commando brothers on the other side of town.

We parked before what appeared to be the main door of the compound and left the bright sunlight to find ourselves in the shaded interior of the Special Forces dayroom. To our right were sturdy tables made by the local carpenters, a few comfortable chairs, a small library and a pool table. A large print dominated the wall over the pool table — the same painting that was in the day room at FOB and in the day room in Nha Trang. In the painting a shapely, beautiful, dark-haired woman wearing a green beret and a Special Forces shirt with all the patches gazed at us from the canvas. As we glanced about, an SF sergeant met us at the door. He had a weeping bandage on his cheek and was daubing it with a cloth when we entered. He started to smile as he greeted us and winced as the movement pulled on his wound.

"Come on in."

Fresh blood appeared on the dressing and mixed with the seeping antibodies and older crusted brown blood. He glanced at our berets and the red SOG crests on our chests and held out his hand.

"Glad to see you boys. You must be from the FOB, I take it."

"We are. We have no official business here. We just wanted to meet you guys — our brothers down the street. We aren't disturbing anything, I hope."

"Nah, I can use the company. I am the only one here, just me an' Phan, our cook, and a handful of strikers guarding the perimeter. I am happy to see you boys. Come inside. I'm Rodriguez."

The sergeant was slim and short and had black hair. He braced himself by putting his weight on a nearby table and hobbled to the closest chair. "Have you boys eaten breakfast? Phan is a good cook and loves to take care of us. We have so much food here now it will spoil if I don't feed you. How about bacon and real eggs and American fried potatoes. Phan makes biscuits too.

"Phan!" he called.

A thin Montagnard in his fifties instantly appeared. One side of his jaw was miss-shaped as if it had been broken and did not heal in line. His eyes were dark and clouded over like smoke and his smile revealed that his front teeth had been filed to the gum line in his youth. "This is Phan. He has fought the Communists since the French in Den Bien Phu. He parachuted in during the siege and was one of the groups that fought its way out of that meat grinder. He then fought on our side in the A camps and with the Mike Forces."

Phan waited before us, and I rose from my chair in respect. "Phan, could you make three breakfasts for us?"

The old fighter smiled in delight and returned to the kitchen.

"And you," I said to the sergeant, "What happened to you?"

"Shrapnel outside of Ben Het. Got it in my face and thigh. Lucky though, the blast was pretty spent when it hit me, so it didn't go in too deep. Irritating though. The one on my face stuck in my jaw and sliced my tongue. Didn't know there was so much blood in a tongue. The other piece of metal poked through my pant leg and was embedded in my thigh bone. That one was stuck there pretty good. I didn't have a plier to pull it out so a couple of my Yards had to wriggle it out. I need to heal up quick so I can get back out there with my people."

Phan brought us a huge breakfast and we thanked him and began to eat.

"I guess I am ignorant, Sergeant Rodriguez."

His look at us was one of sadness and wonder. He was dismayed that we were unaware of the sacrifice and danger his people had gone through and was baffled that Mike and I seemed unaware of that struggle.

Rodriguez winced again as he placed food into his mouth, and he daubed the dressing on his jaw with a gauze pad.

"This Mike Force has been fighting a North Vietnamese regiment at Ben Het for ten days now. We have a hundred percent casualties. We have been plugging the gaps with squads and platoons where we could get them. Who knows how many of our little people we have lost? As far as I know, I am the only one left and I am just waiting for word to rejoin the Mike Force. I feel guilty every minute that I sit here."

Rodriguez' eyes watered from the wound in his cheek, and he daubed it with the cloth that lay on his lap like a napkin. He spooned salsa on his eggs and continued. "Our people are not inside Ben Het itself. We are engaging some of the nearby NVA units to pull them off the fight. They tell me that the situation in the camp is desperate. They are being hammered by the enemy artillery. They figure there are more than three thousand charging the camp and they are tunneling under the wire."

He looked up at us. "Do you think FOB will be sending anyone?"

Mike looked at me for confirmation and said, "I think we are doing our own missions. They will not let Ben Het fall, that's for sure."

There was movement at the door to the kitchen. Phan stood at attention in his bare feet in torn jungle fatigues and a beret on his head — a modern day Gunga Din. A crossbow and quiver were strapped over one shoulder and a bolt action rifle was at his side.

"Phan will go to the fight," the Montagnard said. "Not too old to fight."

Chapter Fourteen

BEN HET AND JULIET NINE

He was ugly and scarred, with sad, milky eyes, and bags under them that were rimmed in red. He had an ungainly stride that spoke of old injury, like the walk of a moonshiner of old who rushed to a hiding place with a jug under each arm. His skin was the color of old liver that had bleached in the rain and when he moved, his bones seemed loose under his skin. But for his appearance, he was a creature of loyalty, calmness, and dependability. He was as sure and easygoing as the pendulum of an old grandfather clock, and to the men of Special Forces camp A-244 at Ben Het, this dog was their mascot.

It was Staff Sergeant Neil Kline who found him. Kline was leading a patrol into a friendly Montagnard village with an observer from Saigon when he heard the snap of a breaking bone and a croaking-choking sound in the grass along the trail. A large boa constrictor had its last coils around its victim and Kline simultaneously saw the shiny scales tighten together and the furry, floppy ears and nose of a small dog. The eyes seemed to plead. With a flash, he drew his KA-BAR knife and drove it through the skull of the snake, the end of its blade crunching into the gravel on the other side of its head. He flew to his knees and unwrapped the thrashing snake and blew life-saving breath into the dog's nostrils.

With his eyes on the wounded dog in his arms, he spoke to the visitor from Saigon. "Had to intervene," he said, "We haven't eaten yet."

The headquarters man from Saigon, recalling that one of the euphemisms for Special Forces was, "snake eaters," asked with a shaky voice, "The snake or the dog?"

Kline slowly faced him and winked. "Coming to dinner?"

So, he became the camp mascot and with his escape from the boa constrictor he acquired the name Boa. When he was grown, Boa's happy loose walk said, "I am a bachelor, an eligible bachelor." One of the old Montagnard strikers from Dien Bien Phu days was sitting beside Kline on the wall and watching Boa walk by like the cock of the walk. "*Trung Si* Kline, Dog him walk same same French boy when he look look for girl. Him same same, '*beau*.'"

So, Boa became Beau. He hated Vietnamese. He might have sensed their attitude toward him, or it was a smell about them, but Beau avoided them. Beau also was careful around the strikers for he seemed to know they regarded him as food on the hoof. One of the strikers laughed when the dog looked into his eyes, "You safe, Beau. You too skinny and boney for Montagnard. You no come my kitchen." But Beau loved Kline and the other Americans in the camp. Each night he made the rounds to every Green Beret, stopping at each hooch, each bunker, and the day room. His loyalty was an invisible chain between him and his soldiers. Twice when Kline and his reconnaissance team were miles beyond the perimeter of Ben Het, Beau had passed through the mined perimeter and made his way through enemy territory and found his location in the field and eased his way into the team's night position. He licked Kline's hand and curled up beside him for the night.

February 21st, was a Monday and they had steaks in the mess hall, two days in a row and Kline wondered if that was a preparation for something. He unwrapped kitchen scraps and fed them to Beau, then raised his binoculars and glassed the area to the west toward the NVA sanctuaries in Cambodia. Kline could not shake the feeling of foreboding. Every report of their recon teams, and intelligence reports indicated significant enemy movement toward the camp. Then, it was as if the enemy had vanished. Kline did not like it. He could not put his finger on why he felt impending conflict — certainly he would not be able to articulate any of this to the others. It reminded Kline of the complete stillness before a tornado, before the sky turns black with streaks of lightning, and the grain fields blow flat in an instant and then the wind shrieks in your ears and you force your eyes shut against straw that has been turned to yellow needles.

Beau put his muzzle under his hand and whined. "You too, huh boy?"

He studied the distance again and saw a small flash in the sunlight — cobalt blue like the lens of binoculars. Was an enemy commander watching him in turn from the other side of the clear cut?

"You too, Sergeant Kline?'

Kline flinched. He had so concentrated on the west that he did not notice the officer's approach. "I'm afraid so, Lieutenant. It's just a feeling that I have."

"Well, if it is any consolation, I feel the same way. We had every indication of something brewing and now nothing."

The sergeant set the binoculars on the window ledge. "I have a friend in Alaska that told me about that big earthquake they had when the tsunami wiped out those towns. They said it was completely calm and then all the water left the harbors and then without warning the big wave came in and up and up. It feels like that now. I think I will stay here on the perimeter tonight."

"Well, I think we are ready for the fight when it comes. Hey, isn't that Beau there in the wire?"

Kline glanced down at his side and saw that Beau was gone. "Augh! It is. I think he has a girlfriend out there somewhere. I thought he would get blown up the first time he did it, but I think he can smell the explosives. That first time, he would come up to a mine, stop and sniff, and then back up and go around. He has his little route that he goes. Sometimes he comes back with a rat or something."

Lieutenant Linnane smiled and nodded. I think I will try get a few more people on perimeter with you. See you later Sergeant."

Beau returned to the camp just before dark with a rodent in his mouth. He set it down at Kline's feet but did not eat it. It was the chase that he wanted, not the meat. The sky was starless and opaque, and Kline saw it as a curtain behind which things were occurring. Around midnight, like the tornado on the grain fields, the battle began and for the next ten days Ben Het was in continuous siege. It started with a massive barrage of artillery, mortar and recoilless rifle fire into the camp — hundreds of rounds exploded inside the perimeter. An enemy regiment charged the wire along with hundreds of sappers whose duty it was to penetrate the concertina wire. Some of them had studied Beau's route through the wire and crawled on his narrow path, but it was narrow and only one soldier at a time could feel his way through in the dark and the camp's rifle fire stopped them at the place.

Captain Franceour called for "Spooky," the airplane that could lock in and fire 6,000 rounds a minute from each gun. Its flares converted night to daylight and lit up the charging enemy. The captain called in artillery and fighter airplanes on the NVA and by morning the enemy had left the field with heavy losses. For the next ten days the camp was bombarded with hundreds of artillery rounds each day. Ben Het was surrounded and outnumbered by ten to one, but the camp held.

It was a cloudless Monday, and there was a lull in the fighting when Beau passed through the perimeter wire to the outside again, perhaps to check on his girlfriend. He returned midafternoon when the angle of the sun left the hundreds of enemy dead exposed in deep shadow. His return nearly caused his death for he was dragging a prize in his mouth when the end of it caught one of the remaining trip flares in the wire. There was an immediate flash and the nearest striker fired one burst of 30 cal., the rounds striking all around the dog.

"No, no, no!" Shouted a nearby striker. "Him no VC, him Beau." Beau continued to drag his prize, tugging it from the barbed wire when it tangled, and when he was free of the concertina wire, proudly dragged it to the feet of his master, Sergeant Kline.

"What do you have there, boy?"

Kline started to pick up the object but froze mid-reach. Before him was a length of flesh, an upper arm and elbow, wrapped in a shredded sleeve. Kline hooked the sleeve with a stick and held it up to his eyes. His eyes watered with the stink, but he flattened the cloth with the stick. At a place just below where a shoulder would have been was the shoulder patch of the 66th NVA regiment — hardcore NVA.

March 3rd. They heard tanks moving toward the camp. They were around a bend on the far side of a hill and could not be seen, but the men clearly heard tanks. A huge barrage of artillery fire fell on the camp smashing fortifications and buildings. Thousands of enemy shot and screamed at the camp as they charged toward the perimeter behind ten T-76 Russian tanks.

Lieutenant Linnane shouted into the radio to be heard above the fighting, "I need Spooky. I have tanks in the wire. Ten of them." The camp was a mass of explosions from artillery fired from the sanctuaries in Cambodia and from mortars near the camp. Machine gun and rifle fire poured into the camp. "I repeat, I have tanks in the wire."

"No. you must be hearing road building equipment."

"I have tanks I tell you."

"Say again what you have."

"Tanks. Tango-alpha-November-kilo-sierra. Tanks. You got that?"

"Roger. Understand tanks."

There was heavy, but broken cloud cover and the pilot was unsure if he could get through to the beleaguered camp but when he found one break in the overcast, he flew through the opening and remained under the ceiling until he was relieved. Spooky sprayed the tanks with 40mm cannon and two tanks and a troop carrier exploded and burned on the field. One enemy tank made it to the perimeter wire where it stuck in soft mud and the tracks wrapped themselves in miles of barbed wire. Throughout the morning Spooky and fighter jets dropped bombs and napalm on the battlefield until the NVA pulled back with the surviving tanks but artillery continued to land in the compound. The siege would continue.

Sergeants Kline and Rivera leaned against one of the bunkers. Their legs were splayed straight out before them, their rifles across their legs. Kline held out his arms for Rivera to see.

"Kinda looks like freckles, don't it?"

Rivera stopped picking at his arms and held his up next to Kline's. "Mine don't show up good like yours."

They both resumed to pick tiny pieces of shrapnel from their skin.

"I could sleep a year. Can't remember when I have slept an hour over these weeks."

Rivera stopped picking long enough to show a piece of metal to Kline. "This is a big one. That would get you a purple heart in a leg outfit for sure."

Staff Sergeant Kline did not answer. He had a piece of his own shrapnel between his thumb and forefinger, and he was asleep.

The Communists changed tactics slightly over the next weeks. They still hammered the camp with artillery from the sanctuaries hidden somewhere in Cambodia, but they began most of their attacks during daylight. They considered that we could see their muzzle flashes in the dark and could train fire on them more easily. It was a Sunday, another no-steak Sunday. The Communists began another probe on the compound with artillery pouring in to support the effort.

The last thing Kline remembered was being thrown high into the air, wrapped in a shroud of shredded sandbags and gravel and dirt. It was dark, but he did not know if he was sensing the black night of Ben Het or if he was losing consciousness. He had seen the flash of the incoming artillery when it sunk into the earth next to him and his interpreter and exploded. Arms and legs flailed around him as he spun in the air above the bunker. "Please let them be still attached to me," he prayed. His body bounced when he landed on the ground. The first bounce took the air from his lungs, and he heard its leaving, "Huuumh!"

He came to, face down in the gravel with his nose flattened against his cheek. Small stones were embedded in his flesh and debris lifted his upper lip from his teeth and filled his mouth with dirt. His face lay in a pool of blood and he was smothering. His lungs screamed for air, and he convulsed as he gasped and choked on dirt. Something pulled him by the back of his collar. He heard Beau whine and felt the tug as his dog braced his legs and jerked and pulled on his collar. He heard a yelp and felt his face free from the pool of blood. He smelled moist gravel and the iodine of his own blood, and he smelled sweat and fear and vomit.

"Auugh! Auuugh!"

Kline rolled to his back and opened his eyes and saw the brown anxious eyes of his dog. He was alive. He glanced to his side and saw a crater where his interpreter had been.

Red and green tracer bullets crisscrossed above his head. Nearby, a North Vietnamese artillery round slammed into a building and the sagging timbers groaned like a dying thing. Something hissed inside and flames crackled from the burning wood. A mortar flare lighted his place as it swayed back and forth in its parachute.

His hearing was coming back. Machine guns fired from the bunker next to him. One of the barrels was see-through red hot and he saw the bullets pass inside the barrel. Kline heard the thumping of the mortars the enemy was firing at the camp from just outside the wire. "Krump, krump, krump." The rounds impacted along the perimeter like railroad cars slamming together.

Kline wondered how badly he was hurt and gingerly felt his face. He felt no deep wounds, nothing pierced his skull, but he dared not feel further. He could not feel his right leg. Kline was horrified. There was only a left leg visible in the dark. In a panic he clawed the ground. Nothing. This time he started at his groin and felt downward, following the flesh toward his feet, feeling along his pant leg under the soil. His shaking fingers tore away the earth around the limb to where his knee would be. With both hands he grasped the cloth and with a groan pulled on the trouser leg. He rocked backward and freed it from the ground. His leg was there. But it seemed far away and lifeless.

"Get back in the fight. Get back in the fight," he ordered himself. He clawed his rifle out of the dirt and half stood to get to the perimeter, but the leg would not move. He placed his forearm under his thigh and lifted it and lunged toward the trench, falling headlong into it and landed on a body. There was a shriek. The body was alive and pummeled Kline with his fists.

"*Kaka dau! Kaka dau!*" the Montagnard screamed at Kline. Kill! Kill!

"No! No! American. *Trung Si* Kline."

"Ahh, Kline." There was relief in the voice. "Think you VC."

"Yes, no sweat." Kline clamped one hand on the soldier's shoulder and spun him around to face the bunker. Using his rifle as a long index finger, he pointed at the machine gun."

"Help me get there. My leg number ten."

The little soldier saw the transparent glowing barrel and gasped to see the shadows of bullets passing through the length.

"Help me get there. Soldier needs to change barrel or bullets cook off and kill soldier."

Kline leaned on the tribesman's shoulder and together, they hobbled toward the bunker, the Green Beret's bum leg dragging along. Inside, the floor was inches deep in sliding shell casings and they swept Kline's good leg from under him. He lay sprawled on his back with the air knocked out of him. He shouted up at the silhouettes behind the gun.

"Hey, you need to change barrel. Where is the asbestos glove? Find now."

"No, no, *Trung Si*! Look, look." The soldier's face was white in the flare light with his eye sockets skulled by shadow. The gunner pointed through the opening. "*Trung Si*, Look. *Beaucoup* VC. Look!"

One glance through the opening told the story. As far as he could see beyond the concertina wire were hundreds of advancing enemy soldiers. The flares from Spooky, the C-130, lit up the massive attack. Charred enemy dead hung in the wire entanglements, the razor wire holding them at their waists and bending them double. The white teeth of one dead sapper grinned from a head of cinder in the light of a flare. Artillery rounds fell inside the camp in a rain of explosions. Across the clearing, the tree line blinked where mortar rounds left their tubes and from the barrels of their support machine guns. Perhaps a regiment of enemy charged the defenders of Ben Het.

Kline pulled his eyes from the opening and shouted at the Montagnard. "Change barrel! Do it!"

The Montagnard striker looked at Kline unbelieving, then at the advancing hoard.

"Must do!" Kline insisted.

The striker seemed uncapable to decide.

"Must do or VC fini Montagnard."

The tribesman then knew the gravity of the situation. He dashed to a shelf and put on the gloves and shouted to his assistant gunner. "Get barrel," he ordered.

Kline was weary, so weary that it took all his strength to form words, but he hobbled and dragged himself from bunker to bunker to direct his people. At the west-most point of the perimeter he was knocked down by a blast and crawled the remainder of the way to the next strongpoint. He and his striker did what most of the defenders of Ben Het were doing — fighting on. The striker helped Kline to his feet, and they half walked, half crawled into a bunker. One wall and part of the roof had collapsed. The machine gun was on its side and the gunners who had fired it lay behind it in a heap.

"Help me set this up," he told his striker. "We fight here."

With both hands on the bloody shirt, Kline dragged the nearest gunner from the weapon while the Montagnard righted it on its pod and fed the belt for the Green Beret to fire. Kline heard a whine, and saw Beau take his place at his other side. A patch of blood oozed on his shoulder. He sighted on the nearest group of enemies. In the light of the flares, it was clear that they had dug a trench along the outer perimeter wire. Pith helmets and rifles lined the top and the muzzle flashes from their weapons revealed a continuous line. Shown also in the shadows of the flares was a depression of collapsed earth where the NVA had tunneled under the perimeter into the camp. Kline and the striker engaged the leading edge of the attackers, but it seemed that there was always another mustard-colored uniform to replace the one just knocked down. Then all along the west side of the perimeter, a white inferno of napalm erupted as a jet made a low pass across his vision.

"We are beating them back," he shouted to the dog. In the illumination flares many soldiers turned and ran while others walked backwards with discipline, shooting as they moved. At the nearest line of advance, one soldier who had been buried under the bodies of comrades, thrashed himself free and stood on shaky legs. He faced the camp and with deliberate aim emptied his rifle toward Klein and his men. He patted his ammo pouches and finding them empty, he dropped to his knees tearing into the pouches of the dead. Finding one more magazine he reloaded his rifle, made careful aim and fired until all cartridges were gone. He sighed — Klein could see the heaving of his chest — then slowly turned and walked off the field, unscathed.

Kline eased his head down on the sandbag and closed his eyes in deep sleep. He did not hear the artillery that continued to fall on SF Camp Ben Het.

Morning stretched from her sleep and slipped from the blankets of fog that surrounded the relative peace of Kontum, then strolled in her yellow gown to the gravel pad where Recon Team Florida assembled. Our rucksacks were in a row in the order of our march in the field where we waited for the last of the fog to burn off the hills and permit the helicopters to arrive. I did not sleep well during the night — I never really did before a mission. Every sound in the night invaded my mind and had to be deciphered and dismissed before I resumed slumber. The occasional flare would go up in the dark with its "fssst," and I would wait, half asleep, listening for gunshots after the flare. When the old dog barked in the village where the charcoal maker lived, I imagined black-clad VC had disturbed it and were moving with the stealth and quiet of the shadows that advanced ahead of the movement of the moon. But in the end, I slept and had to be wakened.

Except for Chin, our point man, we were all putting camouflage on our faces and hands in front of the Recon HQ when Chin and Nhoc said they forgot something. Doney nodded his okay and they ran to Supply and presently came back with a thick felt marker.

"Han-Son. You no can go to field before we fini you,"

Chin held the marker in the air like a trophy. "You have Chinese name. When you go field now, we always write on your back this — Han-Son, *Kam Bow Ya Chin.*"

Chin found a piece of cardboard from a C-Ration box and wrote four Chinese characters and held it up for me to see. Nhoc, the scholar, explained as Doney and Jim Morris looked on: "First two say your name, Han-Son. Next two say, *Kam Bow Ya Chin*. That mean, 'eternal life, never die.' It mean that God see you down there fighting and he sees Hanson on your shirt and 'never die.' And God, him say, 'That is my man. Hanson, him no die.'"

Then with ceremony they wrote the Chinese characters on the back of my shirt, just below my collar where God could see it above my rucksack, 'Hanson never die.'" As long as we were together on the team, they never let me go to the field without alerting God.

Bob Howard stepped out of the Recon building and said, "Choppers twenty minutes out. Are you guys ready?"

"Ready," Doney told him.

"I have the jeep and the three-quarter-ton laid on." There was sudden activity and the engines started and we hefted our gear into the bed. The commo man ran out to confirm again that we had the one-time codes and frequencies and all the call signs. We passed through the first gate and picked up the "chase medic" on the way and arrived on the steel helicopter pad as the squadron of five was still a single dot on the horizon.

Team Florida would ride in two Hueys to the remote landing zone deep in enemy territory. Three Americans and eight SCU were slated for this mission — perhaps a little light for a full-blown prisoner snatch, a little heavy for strictly intelligence gathering but just heavy enough to help us survive a scrap behind the lines until help arrived — and that, with the marginal weather and hot target, was a real possibility. Half of our people were Chinese and the rest were Vietnamese who we had trained. A third Huey was for the chase medic, the very highly trained Special Forces medic. If we got into any trouble, he could take on our wounded from the field and care for them en route to a field hospital, or if we were fixed in place with multiple wounded or surrounded, could land on our location and render aid. There were two chase medics going in on this mission.

"Expecting anything special?" I asked.

"Just showing the new guy what we do. Anyway, you might need us."

Next to the "slicks," just to the side of us, were two narrow Cobra

Gunships. Even motionless on the pad they were an image of lethality, a northern pike fish finning in the shadow of a rock ready to attack with blinding speed and ferocity.

Another jeep pulled up to us and SFC Daniels hopped out.

"Just wanted to let you know that I am flying Covey for you today. My pilot is warming up the Bird Dog now, but we will be over the target before you get there. I made a pass of the area yesterday. Lots of activity."

Daniels glanced at our team. Like all covey riders, he had spent his time on the ground and knew what a team was going through. The Special Forces Covey Rider in the plane took the wisdom learned on the ground to where he sat in the airplane. "I am glad you are going in a little heavy. If it gets hot in your target, and we have more than one team in trouble you may have to hang in there for help to arrive. I'll keep an eye out for you. I have a couple of other teams in the field to look after too so I will be around."

He patted us on the back and waved to our Indig and then sped off in his jeep.

We were all seated in the two Hueys; Chin and Doney in the first, followed by Hu, the interpreter, then Joe with the radio and two of our Viets. I followed with four of our little people. Three were Chinese and I had Ba, my Vietnamese tail gunner. The pilot looked to the side at the next chopper and seeing that all were ready, we lifted off the ground, leaned ahead and sped toward our target, "Juliet Nine."

We flew high — five thousand feet — and to the west. Cresting the Central Highlands, the ground crawled up under us and we changed course several times so any watching enemy could not anticipate our target. It was early enough in the war that the Communists did not have every LZ monitored, but the plan was that if we were shot out of the first two landing zones, we would return the following day to a smaller opening in the jungle and rappel in. We made a pass at the first LZ. The first aircraft came in trying to draw fire, then the rest of us came in low, brushing the grass as if we were landing, then veered off and we continued to the next LZ. At the second opening in our target area, we flew in a gentle circle, and I saw the Bird Dog make a low pass just above the trees. Our engine changed pitch and we banked into an acute turn. It was a tight descending spiral that lifted me slightly off the seat. In the blur of the turn, I saw that Doney's group had already landed and were running for the tree line. Seconds later we found ourselves a foot above the blowing grass of the opening. We jumped out and ran for the edge of the field where we joined the rest of the team under a hardwood tree.

We used the engine noise to cover our rush from the LZ and when the squadron left for the next valley we waited like green statues and listened. When it seemed certain that our landing was not compromised, Doney nodded to Joe and he whispered, "Good day," into the radio and the squadron left completely. We were on our own.

At a sign, Florida rose to its feet and crept toward the west, the Ho Chi Minh Trail, and the sanctuaries the Communists kept in "neutral" Cambodia. Ambush was always possible moving off the LZ after we had dismissed our air protection. Many teams in the past fought desperate battles with a waiting enemy just after inserting into a target. The enemy sought to wipe out an entire team or capture a SOG man for torture and interrogation. But we moved with stealth, changed direction often, made many security stops, ambushed our back trail, and so slipped deep into the enemy sanctuary for our seven to ten-day mission.

By the third day it was very hot and dry, and the air was death-still. The jungle floor was dry, brown and brittle. A slight brush of cloth against the dense foliage mimicked the sound of a crinkling empty paper bag. Fallen leaves curled themselves into brown megaphones and waited for a careless boot. A yellow bird ate seeds in a tree, and I was amazed at how much sound the falling seed pods made in the stillness. It seemed the forest itself held its breath to hear us pass. We came through one of these patches and I know that some sounds must have attested our passage, when Chin froze in place. He clinched one hand into a fist and held it behind him for us to see — "Stop, freeze, danger." Doney inched forward. We had been moving parallel to an unseen high-speed trail and only now converged on its presence. It was hard-packed black clay with not a blade of vegetation on the surface.

Hundreds of soldiers may have walked only yards beside us, and we would have been unaware of their presence. But they certainly could have heard us moving in the thick vegetation.

We froze in place and monitored the trail. There would be no sounds of footfall to warn of enemy approach on this trail — we could be looking to a place where the trail became obscured by the vegetation, and they would just appear.

We hovered along the trail and watched for enemy activity, noting the location and orientation for our notebooks. There was a shout from somewhere beyond the bend. I glanced first at Ba, then at Nhoc to see if they got anything out of the shout. Nhoc shrugged that he did not know. Ba did not take his eyes from the bushes. His eyes focused along his rifle at our back path. Something had alerted him, a sound as slight as two leaves pressing each other. Covey was not available to us as they were inserting a team.

I looked toward Doney. I knew that we needed to make our way from the trail while we had light to see and find a place from which to give a SITREP (situation report) when Covey passed through. We also had to pick a place to RON. He pointed a direction to the point man, and we peeled off and slowly followed, all of us facing the trail until it was our turn to go. Ba was tense, expecting desperate combat at any moment. He moved as if his foot was about to press the plunger that would start it all. He and I covered the backtrail of the team long enough to ensure that we had not been discovered and pursued.

That night it rained for an hour. We were in the highlands and nights were chilly and we were soaked and shivered. When the shower ended, the trees dripped and mimicked searchers moving through the foliage. I watched through an opening in the leaves where the sky was just a few shades lighter than the forest and saw my breath and I felt exposed. I had but a thin, small square of tarp that I used to cover my rifle, but in the end, I hovered over my weapon with the tarp over my shoulders. I listened for movement but only heard the dripping in the leaves.

Back in Ben Het, a young Green Beret sergeant peered through a window slot of a bunker at the hundred yards of churned mud and tangled barbed wire and the bodies of dead enemy soldiers whose existence had been reduced to pieces of uniforms and the bones inside them that gave them shape. It had rained — a shower that had lasted an hour and he sheltered in the enclosure looking for signs that the enemy was using the downpour to hide an advance. Perhaps flare light on the mud would show drag marks of a crawling sapper. The young sergeant would shortly make his rounds to be sure his strikers were alert, but only after he saw no signs of infiltration through his window. There was still a light rain, not much more than a drizzle, but enough to keep the sky overcast and prevent close air support. They would have to rely on tank or artillery fire to stave off any probe.

The downpour, when it came then, drowned out the sounds of the shovels that dug trenches ever closer to the camp. For some time, Ben Het had been aware that tunnels were also being dug under the wire and deep into the camp for the big assault.

Artillery rounds were landing on the west hill. They were not a barrage — that would come later, but now, the rounds taunted, "We are still here." The intent was to harass, to lay siege, to say, "No point in the camp is safe from us, you will not relax, you will not sleep."

It was impossible to anticipate where one of the two to four hundred rounds that exploded on Ben Het every day, would land. Someone said that Sergeant Kline's dog knew when a round would hit. The strikers would watch Beau when he was around. He would whine and head for cover and one or two minutes later the explosion came. No one knew if he could hear the shell when it left the mouth of the cannon, felt the air pressure change, or if God told him — but when Beau ran for shelter, strikers and Green Berets alike also dove for cover.

Outside, in the open air, the living always had a refuge in mind at the first sign of incoming. Strikers and their families in the camp lived in underground bunkers roofed in timber and sandbags. Life underground for these Montagnards was a new norm. Yesterday the sergeant finished carving a water buffalo out of the local hardwood. He carved the buffalo in a reclining, peaceful posture with its four legs under its body so it would not easily break. It was with both pleasure and blisters on his carving hand that he gave it to a Montagnard boy who day after day sat alone in the sandbag doorway of his house.

He looked through the slot again and watched the hills blink as squadrons of B-52 bombers dropped their ordinance on staging areas and artillery positions of the NVA. Intelligence told him that artillery pieces were dug into the hillsides in tunnels. It would take an exact location to effectively eliminate them, but until then they could only do their best.

Without preamble, the rain came suddenly our fifth night in the field. We were listening to the normal jungle sounds; a flutter of a small bird as it flew to its nest, the scurry of a rodent, bamboo shifting in the thicket. We were memorizing the visual world around us in case we had to move in the dark. Then it poured. It was as if the clouds could carry no more water, tripped and spilled it all. None of us on Florida ever took our web gear off in the field and I leaned my back against a tree with my rifle cradled across the ammo pouches in front of me and stretched my tarp over my shoulders and across my weapon. But even then, the rain poured down my neck, and soaked my legs and rolled down my face and carried the oils of my camouflage into my mouth. We had Claymores out and I held the detonators next to me out of the rain.

Morning, when it arrived, was grey and dripping, and my back ached from shivering. The soaked vegetation brought the odor of humid, fecund jungle to my nostrils. Although the sky was still overcast, I sensed that the day would be clear. I was stiff and sore from not moving and the chill that came with the night. We ate in silence. This was a time of absolute quiet when we listened for signs that the NVA may have moved up on us in the night. Doney made a SITREP from the code in the one-time pad and waited for Covey.

Noi, the Vietnamese playboy of the team, offered me local spices to add to my rations. Noi was handsome, dressed like James Dean, drove a motorcycle, and always had a pretty girl on the back. His spoon stopped part way to his mouth. Noi turned his good ear toward the nearest hills and cupped his ear with the other hand. He stretched out his thumb and little finger in the shape of an airplane and wiggled his hand like wings. Then I also heard the distant drone of the Bird Dog. It flew several ridges away but did not come near us. Doney gave the coded message to Joe, and he lay on his stomach under a tarp to muffle all sound and gave the message to Covey. Doney nodded that it was time to go. We retrieved our claymores and stood to leave.

There was a shot. We had trackers and they were telling their people that we were moving.

Not far from Recon Team Florida, on the tri-border where Laos, Cambodia and Vietnam all touch, at the densely packed Communist base area 609, another Green Beret unit was about to enter battle. They were the fourth battalion of the II Corps Mike Force led by a handful of Special Forces soldiers. Two companies of well-trained Montagnard strikers and a recon element filled their ranks. Their mission was a reconnaissance in force to find the artillery that was bombarding Ben Het, and to interdict and destroy the enemy as located. As they moved in tactical formation up a narrow finger of land deep into enemy controlled territory, they observed a large enemy unit coming down the same narrow ridge they were climbing. It proved to be a full Communist artillery company descending with the sleep of being deep in their own sanctuary. They stumbled and staggered down the trail under the weight of a six-hundred-pound M-43 120mm mortar which, even disassembled, took dozens of soldiers to carry the parts. Mortar parts were slung from poles and carried on the rag protected shoulders of a half dozen men for each part. Even the mortar rounds they carried over their shoulders or in pack cradles weighed thirty-four pounds each.

This mortar was an important weapon in the siege of Ben Het. It was comparable to a 152mm howitzer. In a fight it could fire ten to fifteen rounds a minute nearly three miles.

At the right moment the Mike Force opened fire and attacked the enemy company and overwhelmed it by surprise, superior weapons and leadership. Those that survived the attack fled the area abandoning the mortar, all equipment and even their rifles. A sweep of the area found a treasure trove of top secret orders, maps, troop dispositions and numerous documents written in Chinese. A study of the documents in the rucksacks presented a significant amount of intelligence. Radio contact with HQ brought rapid helicopter support to the site of the battle. Jungle penetrators were used to get through the thick jungle canopy to the force and they sent off the mortar, ammo and all documents to the base. The Mike Force had one casualty, a striker who was shot in the head but alive. A jungle penetrator was sent through the trees, and he was lifted off to an aid station.

That night there was heavy enemy activity and the Green Berets requested Spooky for support. On arrival it was found that they could not get a firm fix on the team, so John Padget stood on a stump and exposed himself as he shined his flashlight into the sky until Spooky learned their exact location.

The shot that the enemy tracker fired to signal our departure from our RON was very close, certainly less than forty yards away. It sounded like it was just on the other side of the thicket. It was certainly not shot from several thickets away for the report was not muffled by foliage, but crisp and clear.

I had been in-country enough to recognize that the shot was not the "pop" sound of an AK-47 but rather that of the older SKS the Viet Cong used. I imagined a Communist Montagnard tracker held the rifle and trailed us like a bloodhound. I glanced at my people. Ba, Noi and Nhoc on either side of me expected an immediate fight. I slowly looked toward Chin, at the front of our column. He looked at Doney and smiled. He signaled a direction and RT Florida continued its mission.

We had been fortunate that we had not been discovered, for we gathered intelligence in the backyard of the enemy sanctuary. We discovered numerous trails before we gained a hillside that overlooked the Ho Chi Minh Trail with its bunkers and convoys and patrols. When we made a security stop, we heard the enemy. We heard construction, the chopping of wood and occasional shouts from all directions. An engine would start. More shouts. Twice when we stopped at a trail, we heard them pass on the other side of the bushes. They moved swiftly with a destination in mind, never talking — so much ground to cover in a limited time. We heard the brushing of their cloth uniforms — arms brushing against their sides — hundreds of them. There was the squeak of leather from the boots of army regulars and not the tire sandals of the old Viet Cong. The tapping of metal hinges on rifle slings marked the time of the footfalls. But now the enemy was aware of us and would not ignore our presence.

Our movement was soundless in the moist soil, and we used that to maneuver close to the enemy. We looked for signs of supply depots, headquarters facilities, a chance to catch a prisoner.

We stopped at a stream to monitor a trail. There was a shot.

We changed direction and moved toward a ridge. Another shot.

We hovered near a high-speed trail, and I heard the clicking of bamboo part way up a hillside. Doney changed directions and we found ourselves at a junction of trails. There was a shot. We evaded and found a defensive place where we could do a SITREP in case Covey came over our area. The sun came out and I saw that any movement in the foliage shimmered in shine and shadow, and I thought even the tracker could not get close without us seeing him. I heard shouts from two sides, a hundred yards away. A glance at Chin — there was no smile. Doney gave a direction for us to go — right through the middle of them.

With absolute stealth we moved toward the enemy and when we were near, we lowered ourselves to the ground and let them pass us by. When they were gone, we moved to the west until we hit a high-speed trail. As we paused at the site, I thought I saw something like a thin black snake. When it did not move, I realized what I was looking at. I clicked my tongue and Norm Doney caught my eye. I nodded to the place. He looked at me and I nodded again and pointed.

"What?' he said when he came up to me.

"There," I said pointing again.

We crept down to the place and touched what I had seen. It was black cable and commo wire. We were at some kind of headquarters area. It was big and secure enough that they had telephones to their outposts. We backed off and Doney took notes for his log.

We started to move away from the danger area when I heard something in the distance. It was a muffled, "Boom, boom, boom," and sounded like it was over the hill. I heard trucks passing along the ridge below us, but I could not see the road. Again, I clicked to Doney.

I cupped my ear and cocked my head, meaning, "Come here."

"Hear that?" I said when he got to me. "I think that is artillery. Listen."

He listened carefully. There was surprise in his eyes when he said, "It is. It is artillery."

He put us into a defensive perimeter and he, Chin and I left on our own. We low crawled some of the way, let patrols go by, and twice sped across a road and high-speed trails. It took nearly an hour to quietly crest a ridge and when we neared the top the "Boom, boom," was loud. We studied the ridge on the other side of the road. I heard an artillery shell go off and saw the leaves blow around the barrel. After a time, it was clear that I was looking at camouflage and there were many artillery pieces in a line deep into the opening beyond our view. Many soldiers hovered around the weapons and there were trucks supplying the unit.

"They have to be firing at Ben Het," I said, "There is nothing else."

Doney studied his map. We have to get this location exactly right. We went over the map together. "Here is the road on the map...and the ridge in front of us...and the river we crossed this morning. That," he said tapping the map with his finger, pointing at a cliff-shaped hill, "Is over there. That is the exact place of the artillery. Do you agree?"

"Yes," I confirmed.

"Let's get back to the rest and find a place where we can wait for Covey."

We found a place tucked into some cover to conceal us. It had a slight elevation and was easy to defend and afforded us several avenues to evade. It seemed that we had evaded our tracker. Doney prepared a SITREP while I set out Claymore mines. Ba took a position several feet from the rest of us to watch our back trail. I glanced around the circle of our people. There was nothing to do but to wait — either for the enemy to come for us or for Covey to arrive. It was hot and quiet. It seemed that I could hear the moisture evaporate from the leaves. It also seemed that there were no natural sounds in the area, only suspicious ones that could only be dismissed after consideration. I listened to a bee, and it irritated me that its weight on a flower settled the leaf and in departing made movement where I tried to be motionless. Then the buzz of the bee was replaced by another buzz. It was the sound of an airplane over the ridge. It was Covey.

Doney sent the SITREP.

"Standby," was the immediate reply. "Will send off and come back."

Twenty minutes later Covey returned. Joe Morris took down the coded message and translated it from the one-time pad. He crawled on his knees to Doney and whispered the message in his ear. I could not hear but read his lips, "Go rapidly to nearest LZ for immediate extraction. Suggest…" and he gave the coordinates. Doney consulted his map and planned a route and Florida stood and pushed our way through the undergrowth to the rendezvous place.

We were there in an hour and set up security as we waited for the helicopters to arrive. Covey arrived fist. "We have Cobras and a pair of A-1 Spads on station to cover us."

The Cobra gunships made a pass along the tree line with their miniguns followed by another and when it did not draw fire, the first slick sloped in and hovered over the elephant grass, and my half of the team boarded. Before we cleared the trees, the second Huey hovered over the grass and the rest of Florida piled aboard. Recon people usually say that when they leave an LZ there is always a sense of relief but as I looked at the pilots and recalled how quickly they got us out of the target area, I sensed an urgency about it all.

The Mike Force got the word at nearly the same time. "Proceed immediately and as quickly as possible to a point seven clicks south of your position." Words like, "immediate," and "expeditiously," presented the urgency in which they moved. Simultaneous with their arrival three and a half miles south, the bombs of a massive B-52 strike began to fall where they and Florida had been. It was possible to pluck out a small unit such as Florida, but not a Mike Force battalion. The men in the

Mike Force said that it was like being in a strongest earthquake they had ever been in. "If you dared to stand, you would not be able to."

When I asked John Padget what it was like to be near the strike, he could only reply, "Good Lord!"

After the mission, Norm Doney confided in me that they had diverted a massive Arc Light strike of a hundred B-52s on the area. It is said that ten thousand B-52 bombs fell around Ben Het before, but after this strike the Communist guns fell silent on Ben Het and the NVA melted into the jungle.

Chapter Fifteen

FROM BRIGHT LIGHT TO ONE ZERO SCHOOL

It was on the sixth day of our Bright Light mission at the Dak To launch site when we received the alert. The sergeant from the commo shack thrust open the door of our Spartan barracks and peered inside. When his eyes adjusted to the dimness and he located us Americans he nodded solemnly and announced, "A team is in trouble. They are in heavy contact and on the run." It was a simple statement of fact given clearly, precisely and without urgency. Had his words been delivered with the dots and dashes of the Morse code which he mastered in commo school, they would not have carried less emotion. But for us who waited for such a call and understood the significance of it all, it was a notice of great peril. Somewhere in the jungle before us, a team made up of our brothers-in-arms was in grave jeopardy and faced capture or annihilation. If called upon, it was the duty of us on the Bright Light team to be inserted into the center of that maelstrom of bullets and explosions to aid in their rescue, continue their mission, or on occasion, to find and recover the bodies of the men where they fell.

"Are we going in?" Doney asked.

"Don't know yet."

"Casualties?"

The commo sergeant had already started to go but turned back to answer. "Yes. But with all that is happening on the radio we don't know the extent of them."

We followed him out the door as he returned to his radios. "Assets in the air?"

He answered over his shoulder. "Covey is in the air with a pair of Spads on station. Choppers are on the way here to refuel and then go in. Should be here shortly."

"Got it."

Doney turned to us and with an even voice said, "Joe, Dale, get the team ready to go in, I'll see what I can pick up on the radios."

It took nothing to get the team ready, as our purpose for being there on Bright Light was to be in readiness for instant combat. We were no less set than if we ourselves sat on a launch pad waiting to be inserted on a mission of our own. We put on our web gear and rucksacks, and trooped outside with our weapons as if we were walking to a pair of Hueys. The sun was blistering hot alongside our quarters, so I had our team sit at the side of the commo shack in the shade of the eaves. I looked at Team Florida as they sat there in a row. There was no question in any of their faces that we would be going in. It would be a time of desperation and last resort for the team on the ground that would commit us — a team surrounded, unable to move because even the jets and Spooky and gunships were unable to dislodge the enemy, or when the team had either too many or too massive wounds to move, or when the radios became silent as our people called, "Bra Strap, Bra Strap," over and over to be answered only by static or worse, the voices of enemy soldiers from an open mic.

My people leaned back on their rucksacks and waited for us to tell them what to do, their hands folded on top of the canteen covers full of ammunition. Ba absently flicked the safety of his rifle on and off, on and off. One or two of them closed their eyes and sunk into themselves in that quiet sanctuary many of us have prior to battle. Noi held one rifle magazine in his hand and absently tapped it against the palm of his other hand seating the rounds repeatedly. I caught Chin's eye and he smiled his ubiquitous smile, and tapping the back of his collar said, "Han-Son, *Kam Bow Ya Chin*, you have?" I laughed and turned so he could see my collar. "See, it's faded but it is still there."

Chin smiled, nodded and closed his eyes — the corners wrinkled into lines like furrows in a farmer's field.

We leaned against the wall of the commo shack, and I felt the vibrations of the radios on the other side. The exact words were unclear, but tones of desperation shouted through the walls. There were stretches when we only heard static and squelch in the background. Then the transmissions were shorter in duration but closer together. "Joe, I'm going inside to listen for a bit. Maybe I can see what's going on."

I slipped inside and found a place where I would not be in the way. Doney saw me come in and came over to me. "It sounds pretty grim, but they have a good One Zero. He has the experience and calmness to get them through this. Nothing is hopeless." Then Doney looked at me as my mentor, "If you spend any amount of time in recon, you will face this yourself. It will happen to all of us." He paused and gave me an update, "They have three casualties. They are carrying one. Covey gave them directions to an LZ. I think the One Zero suspects the NVA are monitoring his radio. He keeps changing his direction even after Covey advises."

The One Zero's voice came over the radio. "Covey, Covey, this is Bra Strap," I heard loud crackling over the radio. The One Zero's voice was high pitched, and he was talking very fast. "Is that static or small arms fire?" I asked Doney

Doney had his head down when he spoke. "Small arms fire. They are in very heavy contact. Very heavy. Not good. This could be the end."

Covey spoke. His voice was calm and assuring and he used the One Zero's first name now to say, "I am with you. I will not leave you."

"Bra strap this is Covey. I am with you Ted. We've got you. We'll talk you through this. You are only fifty yards from an LZ."

There was a long pause before Bra Strap came back over the radio. His voice was more controlled this time. "I don't know if we can make it that far. One just got shot that last contact. How far out is support?"

A second sergeant in the room, who monitored another set of radios pulled off his headset. "That was the control tower. Our assets are coming in now from Kontum. Should be here in a minute."

I looked to Doney. "Will they need help?"

"You can see. You can watch for them at the control tower."

Outside, I gave Joe the heads up and we climbed the nearby tower. It was not much of an affair, just high enough to see over the base and direct our air support. Our launch site was a small, fenced perimeter surrounding only three, one-story buildings. As we entered the tower the sergeant pointed toward a break in the hills to the south. "Should be coming from over there. It is the most direct route when the weather is decent. There," he said, pointing, and he handed me his binoculars. "At least six or eight of them, I think. I assume there will be slicks and a chase medic for the wounded, probably a couple Charlie models and the cobras."

"Will we be able to help them at all?"

"We can see. Let 'em land first and then check. Be careful though. If the Communists in the hills see a bunch of choppers on the pad all at once and you guys out there with them, they might hit us with rockets. Listen for them. Sometimes you can hear them shoot before the rounds land."

The Cobra gunships landed first and fueled while the others remained in the air so they would not draw fire. As soon as the Cobras fueled, they lifted off to the west to get in the fight.

We ran out to the Hueys and the Chase Medic's helicopter to see if they needed help.

"Are you guys from Team Florida? If you guys get committed, we will be the ones to come back to bring you in. We'll know more soon." And then they were gone — just dots in the sky.

Back at the radio shack I listened to the battle. "Covey, Covey, this is Bra Strap." There was static again that I recognized now as small arms fire.

"Bra Strap. Go ahead."

He came back, and this time we heard the "Krump, krump" of

exploding grenades in the background. The enemy was close. "We must be close to that LZ, but we are hard pushed. And we don't know what is in front of us"

"Bra Strap, I have assets on scene. I have to fix your location, so they don't hit you. Toss smoke."

There was a pause, and the One Zero came back, "Smoke tossed. How do you see?"

Another pause, and Covey came back, "I see two smokes in two locations, one red and one yellow."

The one zero then shouted over the radio. "Shoot 'em up then, 'cause I didn't throw any!"

As Covey marked the smoke with his own smoke, the Spads and Cobras worked the sites over and Doney emerged from the commo shack with maps and a slip of paper with call signs and frequencies and stopped before us.

"FOB is sending a pair of helicopters to pick us up and take us to the site. They want us in the air and on scene for immediate insert."

The moment they landed we ran across the pad and boarded and before we even were seated, were airborne and heading west.

"Bra Strap, this is Covey."

A weary voice answered. "This is Bra Strap." His voice sounded like one that was called from deep sleep, the inside of his mouth, dry and stuck together.

"I believe we got your two friends with the smoke. Can you toss smoke?"

"Smoke out. Identify."

"I see red smoke."

"Confirm, red"

"Got you. You are so close. Only twenty meters to go. I am going to work the area all around the LZ then get you in for pick up. Hunker down."

"Copy."

Spads dropped 500-pound bombs around the perimeter of the small LZ and the Cobras followed firing up the back trail of the team.

"Bra Strap."

"Here."

"Let's get you home. I have slicks coming in and Bright Light is standing by to help you if you need it."

In minutes Cobra could see the team at the edge of the LZ. The heavy casualty lay on his back in the grass, one arm across his chest, the other outstretched to one side. He faced skyward, unmoving. The One sat upright next to him, and his pale face looked side to side for the pursuing enemy. Even from the air his bandages could be seen. Two tribesmen with lesser wounds kneeled at the edge, their backs sheltering the other wounded, daring with their rifles the enemy to come. The rest of the team readied themselves in a semicircle facing the back trail. The first slick came, and the rotors raised a dust that clung to the dressings and browned the red bandages. The door gunner of the helicopter did not help the wounded enter the craft but fired off belt after belt of rounds into the brush. Seeing that the severely wounded were helpless to get in, the One Zero and a Montagnard that was not wounded stumbled to the wounded and tried to lift them into the slick. They could not heft the worst wounded all the way in, getting only as far as the strut. They propped the body on the strut, repositioned themselves, shoved the limp body the rest of the way in, then slid the form on the floor where it would not roll out. The two ran back to join the others on the edge of the field. Gunships worked the edge of the tree line. As the second slick came in, they received 12.7 fire from a nearby rise in the terrain and the Spads attacked the site. The helicopter cleared and the harried team proceeded to safety.

The A-1 Spads were the first to leave the area, followed by the slicks and then the gunships which flew at our flanks on the way back. Covey made one pass over the site, over smoldering bomb craters and trees that were shredded of leaves and limbs and debarked. Just in case the NVA were watching from someplace in the shrubbery, he tipped his wings to wave goodbye.

Our two slicks departed the formation and dropped us off at the launch site. We still had a few days of duty to serve. Looking down as the slicks descended to our air strip, I was struck with the empty bleakness of our Bright Light location. Our small compound consisted of but three single-story structures, small ones, and the one in which Recon Team Florida stayed did not even have solid walls to the ceiling. The walls were four feet high, and canvas completed the rest and joined with a canvas ceiling. During our stay, there were no cots, chairs, tables, fans or a place to cook. There was no shower. Although the upper walls and ceiling were of flimsy canvas, the floor was solid concrete. The floor from all sides sloped to the center of the room, to a large drain hole and grate. The canvas could be raised for ventilation and the elimination of odor. During times of siege, our building was the mortuary of the base.

When the sun was on the roof, the barracks was a humid sauna. To relieve boredom, we exercised, practiced immediate action drills, read books and waited. It is said that war can be defined as long stretches of great boredom followed by short periods of extreme terror. Bright Light duty is like that; however, even in the periods of boredom there is a tenseness that superintends everything. Doney spent hours in the commo shack monitoring the progress of the teams on the ground. When any team was in jeopardy, Joe and I made frequent trips to the radios for status reports and to gauge the probability of us going in. We slept on the cement floor with our heads toward the wall and our feet sloped toward the center drain. To keep in military trim, we exercised and trained and maintained hygiene as much as possible. I read and studied a book called *Memory by Furst*. I did my personal workout and one afternoon when the heat was oppressive, I pulled out my pocketknife and carved the entire motto of many Special Forces people by John Stuart Mill on the edges of my nunchaku:

"War is an ugly thing but not the ugliest of things: The decayed and degraded state of moral and patriotic feeling which thinks that nothing is worth war is much worse. A man who has nothing for which he is willing to fight, nothing he cares for more than his own safety, is a miserable creature who can never be free, unless made and kept so by the exertions of better men than himself."

After a morning rain shower and a cleansing bar of soap we lazed in the shadow of the overhang of the commo shack, and watched the deep-brown rain-wet pebbles dry to pale-ochre and we talked as a team, shedding doubt on Kipling's "Oh, East is East, and West is

West and never the twain shall meet." As we leaned there against the wall, we could not hear the words of the radios through the wall, but the squelching and hissing reminded us that even in the quiet and boredom of the day there was always a tension in the air of being thrust into battle at any moment.

It was our eighth day of Bright Light. We had two more calls to be ready for insert but both teams were exfiltrated from the target before we boarded the helicopters; one of them was pulled out on strings, and the other team blew their own LZ where they were using C4 explosives.

Mid-afternoon that last day felt like the monsoon clouds hovered over us to prove that it had arrived. The water in the air was as dense and heavy as that filling the ground and the gutters. Its presence was felt, but the downpour had not yet begun. The heat of the day was still oppressive and Florida tried not to move.

The commo sergeant emerged from the shaded recesses of the shack and stretched in the doorway. He was stiff from hours spent bent over code books and speaking through the squelch, for the thick clouds played havoc with reception. His eyes watered from the glare, and he held one hand over his eyes like a salute as he looked left and right and found us where we sprawled under the shadow of a roof. We did not appear military at that moment, more melted than anything.

"Hey, Sarge, choppers on the way."

Doney was in the control tower, so I stood up for the message.

"Wounded coming in?" I asked.

"No. They're coming for you."

I felt that familiar electricity that always went through me for a moment at an alert.

"I'll get the team ready. Doney and Joe are in the tower. We will need the maps and call signs of course."

When the sergeant saw that I misunderstood, the hands that shaded his eyes became the signal for "Stop."

"No. No. FOB is sending a chopper out to get you guys. Another team is coming to take your place. About an hour ETA. Let Doney know."

It was a pair of Hueys that picked us up for the ride back to base.

The pilots said that they wanted to split the load between the two. "Our birds are getting a bit old and tired and don't like to carry so much." Doney briefed the One Zero of the incoming team. I told the Americans that we left their quarters clean and ready for them.

Once aboard, the rotors sped up and the aircraft lurched like it wanted to be off. We lifted into the air, and I looked below and watched a bullseye of red dust spread out and then disappear.

Monday morning was clear and sunny, but not hot, and it seemed that the monsoon had left for a time — perhaps to gather more water. Recon company was in formation at 7:00 a.m. and Bob Howard led the assembled recon teams in the "daily dozen" exercises. When the last exercise was completed, he shouted, "Right face, forward march," and as we passed through the gates of the compound, the command was, "Double time, march." We jogged the three-mile circuit from the FOB, across the Dak Bla River bridge to the outskirts of Kontum and back. Part way there, just before the bridge, from the trees beyond a farmer's field, a bullet buzzed over the formation. The round was high, perhaps ten feet high, and there was only one round fired. It was as if the Viet Cong had discharged his weapon once, then quickly hid it, perhaps wrapped in canvas and shoved under a furrow, then took his place behind a plow behind his plodding water buffalo.

For the last few weeks, the sniper took a pot shot or two as we jogged. We considered having a couple of us hide near the place and kill him the next time he aimed at us. We mulled it over with Howard, and the concern was that if we eliminated the shooter — and he was not a very good marksman — that they would replace him with someone who was. We envisioned the shooter as an aged farmer type with an ancient rifle and cataracts on his eyes. We kind of liked that guy out there who was hiding in a field, or wormed into the clay of the riverbank, as long as he couldn't shoot well. But someday the old buzzard might get lucky and actually get one of us. A couple of the guys were recuperating from wounds and not ready for Howard's workout, so we rigged up our three-quarter-ton truck with a 60-cal. machine gun to shoot over the hood, and a second one to shoot from the bed. He stationed a few of our SCU to stand in the bed and appear to be ready to run any sniper down. With that incentive, the Dak Bla sniper chose to retire.

The heavy rains held off, and days of clear sky were forecast, a respite for teams on the ground that waited for air support to stand by. Teams had been poised at a target, ready to spring when the torrent came without warning, a thick grey soup that erased everything from view beyond a few feet. Nothing could fly. Team leaders chose to hunker down. Support had to be in the area before they struck. When they "kicked the hive," angry retaliation would be immediate and deadly. Some teams spent tense and tenuous nights surrounded by enemy patrols and welcomed the friendly purr of Covey as it flew by along the next ridge, the sun laying the plane's shadow over the team, lending comfort as the shadows of the New Testament apostles did over needy souls. Recon teams that were between missions in garrison also took advantage of the break from the downpour.

This sunny Thursday was committed to rappelling from the Dak Bla bridge. Bob Howard parked the three-quarter-ton truck with attached machine guns near the crown of the bridge where we could see beyond the river and its sandy banks all the way to the leprosarium in one direction, and in the other, to a farmer on the far side of the fields who followed behind his plow and plodding oxen. To the east we could see across the slash-burn to the Montagnard village and the vertical posts that supported the houses, barely seen among the trees. All the recon teams came with web gear and rifles for training.

It was said that at the time SOG began operations "over the fence," the Communists utilized about twenty-five thousand troops to guard and maintain the Ho Chi Minh Trail the entire distance from Hanoi to the terminus in Vietnam. Now it was believed that over a hundred thousand enemy troops were committed to guard and protect the trail. Our few SOG teams tied down the equivalent of ten enemy divisions. Without realizing it, the enemy proved the effectiveness of our operations by the measures they took to combat them. An entire NVA regiment of specialized troops were committed just to find and kill Special Forces soldiers on a SOG mission. In the thousands of square miles of enemy controlled territory, they stationed forces at nearly every opening in the jungle large enough for a helicopter to descend and drop off troops. It was becoming necessary to use alternate means of entry. One of those methods was to find a very small break in the trees and rappel in.

The training of the morning was "Hollywood," which meant that we would rappel with our rifles and web belts but not with our rucksacks. We looped the running line through the carabiner of our seat, backed off the bridge and leaned out. We pushed off with our legs and zipped down the line braking once just before the ground. We allowed two seconds from the push off to the ground below. Some of the SCU had never rappelled and the morning was given to make each team proficient.

For the training in the afternoon, we added another turn of the line through our carabiners as we rappelled, to compensate for additional weight. In addition to our web gear, a bag of sand was placed in our rucksacks to simulate the weight we carried in the field. As I waited for my turn, I gazed across the field and saw the farmer stopped behind his plow and oxen. They were the color of the soil, but their shadows lay black and left them easy to see. He stood behind his beast and leaned across its back and watched us at the bridge. From time to time he lifted a hoof and examined it as he peered from under its belly. He stroked the animal's back and the hump behind its neck as he studied us. I took a step closer to the edge of the bridge and he saw me watching him. He quickly grasped the handles of his plow and tapped the animal's back with the tip of a thin prod and clicked his tongue as they proceeded down the furrow. It was quiet where I stood at the edge of the bridge and the click of his tongue was clear in my ears. I may have been caught up in the scene, but I was certain I heard the creaking wood plow and the hooves as they lifted out of the moist soil.

"What do you think, Dale?" I hadn't noticed Doney beside me. "What intelligence do you think our shooter has learned?"

I was still watching the Viet man as he came to the end of the row, and I fought an urge to wave at him and smile at his predicament. "Obviously he can tell the higher ups that recon is practicing our rappelling skills." I looked over to Doney. "Can you imagine that this sliver of information will filter all the way to the sanctuaries in Laos or Cambodia and a couple of generals in some thatched bamboo headquarters will ponder the significance of what we are doing?"

Master Sergeant Norman Doney smiled, "Oh they know what we are doing."

Florida did well with the training but some of the teams had tribesmen who had never infiltrated this way. Montagnards learn quickly but some discovered that when they pushed off with their feet, their rucksacks made them top heavy. They flipped upside-down creating a knot in the snap link and they were stuck in the air halfway down the rope. The only remedy was for them to thrust their feet downward until they righted themselves and could continue down. By late afternoon even the new tribesmen were comfortable enough to rappel into combat. We dumped the sand from the bags and gathered our gear for the walk to base. A glance to the west showed the gravel river banks to be golden in the sun. Smoke from the charcoal fires rose at the leprosarium where nuns prepared meals for the stricken residents. To the east, the plowed fields resembled corduroy in the light and shade, and though there were hours until curfew, the man and oxen were gone.

Friday morning was again clear, and Recon Company trucked to the "Yard Range" where a pair of helicopters waited to complete our training. Away from prying eyes and watching farmers, we rappelled from choppers a hundred feet in the air into very small openings in the nearby jungle, and team by team slid into the thick foliage. The choppers would dip above the thickness and in not much longer than a hesitation, be gone. The foliage folded back into itself. Troops of monkeys briefly complained and were silent, as lizards once again elbowed through the grass and birds again trilled among the leaves.

It was evening, and I lay on my bunk with my clothes on. It was one of those times we all get when we think something will happen. I had shuttered the windows against the possibility of someone tossing a grenade inside, so the room was stuffy and I could not sleep. I was reading Ian Fleming and as I read the words of the book, I recalled seeing the movie somewhere between Fort Bragg and Vietnam with Mike Buckland, Dennis Bingham, Randy Rhea and a few others, and the images of the movie filled in between the sentences. Blofeld turns slowly toward Bond holding his fluffy white cat and faces him with the long vertical scar across the right side of his face. "James Bond. Allow me to introduce myself. I am Ernst Stavro Blofeld. They told me you were assassinated in Hong Kong," he says in mild surprise. Bond replies, "Yes, this is my second life." A hint of a smile faintly appears in the slit of Blofeld's mouth. "You only live twice, Mr. Bond."

"We certainly do not look like Sean Connery on our missions. Our faces are blotched under greasy camouflage and sweat. No one writes beautiful musical scores to accompany us when we fight for our lives either," I was thinking. That is when the shooting started just outside of my window. It sounded muffled but nearby — several rifles fired on full-automatic followed by shouting and thumping, like a brawl with baseball bats and fists.

I threw on my web gear, grabbed my rifle and ran to the side door. A couple other SF guys were also in the building and joined me and we leapfrogged toward the shots covering each other as we moved. All the shooting came from the Chinese quarters just behind ours. As we approached the building the front door cracked open and smoke-filled yellow light from inside lay prone in the dirt like a naked wounded man. There was coughing and the sliding of wood chairs on the floor and one by one, Chinese men stumbled out in shocked silence. They had no weapons. Some wore wife-beater undershirts. A few others followed in unbuttoned long-sleeve shirts with their heads hanging, mumbling as they stumbled out. I saw no blood or wounds, but I expected carnage inside the small one-room building. I recognized one of the men who walked trance-like out of the room.

"Chan. What happened? VC come?"

He looked up at me. His face was moon-white in the light, and he seemed shaken, angry, and relieved at the same time. "No, no," he stuttered. "No VC. All finny now. No worry. All finny. No problem."

Hundreds of rounds had been fired in the small, cramped space.

Singly and in pairs and small groups, a dozen Chinese emerged from the space. Blood had to be thick on the floor and many would be dead or severely wounded. "Chan, will Chinese men still shoot? Are there *beaucoup dao* — many dead?"

Before he could answer, my Chinese Nungs from Florida who heard the shooting joined us outside of the hooch. Chin appeared at my side and placed his hand on my shoulder — a gesture which said, "Do not shoot yet." Concern was clear in his voice. "Han-Son, I talk him." After an animated exchange in rapid Chinese, Chin shook his head in disgust, and he strode boldly into the building. Moments later he came outside and joined us.

"Han-Son, all fini now. Everybody is okay. Nobody dead. Nobody wounded. Everyone can go home."

"First tell me what happened, Chin."

"Not much, Chinese just play poker and somebody cheat, then everybody shoot, but finny now. Nobody hurt."

"Chin, do you mean to tell me that a dozen Chinese men emptied their rifles at each other in that tiny room and not one person got shot."

Chin looked at me in the dim light and he shook his head for he could not believe it either. "Think maybe that Chinese men just lucky in poker."

Florida's next mission across the fence was a northern target in Laos. The target was designated as "India Six." It was a hot target, and most teams were shot out in just a few days. I talked with the One Zero of the last team that was sent in that general area.

"Hanson, I told Doney this: The area is hot, and they seem to know you are coming. As if there is a snitch that lets 'em know. We came in on our LZ and there was a sign on the LZ. A real sign, I tell you. It says, 'Welcome to LZ number two,' and below it there is our team name."

"You're kidding!"

"Not kidding. They were on us right from the beginning and we got shot out within two days. Thank God we didn't lose anybody."

Doney chose a small break in the trees a couple of miles from the compromised LZ, and we rappelled into Laos. There was no "Welcome

Team Florida" sign, but the area was dense with enemy. Doney tried everything to shake them, but the movement and signal shots remained around us and we never got to the main target. At one point the NVA were massed and about to come for us on line. Some of our team were Buddhist and they always wore a gold chain around their neck with a gold Buddha on it. When they believed that death was imminent, they would put the Buddha in their mouth. If they died with Buddha in their mouth they would go to Heaven.

"Hanson, I know you say Jesus is number one. Buddha-man me. I like Buddha number one. VC come, Ba put Buddha here," and he placed the gold cast into his mouth, "Buddha, friend me. He see Ba number one Buddha and he save me."

It was certain to me that they were about to assault us. They did not hide their movement through brush. Metal clacked against the stocks of their weapons without any concern that we might hear. On the other side of a dip in the terrain, nervous soldiers pulled back the receivers of their rifles to ensure a round was indeed in the chamber, as they waited for the order to go. A muted squelch of a radio was clear on the other side of the shrubbery. We were likely to be overrun, and I looked to the side and saw Ba. The gold Buddha was in his mouth and its chain hung from the sides of his mouth like thin tusks.

He was near me, and I edged to his side. He was pale and he kept licking his lips and his eyes glanced left and right, left and right, as if the pupils were bouncing off the sides of his orbit. His hands shook.

"*Beaucoup, beaucoup* VC," he whispered. Many, many VC.

I was nervous too, but I whispered to him, "Lots of targets," and I winked.

That mission only lasted two days, about average for that part of Laos near the enemy sanctuaries. We were pursued and we maneuvered until we found a slight rise in elevation where the trees thinned, and grey daylight shouldered in between a dozen scraggly trees. Thick stands of bamboo grew in patches, and I knew they would funnel the enemy where we would concentrate our fire, but that advantage also limited our own avenues of escape. We planned for this to be our stand. Covey was on the way with assets. Including the various helicopters and jets and Spooky, perhaps twenty aircraft would be involved in getting us out. Doney caught my eye and motioned me over to him.

"We'll have to blow us an LZ. Take a couple of the guys and rig all the trees so we can blow them when the time comes."

Joe gave me the C-4 from his rucksack, and I added mine. With Nhoc and Noi, I belly crawled from tree to tree and strapped the clay-like explosives to their backs, connecting them with det chord. I joined them all with the main cord and crawled with it to the edge of the opening and attached it to the detonator.

I heard the mosquito-like hum of Covey in the area. I felt immediate relief knowing that we were not alone. But Charlie heard it too and they wanted to finish us off before we got air support. They opened up on us just as two Spads flew over us just above the trees. I could no longer hear, but across the space between the trees, I saw Doney gesture with his hands — like someone wringing water out of a rag, "Blow the LZ." The start of the battle had all of us prone to the ground and when I blew the C-4 there was a massive explosion to our center and the trees slammed to the ground. Limbs and debris became shrapnel. There was a cloud of brown dust in the air. Joe tossed smoke and I lay on my back and directed my mirror toward Covey.

"I see red smoke and shiny," acknowledged Covey over the radio, but I did not hear it. Florida lay flat on the ground using our rucksacks for shields and shot toward the massed enemy. Our efforts were joined by the Spads and Cobra gunships. Twenty minutes later I heard a shout above the battle and saw Doney point toward the center of our new-blown LZ. A Charlie gunship was descending to pick us up. Its rotor blades clipped limbs at the edge of the circle. We stumbled over the fallen trees and branches to the side of the helicopter, and I helped my people get aboard. Ba stepped on the strut and looked back at me — and spit the Buddha out of his mouth.

I was throwing my knife one evening — actually, three of them, as I had gotten a set of three Pro-Throw knives somewhere. I did not have to spend half of my time walking up to the lumber pile to retrieve them. Sergeant First Class Newman Ruff was another one of us that found it relaxing to throw.

"If I were to start throwing knives all over again," I told him, "I would probably do it by throwing from the handle instead of the blade. I like throwing from the blade because it has much more power."

Newman tossed his Special Forces KA-BAR into the end of a board and waited for me to finish with my three throws. Newman Ruff was a small guy, slim, not five-six, and full of energy. I always knew when I talked with him that everything was well thought-out and then pursued with vigor.

"By the blade has disadvantages. I have to pull it out of my holster and then change hands to hold it by the blade before I throw. Also, I can't throw a knife that is sharpened on both sides of the blade — like yours. I tried throwing the KA-BAR and sliced my finger."

Newman worked the blade back and forth out of the wood. "And mine is a better tool and I can use both sides before it needs to be sharpened," he said.

"Actually, I do carry one like yours in the field. You are going out tomorrow?"

"Yep, just the four of us."

"Four?"

"That's all I take. They send me out for recon — to get intelligence. I don't even give my people M-16s. We carry 30-cal. carbines. My people don't dare get into combat. RT Arizona goes in light and small and we 'sneaky Pete' all over the enemy's backyard and they don't even know we are there."

I remembered the mission we just came in from. I would not like to have been there with just four of us. We would not have survived. "Joe Walker just went out with RT California. He left with at least a dozen people. And he had two machine guns and a mortar tube. His people had special pockets sewn to their pantlegs so they could each carry two mortar rounds."

Newman smiled. "Each of the teams has a personality. When a team like California gets compromised, they can just slug it out. They have blocked all traffic on the Ho Chi Minh Trail before."

Ruff threw his knife square into the end of a two by four. "What I like about having them around is that when the enemy finds me, they are careful because they do not know that I am not Joe Walker."

We were having karate practice in the empty field behind the barracks — two or three dozen of us. We were practicing kata with our nunchaku when we heard incoming break the sound barrier above us. We all froze in place as the first artillery round landed and exploded at the far edge of the field. It was followed by a second, then a third, making their way across the field in a straight line. The impact of the rounds went right through us. A fourth round landed at the center of the class, then a fifth. The sixth landed next to our barracks at the opposite end of the field. Six rounds landed in the center of our karate class and none of us took a sliver of shrapnel. Our only casualty was when one of the guys slammed into an open window shutter as he ran for his weapons.

The word was that we were about to receive a massive attack. All intelligence pointed to that probability. The settlement near us where the charcoal maker lived disappeared. The Montagnard village just to the east, in eye shot of our camp, was deserted. Our recon teams explored the environs of the FOB. We, on Florida, checked out the Montagnard village and did not find a living thing — dogs, pigs, chickens — all gone. The floors above the stilts were swept bare with not a single grain of rice left for the hated Viet Cong. In my mind I could see the villagers fleeing the advancing enemy regiments, padding barefoot down the hard clay paths, their backs bent under all their belongings. Somehow, I believe that the villagers at great risk got word to striker-sons in our camp, "VC come, attack FOB." And I felt the anguish that sons must have had to think of loved ones left to the enemy outside our gate.

The Communists were cruel and without mercy to the helpless people in the villages. I recalled the Montagnard boy who came shrieking down the path to Doc Smith's hospital on the outskirts of Kontum. The Communists had pounded chopsticks into his ears because the child had listened to the missionary; the village elder with white hair was disemboweled at a stake in the center of the hamlet because he would not give up the young men into their army; the young girl with every bone broken because they had no rice to give.

All of us were in the trenches and blockhouses all night; half of us always awake. Flares were continuously in the sky. A couple of mortar rounds were directed into the shadow of a defilade, but only a black cat screamed and shot out of the place. But the NVA did not attack that night, dissuaded perhaps by our readiness.

In the morning, all recon company that were not in the field were on the banks of the Dak Bla with web gear and weapons filling sandbags. Howard had security out and we filled the five-ton truck twice and overhauled our bunkers in the afternoon. He brought tubs of soft drinks and beer in ice water, and we worked for a time without our shirts until he reminded us with a grin that we were government property and could not damage our backs with sunburn.

We continued our vigil for several more days with twenty-five percent alert. Then one morning loud music poured from the cat houses outside the gate to let everyone know that they were open for business and all was safe. The "Green Door" was open, and the rock band belted its lyrics:

> *...And when you ask 'em: 'How much should we give?'*
> *They only answer, 'More, more, more.'*
> *It ain't me, it ain't me*
> *I ain't no military son...*

Tribesmen returned to work in the slash-burn area by the village where we could plainly see them and know that they were back. As we walked with our rifles to the mess hall in the morning, acrid smoke drifted to us from the village at our south wall. The charcoal burner had returned home.

"A team is in trouble!" I had been crossing the road that divided our compound and I paused to watch two boys, sons of the gate guards, play with a pair of scorpions. They had them in a paper lid from a mortar-round container which they had shoved into the gravel on the shoulder of the road, safe from truck convoys and dust. The children watched as the two creatures maneuvered round and around the perimeter, facing off at each other with their poisonous tails poised over their backs. Both the boys and the scorpions were oblivious to any world around them apart from the drama about to unfold in the cardboard container.

"A team is in trouble." It was Mike Buckland talking to me. He bent over to speak in my ear. "They called a Prairie Fire," the code word for extreme emergency. It often meant that the One Zero had been killed, or that the team was about to be overrun. "It's Team Ohio," he said with a low voice.

That familiar jolt of electricity went through me as I heard his words. I felt immediate dread and sorrow for what they must be going through. In my limited experience I empathized with them. I imagined them being chased and being exhausted and barely able to think, much less lift their feet. Their mouths dry, panting, not able to catch their breath. If they had wounds, those wounds would be of no consequence compared to what else they could expect from the enemy. Capture and torture, gaping wounds and perhaps death could be imminent. I felt helpless. We could only watch and pray for them.

I did not even know the questions to ask Mike. "Are there casualties? Who has been hit? How desperate is their situation?" But Mike saved my dumbness.

"I'm heading over to recon to find out what I can."

"I'll go too," I said aloud, and as we briskly walked, I prayed, "Oh, Lord God, please look after the team and bring them out of this and keep them safe."

We were not the first to arrive. John Plaster was the first recon man we met. John was pale and thin, as he had just gotten out of the hospital weeks before. If dread was a color, it would have been found on his face before us. "Those are my people out there. Rich Ryan is the One Zero. Charlie Bless and Bernie Mims are with him. We have been training together. I want to know the situation out there." At least a dozen other recon men were there as the First Sergeant stepped out of the doorway and addressed us.

"This is what we know so far. Recon Team Ohio has called a Prairie Fire Emergency. We are in radio contact with the team. Just before dark they found at least fifty NVA bathing in a stream and tried to direct an airstrike on them. Assets arrived and were about to take out the target when they ran out of daylight. The team hunkered down for the night, but the enemy moved in on the team, surrounded them, and hit them with a massive attack before daylight and the team got split up. Bless is missing. Ohio is being hard-pressed, and they are evading and trying to get to an LZ. When we have contact on the radio, we can hear heavy gunfire in the background. That is all so far."

I prayed again, "Lord, protect them and get them back safe."

Each of us wanted to be with the team and the closest that we could be was to go to the commo shack and listen to the radio traffic. We slipped into the room uninvited and sat in a circle around the radios, some of us sitting on the floor or along the wall.

Static...The voice of Covey to the team, "Situation? How are you doing?"

Ohio to Covey — Rich Ryan talking. His voice was high-pitched and he was talking very fast. "Heavy contact. We are being pushed. Need help or it is over." There was static and a heavy volume of rifle fire in the background and the "krump" of grenades.

"Trying to get assets to you. Need your location. Give smoke."

"Roger. What do you see?"

"I see white smoke."

"Roger. I just threw a white phosphorous grenade at the enemy."

Covey switched frequencies and talked to us at the FOB. "Here is their location," and he gave the coordinates.

We listened to the running firefight and the changing coordinates as the team was pushed by the enemy. I was writing the coordinates down as they were given. Ohio moved and set up an ambush, then fought until they were pressed again and had to move. We did not hear anything about missing Charlie Bless. Was he dead or captured?

"Let's go to S-2 and see where intelligence has them on their maps," someone said. Several of us signed in and we plotted the coordinates that I had written on the latex map. Ohio was being hard-pressed by the enemy, but we could tell that the NVA were steering the team. For the past two hours they had been pushed up a ridge. The map showed very steep sides. Soon they would get to the end of the ridge and the map showed that they would be at a cliff face. Ohio would no longer be able to move, and it would be over.

We looked up. "Operations" was in the room, as was the CO of the camp. Our recon commander was also there. All of us can read the script that was portrayed under the grease pencil. Even with all our air support, Ohio would be doomed if not rescued soon.

Someone from Commo entered the room. "Lots of casualties. Ryan has been shot in the chest."

"That's it for him," we were all thinking.

The recon First Sergeant looked over at the CO. "We can get up a Bright Light Team from here to go in after them." The CO nodded to go ahead.

"I'll go," I said. Several others also volunteered, and we gathered our weapons and web gear and met back at the Recon office. The First Sergeant said that he would lead us in to get what was left of the team and he got maps and the latest information. Choppers were on their way to get us.

I leaned back against my rucksack beside the recon wall. My mouth was dry. I was nervous and my heart was pumping. It seemed my vision was dim as I waited there. I remembered one time before, when I similarly waited for a dangerous mission, how keyed up I was. I could not sleep or relax. I was in barracks and was reading a book that Jan Novey gave me. It was a collection of poetry written during some of the wars around the world. There was an Italian or Spanish one that was translated into English that I read back then. I memorized it just to occupy my mind. It read:

> *All night long*
> *Thrown against a buddy,*
> *Slain*
> *With his gnashing teeth*
> *Bared to the full moon.*
> *I was writing letters full of love.*
> *Never had I hugged life so dear.*

I recited it to myself just to prove that I was not bothered by it all. I prayed for RT Ohio, that God would bring them out alive. I was glad that no one could see how nervous I was. I was always amazed that everyone who saw me in combat said I always looked so calm and that I always knew what to do. I guess it was just the first moments leading into danger that unnerved me — but it must be that way with the others too. Then I thought of Ohio and the turmoil they were going through, and I was ashamed, and after considering their peril, I became calm and ready to board the chopper and do what needed to be done. I could not sit still any longer and I got up to learn the latest.

I collided with John Plaster as he was coming out of the door. "Dale, they got Charlie Bless. He has been shot in the chest too, but he is alive and coming in." We rushed to the heli-pad to meet the choppers that would take us to where RT Ohio was holding out, and one of the commo guys ran over to us. "They got 'em. They got the whole team out and they are on their way in." We were standing on the pad facing "Indian country" with our hands over our eyes against the sun, and we heard a distant rumble. I was amazed that they were coming here to the FOB instead of going to Pleiku and the big hospital and surgeons.

The first slick landed and we all rushed to the helicopter and saw Charlie Bless. He had been shot multiple times in the chest but was sitting upright next to the door gunner. He raised his hand in greeting as the medics rushed to him with their stretcher. He waved them off and slid his feet down to the strut and slowly stood. His exhaustion was apparent. He tried to smile but the effort was too great. The medics propped him up to keep him from falling, but there was no blood. He had been shot in the chest but no blood poured from any wounds.

His voice was that of someone who was sleeping. "I am just so tired fellas."

The second helicopter sloped in for a landing and settled next to the first. Rich Ryan slid off the slick and turned to help the others get off the aircraft. Rich had been shot three times in the chest and I could see the holes in his shirt, but there was no blood. I took his rucksack and rifle to relieve him of the weight and he saw me looking at the bullet holes in his shirt. He parted his shirt so I could see. There were huge welts where the slugs struck his body. They pierced his clothing but stopped at his skin.

He faces us, "I know I was shot. The guy jumped up in front of me as I was reloading and pointed his AK right at me. I saw the flash and smoke and the rifle bounced with the recoil, and I felt myself being hit. I can't explain it."

Intelligence would later suggest that our efforts behind the lines was so effective that PAVN had only enough gun powder to do half loads in their ammunition. That might have been true. The only explanation I could give was that Ohio was protected by the hand of God. Many years later I was talking with an old Montagnard man at a Special Operations Association meeting. He was a part of the third wave of tribesmen and their families who made the long trek to freedom. His people were Christian, not animists, and the 5,000 people in the group who began the trek (only 200 made it all the way to freedom) shared one Bible. It was precious to them, and one strong man was chosen to carry and safeguard the treasure each day. One Sunday the North Vietnamese who pursued them shot at the group as they stopped on a ridgetop for church. Several bullets penetrated the shirt of the young man who carried the Bible. In the concern for the Scriptures, they opened his shirt. Copper-sheathed bullets lay mushroomed on the cover of the book. The bullets penetrated the cloth but stopped at the edge of the Bible and left it unharmed. Perhaps the same happened to Rich and Charles and the rest of RT Ohio.

Some of us ambled across the compound, our minds filled with wonder and gratitude. We would experience one other wonder to end the day. The 189th helicopter squadron, who supported us, knew that this was a time to celebrate. It was a day of victory. I heard a rumble of helicopters coming from the west and the place of battle. Then, just yards above my head, I saw what I thought could not be done: Huey helicopters passed over the compound and did an aerobatic victory roll over the camp — helicopters flying upside down. As with the Hebrew slaves said when they were leaving Egypt, "It was a day to be remembered."

It was the 5th of July. The date is clear in my mind because the day before was Independence Day. The Communists did not probe our CCC compound during the night. No one slipped in to attack us on the side of the perimeter that faced the Montagnard village, counting on stray bullets of our return fire to maim innocent villagers and create a divide between us. No sappers slipped through the wire with explosives wrapped around their bodies just to take out one American. And no rounds were lobbed in with timed air bursts to throw shrapnel into the compound — their imitation of 4th of July fireworks. Instead, I spent the night on our perimeter in a newly sandbagged corner-bunker with Ba and Noi and I told them that rights in America were inalienable and endowed by our creator, and that meant those rights should be obvious to all, that they derived from God and were not a thing bestowed by government, and therefore government could not take them away. So, when morning came without event on the fifth, we brushed the grit of the seeping sandbags from our clothing and faced a new day.

It would be a hot one. We were at the motor pool and maintenance area, and this Vietnamese craftsman and I were leaning against one of the trucks. The sun beat down on the metal hood and the vehicle "ticked" as we talked, as if it had just been driven and not parked in the shade of the night. I was negotiating to have him mill me a couple more pairs of nunchakus, shorter than the ones he made before so I could carry them more easily in the small of my back under my fatigue shirt. Correctly made nunchaku are six-sided and tapered, not round like you see on the movie screen. They are made of dense hardwood, and with three correctly spaced holes drilled at the narrow end to receive the parachute cord which paired the sides together. My Vietnamese friend had access to the milling machine in our shops. "Same price as before?" I asked. And he smiled and spit betel nut through his black teeth. He was satisfied with the price. I had not asked him to countersink bolts into the ends this time.

Jan Novey saw me there and walked over in his shapeless fatigues. I remembered that day when he spoke to our 11-F class and erased all the glamour of war and wrote on the blackboard of my mind the harsh reality — of the probability of torture if captured, and the reality that if we were still prisoners at the end of the war, all but our families would forget that we were even there. I remembered his nail-less mutilated hands and scars and how much I admired and respected him. From the short time that I spent with him in Vietnam, I added this to my feelings for this tired, old man — I was genuinely fond of him, like a father.

He reminded me of my grandmother in a way — not that he looked in any regard effeminate, or that Grandma looked manly. Both had the same drawn, tired look of having suffered adversity and struggle, and persevered through the demands of life. Grandma Hecker had been run over by a trolly car in Berlin when she was a little girl, and it crushed her legs and she hobbled and walked in pain the rest of her life. Jan Novey had that same drawn look about him. It seemed to me that the streetcar of tyranny had made its passage across his soul and destroyed his smile. But Jan Novey returned my affection in that he noticed a young Special Forces soldier and took the time to be his friend. His open smile was replaced by concern and compassion.

"Vell, I suppose dat you tink my Viet vorks for you now, eh?"

"Well, if you want him back, all you have to do is sell your milling machine and we will all leave him alone."

He thought for a moment and nodded, "Vell dat makes a lot of sense, doesn't it?"

"Thank you again for the book of war poems. I read some of it again the other day."

"Yah, but don't tell anybody dat Jan Novey reads poetry."

Novey leaned against the metal of the truck and quickly pulled his arm away. "Woosh, it is hot already. Vell, dey didn't come at us last night, did dey?"

"No, I sat with some of our team in one of the bunkers and I was telling them about freedom and liberty. I told them about 'inalienable' and how that meant that freedom was obvious and that since the source of rights and freedom is God himself, government did not have the right to take it away."

"And how did dey respond?"

"You know, Sergeant Novey, the right to freedom is obvious to them too."

"Yes, of course."

"Of course?"

"Yes, you said it was inalienable. Everyone should know that."

"Sergeant Novey, you saw your country made into slaves. Why do they not seem to resist or be more vocal to the West?"

Novey leaned against the wood frame of the truck and stared at the dirt as he thought how to answer. "Dey try, Sergeant Hanson. Dey try. But dey dare not speak. Dey vill be imprisoned. Sometimes dey put all the family in concentration camps for von vord that de fadder has said."

There was a pause, as he collected his thoughts, and I did not interrupt him.

"I have fought the Communists for more dan thirty years. So many times, I swam de Rhine on missions behind the Iron Curtain. De government is brutal. Da people live in terror."

Then Novey raised a finger, as he remembered something. "Hey, let me read you something. I vas reading a book da odder day and I read something dat I don't forget. I don't know why I saved it, but I wrote it down just as it vas in the book. The book was written by Sax Rohmer, and he was writing a story about secret Egypt. It seems that in Cairo about the turn of the century there were enclaves. (You would not tink dat an immigrant like me would know a word like enclave, vood you?) Vel in those enclaves were tyrants of de old way. Servants could be whipped to death or their tongues cut out just because dey whispered."

"Wait," he said as he pulled a flat and battered wallet from his pocket. He opened a flap and retrieved a piece of yellowed paper. He held it so the sun did not overshadow the writing. "Listen.

"The harem of the Pasha is well guarded; not only by such as he, but by the Nubians and by the other mutes."

"Mutes!"

"He has many slaves. His agent in Mecca procures for him the pick of the market."

"But there is no such thing as slavery in Egypt!"

"Do the slaves know that, effendim?" he asked simply. "Those who have tongues are never seen outside de walls-unless dey are guarded by those who have no tongue!"

We were both silent — me, as I soaked it in, and he to be sure that I did.

A jeep with two senior sergeants drove up to us. "Jan, time for us to go to Pleiku."

Jan Novey crawled into the back of the jeep and waved goodbye with his nail-less fingers.

It had not been two hours since the three sergeants left for Pleiku, when Dennis Bingham found me. Dennis was one of my roommates throughout SF training. He had what they call "rosy cheeks" and a great mind. Dennis read a book a day, thought logically, and as far as I know had never uttered a curse word. He stood before me, clearly agitated, but he looked directly into my eyes and calmed himself before he spoke. "Our jeep that was heading for Pleiku was just ambushed. Richard Smith, the club manager, and George Lichchynski are dead, and Novey is wounded in Pleiku hospital."

I did not know what to say. They were not on a dangerous mission. It was a quiet, sunny day on a paved road with tanks and halftracks spaced along the length. Our people who were ambushed were those who no longer went to the field. There were no radio communications, or air support, or Bright Light teams to prepare us for this.

Doney let me go to Pleiku the next day to see Novey. We waited until ten when the 4th Infantry Division had cleared the road of mines and a couple convoys had passed. We took a three-quarter-ton truck and some of our people in back to make us a less tempting target.

Novey's bed was near the end of a long hall, with hospital beds on both sides. He was propped up in bed with his hand resting on a pillow elevated above his heart. A clear plastic container of fluid hung from a stand and a tube from it fed into his arm. A very large bandage was wrapped around his brow like a turban. His hair was still matted with blood where the nurse was unable to wash it away. Novey looked grey and shriveled under the sheets and appeared to be asleep and I did not want to disturb him, so I turned to walk away.

"Hey," he said, opening his eyes and looking my way without turning his head. "You come all dis vay through Indian country and don't say hi to me?" His voice was quiet and seemed far away.

"I don't want to bother you, Sergeant Novey."

"You call me 'Jan' now."

"What can I do for you? Can I get you anything?"

"Nothing for me. At a time like dis I am just tankful to be alive."

"I haven't heard how serious your wounds are. Will you heal in one piece?"

Jan lifted the fingers of the hand that rested on his chest, keeping the palm on the covers. "Just dis," he said. "I tink that I need to tell you what happened so it doesn't stay in my mind."

He pointed his chin to a glass.

"Water?" I asked

"Yes." And I poured it half-full so it would not spill and gave it to him.

"I don't know vat dey hit us with. I don't tink it was a road mine or ve would not be here — maybe B-40 rocket. Anyway, the jeep flew into da air and landed upside-down. I landed beside the jeep. I was sitting upright with my back against something. I was frozen... I could not move." Novey looked upward toward the ceiling as if he were watching a film of it all there. "I vas paralyzed. My eyes ver wide open, but it was as if I ver dead. I could see everything... I could hear... I could see. But I could not move." Jan paused to catch his breath.

Jan Novey turned his face toward me. "I vas shot across the forehead and blood vas pouring down my face. I could feel it pour down my face and into my collar and I hoped dat it was not my brains too... I could see everything, but I could not move.

"George had been driving and started to sit up and the Viet Cong walked up to him and shot him in the head. His blood and bones splattered on me. I just sat there and waited for dem to come over to me and shoot me too.

"Richard was mostly under the jeep. I tink he vas awake and saw their feet when dey walked up to the jeep. I saw him pull his foot under the jeep so dey wouldn't see him. But they saw him move and one of them pointed his AK under the jeep and shot it full-automatic and killed Sergeant Smith."

Jan was out of breath and was nearly asleep. Perhaps the shot the nurse gave him was taking effect. He took a long breath and continued.

"Den it vas my turn. I know my eyes were vide open and I wondered if they would gouge them out with a stick, but dey did not. I tink, with all the blood that poured down my face and because I could not move, dey thought dat I vas dead already. One of dem saw my ring and tried to pull it off but he could not get it past da knuckle.

"'*Di bay gio*,' said one of dem. I tink dey heard a motor of something coming and dey told him to hurry up. He pulled on my ring again but it vood not come off. So, he pulled out his knife and started to saw off my finger. Even if I could have moved, I would not have — I would just pretend dat I was dead and let him cut on me. My eyes were wide open and I vatched him cut, but it could not cut through de bone." Jan stopped to catch his breath again and when he began again his voice was soft and quiet, as if the words emanated from a dream. "So he broke it. He put my finger in de palm of his hand and broke it. I heard him grunt when he did it. Then I heard de snap, and he finished with de knife. He wiped de blade on my shirt and put it in de sheath. Then he held my ring up with both hands to look at it in de light."

"'*Di*,' dey told him again. So he slowly stood up, still looking at my star sapphire ring, and slowly walked away. And dat vas it."

Jan turned his face to the other side and closed his eyes. He was sent to Japan the next day. I never saw Jan Novey again.

Afternoon shadows raced beside our truck as we returned from Pleiku hospital and parked at the motor pool — in the very spot where Novey read the wrinkled paper from his wallet. Those words which he had written in grey carpenter's pencil took on new life as I pondered them — that tongueless slaves cannot speak of their slavery. When Jan Novey closed his eyes the last time that I would see him in this life, I remained a moment and gazed at the face of this tired old knight. I could not tell the difference between the scars and wrinkles that his crusades had placed there. I did not salute, but I did utter a silent prayer for my old soldier friend.

It was six miles back to CCC through Indian country, plenty of time to remove my mind from the side of that bed and get back to task. A tank and a halftrack were parked at the edge of the road with a green tarp stretched between them and GIs were cooking with C-4 in its shade. Then we came to the place of ambush. They had already removed the wrecked vehicle, but the location was plain with the spilled oil and small debris at the shoulder of the road. Scavenger birds swaggered and pecked at the ground. None of us wanted to stop but we slowed down in readiness, our eyes searching the tree line and shrubs from which the attack was carried out. I rode shotgun as I am left-handed, and it was easier for me to shoot to the right. My thumb was on the selector switch as we passed by. None of us spoke the rest of the way back.

That changed. There were children's voices. Excited voices. Like a school playground. I was crossing the road that divided our compound and children ran past with wide, excited eyes and happy smiles. "Huey! Huey!" they cried. As a group they ran to a tall, powerful-looking sergeant who crossed just ahead of me. "Huey!" they cried. One boy, a little older than the rest, about seven or eight, corrected the younger children — "Baby Huey," he said emphasizing the word "baby." And the little ones called, "Baby Huey!"

SFC David Hayes stopped mid-street and shyly began to hug them. "*Chao um,*" he said to the boys. And to the littlest girls, "*Chao Co dep long,*" Hello pretty girls. They giggled.

A five-ton truck honked its horn and David Hughes feigned fear and surprise and ushered his flock off the road. These were the children of camp workers and they waited outside the gate for the workday to end. Hughes was tall and powerful, far stronger than he himself realized. Someone in camp once said that he was like "Baby Huey," the cartoon character, and the children heard it. "What is Baby Huey?" they asked, and the next day someone showed the children the cartoon. He was a very large yellow duck in a diaper. He was trusting and very strong and did not know it. So SFC David Hughes of Recon Team California, Special Operations Group, 5th Special Forces Group, (Airborne) became "Baby Huey."

I stopped to enjoy the scene and noticed that Baby Huey was in sterile fatigues, and I remembered that his team was scheduled for a mission. David Hughes dropped to one knee to be on their level and chatted with his flock. Indeed, he was a powerful man, for when he patted their backs, his hands were large like wings. He waved at them "Goodbye," and they shouted, "*Chao um, Chao um.*" And the older boy shouted, "*Chao um,* Baby Huey."

It had been only a few days when the word came out. Team California was in trouble. The One Zero had called a Prairie Fire Emergency. "At least a company size force is attacking us now," said the tense voice. "We have casualties." Silence followed for several seconds before we heard the One Zero again. This time the rifle fire was loud and close in the background. "We have…" and there was nothing more.

We followed the progress of the team from bits and pieces of radio traffic gathered from the commo center. There were gasps of traffic in which we heard rapid muffled voices of desperation, smothered in the background of explosions and rifle fire.

We hustled to Recon Company, and they relayed what they heard from Covey. Spads, and Spooky and gunships were on scene engaging the enemy.

"Hughes is seriously wounded." Those solemn words came from one of our out-of-breath recon guys, who had just run from the commo shack. "They were surrounded and attacked from the rear. Hughes held them off until he was hit." Each of us recalled a personal image of him. I remembered him kneeling, surrounded by children.

Covey called. "We are going in for them now."

We heard five hundred-pound bombs exploding in the background and the ripping sound of Spooky's mini guns. Minutes later, it seemed an hour, Covey came back, "We're trying to get them out on strings. First chopper is going in now."

We ran across the compound to the helicopter pad and waited, watching the sky to the west. A pair of trucks outfitted with stretchers braked and skidded to a halt at the edge of the pad. The medics cut the engines to listen for the approach of the team and leaped to the ground with their medical kits. Most of recon lined the pad and waited without talking. A tiny speck, a dot, appeared in the distance. It was too far away for us to hear anything. The dot seemed never to grow larger or closer. We stared at the place. It was still only a dot, a blur on my retina. Then finally the dot began to grow and we could hear the faint sound of the rotors. My eyes were dry from staring without blinking and I closed them for a moment. When I opened my eyes, the dots had taken the shape of helicopters a little to the north of the White Mice building. The Hueys did not pass directly over Kontum but skirted around the outer limit of the town, away from curious eyes and out of respect for our stricken men. Below the belly of the craft, hanging from ropes, were the shapes of men.

I stared at the first aircraft. From one rope, three of our people clung together, their arms wrapped tightly around each other lest one of them fall. Below them, suspended by himself on a separate rope, hung a single large soldier. The wind whipped his sleeves and pressed back his hair. His head was slumped forward in death. Below his waist, the wind thrust one empty pant leg straight back, the ends flapping like a tattered flag. It was Baby Huey.

The next day, the 14th of July, I flew out of Kontum on a Blackbird. I wore sterile fatigues and waited on the tarmac with my rifle and web gear wearing a flop-hat instead of my beret. SOG headquarters did not want it known that the Green Berets and their secret projects were associated with the compound where I was headed. I watched as the very large four-engine airplane rumbled off the active runway and taxied toward me, hissing and growling as it came. I had jumped from a C-130 several times in the past and I was always awed at its presence, especially when I was boarding one, all chuted up to parachute on a distant LZ.

This airplane in particular carried a special awe. It was called a "Blackbird" because it was painted a sinister black with just a few very dark green patterns to break up its profile. There were no markings on the fuselage — no country of origin or numbers, no parent squadron — nothing to identify it. The Blackbird was deniable. It did not exist.

It was sterile, like we SOG people were on a mission. Across the nose of the Blackbird was the yoke of the "skyhook" assembly seen later in James Bond movies and in the Green Beret movie. Inside the Blackbird was a crew of ten or twelve — a lieutenant colonel, a few majors and captains, and a few senior NCOs. The missions and instrumentation of a Blackbird were so classified that maintenance of the aircraft was not performed in Vietnam. Instead, it was flown to a secure base in a certain friendly country. Prior to leaving, removable insignia of the host nation was attached to the surface of the plane. No person of the host nation ever saw a Blackbird arrive as a Blackbird.

As it hissed and rumbled my way, I imagined what missions they had accomplished prior to picking me up that day at Kontum airport. Perhaps in the partial moon they had parachuted a team along the Ho Chi Minh Trail or re-supplied a Stay-Behind team somewhere in the jungles of Laos or Cambodia or North Vietnam. They may have used its advanced radar to fly a mission at treetop level through winding valleys deep into Red China or near Hanoi. The moon was right for that now, and they had sophisticated instruments that the public did not know existed. Perhaps, when the morning sun painted layers of cloud the hue of Buddhist monks' saffron robes, this very airplane was resupplying a secret army in a hidden sanctuary deep into enemy territory. All of this before breakfast.

Quickly, before any Viet Cong could rush to his tube and send a mortar round our way, we were airborne, flying above the red roofs of the city and squares of rice paddies. We banked, and through the window I watched the Dak Bla slide snakelike under the belly of the plane as I held a mug of coffee that the crew gave me — real coffee made from beans from a special place they had been. Our next stop was Long Thanh, the location of SOG's One Zero School. I was the only passenger.

A five-day all Green Beret mission marked the end of One Zero School. Fifteen men were in our class from SOG operations throughout Indochina and the plan was to break us into three teams of five men each to infiltrate and recon Communist sanctuaries in the Australian sector of Vietnam. Briefing was at a remote, isolated location that was far from their air-conditioned headquarters and secure from moles or listening devices.

They brought us by three-quarter-ton trucks down a narrow paved road that served French farmers before the Indochina war but had fallen into deep disrepair. We left the main road and crossed a field, following in the tire paths of other vehicles. The grass was worn off the ruts and sand had sifted into the prints. We stopped beside the awning of a canvas tent set near the edge of a large grassy field. The day was warm and sunny and a soft breeze that barely bent the grass whispered as it passed. Spaced trees with no vines or underbrush margined the field — left from the days of the French rubber plantations. Michelin Rubber grew miles of rubber trees nearby and it was said that they paid off the Viet Cong to stay away from their enterprises. Notwithstanding, the Australians fought their fiercest battle in a nearby rubber plantation at Long Tan.

We were pointed to a row of chairs under the awning. A large easel, like a blackboard, stood before the row of chairs, covered with a drape and I assumed that it was a map. There was no activity one would associate with a headquarters, and the only soldier that I observed was an Australian sergeant major with a fierce red mustache. Looking straight ahead he snapped to attention. "Attention!" he commanded, and we did the American version of coming to attention.

As we stood, an Australian major marched to the front, passing alongside us. He was average height and slim, almost skinny, with a brown mustache that was little more than a line between his nose and lip. He had a baton cocked under his right arm at exactly the horizontal. Military socks covered his calves and authorized shorts extended down to just above his knees.

"Gentlemen, at ease," he said, and the sergeant major assumed the "parade rest" position. "Take your seats."

"Welcome to the Australian sector," he said, looking at us one at a time. It was his concession to informality with the Yanks. "I will hope that our jungle will be a pleasant challenge to you Green Berets. We have selected a few targets which may be worthy of your skills."

The baton became a pointer as the sergeant major lifted the cloth from the easel and the major gave the macro view of the sector, pointing out hamlets, friendlies and suspected enemy locations. Following the five-point patrol order outline, he cleanly and clearly laid out everything we needed to know for the task ahead. At the end, he gave a synopsis of our mission:

"By now you must have heard the rumor that the rubber producers and the tire companies like Michelin have bought off the Viet Cong to leave their plantations alone. The Vietnamese government is probably paying them off also. We think that the trade-off is more than just money. The Vietnamese government will not bomb the rubber trees because they make money off them. Because they are not bombed, it is a safe place for Charlie to hide."

The major laid his baton across the bottom of the easel and placed his hands behind his back. He stepped forward and lowered his voice, engaging us as professionals who would understand the situation. "And so you see, my American friends, why I am talking with you out here instead of in my headquarters. It has occurred to us that our Vietnamese friends do not want us to find Charlie here. They might even tip him off if they knew we were coming."

"You can see from the maps and intelligence that we have shown you, that we are committing you to some impenetrable jungle where we think Charlie's sanctuary is located. We do not want you to engage them unless you must. Just find them and we will do the rest.

"I have only one other thing that I must tell you: When it is time to extract you from the mission and you call for a helicopter to pick you up, we must insist that the LZ is completely secure. You must ensure there are no enemy around the entire perimeter. You must recon all the way around it. My headquarters insists that we do not lose any of our helicopters."

The major cleared his throat, for his next words did not correspond to an order, and he probably did not know that he would say them. "I will be grateful to you."

Before his sergeant major could call us to attention, the major saluted us, and left the awning.

It was late in the day, when shadows lay flat on the ground, unmoving and black like burnt corpses, that a helicopter inserted us into our area of operations. We had them drop us several "klicks" (kilometers) from the suspected enemy base camp so if they observed us coming in, they would not guess our objective. To increase our own chances, we asked the chopper crew to make a couple of fake landings in other LZs, and we watched them clear the trees that surrounded our LZ and we heard them drop into an opening over the next ridge. We went in a few hours before last light to give us enough time to find a good RON but not enough time for the Viet Cong to locate us. I walked point and found a good place for the night which they could not easily or quietly approach in the dark without us knowing, and which had several ways for us to maneuver away. Five men makes for a very small perimeter, but also a harder one for the enemy to find. As I was point for the mission, I took the place on our circle which would be our likely direction to move and evade if we were hit during the night, and waited for the morning.

Leaning there with my back against a tree, I considered our mission for the Australians and compared it to our SOG experience and One Zero school. SOG was the elite of the elites and the school capped off our preparation to lead those SOG teams. Nothing was left un-taught — caring for multiple horrendous wounds, prisoner snatch techniques, communications, evading the enemy, ambush techniques, intelligence gathering equipment, calling in air strikes under extreme pressure, and dozens of other topics. It seemed however, that our mission lacked the support we were used to — but that was just an impression. Our insertion did not involve numerous aircraft, support aircraft or Covey. Given the words of the major about not losing a helicopter, I was not certain what assets we could rely on if we got into significant trouble.

Three days of stealth took us to the place on our map the major suspected to be a Communist sanctuary secure in a protected rubber plantation. The underbrush was nearly impenetrable but had to be crossed until we found signs of heavy enemy activity — highspeed trails made by the Viet Cong or indications that the old plantation roads were being used by them. We were near some of the old roads and during the night we heard truck engines. Once or twice, I saw faint light flicker on the side of a low ridge, perhaps dimmed headlights filtered through the branches of the trees. I stared at the spot and wished it to reappear to be sure, but it did not. Deep into the night, well after midnight, a single shot startled a tree full of hanging bats. They rose in unison. I heard their chirping sonar as they flew in a large circle in the blind sky before returning to their roost. Even the Montagnards did not hunt in the dark and I assumed the shot was from a signaling road watcher or tracker.

The next morning, we moved across a dense tangle of crisscrossed logs, brush and vines. From the other side of that thickness, small sounds of human activity filtered through; the low hum of a generator, a few shouts, a door shutting, a truck motor, but it was all very faint. The ground was littered with debris — empty shell casings and cans and garbage. To move quietly and with stealth, I reduced our speed to a crawl, and at times I found myself on my belly. A chance ray of sunlight fell on a "spider's thread" and I froze. I studied the thread and my eyes followed it to its source — a green army C-ration can that had been wired to a tree, and I knew that a grenade was inside ready to be tugged free and explode. Twice more I found booby traps and I knew we must be near their base. I saw faint skylight ahead through the weeds and tangle and sensed an opening. I inched forward. I had not moved ten feet in the last hour. I froze. Something was dead wrong, and I did not know what it was. Then I realized what alarmed me. *Nuoc mam.* Somewhere very close by in the underbrush before me, an enemy was hiding. I could smell that soldier's breath.

Many odors had passed my nostrils over the hours; vegetation crushed under my knees, a plant in bloom, stagnant water that festered in the way, dead logs that were turning to mush, something rotting unseen in the shrubs to one side, but this was *nuoc mam.* No other odor was like it. It was the Vietnamese version of soy sauce. The word would literally translate to "fish water." Fish were hung and the liquid that dripped from them was collected and fermented and became the seasoning of the people. I did not mistake it — the smell could only come from the breath of someone very close to me. I froze and deciphered every blade of grass until I saw him. He moved slightly and that movement revealed his profile. His shadow moved side to side as he sought for us. He looked in my direction a moment then faced the other way. Perhaps he watched a trail or meadow and did not expect anyone coming through the tangle behind him. I willed him to look the other way and froze until I was sure he faced away. Then I saw the shadow of his hand move to his mouth and I could hear him. He was eating. I listened in the stillness and heard a rustle in the leaves a few feet from the eater and I knew that he was not alone. I backed myself, moving in the very places I had been before. I know my movements were imperceptibly slow and I was glad we had space between us Americans as we moved. My eyes never left the form as I backed, my rifle ready to fire.

When I dared look behind me, I slowly signaled, a pushing motion of one hand, palm down in a slow pressing motion, "easy, easy." I did not dare signal "enemy," placing my open hand behind the back of my head — I would not risk so large a movement. I pointed at the nearest man and looked in his eyes and with the speed of a clock hand I pointed a direction for him to lead.

"Enemy?" he mouthed.

I nodded with a speed that communicated "danger, very grave."

He turned at sloth speed and maneuvered away through the tangle.

My immediate problem was to get myself turned around in the mess and tangle around me without making the slightest sound while keeping my weapon on that form on the other side of the bushes.

"Lord help," I silently prayed, and as I finished, a two-engine military plane appeared on the horizon. It must have just taken off from a nearby base for it was climbing and the pilot had not yet cut back his engines. I saw the shadow turn his head and follow the passing airplane. Under the cover of that engine noise, we extricated ourselves and put distance between us and the ambush site.

An hour found us far enough from the danger area to appraise what we had learned so far. One of the guys from CCN whispered, "We know the roads that they are using and where they converge."

"The booby traps we have seen are all theirs and they would be close to their base. And the ambush site too," another one of the guys said softly so only we could hear.

I added, "The thing I notice most is that every sighting of the enemy we have had, they have moved like someone in their own backyard. They talk. They do not whisper. They do not move like someone on patrol where there might be enemy."

"And they are not afraid to walk in the open," said CCN.

A buck sergeant from CCS whispered. "Well, we didn't get to stand in their chow line, or listen in on their briefing at their headquarters, but I think we have learned what they sent us out here for. The Aussies will have to connect those dots. At least we can go in with information while it is still fresh and usable."

We looked at each other in silent agreement — it was time to make our way to an extraction LZ.

Our maps they gave us were old, from the time of the French, long before satellites were producing accurate maps. The first patch of white on the mostly green map that indicated a break in the forest where we could be picked up, was only a few klicks away. It was far enough from where we had scouted but there were two smaller LZs we would have to go around to get to it. We would do a careful reconnaissance around them searching for enemy "watchers" and possible ambush sites in case the Aussies followed up on our recon.

By the time we scouted the first opening in the jumble of brush and trees, the day was far too advanced to continue to the next opening. There were trails on the circumference of this one, but they showed no recent use, and there was a trench line with several bunkers. The roofs of some of them were timber from old railroad ties that had rotted through and had collapsed. There were no railroads in Vietnam and those timbers served a life elsewhere and were on their final life in Indochina. The ties gave way and the sandbags molded through and the sand inside them poured into piles inside. We spent the night on a grassy rise which was removed from the trails we found, but close enough to monitor the activities of the field by listening. Well after dark I heard several voices talking at the same time. They were low and conversational but not the voices of those who were careful of being heard. The hum of talking continued for a couple of minutes and stopped. Apart from a few monkeys in the trees it was quiet the rest of the night.

We ate at first light, when darkness surrendered to grey but before color had arrived. I ate from my PIR (personal indigenous rations) and squeezed it into my mouth, and I recalled the soldier's *nuoc mam* breath, and wondered if an enemy could smell the food we ate. Midmorning we surveilled the second opening, skirting our edge of the field and listened for traces of enemy presence. As we rose to leave the meadow, we were startled by loud grunting. Something hidden in the deep grass charged us. It crashed toward us through the field, grunting and breaking twigs, the grass hissing against its legs. Though our attacker could not be seen, its route was clear, for the tall reeds became flat and broken, leaving a trench of shadow in its wake. It stopped, adjusted its direction more directly at us, and rushed toward us again. We were ready to shoot when I saw the sun on a pair of curved white tusks. The creature was a black, hairy, feral hog and for all appearance and mannerisms could have been an African warthog. It looked at us with black beady eyes and made a short, fake charge. When it saw that we did not flee, it seemed to turn itself clean around on a hop without moving its feet, it lifted its tail straight up, and trotted off with a snort.

The field we had picked from the map opened before us, picnic-like and peaceful, especially because we left the dark tangle of underbrush and bugs and spiderwebs and sogginess that defined its edge. But as calm and pristine as the meadow was, we knew better than walk on it and expose ourselves until the helicopter arrived. The size and shape of the clearing surprised us. It was far larger than indicated on the map and we could never recon the entire perimeter as the Australian major wanted, especially through the tangle we had experienced so far. Even if we did make it completely around, there would be no confidence that Charlie had not moved in on a side we had already patrolled while we were on the other side.

The shape of the field concerned me also. The outline was that of an hourglass — two hemispheres joined by a narrow grassy area in the middle. I set up in the narrow strip between the two halves. It was the only way that we could watch both halves until our liftoff arrived. We visually monitored the halves and called the Australians for a pickup.

"ETA three zero minutes, Yank," the radio man said, and we slid back into the weeds to wait.

It had not been five minutes. We had barely whispered into our handpiece when loud voices speaking Vietnamese came into our ears. Several of them were in animated conversation on the far side of one of the two fields. At first, I could only follow the movement by the voices, moving along the far side of the one hemisphere of the field before us. The speed was rapid and steady, at a pace that could only be accomplished on a trail. Soon, I began to catch the movements of the group — the bleached color of a wood gunstock, the straw-colored shape of a peasant's hat. At least six or eight were in the number, but spaced behind them fifty meters back, was a very large body of soldiers. With that great number of men who followed, the sound of squeaking leather, and the swishing of fabric pant legs, and padding of feet, it was clear that the first group of soldiers was the point element of a larger unit — at least company size.

Then in that moment I realized the great peril we were in. I had chosen the narrow strip between the two halves as the only place for me to watch both. The enemy saw those same two halves of open field as a danger area that exposed them to passing military aircraft. They decided to cross it at the narrow place — the very place I had picked for the five of us to set up. Before I had time to whisper what was about to happen, the VC were at the far side of the strip, ready to walk right over me.

We slid back on our bellies into the ooze and mud and weeds. A firefight seemed inevitable as they headed toward us. I raised my head just high enough to peer through the reeds. There were eight in this first group, five were all in black and wore conical straw hats. They wore bandoleers of ammunition and carried SKS rifles slung over their shoulders. They moved with a familiarity of the area and without concern and were in animated conversation. The other three were NVA regulars in yellow-green uniforms and chest bandoleers. The three were alert, looking side to side for danger with the AK-47 rifles in their hands following their eyes. The uniforms of the NVA were clean and their hair was trimmed, and every indication was that they were well disciplined troops. If they did not pass us by, I would shoot them first and go for the VC after that.

The grassy field was slightly higher than where we lay, and I slid back and felt the muck and water cover my legs. I looked to the team beside me and touched my watch and held up two fingers — we had two minutes until they would be on us, and we would fire. I held my four fingers up, closed my hand and repeated the motion — "There are eight of them in the first group." As I rolled back to my stomach, I noticed my blond-haired team member from Anchorage, Alaska. He lay next to a pool of water in the mud and grass that was full of water bugs. He toyed with them with a thin stick for a moment. Another minute to go. He rolled to his stomach and prepared to fire.

The voices stopped. My heart thumped in my ears. Did they sense us waiting at the edge of the field only a few dozen feet away? I would wait until we would be forced to fire. I listened. I did not hear anything. Where were they?

Then I heard the grass complain of passing feet just over my head. They were almost on top of me. The grass hissed and I saw the blades of grass part to make room for their feet. Any second now! We would wait until we had to shoot.

I was certain that we could take out this first group, but the following company was only forty or fifty yards behind and could overpower us from there. I remembered our helicopter lift-off on the way. Would they come alone, or would they have an escort that we could call on for support when our fight with the second element began?

The sound of movement in the weeds passed along our front to the side and followed a trail into the jungle. How could they not have noticed us? There was a point that I could have reached up and tapped the sandal of a soldier passing by.

We waited in the muck, barely breathing, not knowing if all the point elements had passed by. I listened for the approach of the main body and my mind wildly planned how to engage them. We could not let them get so close this time before we fired. I would take out as many as I could with my rifle before they reacted, then duck behind the shallow bank where we lay, and toss grenades from there. I would yell at our radioman to call for air support. From there I would shoot a grazing fire from the muck across the field. Hopefully by not exposing ourselves at length to the much larger force we could survive until support arrived. At least that is what went through my mind.

I looked to the side at my people. Their legs were barely seen in the mud and were drawn up in preparation to stand and fire. I caught their eyes. We were all on the same page. I would only nod when it was time.

The approach of the large force was loud and apparent. I hoped that they relied on the point element for their security and marched with slung rifles.

I gauged the time we would fire. I did not want them right on top of us. Twenty seconds and I would shoot. I looked to our people and signaled "twenty," then with a forefinger began the pace. "Nineteen, eighteen," and returned to my rifle.

"Fourteen," I counted in my mind. "Thirteen."

The sound of an airplane filtered over us. It flew low and its path would take it directly over the twin fields. The plane flew as if they were searching below. Its wings tilted side to side to let the pilot see over the wings.

"*Hep!*" someone in the enemy force shouted, and I could imagine him pointing to at a place and ordering his men to rush off the field before they were seen by the plane. "*Di,*" he yelled, "*Di mau.*"

There followed the sound of a mass of men running off the field in the direction the point element had gone. The ground thumped with running feet. Metal slings tapped against wooden stocks. Canvas fabric rubbed together and as the last of the unit passed us, I heard heavy breathing and grunting from those who lagged with the heavy weapons of the company.

I wondered at first if they only went far enough into the jungle as not to be seen, but I heard snapping twigs in the distant thickness and considered that the unit had passed.

As it was, we listened for ten minutes before we looked up at the field to find it pristine and empty once again. If it were on time, our pickup was only ten minutes out.

"We better check out the area they passed to be sure they do not set up and wait."

They nodded their agreement, and we scouted the area. We found a shirt sleeve a soldier had dropped in his rush. It was tied at both ends and full of rice. It was not booby trapped and we saved it. Intelligence would soon know where the rice was grown and what field produced the cotton for the sleeve. A few meters deeper into the woods we found a magazine for an AK-47 with three rounds inside, and we wondered if the Communists were running short of ammunition or if this unit had been recently in combat and expended their rounds. We smiled as we imagined the face of that fearless NVA soldier when he learned he had been on patrol with an empty rifle.

We had no sooner reclaimed our position at the narrow strip when we heard rotor blades over the ridge. Two of our people moved to protect the side where the enemy column had disappeared and a minute later an off-green Huey with the beautiful roundel and red kangaroo glided down to our smoke.

Fourteen of the fifteen of us were at final debriefing. One of the teams had significant contact and a sergeant was shot in the shoulder. In all, when all the information was transferred to the major's map, the elements he needed to mount up an operation were there. We never learned how the Aussies used what we learned.

The next day I flew out on an Air America Curtiss C-46, designated for "black ops" missions. At the time it was believed that Air America was the largest airlines in the world. It was the airline of the CIA and as its cover, it ran a legitimate service for that part of the world, complete with terminals, pilots and paying passengers. The slogan of the company was, "Anything, Anywhere, Anytime, Professionally." That motto certainly fit the "dark side" of the airline, for it supplied private wars, dropped paratroopers at secret airstrips, supplied arms to secret armies, and ran a civilian counterpart to SOG.

Some of their operations began in the last days of the Chinese civil war, when Mao and the Communists captured the bulk of the mainland. Chang Kai-Shek and the Kuomintang had armies far to Mao's flanks ready to spring. But Mao made a major thrust that sent Chang's army reeling and retreating to the island of Taiwan, which became Nationalist China. Chang's armies that did not make it off the mainland were stranded. They could not get to Taiwan, and they would not go to the mainland and certain death. The "Agency" made a deal with those stranded armies: "If you keep Communism out of your part of the world, we will not bomb your poppy fields and we will fly back your commerce." So, Air America took on the mission of supplying weapons and supplies to the warlords, and they returned with the cargoes of the warlords. The presumed hard currency of the East — the poppy, was always bundled in a manner the pilots could say that they were unaware of the cargo.

There were three of us from One Zero school on an airplane heading back to our parent units. Our pilot was old enough to have flown the "Golden Triangle," the warlord run. "We are going to fly slightly east of north, not directly to Kontum, and points north," he told us. "We have something to drop off on the way. We won't have to land, just bank low over a certain field and toss it out of the window."

It happened as he said. We passed a field a distance from a small hamlet where a dozen people waited in camouflage at one corner. We would not have seen them at all had their morning shadows not pointed them out. Yellow smoke snaked up and the pilot make a "turn on pilon" so the package would not strike the propeller. The plane leveled and climbed and continued northeast. A couple of dozen miles later, at a bend in the river where rice paddies met the tree line, we watched a firefight below. An attack on a position was in progress and I hoped that it was not friendlies who were charging across the open rice paddies. A flash, like lightning, followed by billowing white smoke rose along the tree line and I knew that our people were running air support for some friendlies.

"We are going to veer east of here, so we aren't in the way of the jets. I would just as soon fly the coast anyway," the grey-haired pilot said.

My two classmates sprawled out and went to sleep and I looked out of the window. We had been flying over the South China Sea for twenty minutes and the captain yelled back at me. "Hey sarge, come up here. Look at this."

I climbed into the cockpit, glad for the front row seat. "Look at this. Down there." He pointed and banked slightly to the right. "Down there. See that?"

The younger pilot moved so I could see better. He had taken the wire out of his pilot's hat, and it looked crumpled and used and old like the one in *Terry and the Pirates.* "All that white," he said.

I did not get what the fuss was about. "It kinda looks like shallow water over a sandy bottom," I offered.

He looked back at me and smiled. "Not way out here though. Looks like that, but you will never guess what that is. You won't believe it." And he gave me a clue. "That white is two miles wide and six miles long."

Now I could not imagine what it was other than shallow water over a white sandy bottom. "And my sonar says that that mass is a thousand feet thick. He laughed out loud at my perplexity.

"Give up?"

"I haven't a clue."

"That, Sarge, is a solid mass of mating sea snakes!"

I was horrified. I could not imagine it. I remember a boiling mass of white maggots that exploded from a dead cow's belly — how they wiggled in a mass and crawled in a frenzy of activity, and I imagined those maggots being one or two meters long. "Aaugh!" I said aloud.

The co-pilot took off his cap as the bill pushed against the window. He was young and slim with a big Adams apple that moved up and down when he talked. I watched it go up and down a couple of times and I knew that he was swallowing. "How long would a guy live if he fell into that mess?"

"I think you would be dead before you stopped the downward fall," I offered.

"No kidding," he said as the veteran pilot banked the other way.

"Been in the Agency long?"

He looked back and smiled when I used that term. "I mean, have you been flying long?"

"No, you're right, sarge. I started out with Chennault's Flying Tigers helping the Chinese against the Japanese. Later, after that war came the Chinese civil war and Chiang and the Kuomintang were fleeing Mao and the Communists. I could not count how many flights I made helping the people escape to the island. I even flew out Chiang's treasures. All those beautiful jade carvings you see in the museum in Taipei were once in my plane."

The co-pilot was flying now, and he banked left and flew generally west. "We will be at your stop in a few minutes. Then we will drop your friends off at CCN."

"Will that be the end of your day?"

"We have one more stop at a dirt strip in a certain country you have probably visited already. Half of the airstrip is a gravel riverbank, and the rest is hidden in the trees. On a certain window of time, we will make a pass over them to let them know we are there, and they will run out and pull away the bushes that camouflage the rest of the strip. They pop a smoke, so we know which way the wind is blowing and if the smoke isn't the right color, we know they are compromised."

We talked in the front cabin for the next half hour. As we flew over various hamlets and Special Forces camps, he relayed their history and anecdotes about the battles that surrounded them. He would point and I could see the gold Rolex watch shine against the copper color of his tanned forearm. I compared it to the one on my own arm — a cheap, olive-drab plastic Seiko.

"I am getting old and long in the tooth — the time a man would retire in any other job. I do not think of myself as old, just highly experienced. I could not imagine living in a quiet world. Some day they will shoot me out of the sky and you Green Berets will come to rescue me. I hope the end is quick and that I am never captured."

He was quiet for a minute. "That is Kontum over there just past the curve of the river. Sarge, land this thing, will you? The co-pilot will talk you through it." He winked and pointed me to his seat.

Mike Buckland met me halfway across the compound, a few paces outside of Recon Headquarters. We exchanged hugs. Best friends in a war that took friends away. His smile was quickly replaced with sadness.

"What?"

"Bad news, Dale. Dennis Bingham was killed on a mission while you were gone."

I just stood there stupefied. "What happened?"

"They had just finished a horrendous fire fight and were chased until they broke contact and thought they had lost their pursuers. They were in a little circle catching their breath and they all looked at each other and could not believe their escape. Dennis shook his head and smiled in relief at their great adventure, and a sniper bullet got him in the head just as he smiled. And that was that."

An image of Dennis with his boyish looks and rosy cheeks filled my mind. We had gone through jump school together. He was our roommate for the year at training group, and we were close friends at CCC. I wept. I felt my shoulders shake and I covered my eyes, and I was embarrassed to be crying in the middle of the parade field. Mike stood in front of me to shield me from view. When I composed myself, I checked in at Recon. While I was gone, Bob Howard had flown out to receive the Medal of Honor and Doney, my team leader, was the new First Sergeant. He was not in but would see me later.

I put my gear on my bunk in the Florida team room and left to find Doney. I found him as he was leaving his hootch on the perimeter. He had a handkerchief and was wiping tears from one eye. I stopped and waited so I would not intrude when he looked up at me and smiled holding the cloth to his eye. His smile was fatherlike. "I am glad to have you back, Sergeant Hanson."

"What happened?"

"I caught some shrapnel in my eye while you were gone. The eye is okay, but it cut my tear duct and tears keep flowing from my right eye. I have to daub it every few minutes. You missed a good one. A prisoner snatch that went wild. We had a big firefight and Chin was badly wounded."

We walked across the parade field to his new office. "Chin had shrapnel to his forehead that exposed his brain, and he took a round

238

in the shoulder. He had one hand on a strut of the helicopter, and it started to leave before he got all the way in, so he did a one arm pull-up onto the strut with all of his gear on and lay across the strut all the way back to camp. The surgeons closed the wound in his skull and patched his shoulder and he is back here in camp already."

He daubed his eye.

"Our Chinese on Florida decided that it was time to retire from the field and they all have gotten jobs in Supply. They have been fighting for many years and they may have been the last of the Chinese Nungs left alive. Joe Morris wanted to get off recon and has been reassigned to Commo. He has done more than his share in the field."

We entered his office. "I am the First Sergeant of Recon now, so that makes you the One Zero of Team Florida. When Ken Worthley comes back from extended leave the team will go back to him. For now, you have all the Vietnamese that are left on the team, and you can work on rebuilding. You will be a very capable One Zero."

I met Joe Morris coming out of the mess hall. His skin was pale from days of camouflage paint and jungle canopy, and his red hair and brown eyes were dark in contrast. I had been gone only three weeks and Joe had been in two difficult missions during the time. He was nervous even in the telling. "Florida was all set up to do a prisoner snatch and it wound up in a hellacious fight. I did not think we were going to get out of it alive. Doney was wounded in the face and Chin took one in the head and I could see his brains. We put a bandage on his head, and he kept on fighting, and he got shot again, this time in the shoulder, and he just kept on fighting. When it was over, I told Doney that I couldn't take it anymore. My nerves were shot. Doney said that he understood, and I got a job in Commo — that is my MOS. Well, I heard that that my friend Dilemma on RT Hawaii needed a straphanger to go. What could I do? I told them I would go, and we nearly didn't come out of that one alive either. Dennis Bingham was killed on that one. Dale, my nerves are shot but if I stay here in camp, I will wind up strap-hanging again."

Joe seemed to apologize for leaving recon.

"Joe, I think you are a courageous man and deserve a rest."

"Well, tomorrow they are sending me to Leghorn. It is on the top of an impregnable mountain with a platoon of Montagnards for security. Nothing can happen up there. I think I will monitor the radio and read a few books."

A few days later one of the guys in commo gave me a message from Joe Morris at our radio relay station on the top of Leghorn. "Dale, here I am on the top of leghorn, the safest place in all the SOG operations. Yesterday when I was walking along the perimeter and checking the security, lightning hit a claymore mine beside me and knocked me for a loop. I wasn't hit by any shrapnel, but I know this — there is not a safe place for Joe Morris in all this country."

Chapter Sixteen

LIMA FIFTY AND THE SPY PAYMASTER

July 21. They arrested Colonel Rheault, the commander of all Special Forces in Vietnam. About the time they made him a prisoner I was sitting on one of those folding chairs in One Zero School listening to a lecture on intelligence gathering, setting up spy networks, and techniques for debriefing local agents. It was hot and stuffy in the classroom, and the blades of the ceiling fan made their circuit slowly, as a predator does when it seeks an opening in an enclosure. The fan made no sound that would mask the speaker's voice and the fingers of breeze barely lifted and peeked under the papers on our desks — papers that said in bold letters at the top, "SECRET-NOFORN."

Although Colonel Rheault had been in-country only two months he was already respected and held in high regard among us. But like a street thug or common criminal, he was being held in solitary confinement in the stockade at Long Binh jail. Along with him, seven other Green Berets were jailed in tin roofed cells that were saunas in the blazing sun. Some have described the jail as "prisoner-of-war-like." They were held in the same facility as deserters, rapists, thieves, and those who committed criminal assault. But these Green Berets committed none of those crimes. They were arrested and charged with killing an enemy spy, an enemy agent who caused the torture and deaths of many men. And though the necessity to eliminate the spy was a given conclusion before Colonel Rheault even took command, he was charged with murder. The execution of the dangerous double agent became national news and took on the aura of a spy novel.

It was a certitude that spies were embedded deeply into the South Vietnamese command structure at every level. Security with the South Vietnamese was a porous sieve in which little was secret at the end. Some suggested that, telling the South Vietnamese was not that different than telling the Viet Cong. It became a practice among some commanders to not inform the Viets about sensitive missions. The Communists often had detailed advance knowledge of missions and intelligence gathering programs, and it was believed that a mole had to have been present in either the planning stages or possessed copies of the actual orders that would be later given to commanders in the field. As a result, teams were regularly waited for and ambushed at the LZs. Some teams were wiped out. A few teams and individual agents disappeared entirely. Enemy units disbursed just ahead of a large-scale attack by our forces, clearly with advance knowledge that we were coming. A spy was killing our people.

A fortuitous event occurred that appears to have exposed that spy. For cover he worked as an interpreter for B-57, Project Gamma, which was run in part by the Green Berets. Gamma's mission was to gather information on enemy troop movements and plans, and to find supply dumps and troop staging areas. In addition to being an interpreter, he helped set up teams of agents and send them to gather intelligence in enemy controlled territory. His name was Thai Khac Chuyen and he was one of the top agents of the program. But dark clouds of failure hung over the project as team after team disappeared or were eliminated soon after they arrived on the ground. Individual agents left in place were doubled or killed by the NVA. Most attempts to keep teams in the field ended in compromise, torture, and death. Because of its utter failure to maintain agents in the field, the project was terminated.

The Americans did not know it then, but Chuyen — who recruited and sent those agents into enemy territory — also betrayed them to Communist interrogation and execution. In effect, one enemy double agent singlehandedly shut down an entire program, a program which some intelligence experts said provided up to seventy-five percent of all intelligence in Vietnam. With the project shut down, Chuyen the interpreter faded from notice. Then, an allied unit made a raid on a Viet Cong camp and recovered a series of photographs which were taken in a Communist base camp. The pictures were not grainy, but clear and well-focused. Prominent in them was the missing Mr. Chuyen, smiling and in amicable conversation with high-ranking North Vietnamese officials.

Chuyen was induced to come back to work in a new project, but on arrival was detained for questioning. He was interrogated and given a polygraph and sodium phenethyl, known as truth serum. Those who administered those tests were convinced that Chuyen was a double agent whose chief loyalty was to Hanoi and Communism. The subject stated firmly that he would not cooperate with the Americans. What to do with Mr. Chuyen? They could not release him as they determined him to be a spy. They could not turn him in to the South Vietnamese because the Green Berets had not made them aware of the Gamma Project as they did not trust them. The Green Berets sought advice from the CIA, but the Agency did not want Chuyen as he refused to cooperate and was of no use to them. "He is your baby. You take care of him," was the essence of their response.

"What do you suggest that we do with him?" They asked.

With a yawn, they gave the obvious answer, "Terminate with extreme prejudice, of course." The euphemism always meant execute the subject. According to the Geneva Convention, execution of spies is permissible and expected in war. In fact, all of us Green Berets on a SOG mission would not be given prisoner-of-war status and could be executed as spies if we were captured. We carried no identification, our uniforms were sterile, and our government would deny any knowledge of us. Hundreds of spies such as Chuyen were executed every year in the war. Chuyen would just be another one of them.

The actual deed might have resembled an old Hollywood black and white movie. The street beside the harbor was empty of men and darkness was over all except for the few streetlights of the city that reflected on the water as thick fog rolled in. There was the occasional moan of a marker buoy, a sound that resembles a human groan, and from a blackened shack came the muffled cough of a peasant with TB. In this case, a small boat putted out of the harbor toward the South China Sea where the muddy-bottomed Giang River meets the open water. In the bottom of the boat was a large sack on the floorboards, with the inert body of Mr. Chuyen. He has been sedated with morphine and his body was wrapped with chain and stuffed into the bag. At a place they thought appropriate, the double agent was lifted high enough that he could be shot without the bullets piercing the floorboards of the boat. Two rounds from a silenced .22 Colt Woodsman pistol went through the spy's head and the weighted body was lowered into the sea. Blood oozed from the sack and diffused into the sea and the milling sharks below.

Story over.

At least, it should have been. Hundreds of spies in the fifth column of collaborators and enemy agents were executed in a similar manner every year. In fact, the CIA's "Project Phoenix," later renamed PRU for "Provisional Reconnaissance Unit," executed hundreds of spies like Chuyen as their basic mission. So, in this context of war, it was a shock and bewildering that of the hundreds of terminations, that someone chose to focus on prosecuting a handful of Green Berets. To us in Special Forces, the arrest of Col. Rheault and his staff, was an attack on all Green Berets.

It was Shackley, the head of the CIA in Vietnam, who threw the Green Berets under the bus to distance the agency from accountability. Like Pontius Pilot, he washed his hands before General Creighton Abrams, the commander of all U.S. forces in Vietnam, to say, "I am innocent of the blood of this man." Our suspicions were that Abrams then took his turn at Pilot's bowl and said by arresting Rheault, "I too am innocent of the blood of this man." We in SF were aware of the dislike General Abrams had for the elite forces who operated in the war in Vietnam independently of his direct control. When Abrams heard that the Green Berets had executed a double agent he was heard to say, "We've got to clean those guys up." This would be a message to Special Forces operating in Indochina — "I am in charge of this war"

Abrams had minimal operational control over Special Forces. We, through SOG headquarters, the CIA, or the Country Team planned and directed our missions. We hired our own army, trained and led them. Tens of thousands of Chinese Nungs, Montagnard tribesmen, Laotians and Cambodians fought directly under our command and were paid with funds passed to us from the CIA. Their loyalty was to us, the men in those "funny green hats." SF did not even receive food from the armed forces but bought our own, often by selling captured souvenirs of war and using the money to procure food on the local market.

Abrams had one "thorn in the flesh" that he used. He could and did assign some of the officers who served in our units. Many of our officers were good men, well trained, and often came through the ranks, but many that Abrams assigned were not even SF qualified. They were clueless and even antagonistic to unconventional war techniques. Some, like the colonel that Abrams assigned to replace Col. Rheault, were not even airborne qualified. The ultimate insult to an elite unit.

Abrams proceeded to court-martial Rheault in-country. Proceedings would occur in the fog of war and the results would never be learned stateside or in the press. The eight men would be kept in solitary, in metal Conex containers which measured only five by eight feet, until the "mess was cleaned up."

Back in Kontum with One Zero School behind me, I found that the arcane imprisonment of our people in metal Conex containers — which are sometimes used for transporting garbage — became a seething anger among our people, especially among us enlisted men. Our emotions were a festering boil about to pop, a fuse attached to an explosive. When we thought of that stockade, we were like the case of old dynamite I found in an abandoned gold mine that seeped and sweated in a box and waited for just the right bump to set it off.

We were talking at the club after dinner. One of the old sergeants, I'll call him "Smith," lowered his voice and leaned over the table and said, "Sergeant _____ and his team hopped an Air America plane to Long Binh, and they set up outside the fence. He made his way in through their perimeter wire and through the guards and found the trailer where Colonel Rheault was held. 'We're here to get you out. The way is clear, and my people are all waiting.'" The old sergeant sat upright and took a swallow of whatever it was he was drinking.

"But Rheault says, 'No thank you boys, but we all talked it over and we are going to sit this out. There is no way this nonsense can go on. They have to drop the charges.'"

The sergeant looked at each of us with his watery grey eyes. He had not shaved, and he had white bristles on his face. "I don't think Abrams is going to drop those charges. Our boys are still sitting in those cans like sardines."

Another sergeant across the table from him was off duty and wearing a green T-shirt with the peace symbol on his chest. Printed in a circle around the symbol were the words, "THE FOOTPRINT OF THE AMERICAN CHICKEN." He mashed his cigarette in the ashtray like a bug. "They are treating us like criminals for doing our job. Killing Commies are what we are here for." He shoved the ashtray to the center of the table, and he leaned back in the chair, his breath hissing between his teeth. Anger punctuated every word of his sentence. "The newspapers treat the dopeheads and protesters and draft dodgers like heroes, but they arrest us who are out here fighting a war."

Smith leaned forward and lowered his voice. "I got friends in the Mike Force and some of the A Teams. They are ready to take battalions of little people to Long Binh and get our people by force. The people who fly for us have already said that they work for us, not Abrams. It is all going to come down soon."

His words still charged with anger, Peace Symbol added, "It is criminal what they are doing to Rheault. He is one of us. We never leave our people behind — not in Laos, not in Cambodia, and not in Long Binh."

And this was the atmosphere that hovered over every project and

Mike Force and A Team in the country — the heavy air that proceeds an unseen storm which is sure to happen.

I was talking to a couple of enlisted berets in the open spaces behind the S-1 building where most of the clerical aspects of our camp were done. It was a chance meeting and we had stopped to watch the passing of high-flying jets marked only by their vapor trails. By now everyone in Abram's command was aware of the likelihood that SF and their people would move on Long Binh and take their officers by force. It was not a matter of surprise. They would simply move on the compound and overcome anything that was in their way.

As we were talking, a couple of captains stepped out of the building for a smoke. They were captains assigned to our camp by Abrams. Neither of them was SF qualified but wore the beret. They were aloof from the rest of us and in their off time were either in the officer's club or in their own quarters.

"It is pretty certain that we aren't waiting much longer. Some of the Mike Force people are just about ready to go. Some are going by convoy and the rest by air," I said in a voice just loud enough for the captains to hear, but not so loud they would think I wanted them to do so.

Another sergeant who I came in-country with added, "I know two or three thousand are ready for sure. I can't imagine what the regular soldiers at Long Binh will think when they are told they have to fire on other Americans."

"Well," another one of the guys said, "This will be nothing compared to fighting the hardcore NVA we find on our missions."

I saw the two captains flick their cigarettes and ease back into the administration building, taking care the door did not slam on its spring.

The next day, the word filtered down to SF units that Rheault and the others had been flown out of country to a prison in the States, well out of our reach. We learned much later that it was not true, but at least they were no longer in steel containers.

After One Zero School, RT Florida was a shell of itself. Norm Doney had become the First Sergeant of Recon Company. Joe Morris went to Commo and the top of Leg Horn Mountain where he was reasonably certain the Communists could not get him. Our brave Chinese retired and found work elsewhere in the camp. Lam, at age thirty-six, was the old man of my Vietnamese, and he too was weary of fighting. He and his wife started a tailor shop in the compound where they altered our fatigues and sewed patches on our uniforms. All that was left were our four Vietnamese and me. We needed another American and a few more indigenous people to round us out. Ken Worthley would be back in a few weeks and would resume being the One Zero, giving us a second American. Until then we continued to practice immediate reaction drills and shoot at the range. We pulled only close local missions and tried to rebuild.

Then one morning Ken Worthley rejoined the team, and I became the One. Like me, Ken was a Minnesota boy. He was slim and blond and wholesome. He spoke quietly and never uttered a curse word. Through his church in Minnesota, he collected clothing for the lepers that lived beside the Dak Bla River. One day a dozen large boxes of clothes arrived, and he and I loaded a small truck and brought them to the leprosarium. Although the nuns and residents were delighted with the clothing and our visit, they were shy and reserved, fearing that the Viet Cong would observe them speaking to us.

We did a local training mission, just the six of us. It was a walk-in mission. We got giant pairs of wool socks that we could fit over our boots. After dark and curfew, when we were certain we were not observed, we made our way along the road well into Indian country, the socks muffling our steps in the gravel. We left the road following a fence line into the trees and made our way along a ridge and set up an ambush on a trail. Around three in the morning the enemy set off our trip flares and we blew the claymore mines and tossed grenades into the path below us. We did not fire our weapons and the enemy had no muzzle flashes to locate us in the dark and shoot back. We waited, listening for the cries of wounded men in the kill zone and for movement. A heavy but brief rain followed that masked any sound that would indicate they were maneuvering around us. We did not move but willed our ears to hear everything as we shivered in the wet and cool of the night. In the morning we inspected the trail but found that the shower erased all blood and signs of casualties from our ambush.

We moved north in the direction from which the enemy had come, where the grass was as tall as cane fields all the way to the foot of the next tall hills. Through them, perhaps during the night as we lay in ambush, many men had cut wide swaths for trails making no effort to hide their passage. The smell of green broken stems filled the air, and fecund moisture seeped from freshly trampled stalks, ready to grow again. The wide path did not signal the work of the Viet Cong who tried to move unnoticed, but rather, large military formations of NVA. Their movement was very close to the city, and I wondered if they were positioned nearby. The makers of that road-sized trail were brazen and certainly not concerned with noise or discovery, moving as if they owned the night and challenged the day.

We followed the sign until we found an old French fort, half hidden in encroaching vines and foliage. It was not made of wood or sandbags but looked medieval above the tall grass, of huge permanent squares of stone. My impulse was to go to the fortress to see if the enemy were using it as their own, but Ken warned, "There are mines everywhere. They say the French saturated the place with them before they left so the Viets would not dare use it after they had gone." We reconned our way back to the FOB via the ridgeline and the barbed wire fence to the FOB, debriefing and dinner.

We were crossing the parade field when Doney called us over. "There are four Cambodes outside the gate who are looking for work. They say they have worked for SF in the Mike Force and have run recon before. You are short of indig on Florida. Why don't you check them out?"

Four more SCU was exactly what we needed to round us out and if they were already well trained by Special Forces, they were just what we needed. Ken and I met them at the gate. They were brown and muscular like the Montagnards, fierce looking and powerful as they waited, human weapons of war. No expression marked their faces, and one could easily conclude that when death came to them in his black hood and scythe, their lips would curl in a sneer. They were without weapons, and I wondered how they made it through the jungles of Cambodia and the Communist sanctuaries of the tri-border. They stood unsmiling, ready to strap on weapons and go to war. They were clearly mercenaries for hire, skilled professionals. We signed them in and escorted them to a secure place to meet the team and conduct an interview.

Throughout the interview I could only recall the story that Larry Torn told of some of these Cambodian mercenaries — how they met a group of Buddhist monks on the trail and left their bodies propped up at the edge, each with his severed head tucked in the crook of the respective dead monk's arms. My concern was their loyalty and their position on Communism. I had thoughts that they could easily turn on us in the field and kill us at an opportune time.

Ken was asking them questions regarding their training and the units they had worked for. I glanced at my four Vietnamese. They were tense. I knew that they would trust our judgment whatever we decided but I could not mistake their uneasiness. When Ken concluded his interview, we escorted them to the gate and told them we would get back with them.

"Well, what do you think of them?" Ken asked the team.

The four looked side to side at each other, then at Ken Worthley. "No, no. No trust Cambode. No trust.'

"Ba, what do you think?"

Ba's face was that of the North Vietnamese, high cheekbones and a face that expressed his thoughts. He shook his head and waved his hand back and forth. "No. No like. Maybe they VC. Maybe go field and fini Team Florida. Me no like."

"Does everyone feel the same way?"

"Yes!"

"Okay, but Florida has a mission, and it is just us then."

"No sweat," they all said, relieved to be rid of the Cambodes.

Lima Fifty. They were on us almost right away. Death came in our first two hours on the ground and left his shadow the entire time we were there. Our area was a ten-by-ten-kilometer square of highlands, miles-deep into Communist controlled territory, well beyond the range of our radios. Our target was smack in the backyard of base area 609, that spear-shaped piece of ground formed by the boundaries of Laos, Cambodia and South Vietnam. PAVN used it as a major staging area and sanctuary. When our boots left the struts of our helicopters that morning in Cambodia, they touched ground claimed by the bloody and elusive 66th NVA Regiment. The 66th were the crack shock troops that besieged Ben Het, Dak To and several other Special Forces camps.

Rain squalls delayed our landing until noon, until someone, perhaps it was Covey, suggested we follow a squall in, using the rain and clouds to hide behind until we reached our LZ. That we would survive the first hour was moot, so Covey stacked the sky with gunships and jets on standby. Florida was understrength and the weather was marginal, and as much as I would have liked to have more "guns" with us, I was glad we did not have the untested loyalty of those four Cambodian mercenaries among us.

I sat on the floor of the lead helicopter and leaned back on my pack with the radio's antenna wire looped over my shoulder and tucked under a shoulder strap. Through the open sliding door, I watched the second Huey catch up and position beside us. They flew close. The space between the two sets of spinning rotor blades had to have been a dare. Their pilot gestured to our pilot through his window and laughed at the private joke. The other half of our team was in this second chopper. All except Ba sat in the cloth seats where it was easier to stand when it was time to go. Ba was on his back leaning on his rucksack with his arms draped across his rifle. He looked across at me. He held up his Buddha for me to see and flashed his mouth-open smile then replaced the fat, smiling figure into his pocket. He patted the pocket twice with his hand to show me it was secure and next to his heart. At least it was not in his mouth this time. Bob Garcia sat next to him and waved. Bob ran recon with Ken Worthley before and volunteered to strap-hang with us, giving us another American on the team.

The other Huey dropped back and I felt an abrupt change in pitch.

Our pilot dropped our nose and through the window I saw a Cobra gunship cross our bow a few dozen feet below us — a fast, sleek hunter. We banked into an acute, spinning descent toward the tiny break in the trees that we had chosen for our LZ. It was picked because it was small, so small we hoped it would not warrant watchers to monitor it. I felt pressure in my gut and felt myself become lighter in weight as we spiraled down. The surrounding hills and the treetops blurred with the spinning. About the time I lost all concept of direction, the twisting abruptly ended in a hover just above the ground.

For seconds, the helicopter was low and stationary and vulnerable enough to be shot out of the air by the poorest of shooters. The grass lay flat under the blast of the rotors. Tall shrubs that were not quite trees surrounded the opening were lopped off by the blades. Leaves and branches cycloned in the air. Branches cracked like rifle fire as they were severed by the blades. The Hueys hovered just above the ground as we hopped from the struts. The door gunner wore black leather gloves as he grasped his machine gun and peered over the sights. He was ready to fire until the weapon was too hot to hold. I was slightly disoriented from our spinning descent but trusted that the pilot lined us up correctly and I hopped off the port-side door and ran toward the trees, ducking under the spinning rotor blades.

We waited in a small circle as the second lift descended with Bob and the other two Viets. Before they even cleared the field, the Huey rose and departed our area and disappeared over the hills where they waited for us to dismiss them.

We gave it five minutes. We barely breathed as we listened for signs of enemy. If they heard our landing, they could have forces rushing toward us. I looked at the decapitated bushes. If they came to investigate the sound of the choppers there would be no question that helicopters had descended into that opening in the trees. Ken looked back at me and nodded. I got on my face on the ground and whispered into the headpiece, "Team okay. Good day."

The jets and gunships that had stationed somewhere unseen left their place in the sky. Covey circled over the next set of ridges and waited to be sure his "chicks" were secure from the nest. It was noon.

The sun was high, and our shadows curled around our feet like timid things.

There were many trees down on the ground near our LZ. They were thin and leafless, with spindly limbs and they were dry, so passing through them without making noise was difficult. I felt exposed passing through empty spaces where trees once stood. It felt like we were walking through fields of fire, cleared by the enemy for ambush. We could see far ahead where we walked, but not at all into the shadowed thickness beyond. We entered dark, triple-canopy forest, the place of underbrush and shadow, and concealment. Monsoons were beginning and the streams filled their banks and ran quickly. Deep grass lined the banks and was matted down, but I could not make out individual footprints. Crossing this, our boots sank into wet mud, and I knew that Ba, our tail gunner was challenged to erase our passage and keep up.

We left the wet low area and proceeded along a ridge. An enemy presence was felt, but not evidenced. Like imagined ghosts in an old house, it seemed they were there, waiting and biding their time. We moved at tortoise speed, never moving until every blade of grass and every shadow was investigated. Noi, our Vietnamese cowboy who replaced Chin at point, crouched as he moved. Every twig or dried leaf was potential sound and Noi moved them to the side to clear the way for our feet. It would be left to Ba at the rear to replace them as they were. I heard a signal shot from the area of our LZ, but it was muffled in the brush and was far away and perhaps I did not hear it at all. We had not gone far from our starting place when we found trails. They were established ones and had signs of recent use. We found a trail that was the width of a vehicle. Soldiers could walk abreast if they chose. I looked above and saw that the tops of trees had been tied together and the branches formed an arch. The trail could not be seen from the air.

We slogged up the side of the ridge and our legs were soon like rubber, and we puffed with the weight of our packs and the steepness of the climb. Ken gave the palms down sign, and we sank slowly to the ground and watched and listened for movement.

It was dead quiet. No birds fluttered in the leaves. No insect placed its weight on a slender stalk and betrayed its presence. Nothing disturbed the grass. We waited in our line of march with our weapons ready. Ten minutes. My eyes were dry from looking for the faintest shiver in the grass. I imagined hearing the moisture evaporating from the greenery. Nothing living was in sight.

Nothing is louder than a firefight that erupts from absolute silence. Almost next to my ear, Ba fired half a magazine on full-automatic. The next one of us in line began to shoot. I saw bullets shred leaves next to me but saw no enemy. I scrambled to him with my rifle and tried to see the enemy soldiers. The first body was close and flat on the ground, obscured by the patch of thick leaves I had just watched. Ba shouted at me, "VC come." His eyes were still fast on the spot. He glanced at me only for a second. "Han-Son, VC, him die! Him be VC tracker. Him follow Team Florida."

Ba glanced at me again and back to the spot. "I see two VC. Him die but no see other VC. Where him go?"

Ba was frantic to locate the second enemy tracker. We did not hear him run away, crashing through the undergrowth. He had to still be there just waiting for a clear shot at us.

Then Bob Garcia squatted with an M-79 grenade launcher. His head moved left and right as he tried to look through the bushes in front of us. His head stopped traversing the bush and he slowly raised the launcher and aimed under the nearest limbs of a small tree. He fired and the round exploded, and I heard the body crumple on the ground a short distance away." I couldn't see the other one through the bushes at first," he said. "Then I saw his legs under the branches. I aimed at his legs."

Ba looked at me and reported, "VC trackers follow team. Two VC. Them die."

Bob was not sure if they were trackers. "Their rifles weren't at the ready. One of them had his rifle slung on his shoulder." Then he thought out loud, "They were following us but maybe did not know we were so close."

"Or maybe they needed their hands free to remove twigs from under their feet to move quietly," I wondered.

Ba had his rifle still aimed at the place where the first tracker fell in the grass. I could only see where he lay because his foot showed above the grass. The toes pointed skyward and did not move. Bob and I moved toward the second tracker. Perhaps he was still alive and could be taken prisoner.

Signal shots. Two of them. They came from beyond the belt of brush in front of us. They were not the "pop, pop," of the AK-47, but sounded more like the report of the SKS that some of the trackers carried. The shots were muffled by the leaves, and were close by. Twigs snapped as many men rushed us through the brush. Loud shouts came from two or three places. They were not angry shouts but that of scouts at the front giving direction to those behind. The shouting and the sounds of an advancing enemy grew as at least a company of men began to charge us.

At the front, Ken hissed to get our attention. He looked at Noi and pointed a direction for him to go. The Communists knew where we were. We needed to put distance between us, evade them and continue our mission. With them directly behind us in pursuit, a charge of adrenaline went through my legs. For one moment they were concrete, too heavy to lift. They seemed paralyzed, and I thought for a moment the team would be gone and the enemy would find me there unable to move. Then the moment passed, that five seconds of terror most of us experienced in some form, at some time, at least once, in the field. Blood returned into my core and my blurred vision returned to normal. We moved out in a fast walk, and I knew that Ba would not be able to hide our passage on the ground. We hustled northwest for fifty meters, then changed direction to the northeast. We could not hear pursuit, but knew they were somewhere behind us, following, calling in more soldiers, guessing our movement, setting up ambushes. At a point when we felt we had placed some distance between us, Ken held his hand up to stop. He gave Noi and the rest of us a sign to move now with caution. We fish-hooked to the southeast moving cautiously and slowly toward the enemy. Our new direction would have us converge on our own back trail. We hoped we could find a place of ambush to "fire them up" when they drew alongside. We would give them a reason not to chase us.

We moved at the speed of a glacier. Noi crouched ahead like someone probing the ground for a cobra, certain that explosive contact was imminent. We knew we were in the vicinity of our own backtrail. If the enemy used trackers to follow, they would pass this way. At a place, we found good cover and concealment, and could see a length of the path. If the timing were right, we could take out a dozen of them. We did not have time to set out Claymores, so we settled in and blended into the forest. Our danger was that they might have passed this place already and could emerge behind us.

We waited.

The shrubs and grass betrayed no movement. There was no sound — but then we had not heard the trackers either. A half hour. Nothing. Then, a hundred yards into the trees a dog barked, the sound, muffled by the undergrowth. The image of the death-grey hound the NVA used to find SOG people came to my mind. A voice drifted through the greenery, of a handler talking to his dog. Then I heard the soofing sound that warm Autumn breezes make over brown leaves. No breeze stirred the trees and I pictured dozens of enemy trouser legs brushing against the undergrowth. Two soldiers appeared out of the shrubs, and I heard heavy movement around us. Noi and Ken engaged them, and both went down. I heard a shout and the sound of several men crashing through the brush. To my side, three NVA in mustard-colored uniforms rose and began to shoot at me. I returned fire and two went down. I was out of ammunition and reached for a new magazine. The enemy had AK-47s with their thirty-round magazines, while we men in recon still only had twenty-round magazines.

I had practiced magazine drills a hundred times and could change magazines in two seconds. But in those two seconds, I faced an enemy who still had ten rounds in his weapon. He fired on full automatic, and several rounds hit my hand as it reached for a magazine. My middle finger hung by a piece of skin, the fingernails and ends of the other three fingers were shot off, and the knuckle of my index finger was shot away. The hanging finger got in the way. I glanced down and saw the problem, then I used the tip of my little finger and my thumb to insert a new magazine. Several of us shot at the third man at the same time and he went down. "I think him die," Ba said. I pulled a field dressing from my harness but could not tie the knot. Ken came over and I turned my hand over and flipped the swinging finger into the palm of my hand so I would not lose it, as he tied the knot. There was heavy movement in the brush. Ken pointed a direction for Noi, and we broke contact and began to evade. Bob and I sprinkled CS powder on our backtrail and hoped that when the hounds sniffed it up their noses, they would be ruined the rest of the day.

For the next two hours we evaded our pursuers, switching direction, fish-hooking back to ambush our backtrail, using every trick we had learned from the old SOG warriors. Midafternoon it seemed that we had evaded them, at least for now. We moved along a ridgeline where there were many trails and every indication of heavy enemy activity. We made a security stop to watch our backtrail. My hand ached and I had no way to stop the bleeding. Across a ridgeline that opposed us there was indication of a very heavy enemy presence. From the far left to the right, the North Vietnamese soldiers shouted, their officers and sergeants ordering the movement of their platoons. Dogs barked. Other dogs bayed, hounds on a scent, and I pictured their handlers being yanked ahead by taut leashes.

Our shadows were long. We were at the time of day when the last of the birds make their final peep before they bend their legs on a limb and cause their feet to grasp the branch. Our next step was clear. We needed to evade them and find a place to hole up for the night. The dogs were a problem. Bob laced the area where we had just stopped with a generous amount of his powdered CS. It was his last, but I had some left that we could use when we found an RON.

Noi led us out. From the map there was a shallow hill that led into a steep, narrow gully. We would change direction a time or two, lace the route near the place with a dose of CS, and pass the night. When the dogs sniffed the powder near us, we hoped their yelping would alert us to their nearness. We found a decent place just as we were losing most of the light we would need to set up for the night. We were tucked in and hard to find, and we could anticipate their likely approach and had a means to evade if we had to. We found our places in our little circle and settled in to memorize our surroundings, and we waited for the day.

That night I lay on my belly in the total darkness of the jungle without moving, the detonators of four Claymore mines in my hands, and waited for the Communists to come for us. My hand that was wrapped in the bloody bandage had bled and coagulated repeatedly during the day and dried hard into a red cast with just my thumb and the tip of my little finger sticking out. I felt where the ends of my fingers were shot away and two of the nails were bent backwards and lay across the back of my fingers. The forefinger was stiff with the mangled joint and I felt the hanging finger as it lay there in the palm of my hand like a gathered thing. To make up for the measured use of that hand I braced the detonators on a firmness of earth and positioned the heels of my hands on the triggers. I kept rubbing the fingers of my good hand over the detonators, counting them, keeping them aligned side by side.

My fingers were nervous. "One, two, three, four, one, two, three, four," they counted, over and over as they passed across the plungers and kept them side by side.

When the time came to press those detonators, I hoped that nothing would be living to my front.

The enemy had a general idea where we might be — the direction of our running firefights, the signal shots of their trackers, and the baying of their dogs that chased us said that much. But we always changed the direction we moved, especially after an encounter, so they did not know for certain where we holed up for the night. Throughout the day, however, they massed large forces into the area to seal us off. We were effectively surrounded as they concentrated troops and ambushes into the area and constricted us. When finally the North Vietnamese could fix our location, they would sweep up our hill where it could be our final battle — unless my Claymores cut a swath through the assault, and we could fight our way through the cordon. We would evade, ambush and move, over and over until we made it to "friendlies."

If we could not break out, we would fight in place until the end, and hope that help could arrive with fire support from our aircraft.

Until then the Communists were scouring every inch of ground, of that I was certain. We were miles behind enemy lines, deep into denied territory, and had blooded their people today. Perhaps thousands of NVA were on the other side of the shrubs prepared to kill or capture us.

I heard a thumping sound.

Was my heart beating so loudly that it could be heard? I held my breath to isolate the sound. I shut my eyes so I could focus only on my ears. I listened. My ears probed the blackness for any sound.

It was a still night and sound carried. Most nights behind the lines, if you listened for it, you could hear a sleeping monkey as it shifted its weight in a tree, or the sighing of brown grass when the barking deer passed, or the knuckled legs of two bamboo stalks rubbing together as they gave up the moisture of the day. But this night was utterly still.

It seemed that nature held its breath where we were tucked in a grove of bamboo in the side of a hill. I heard a breaking sound like someone moving in the dense undergrowth, then realized that it came from a length of bamboo that popped with the temperature change of the night. Would the searching enemy think it came from us? But a seasoned tribesman would have shushed the searching soldiers nearby and said, "No, no, bamboo pop. No soldier do."

When I could no longer hold my breath, I let it out as easily as I could, and the passing air seemed loud to me. I shut my eyes again and listened. Dry grass rustled nearby, a long continuous shushing in the weeds. A snake was hunting for prey. Even a cobra was more welcome than an enemy point man closing in.

I continued to listen.

I heard the drone of an engine, faint and far away, and I hoped it was our spotter airplane coming to check on us before leaving for the night so we could advise him of our situation and perhaps get a gunship to circle nearby.

But the sound did not pass over us. Instead the pitch of the engine changed like a burdened truck downshifting for a change in grade. From over the shoulder of a nearby ridge a faint glimmer of light, like a quarter moon shows long before it crests the top, indicated that a truck was coming toward the stand of bamboo where we hid.

Unbeknownst to us, a finger of the Ho Chi Minh Trail — that vital lifeline that the Communists built to carry their soldiers and supplies to the war in South Vietnam — lay below us from left to right. The intervening hills and thick vegetation muted the sound of the engines as they drove across our front.

I heard the thumping sound again. This time I knew it was not my heartbeat. There were several muffled thumps across our front from far down the slope. The engines stopped and there were many thumping sounds. They were very faint and far away, but they were there. At the end, I heard a dull clank of metal. Even in the distance I knew that it was a tailgate.

I imagined hundreds of soldiers in yellow-green uniforms leaping from the truck beds and lining the ditches along the road, waiting for the command to sweep up the hillside.

I heard the muffled woof of a dog, and I remembered the grey, long-legged ones from before. I hoped that the CS powder would work, and I was glad that we had no rain to wash it away. The indications were that they were coming for us, and this would be a fight of desperation. There was a light tap on my shoulder, then a whole hand grasped my shoulder. We could not see each other in the dark so he placed his mouth at my ear.

"Han-Son. Han-Son. VC come. *Beaucoup VC.*" Many enemy soldiers are coming.

I patted his arm twice in the darkness to let him know that I heard it too. I turned and tapped the Viet on the other side of me with the back of my wounded hand so it would not start to bleed again. I could feel him nod his head and he shifted his weight over his weapon.

I aligned the detonators side by side again and counted them, "One, two, three, four."

We listened and we heard nothing. Nothing at all.

None of us in our little recon team moved. Our people did not thrust their rifles farther forward to be ready to shoot. None of them piled grenades in front of them. We were frozen, listening, waiting people.

Not a sound.

Had the enemy changed its mind and decided to not sweep our hill? Were they waiting for us to come down in the morning where they waited?

Perhaps I expected a whistle to sound from below and muted commands and then the crashing of hundreds of feet through the undergrowth as they moved toward us. None of that occurred.

Nothing.

A half hour. An hour. Nothing stirred to our front. Exhaustion had its way. My eyes closed with the plungers cradled in my hands.

I snapped awake. I heard a soft breaking of twigs in the distance to the right. Did I imagine it?

"It could be an animal," I thought. But then as I listened there were other sounds across the front. Several creatures were moving on line toward us. They were moving with stealth in our direction.

I remembered the dogs. They would be among them, their noses skimming just above the ground. But for them, the Communists might sweep through us without finding us.

I began to pray. "Lord, plug the noses of those dogs." My fingers began to count the plungers again: "One, two, three, four...."

I felt Quan stretch forward where he lay beside me. I sensed that he pushed his rifle forward and freed the arm he had been leaning on. Ba was next to him on my right, and I heard the brush of his sleeves as he prepared himself. There was a space between us and the rest of the team and there was no indication that any of them heard anything. We were normally touch-close and able to alert one another. Were they set or unaware? I was concerned that an accidental shift of their bodies or loud breathing in sleep could give us away.

Those of us on the right heard soft movement to our front. I recalled that movement was possible in the darkness without sound. A friend in the Mike Force told me that one night an elephant moved through the jungle completely unnoticed by the team. The elephant stepped on a Montagnard who was watching for movement in the bushes. The elephant felt the tribesman's soft body under his foot, gently lifted his foot, then silently continued its way into the forest.

"Plug the noses of those dogs," I prayed again.

The faint sounds of movement passed our position and from time to time I heard the tread of feet moving away, like the desultory drop of rain after a shower has passed.

An hour or two later the sky began to lighten shade by shade until shrubs showed in silhouette. I wondered if the experience of the night had been shared by the rest of the team. My glance in their direction gave no indication. To my right, Ba was crumpled in exhausted slumber, the flesh of his cheek scrunched up by his forearm. He seemed peaceful as he lay now, but as I looked, a golden chain hung from an object that was in his mouth.

We took stock of our situation as we squeezed rations into our mouth. Ken wrote up a SITREP and waited for Covey to make his presence known. Around seven or eight we heard an engine to the east. With my experience of the night, my first thought was of trucks, but then as the airplane crested the ridgeline, we contacted our lifeline. SITREP completed, we moved to the north, mindful of the possibility the enemy may have located us in the night and were stationed to our front.

Trails were numerous and well used as we moved to the north, deeper into the sanctuary of the NVA. The paths were hard-packed grey clay, as smooth as a city sidewalk. The vegetation was thick at the sides and the trees were full and leafy and hundreds could walk past and never make a sound. We set up along one of these. We did not trust our ears to alert us to coming soldiers, so we watched where the path emerged from the bushes. Then they appeared like magic in front of us — several of them, alert and in full uniform. We opened fire. In moments it was over, and the column was dispatched. We swept the trail and while our Viets secured the ambush site, we Americans charged forward to the place where the trail emerged from the bushes. Ken and Bob dropped down to examine two of the soldiers while I secured the trail ahead, firing my rifle and tossing grenades. I rushed back and joined Ken.

Two enemy lay crumpled on the ground. The markings on their uniforms indicated they were both Colonels. They were taller than most Vietnamese, very well-groomed officers, in clean uniforms. One of the officers had a Tokarov pistol on his belt. The first Colonel had a leather satchel slung over one shoulder. He was a very high-ranking Communist courier. Noi slipped up to us. He seemed astonished as he spoke. "Chinese," he said. "Him Chinese man. No Vietnam."

We began to hear shouting. Dozens of men shouted commands in Vietnamese from numerous locations. There was shooting around us.

I glanced into the satchel. Lists, papers which appeared to be official orders. Bundles of American money. Was he a spy paymaster? "This is a treasure trove," I said.

There was movement all around us and random shots riddled the leaves above our heads. Ken began to undress the Colonel. We had a bag, and we would take everything. In the end, Saigon would know everything to know about him and his equipment.

His shirt came off. Our first shots must have killed him instantly for there was little blood on his chest or in his clothing. I watched the blood rise a half inch above the holes in his torso then sink back into his body as his arms left the shirt and his body fell back to the ground. All went into a bag, shoes, clothes, a sample of hair, the contents of his pockets. As we did so the incoming bullets were impacting just above our heads.

Angry shouts came from all quarters as advancing troops crashed through the bushes. A hound bayed. In the movie, the Baskerville hound's howl echoed through the megaphones of stone caverns, but the hounds behind us were muffled in the thickness of the forest, sounding like nightmares we might hear as children as we hid our heads under flannel blankets. We gathered the bag of clothes and the satchel. Ken pointed a direction to Noi and we quickly moved off the trail. Bob covered while Ba hid our egress from the site. Hundreds of troops began the chase to catch us. It was evident when the NVA found the actual ambush site and found their couriers and the missing satchel. The clamor of the chase filled the woods behind us. Our task now was to contact Covey, evade the enemy and find an LZ.

I gave the radio to Garcia and we raised Covey and declared a Prairie Fire Emergency. All air assets would be diverted to our location. We were given the highest priority. Covey circled over and we popped smoke. "Direct you, Lima Zulu, one hundred meters, zero nine five degrees. How copy?"

"Copy five by. Get here fast!" Garcia shouted into the set.

We fought our way to the LZ for the next twenty minutes. Twice we stopped and ambushed our back trail then ran on. At the edge we felt the fury of the attackers. According to Covey later, there were hundreds of them attacking us. I took out two of them at the very edge and seized the rifle of one of them. It was an M-2 carbine. They were charging us in mass with rifles, machine guns and mortars.

Ken shouted, "Dale, cover us from that side." We had no one on the flank and I ran to the place just as they were rushing us from that side. The ground sloped down from there and I held them off with my rifle. There were numerous explosions and gunshots around me, yet I heard the bullets hiss through the grass. Bullets mowed the grass in front of me. Someone needed my rifle on the other side of the LZ and I gave them my M-16 as I was slow changing magazines with just my thumb and tip of my little finger. I had the carbine. The smell of the soldier's sweat and fear and death clung to the weapon. It was as if his last minute in life was forever stamped on his weapon. I was firing as quickly as I could when a burst was directed at me from the side. One of the rounds would have struck me in the face and broken my cheek-bone but it went between the fingers of my good hand as I aimed the rifle and went through the comb of the rifle and stopped just at my skin. The rifle stock was splintered, flimsy and barely held together.

Years later, I met Rich Ryan who flew Covey that day. He told me that I held off three platoons at that slope.

One of the SCU crouched his way to me and handed me another rifle — my third one on the LZ.

We were under intense fire. Sources later told us that perhaps a thousand soldiers attacked us and sought to recover the leather satchel. Covey directed the gunships to fire danger-close to us and the incoming bullets cut down bushes and trees as well as the enemy. B-40 rockets descended on us as we fought.

"Han-Son, Han-Son, Han-Son"

I heard my name called over all the noise of the fight. "Han-Son, Han-Son."

It was Ba. He was standing straight up under fire and faced me. His face was distraught and in anguish. I faced him and ran a few paces to see what he wanted.

"Han-Son, Han-Son. Worthley, him die. Worthley, him die!"

It took a moment for it to sink in. He lay in a pile at Ba's feet. "Worthley, him die."

In the anguish that I read in his features I completely misunderstood what he wanted of me. I had been their leader and friend. He wanted me to tell him what we had to do. But I misunderstood him. I shouted back at him, "Well, what do you want me to do about it?" I thought Ba wanted me to bring him back to life. In the absurdity of what I thought he said I had blurted out those words. Then the full situation came to me. I glanced around the field. It was a maelstrom of explosions and as far as I could tell it seemed that only Ba and I were left alive. I had to get Ken's body home and save the team and the satchel.

I heard a chopper coming and saw that it was not going to land but they had thrown down ropes so we could go out on strings. "Get him out of here!" I pointed at Ken and made my finger like a hook and pointed to ken's chest. I pointed to the descending chopper than back at Ken. "Get Sergeant Worthley out of here." Then I pointed at the satchel and motioned for him to put it down Ken's shirt and get the briefcase out with his body. "Understand?"

Ba stood there only a moment, not wanting to leave me there alone.

"Do it!" I shouted, and he scrambled to one of the ropes which hung below the hovering helicopter, made a loop in the line and snapped it into the ring on Ken's harness.

The noise on the LZ was that of one long, continuous explosion. They fired a barrage of mortars and RPGs at us as well as machine gun and AK fire. Our gunships fired 6,000 rounds a minute from each of our mini-guns, plus 40mm cannon fire. F-4 Phantom jets dropped 250-pound bombs in the trees all around the opening where Florida fought for its life.

"Dale! Dale!"

I didn't know there was anyone left to call me. It was Bob Garcia.

"Where is Ken?" he screamed above the noise.

"He's dead."

"What?" Bob's voice was that of incredulity and anguish.

"He's dead, Bob. He was shot in the neck. I already sent him out."

He seemed to collapse in a heap, but rather crouched and shouted into the handset at the A-1 SPAD pilot. "I want 500-pound bombs fifty meters out."

I was close enough to hear the jet pilot answer back. "Are you crazy? I can't tell fifty meters from five-hundred meters from up here. You will be killed."

"I tell you we are being overrun. I want it at fifty meters right now."

"Are you sure?"

Bob screamed into the handset, "I said fifty meters and I want it right now. That is an order."

My side of our defensive circle was getting hot again and I ran back with more ammunition and my third rifle of the fight. The enemy kept coming. Their numbers never lessened. There was a roar that shut out all other sound as SPAD crossed low above me, followed by the explosion of 500-pound bombs which fell nearly on us. I felt my fatigues flatten on my body with the pressure of the explosions. My eyes were slammed shut by the blast. Shrapnel shredded the leaves just above my head.

Another Phantom passed over our heads followed by the blast of the bombs. We could barely stand during the runs. Surely, nothing could live in the area around our perimeter. I recalled that when our SOG teams had to call in support around them in the past, the enemy crept as close as possible, thinking it impossible for us to call in air on them without hitting ourselves as well. As the jets dropped their load, the NVA made every effort to get near us — grenade close. And despite the massive casualties they must have been suffering, they seemed to keep coming.

I screamed above the noise of battle. Did anyone hear me? "You people get out. I will hold them off."

I had already thrown nearly all my grenades but could no longer pull the pins, nor throw them with my bandaged hand. I thought I heard a helicopter and when I glanced that way, saw nothing. No one seemed to be left on the ground. I had given the radio to Bob long before. I thought I was alone. Then I remembered the RT-10 radio in my pouch. The frequency was set and all our aircraft in that part of the world monitored it. I did not know what to say and I just blurted out, "Is there anybody out there?"

I know my voice was high with adrenaline and shock, and I know that I talked fast. I needed for that moment to know that I was not alone. Then the voice of Nick Ryan, our Covey of the day, came over the set. It was clear and calm and assuring. "We got you Dale. We will get you out."

That was all that I needed. Our danger was not diminished. I just needed to know someone was out there. A calm settled over me.

"Han-Son, Han-Son!" My name was shouted above the sounds of the fight and I heard it. "Han-Son, Han-Son!" It was Noi. A Huey hovered above the LZ and he and Bob were strapped into one of the ropes that had been thrown from the helicopter. They waved their arms to me to come. Their movements were broad and desperate for we were under intense fire. I rushed toward them, half the time shooting and walking backward, and they waved me to hurry. Would we be shot there on the LZ at just the moment of salvation? I glanced toward them. Three ropes were suspended from the aircraft. I watched as the massive number of bullets directed at us shot through one of the three lines, and I watched as the rope fell through the air like a writhing yellow snake and thud to the ground.

"Dale, hurry, hurry," Bob shouted.

The end of the third rope lay on the ground and I wondered if I could tie myself in with my hand wrapped as it was, but I made a huge loop in the line and pulled it into itself making a loop and snapped it into the snap-link of my McGuire Rig. I know the pilot could not see me or that I was ready, but he began to lift off just the same.

We started to lift off under the helicopter and as we rose, the enemy charged the LZ and they rushed the field trying to get to me to pull me off the rope. I was shooting at them as fast as I could and they were shooting at me. I felt myself get shot in the back of the head. I vividly recall the sound that came out of my mouth: "Nghaah."

I did not pass out, but I knew that I had been shot again. I touched the place with one hand to know how bad the wound was. Did it pierce my skull? My fingernails passed over the place a second time and pulled the pieces of metal from the wound. I would be fine.

The heavy volume of fire directed at us and the Huey was enough for the pilot. He began to leave the area as quickly as he could. But instead of rising high enough for us to clear the trees, we were dragged through them. We knocked against them and we slammed against a tangle of trees and were about to be torn apart. The ropes were stuck fast in a crotch of two trees. The Huey was pulling from above. The rope was stretching and taut and it appeared that the helicopter was about to be pulled out of the sky. I knew that in seconds a frantic pilot would order the door gunner to cut the lines and let us fall to the ground and certain death or capture. I hung below the others on the strings and I hacked desperately with my knife at the tangle. At the moment the crew chief was about to cut the rope, I hacked through the last of the tangle and we sprang free, shot like a rubber band into the sky and in a minute were thousands of feet above the battle.

The noise of battle that was of a volume that I cannot describe, was gone. Below us, thousands of feet below, was a mass of smoke and napalm and the white flash of explosions as our jets and SPAD wasted the area. The regiment that attacked us now fled the other way to escape the fury of the ordnance.

For a time, I spun in the air for my rope was not yet joined to the one from which Bob and Noi hung. I spun clockwise until it seemed that the rope could not take more, then unwound the other direction. I was becoming sick, and when the chopper banked and brought me next to the other rope, I grabbed it and stopped the spinning. The banking to my side lowered my rope and gave the impression that my rope was parting. I recalled the bullets shooting through one rope and I saw myself falling thousands of feet to my death. I glanced under me, then grabbed Bob's rope and held it in a death grip the whole way back.

The choppers had been on station max-time using most of their fuel as they waited for the ordnance to pound the enemy so they could come in and get us. They were nearly out of fuel. Ben Het would be the closest place to go. They took an azimuth and proceeded in that direction. They would come in on fumes. We passed through a storm with heavy rain en route. They did not have the fuel to go around it, and the went directly through the storm with us hanging below. The rain slapped us like needles and stung. They were cold and painful and the wetness and wind made us shiver — but we were alive.

The chopper slowed over Ben Het until we hung directly under the helicopter before it descended. Norm Doney and Mike Buckland steadied us as we touched the ground and helped us out of our harnesses. It was only then that I realized how messed up I was. I staggered like a drunk. My mouth was dry and I could barely form words. I could not say a complete sentence. Doney and Mike both hugged me. I felt stupid at my lack of control. I wanted to know that my people were okay. I stumbled over to Noi and stared at him. I think I said, "Are you okay. Are you hurt anywhere," but the sounds that came out of my mouth were that of someone with a stroke.

It had been only twenty-four hours but I was spent. I was embarrassed and ashamed of my condition, but it had been a time of great pressure — pure adrenaline for all that time. I figured that I had been wounded three times in twenty-four hours, my roommate had been killed, one of my people had been slightly wounded and we faced the 66th NVA regiment in their own backyard — but I was not satisfied with myself. I felt weak and tired, but I wanted this mission to end as it should.

"Choo ga ja sjell?" I asked Doney, looking him straight in the eye speaking with all the sincerity of my being. Doney stared at me for a time. He had to digest this missive I was relaying. And he then smiled. "Yes, we got the satchel, Dale. Bob gave it to us."

Someone gave me a soft drink. It was ice cold and its wetness and carbonation were a thing of unmatched pleasure. I closed my eyes and savored it. I drank again and soofed it between my teeth and lips and I sensed I could perhaps speak a clear sentence. I took two uncertain steps and realized that it was not weariness alone that made me walk like a drunk. My legs had been battered when I was slammed against the trees and I was glad the bones and joints seemed to be intact. I glanced at my pants. They were torn in places and tattered. I willed myself to speak coherently and I framed the thoughts into words before I let them pass my lips.

"Ken… is… dead," I said.

Their eyes commiserated with mine. "Yes. We got him, Dale. His body is safe. He will be sent home to his family."

"He… was brave… and calm," I said.

They nodded, for they knew that he would be so.

I took a long breath and lifted one arm toward Noi. "Everyone…?"

"Everyone got out. One slightly wounded. We will take them to the FOB."

"Satchel," I said the word like a statement, a subject to be discussed.

"We have it and I looked inside. SOG is already on the way with a jet to pick it up." Doney put his hand on my shoulder. "What is inside is massive. The man you got was perhaps the highest-ranking Communist official ever taken behind the lines. It looks like he was a senior Chinese intelligence officer. There were lists of names in the case and with the money, we would guess he was a spy paymaster."

A captain walked over to us. "We are ready gentlemen, all fueled and waiting."

"That's our ride, Dale. We are going to go with you to Pleiku Hospital to make sure that they take care of you and make sure that no unauthorized people try to talk to you."

Mike held my shoulder as we made our way, but I felt my steps grow stronger and I did not stagger.

I woke from my bed in Pleiku hospital from something poking me in the side. It was a sharp poke and annoying enough to wake me from deep slumber. I lifted the sheet and looked at the source. It was the corner of a three by five card that poked the thin skin of my side. With my good hand I picked it up. Pinned through the card was a tiny oak leaf cluster. I nearly laughed out loud. Your first Purple Heart is a beautiful award with the face of George Washington in the top and it is usually received in ceremony. Technically, for your subsequent wounds you receive an oak leaf cluster, one for each of the next four wounds. I had apparently been awarded another Purple Heart. Without ceremony or document, I received the tiny pin affixed to a paper card that had been tossed on my stomach while I slept.

There were two rows of beds in the ward. I was in the same row that Jan Novey occupied, but on the opposite end. The beds beside me and across were empty and I wondered if that was done to isolate me because of our classified mission. I was near the end of the ward and bright daylight shone under the door. I started to get up but an orderly appeared.

"Is it all right to go outside?"

"No, I'm sorry Sergeant. We can't let the patients go out on their own."

"The sun might do me some good."

"Yes, but..." Here he glanced about him toward some of the patients in the beds. "Some of these guys could just wander away.... You know."

I lay back and presently that door opened and out of that great rectangle of light walked Norm Doney and Mike Buckland. It was wonderful to see them and after a time, as the orderly passed by, Doney told him, "We need to talk with the sergeant privately on a classified matter. We will be right outside."

We walked into the warmth of the day and it was wonderful to stretch my battered legs and breathe the outside air. My bandages were clean and white, and I hooked my thumb in a buttonhole of my shirt to hold the ache above my heart.

"I just want you to know about the satchel and what they told us so far," Doney said in his avuncular way. "The price of that piece of leather was the life of Ken Worthley — a good man, a brave man, and we would never trade the two. But we got a lot from his sacrifice. What I am telling you is for you, and it is classified, but you have a right to know."

Mike Buckland handed me a Coke, cold and with wetness sliding down the side.

"The Colonel you shot was perhaps the top intelligence agent in the country. And he was, as we thought, a spy paymaster. He had a list of all his agents in two provinces. The money that was in the leather satchel was for them. There were documents to be given to all his agents that read, 'All agents must lay low because the Americans have unmasked Thai Khac Chuyen.' His name also appears in the list of spies the colonel was to pay."

Doney gave me time to digest the importance of what he had just revealed to me. He spoke to me formally as he finished. "Thai Khac Chuyen was the double agent that Colonel Rheault is accused of murdering. That satchel which you guys captured contained the absolute proof that Mr. Chuyen was no innocent citizen but an embedded spy."

For a moment as I stood outside the hospital walls, my bare feet in the hot sand wearing only hospital pajamas, I considered the enormity of it all. A so-called murder in the crowded capital city of bustle and lights and pedicabs and diplomats and ambassadors and perhaps a million people — resolved by a tiny recon team that fought for its life in a remote and forbidden jungle sanctuary owned by the enemy. It was too improbable to be just serendipity. Perhaps the very guiding hand that protected us also led us to the satchel

Chapter Seventeen

HOSPITALS AND CONVALESCENT LEAVE

I slipped out of the hospital ward just after the orderly made his rounds. I pulled the covers tight where I had been and just walked out the door into the brightness of the day. No crumpled sheets to advertise a bed with no patient in it. In the scheme of things, my wounds were not major, although my body was indeed banged up and stiff. I placed my hand on the edge of the cot to stand and hobbled the first steps but was fine after that.

I needed to be outside the ward for just an hour. I was tired of hearing the continuous snore that came from the soldier with the Charlie Chaplin face across the way. In all the time I had been here he had been on his back, never moving, never opening his eyes. Just before breakfast the orderlies slid a sheet over a soldier farther down the line and rolled him out. He had been burned, I think, as they had a thin sheet around his bed until they wheeled him away. A young man near me in the line of cots saw it. He was a clerk and was here for a hernia and he looked at me with wide, terrified eyes and kept asking me, "Is he? Is he? Is he?" over and over.

So, I slipped out and found a place nearby with a seat with a back on it. I wanted to sit in the sun and see a bird — any kind of bird — fly over. I wanted to hear the swish of its wings when it saw me and changed direction. I wanted to smell the orient drifting in from the paddies with the smell of feces and mud plowed together around the hand-planted rice starts — an honest smell of toil feeding the generations. I wanted to see the walk of the laborers of the fields, who, even as they walked in the streets lifted their knees high as they stepped, as they did in the field, pulling them out of the paddy mud. And I wanted to see young Vietnamese women walk by with the natural grace that only ladies of the orient seem to possess.

Several of our orderlies were gathered under an awning. One of them slipped his transistor radio over a nail and as they listened to the song played, those who knew the words tried to sing. But all of them belted out the chorus.

> *It wasn't me*
> *That started that old crazy Asian war*
> *But I was proud to go*
> *And do my patriotic chore*
> *And yes, it's true that*
> *I'm not the man I used to be*

I might see my bird overhead, but with the singing nearby there was no way that I would hear the free air pass over the stiff feathers. I heard helicopters coming in. The beat of the blades was the same speed a small bird's heart makes when held in the palm of your hand. I watched it descend through the cloud of dust it raised and land on the steel pad — a large red cross was on the side and the orderlies under the awning grabbed stretchers and ran to meet it. The transistor dangled from the nail and as the chopper shut down, I heard the last refrain, "Oh Ruby, for God's sake, turn around."

"So, this is where you hide."

"I guess I better find a better place since you found me so quickly, Sergeant Doney."

Doney smiled that grin that he seemed to reserve for me. He was daubing the tears that continued to seep from where the shrapnel struck just under his right eye. Mike Buckland was beside him and handed me a can of cold Coke. "You can read my mind, Mike."

"That's the third Medivac chopper in an hour," I said. "Something is happening somewhere."

Mike answered, "It's the Fourth Infantry — the firebase that is close to the FOB. Sappers got in through the wire and slugged it out with them. They say they took as many casualties as they dished out."

"Did the intel guys come by yet?"

"A Captain from S-2 came by, but he didn't debrief me about the mission. He just wanted to remind me, as if I did not know, that our missions were classified, and I shouldn't talk to anyone."

Doney said, "Let's go over to that awning. I want you to have an update."

We walked to the place abandoned by the orderlies and Doney reached up and shut off the transistor radio and the singer who sang:

I'm so dizzy, my head is spinnin'
Like a whirlpool, it never ends
And it's you girl, makin' it spin
You're makin' me dizzy...

Doney put his beret into his side pocket and looked around to be sure there was no one in hearing distance. He lowered his voice and said, "Saigon is excited with what you guys found. Worthley would be proud. I am going to update you on what else we have learned so far — it is just beginning, and Saigon will probably not tell us everything. You deserve to know what your sacrifice got us."

Doney daubed his cheek and Mike slid a Coke across to him. "To start with, our Chinese paymaster friend had the list of every spy in Kontum and Binh Dinh province. He was giving them money and was warning them to lie low, as you know."

Mike added, "The CIA Phoenix Program will take months getting rid of them. Just think of the dilemma they are in: When Rheault was arrested, the CIA threw us under the bus and said, 'Oh no, we don't kill spies.' And now we give them a list of spies and double agents they need to get rid of. I'd love to see their faces when they get the list."

"More," Doney said. "Our Chinese Colonel was not only an intelligence official, but he was a political Commissar. Remember the siege of Ben Het we just had? Well, the casualties they were having must have been horrendous. Our Chinaman had a list of more than fifty soldiers who had shot themselves in the arms and legs so they could not be a part of the charges. He was coming to administer punishment. He had the list of names of those he would go after."

As the Medivac lifted off, a pair of the interns left the pad and walked in our direction but when they saw us there, they veered off to one of the wards. Mike watched them as he spoke. "We found a few ID cards from some of our GIs. We haven't heard if they were MIA or prisoners. All we know so far is that their cards were in Cambodia."

He sipped his soft drink and continued, "We found eighty pages of top secret orders in the satchel. Saigon will probably not tell us what those orders were or the significance they will have now that Hanoi knows we have them. What was it? Robert E. Lee's orders of the battle were found wrapped around a bunch of cigars, and no one believed they were real."

We watched as a fourth Medivac helicopter landed on the pad and we were glad when only one cot was needed, and we considered that the toll of loss was ended. Doney looked back at us. "One more thing before we go. You know about the tunnels the Communists have that honeycomb under the whole country. They say that the Cu Chi tunnels alone are 120 miles long. Well, our Chinese colonel was also going to give awards and praise to two underground factories and an underground staging area complete with a hospital. Well, our Colonel needed to be able to find them to give them the awards of the Hanoi government, so the coordinates were there in the satchel. You can bet our B-52 squadrons have them now also."

"Well, get better soon. We will want you back at the FOB.

That afternoon they moved me into another ward. There were no other patients in the room. They had removed my bandages and I was sickened by what I saw. About the time I sat upright in the bed and considered what must be in store for me, two surgeons entered the room, one on either side of my bed. The one on my left was considerably older than the other. He wore hospital scrubs and he had coarse black hair with grey on the tips as if the ends were dusted in flour. The other was thin and young, certainly not thirty. His movements were quick and fidgety and there seemed to be an excitement about him and an electricity about his fingertips. They talked over the top of me as if I were not there. The younger had a marker and he traced it along the back of my hand along the middle bone of my hand.

"See," he said with a measure of excitement to the older doctor, "We could remove that metacarpal and suture the hand together and no one would notice the missing finger."

"What!"

He finally noticed that a person was attached to the hand.

"Yes," he said. Here he retraced the line down the center of the back of my hand. "We will remove that bone and close up the hand."

And before he could continue with his conquest of my hand I said, "And give me a woman's hand. You would take out a perfectly sound bone of a perfectly healthy hand and you would proceed from a bad finger to a ruined hand also. No, you will not."

"We decide what is best for you," he said with the emphasis on *we*.

"Actually, we are talking about my hand," I said, emphasizing *my*. "It belongs to me."

"Soldier, you are the property of the United States Government. You do not get to decide."

"Let me make it clear to you. You will not touch my hand."

The younger surgeon glanced over at the other with a look that communicated to him, "Explain to this ignorant lout." And he short-stepped out of the room.

When he had left, the older doctor said, "It will be up to us to decide, not you."

"Then let me make it clear to you: If you touch my hand, I will kill you."

The major stepped back. Fury fogged his eyes and he spit out the words. "Soldier, I will have you court marshalled for this. You cannot threaten a superior officer. You will be on charges."

"Major, I did not stutter. If you touch my hand, I will kill you. I am a crazed Green Beret who has just come out of the field and has taken whatever meds you have given him. What do you think I will do?"

The major glared at me. If he were a bull, steam would have come out of his nose and ears. Without another word, he turned and left the room.

The next morning, on their orders, I was on a plane for Saigon, far removed from the two doctors, and I was scheduled for the very next jet to Japan.

The aircraft was a commercial airliner chartered by the United States Government, one of the fleets designated to take the wounded from the war zone to hospitals in Japan. We were crammed inside, shoulder touching shoulder in extra narrow seats, seats that were rigid, upright and could not be tilted lest we find ourselves in the lap of the patient behind us. Even the rows were closer together to squeeze in more patients. The baggage bins which are normally found in a commercial airliner were removed and hooks were suspended from the ceiling. Stretchers were hung over the seats of the cabin — two cots on the left side of the aisle and two cots on the right side, the whole length of the airplane. Seriously wounded men were carried down the aisle on stretchers and snapped in place on the hooks. Those men had to be carried in after those who were less seriously wounded and able to sit upright were seated, for once anchored over our heads, there was no room to stand.

Many of the wounded were sedated for the trip but those of us who were not drugged had to endure eight hours of immobility and nothing to pass the time. Some of the men with broken bones and serious wounds to their upper limbs had slings which hung from the cots above to lift them above their heart. In all, it took two or three hours to rig the jet for takeoff.

We landed in Tokyo at dusk where the grey and brown of dense city extended as far as my eyes could see. Those of us on the jet were unloaded and taken directly to waiting helicopters which lifted off as soon as they were filled and proceeded to the various hospitals. A chronic result of being dragged through the trees was that the nerves in my legs were damaged and they quickly went to sleep. Both legs were so after the flight and they were leaden and unresponsive at first, but I was mobile after a time and able to hobble to the waiting helicopter where I took a seat by a window. My destination was the 200th Field Hospital in Yokohama. It was a hundred miles from Tokyo and as we lifted off over the capital, I assumed that we would pass over the outskirts, see countryside, and finally come to a new city and the hospital. But the denseness of the city never diminished, and I could not detect the end of one and the beginning of the next. It was solid city the hundred miles to the hospital.

With great efficiency, we were processed and taken to various wards. Gunshot wounds would be in one ward, broken bones in another. The one on the other side of mine was a burn ward — no one could enter that one lest we contaminate the patients. No sign was needed at the door for the smell alone told you what ward it was. I remembered blackened soldiers and the moaning of their agony, and I would pass that ward with a kind of reverential respect.

My ward was an amputation ward, and I must admit I was one of the least wounded in the ward and it tempered any complaints I would ever have. Every person in the ward was there for one purpose — some part of that person's body would be amputated in a day or two.

The ward was arranged like an army barracks, two rows of beds, twenty or thirty in all, with a nurse's station at the front. Many of the patients were heavily sedated and never left their place. Others, like me, were able to converse and move about. The soldier one bed closer to the nurse's station was with the 173rd Airborne. He had been a professional left-handed bowler prior to the war. A B-40 rocket mangled his left hand and it appeared that he would lose it at the elbow. After dinner, the nurse would pass by with her cart of drugs, pausing at each bed. She and an orderly would verify the person in the bed and the prescription and work their way down the line. During the night men cried out in the darkness from a private nightmare or the throbbing of their wounds. At times, the nurse would return with something to let them sleep.

Amputation day. All of us the same day. It began in the morning when the nurse gave us something to ease our anxiety. Then she and a surgeon would come by with her cart and a bevy of clipboards. She would gaze at the whole of the ward and ensure that the beds were all full, none were missing, and that everyone was in their assigned bed. She would stop at the first bed and say, "Specialist Wilson?" and he would nod at his name, and she would put a check beside his name. When everyone was where they were supposed to be, a bevy of nurses and orderlies passed by with their scissors and cut away our bandages. Men cried and shrieked, "No, no, please." For some of them it was the first time that they saw the carnage of their wounds and they stared at the ceiling and swallowed, their eyes glazed in fear.

The nurse passed again with a surgeon. They stopped at my friend from the 173rd, looked at the clipboard and mumbled, "left forearm amp." One of them took a magic marker and drew a dotted line at the place it would happen. My friend stared at the black lines. By noon he would only have a stub left at the place. At my bed I made sure that the dotted lines were at the base of the finger and not on the back of my hand and that only one finger would be taken.

None of us would be put to sleep. A block was deemed sufficient for the job. They made the next pass with shaving cream, a razor, and a hypodermic. They shaved my armpit and injected me with a nerve block. I soon had the sensation that my arm was asleep.

I had not noticed before, for I had been absorbed with my own procedures, but the beds had been disappearing through the door behind the nurse's station. They passed through the door one after another. It seemed my whole world at that time was taken up with watching the beds round the corner. In an hour or two my own bed rounded the corner and I found myself in the hall at the end of the line of beds.

I knew that my wounds were minor compared to others in the line, yet I was apprehensive as we neared the door. By noon I found myself parked outside the operating rooms. There were no doors, and I could see inside. Things moved like an assembly line. There were two rooms and in each of them there were two beds side by side. On either side of each bed were two surgeons. Four patients were having amputations done at the same time. If you were alert, as I was, you could see amputations in progress. I was looking inside as eight surgeons cut away. I watched as a doctor on one side of an operating table dropped something into a metal basket. It was weighty for I saw the basket skid inches across the floor. Then it was my turn. They rolled me in and transferred me from my bed to the table. The two surgeons never looked at me, only glanced at the chart and my hand and began to work.

It hurt. Perhaps the arm block had not taken effect. I watched one of the two doctors press down hard as he scraped my knuckle. "Hey, it hurts."

The surgeon on my left seemed surprised that I could communicate. "You really can't feel anything soldier. It's just your imagination."

"No, it hurts."

"No, you have a block. It can't hurt."

"No, it hurts. I know exactly what you are doing. You are scraping the gristle from the round part of the bone and you're sewing the skin together like a baseball."

The surgeon on the left seemed astonished at my description and he stopped with a suture tool held in mid-air. He looked at the other surgeon. "He can't feel that, can he?"

The other doctor hesitated, then held my hand high up in the air and let it go. For an instant I had a vision of an old leather baseball unraveling at the stitches. My hand fell on my chest with a thud. "Nah, he can't feel anything."

By afternoon we all lay in our places staring at the fan that rotated in the ceiling, all of us feeling our ghost limbs and trying to convince ourselves that they did not remove them after all. One soldier who had stepped on a toe-popper mine while on patrol did not take his eyes from the foot of his bed. A rolled blanket was propped under his stub, and he rocked the good foot back and forth under the covering. Many of the patients would not look at the place where the rest of them had been the day before. The nurse rolled from bed to bed with pain medicine. None of us wanted dinner.

Bandage changing was the horror we dreaded each day. Weeping and pleading began before the attendants even came into the ward with their carts. We could hear the clanging of the scissors and sliding of instruments against the metal carts before they entered the doorway. It was here that resolve to endure it all evaporated. They came down both rows of cots at the same time. The great pain of tending to tender wounds was worse at times than the receiving of the initial wound. Here there was no adrenaline or shock or still being in battle to dull the pain. Bloody bandages were dried and stuck to wounds and had to be peeled away. When I could, I slipped away and left the ward.

In my escapes from the ward, I often noticed a soldier in a wheelchair outside one of the wards. Both of his legs and one arm were gone. He was scarred from shrapnel, and he held his insides in a plastic bag in his lap. I would push him in his chair around the hospital and visit with him. I shared my faith and tried to be an encouragement to him. He would look at me and say, "I am just glad no one else was hurt."

One night in my sleep I relived that night at Lima Fifty and remembered that we placed toe-popper mines in our RON when we left. In the morning. I could not get it out of my mind, and I resolved to try to call Doney. I assumed that the task would be hopeless. I did not have a number to call. CCC was top secret, and I was clueless how to direct the call. I just got on the hospital phone and told them I wanted to call Vietnam and speak to Recon Company of CCC in Kontum. I had no confidence that the operator could navigate the maze that must isolate the security of SOG. I did not wait two minutes before a clear voice came on the line, "This is Sergeant Doney."

For ten minutes, in guarded terms we exchanged the news, recalling that we were not on a secured line. I told him that I would be signing the forms to return to the FOB.

"I dreamed about the mission," I told him, "And remembered that we left toe-poppers in the RON. Did you know that?"

"No, I'm glad you told me in case we send people in there. Exactly where?"

In the RON on the slope of the hill, but I don't know the coordinates."

"I will get with Sergeant Garcia. We will try get it to eight digits. Thank you."

I also called my mother. I had made it a practice to write home at least once a week so they would not worry, and I knew that they had not heard from me for much longer than that. Once again, the phone call from Japan went through quickly and she answered clearly.

"Hi Mom."

"Dale!"

"I'm just calling so you don't worry because you hadn't heard from me. I just want you to know that I am okay. I am in Japan in a hospital. I got wounded but it wasn't bad. I'm fine."

"Dale, they said you were missing in action."

"I don't know about that but I'm here and doing good."

"Where are you hurt?'

Before I could answer I heard my brother in the room. He had finished his tour with the 173rd Airborne in Vietnam and was home. Del and I were close. One time when we were kids, I had a dream and my heart pounded in my chest and the thumping became the thud of footsteps. Then in the dream I saw a huge brown bear under the clothesline pigeon-toeing toward the outhouse with my brother trapped inside. I ran down the stairs two at a time screaming, "Mom, Dad, a bear has Del trapped in the outhouse!"

Dad sensed that my sincerity was more than just a dream and ran to the screen window and peered outside. A huge cinnamon colored bear was indeed ambling to the privy. "Hey!" he shouted. The bear slowly looked up and ambled away.

"I know where you were hurt," I heard him say.

"Where?"

"Your head and your hand."

I was amazed. "How could you know that?

"I felt it," he said.

I was a month at that hospital in Yokohama. They wouldn't let us out of the hospital to see the city because we had open wounds. Our paychecks had caught up with us and we frequented the commissary and snack bar. My legs went to sleep when I sat for any length of time, so I wandered the halls of the hospital grounds. One day as I strolled by, I peered out at the outside world through the small window between the wards and saw a Japanese funeral pass by. Everything was white — the carriage, the two horses that pulled it, the plumes of feathers on the horses' harnesses, the box of remains, and the mourners who followed walking in step to the muted beat of a single leather drum. Other than the helicopter flight to the ward, this was my only interface with Japan.

"Let's bowl."

It was my friend from the 173rd who was a professional bowler before the war. They had an alley in the basement of the facility. I was stir-crazy with inactivity as my attempts to work out only brought excruciating pain. "I'm for it."

We went to the bowling alley and got our shoes and sat down in the chairs and stared at the laces. It had not occurred to us at first that we could not tie them. "Well, I have a left hand that works," I said.

"And my right hand works fine." So, each of us supplied a hand and put on our shoes and proceeded to bowl. He had been a pro — with the other hand. I never could bowl well with my good hand and did worse with the other. Half of our attempts were gutter balls, but it was a welcome change from the dreariness of the routine.

I received a letter from Norm Doney with all the updates he could relate considering classification. Inside the envelope was a page from, "Stars and Stripes," the chief magazine for the army. The headline of the article said, "Informed sources, Kontum Province, reveal that numerous NVA soldiers had shot themselves to keep them from the attacks on Ben Het." A large circle had been drawn around the words, "informed sources." Doney wrote, "That was you," and he drew an arrow to the words.

The next month was at Fitzsimons Army Hospital in Denver, Colorado. "You will like it there," someone told me, "That is where President Eisenhower stayed." My expectations were dashed on arrival. It was crowded and dreary with poor food. It was a place of bustling activity, a beehive that prevented sleep. Fortunately, I knew a Baptist pastor from Minnesota who was now a pastor in the Denver area. He checked me out of Fitsimmons for church and every activity he could think of.

It was at Fitsimmons that I filed the paperwork to return to my unit in Vietnam. It was here also that they de-wormed me — a few red jellybean-like pills. "Stay close to the john," the doctor warned, "These pills don't kill the worms, they just get them so drunk they forget to hang on." As I waited in bed for it all to happen, I read *Colonel Sun*, the first James Bond book written after Ian Fleming died a few years before.

"We are going to send you to the hospital at Minot Airforce Base," the hospital director told me. "It is in Minot, North Dakota. They won't know what to do with you there, you being Army and they are Air Force, but it will get you closer to your home. I think they will give you convalescent leave from there until it is time to go back to Nam. Are you sure you don't want to see a psychiatrist?"

It was early November and cold and the prairie wind made it bitter to be outside the hospital. The man at Fitsimmons was right — the Air Force did not know what to do with an army casualty. I was given a bed in a ward, but I felt far too healthy to stay in a bed. The ends of the remaining fingers of my hand were still scabbed where fingernails had been and my legs still went to sleep — as they would for many years, but the bruising, stiffness, and pain of being slammed against the Central Highlands Forest were about gone. I was decorated at Minot Air Force Base. The commander of the base gave me the awards in a ceremony and although they were not particularly high medals, he stated that they were the highest awards ever given at the base. The press was there, and they sent the press releases to the farm-town newspapers of both of my grandparents, and I was pleased for them.

I checked myself out of the hospital to see a rodeo near Minot and walked to the arena. It was blowing cold even among the bleachers, but I bathed in the warmth of Americana and treasured the evening. It was a thirteen mile walk and I was fortunate to catch a ride with a trucker making his run across country. I was grateful for the ride in the warm truck, but he said he was grateful for the chance to help a soldier. A couple weeks later there was a "Grand Ole Opry," held in a covered arena at Minot, and again I held America by the hand.

They transferred me to a nearby veteran's hospital and said that I would shortly have orders for convalescent leave before my final orders came for Vietnam. The ward smelled of urine and was not the caliber of the hospitals I had experienced. As I placed my bag beside my cot, the tenants of the ward stared at me as a strange thing that slipped into their world. Their faces were parchment-white and lined with grey wrinkles. Around their faces, unwashed hair lay flat against their skulls as thin greasy strings. Their milky eyes slowly opened and gazed at me without interest as I entered. None of them sat up in bed or exerted the energy to engage this young, healthy-looking soldier who had just entered the room. "Hello, my name is Hanson," I said to the man in the bed next to mine. I extended my wounded hand and took his limp moist hand hoping that he would not squeeze it too hard, but his hand was lifeless — just bones wrapped in loose skin. A few old half-awake vets asked about the war but their minds quickly wandered, and they could not take it in. They would lay back in their beds, and with their shaking, boney hands draw the sheets up to their chins and shrink into their covers. As a Christian I wanted to talk about their futures and be of help, but "future" to them was the next meal that they brought to the ward. They would hunch over their bowls with their elbows set on either side and spoon their meals without talking or looking about.

Orders authorizing convalescent leave arrived and I purchased an airplane ticket to my hometown, International Falls, Minnesota. I did not tell anyone that I was coming so there was no one there to greet me when I arrived. It was cold at the airport, and night had fallen, and the terminal was deserted when the commuter plane landed. I found a pay phone and called for a taxi. For some reason as the taxi pulled into our driveway and gravel crunched loudly under the tires, and the engine droned there with the lights on, I half expected people to pour from the houses to welcome me. Although I knew it would not be, as my arrival would be a surprise even to my family, I felt a twinge of disappointment. I paid the driver and retrieved my duffle bag and faced my home. Absence always sees the peeled paint and the sagging door. I walked in and dropped my bag on the floor and noticed how our feet had faded the linoleum. My home. The chair at the table where I always sat. The hum of the refrigerator. The faint smell of dinner mom made hours before. Corned beef?

"Anyone home?"

There was no answer. I went to my parents' bedroom. My dad was there, asleep, for he would be getting up for the midnight shift at the mill. "Hi Dad."

He flinched in his sleep. "It's me, Dad."

He came fully awake. I reached out my hand to shake his as I leaned to hug him. He would not take my hand, would not look at it. His boy had been hurt and he could not bear to touch the place or see my hand still wrapped in bandage. He had been through Iwo Jima, and Guadalcanal and other battles and knew what bullets did. "I'm home dad. I'm back."

And so began my time at home. I was bathed in the love of my family. I visited friends. I went to church when the doors opened. I did what I could not do in the war — I went for a walk after dark and did not fear that someone might shoot at me. We skated at the rink under the streetlight, fished through the ice and tried to catch a walleye, sang in church, drove on country roads and did not worry that they had not been cleared of mines, and drove a hundred miles to see grandparents.

But I could not set aside my training and reflexes. I did not like to have anyone walking up behind me. I did not want my back to a door or be in a lighted doorway or window. I needed to know the source of all sounds. I found it hard to sleep at first because my mind tested every sound. For the first few nights I had to block out the sounds of the night or I could not sleep. I had a reel-to-reel tape player and I put on eighty minutes of classical music and was soon sound asleep. One time I heard voices in the room. They whispered. I came wide awake but did not move until I discovered the source of the sound.

"There he is," one voice said. "He is sleeping in the bed."

"Yes," the second voice said, "We can kill him now."

"Be quiet now. We will sneak up on him and kill him."

"Yes, we'll cut off his head."

"Now," said the first voice.

I rolled from the bed and came up in a karate stance and charged the voice in the dark. As I was in striking distance of the voice and my hand was descending in a chop, when I realized what it was. I had inadvertently played a cut of classical music by Prokofiev called *Peter and the Wolf.* It was at the place when the children found and were about to slay the wolf that I burst from the blankets.

The convalescent leave required that once a month I return in person to the hospital in Minot to check my wounds and for orders. Mom decided to accompany me for the ride to Minot. It was early January and cold and we were driving through the prairie farmland of Minnesota and the Dakotas when it hit. The temperature dropped drastically, and violent wind gusted across the plains bringing hard snow. We could not see beyond the edges of the highway, so I followed the centerline down the blacktop. The wind howled and the snow was crusty and pelted the windows. The west wind shoved against the side of the car. We were in farm country when the engine stopped, and I coasted to the shoulder. I tried the starter, and the motor would not turn over. I had power and lights and gas, but the engine had frozen as we drove. The temperature in the car was instantly below zero. We would soon freeze in place. We were dressed for winter, but not for a blizzard.

"Mom, I have to go find help or we will freeze here."

I put on all the clothes that I could. I strung pairs of socks to cover my ears and used socks for gloves. "I will hurry back, Mom."

I stepped out of the car and the wind nearly toppled me. With the blinding snow I could not see across the road. I knew right away that it was possible to walk in circles ten feet in front of the car until I froze to death. The wind blew the snow clear of the blacktop but the shoulder, fields, and ditches where drifted. To walk a straight line down the highway I placed my left foot on the black pavement and my right foot on the crusted shoulder and walked as fast as I could. My face was nearly instantly frozen, and I could feel the flesh become solid and jiggled when I walked. My eyes burned with the cutting wind. I had to hurry before I froze on the road, but I dared not run and freeze my lungs.

In the distance I saw the haze of farmhouse lights through the blizzard. I found the edge of a driveway and a barbed wire fence that ran along it. Sliding my hands along the wire, barbs and all, I felt my way to a yard and the front door. I banged on the door and when they opened it, I stumbled in. "My car stalled on the road and my mom is in the car and freezing."

The wife pulled me in by my coat. "Harold will get your mom."

Harold was rushing into his clothing. "I'll get your mom. My tractor is just outside."

In a very short order, he had mom safely in the house and warm. The farmers were very kind and gracious. The blizzard lasted two days. Harold pulled my car into the yard during a break in the weather. We found that the wind had forced snow through the cracks of the hood and filled the engine compartment with snow compressing it into a solid block of ice. When the storm was past, we towed the car to a heated garage. It took two days to melt enough to free the motor.

At the Minot air base, I received my orders for Vietnam. It was a "delay-in-route" which meant that it did not count against my leave time. I could fly commercially on my own and they would pick up the tab for the fare. "Pick the place you want to go as your destination. They pay your way there, and from there to Vietnam." I placed one finger on International Falls and the other finger on the other side of the globe. Cape Town, South Africa. Every place the plane touched down would be a hub of exploration until I got to Kontum.

London was the first hub. The airline jet descended through a misty grey sky and landed on the wet runway of Heathrow Airport. In my pocket was a list of relatives I planned to visit in the old country — the old country for Grandma Hanson were those still living in Norway and Sweden. Viking graves with headstones inscribed with ancient runes still stood in the grass of her front yard. From Grandma Hecker I had a list of relatives who lived in a village along the Rhine next to a castle. I taxied to an inn in central London where I planned to spend one day and be off with my list.

It was more like an Englishman's Club that one would find in Africa, with a huge gathering area complete with a massive fireplace and comfortable furniture and library — a gigantic living room. Six inches of quilts and blankets were on the bed, and it reminded me of home rather than a place to rent for a few days. Through the window of my room, drops of rain dripped down the glass, and the grey fog and clouds matched and nearly hid the grey stone of London architecture.

I slept soundly in the comfortable bed and in the morning asked for and ate a breakfast such as the locals would eat. From the lounge I called the airline to confirm my flight — the airlines were on strike. There would be no flights. So, I saw the sights of the city, heard Big Ben, and put my thumb on the pulse of the British people — and I folded the list of relatives I had hoped to meet, and placed it in my pocket.

The next leg ended in Athens, Greece, the ancient city of art, sculpture and learning. Athens was white. All that was of stone was white marble, the stone of the great master sculptors and unparalleled architecture. Stone from the quarries a few miles away was in its turn carved into breathtaking statues to be breathlessly gazed upon or when used as pavement, walked upon. I remembered studying the Peloponnesian War fought between Athens and Sparta. Sparta was the city-state in which one lived and sacrificed for the state. It was a place of a patriotism that had no place for the aspirations of the individual. These were the people of the great Spartan legions. A commander could call attention to his troops, then go inside for dinner and a night's sleep and in the morning would go out to the parade field to find that it had snowed in the night but that his soldiers were still standing at attention. No wonder three hundred of them could withstand Xerxes and the Medo-Persians at Thermopylae.

Athens, on the other hand, was the city-state that celebrated the individual. Here art, architecture, and literature, knowledge and philosophy flourished. But radical individualism erased the concepts of duty, sacrifice, service and discipline, and contributed to unbridled lust. That war fought so long go in history could well be an allegory to ponder.

I roamed about the ancient Acropolis with the Parthenon and the Areopagus with the ionic columns and carved frescoes. Here was the ultimate expression of human achievement of the times. Some of the philosophers who shaped western philosophy walked these floors. Socrates taught by asking probing questions. Plato was his prize student who wrote dialogues and wrote *The Republic*. His most famous student was Aristotle who founded logical theory, and tutored Alexander the Great, who conquered the known world and lamented that there were no more worlds to conquer, then died of syphilis at age twenty-six.

I recalled also as I stood at the Areopagus, an even greater mind than these philosophers spoke here. Athens believed in the existence of God — a whole bevy of them in fact. Every street had an altar or temple for a god. In fact, they were afraid that they missed one so at the gate of the city of Athens they erected a sign, "To the Unknown God." The Christian apostle Paul on entering the city, saw the sign and disputed with the intellectuals of the city. They brought him to the Areopagus to present his argument. "Ye men of Athens, I perceive that in all things ye are too superstitious. For as I passed by, and beheld your devotions, I found an altar with this inscription, TO THE UNKNOWN GOD. Whom therefore ye ignorantly worship, him declare I unto you." The apostle Paul's entire sermon is written on a bronze plaque and affixed to the base of Mars Hill.

I wanted Greek food and found myself in a dimly lit restaurant which had the feel of a quiet retreat for locals. I was clearly American and a couple men came over and introduced themselves. "Hey, you America, yes?"

"Yes."

"Soldier, yes?"

"Yes. How do you know?"

"You walk like. How you say... ?"

His friend supplied the word, "Bearing. You have bearing."

"Yes. That is the word I mean. You have bearing. You walk like soldier."

I did not know what to say about that. I had not realized my posture was erect. I had worked out before I came for dinner and my hand ached and I had elevated it on the table.

"You have wound. You go home now, yes?"

"No."

"No? Why you go back?"

"Because I am anti-Communist. I will fight until we win."

"Hey, hey," they cheered. "You come sit with us. We are anti-Communist too. We fought in the Civil War."

They were all veterans of the Greek Civil War that occurred when the Germans were expelled from Greece at the end of WWII and the Communists tried to fill the void. The men around me were in their late forties and fifties. "We fought against the Communists. Eighty thousand Greeks died. America helped us win it and we joined NATO after the war."

For the next four hours we spoke of Communism and the bitter hatred the people have for it still. We talked about war and guerilla warfare and freedom. We ate Greek food. I told them I took Greek in college, but it was koine Greek of two thousand years ago.

"Anthropos — man," I said.

"Yes, yes, 'man.' Word mean man." And they all laughed at my child-like attempt to talk with them in Greek.

"You look very strong." It was Nicholas who spoke. He was under fifty, fit, with short black hair and trimmed mustache. "Arm wrestle," he said as he placed his elbow on the table. I was very strong, as I had been working out after my wounds. I could curl 155 pounds and do thirty-five pull-ups.

"Okay."

For the next fifteen minutes I tried to put him down. I could not budge him. I know there was a trick to it but I could not see what it was. Perhaps it was that his right side was against the table and supported that arm. The other freedom fighters surrounded us and smiled at the contest. Nicholas just smiled at me. I just smiled back. "I don't know how you are doing it, but I give up."

Some of them had wounds, and like the St. Crispin's Day veterans, rolled up their sleeves and bared their arms and said, "These wounds received I on...."

Born Twice

When I left the city, I saw no Helen of Troy, or lithe young women who could have posed for Michelangelo, and no maidens crushing grapes into wine with their feet, but I did see kindred soldiers and shared in their comradery.

Rome was the place the romantics want to see. The apostle Paul said, "I must see Rome," but to him, it was the share the gospel to the then capital of the world. Caesar from Rome made "a decree that all the world would be taxed," and had the authority to do so. Paul undoubtedly saw the Colosseum, as did I, but may have been in it as a victim and been delivered, for the scriptures state, "And I was delivered out of the mouth of the lion." In time however, Caesar had Paul beheaded. I roamed the Colosseum and although I admired the architecture, I marveled also at the depravity of a culture that built it to watch the torture of people for entertainment. I thought of the color of the buildings of England — grey because the stone is grey, Greece is white because it is made of white marble, and I could not help noticing the red brown of Rome — the color of dried blood.

Under the city are the catacombs and crypts. The catacombs are long tunnels cut through the rock, and on either side, slots large enough to hold a corpse were cut, one above the other where the dead had been left. They told me that there were at least two thousand miles of them and that only a tenth of them had been explored. I read that Christians had hidden in them from Roman persecution. In some of the crypts are macabre art galleries — priests had been fastened standing upright against the wall in their heavy brown robes. Their heads had sagged to their chests and their flesh had rotted away leaving their bare skeletons inside the cloth. Their hoods were drawn over their heads and their sockets and grinning teeth show. Their finger bones reach from the sleeves in gesture. Around them are vast mosaics of design, not using colored stone or glass, but human skulls.

In contrast to these things is the architecture, painting and sculpture of Rome. Bernini's sculpture of Apollo and Daphne left me breathless, as did Michelangelo's sculptures of Moses or David. The Sistine Chapel held me in awe, and I marveled a culture that could produce such beauty could also produce the Colosseum.

I rented a car in South Africa and passing through the gates of the agency I felt like a bird leaving its cage, flying into the warm sun passing over the soil of boyhood dreams with only the sky for my limitation. Every mile that I traveled was a page from books that I read as a youth: Hemingway, Robert Ruark, J.A. Hunter, Laurens van der Post and Frederick Selous. Sometimes as I read, my fingers brushed across the words as if they were fur or feathers as I sounded them out: greater kudo, eland, Thompson's gazelle, safari, rogue elephant, cape buffalo. I took in South Africa with all my senses. I smelled the brown grass, saw the mountains purple in the distance, listened to the bark of a hyena and the rustle in dry pasture.

It seems that God has always placed good and gracious people in my path. Some were mentors. Some were great examples to follow — paragons and not paradigms. Some were just good, kind and gracious people. I do not remember how I met the first one in Africa. He was older, more my father's age. He wore khaki clothing and a broad-brimmed hat to keep out the sun. His shirt had the loops to hold bullets on safari but were empty now and iron pressed. He was a colonel in the South African Army and both of his sons were away in the military. We talked about Vietnam and Special Forces and the challenges South Africa faced. I will call him Johnson and give you his town as Nelspruit only because at the time of this writing the blacks are murdering the whites especially on the farms and trying to drive them from the country.

"Stay with us for the night or as long as you like," he and his wife told me. I slept the night in one of their boy's rooms. Beside the bed was a waste basket made of an elephant's foot and the walls had memorabilia of past hunts. Mrs. Johnson prepared us a dinner of oysters that were brought in fresh from the coast. When I left their home Mrs. Johnson wrote a letter to my parents, "We met your charming son and he stayed the night with us in Nelspruit, South Africa."

We talked long into the night. We talked of conventional war and the kind of missions we did in Special Forces. Before the first shades of dawn touched the house, he offered me a direct commission to major to set up a unit to conduct commando raids behind lines. Some of our conversation which led to that went like this:

"We get the news of the United States and hear what the newspapers say. Let me say the people who are writing the stories about us are not telling the truth about South Africa. The press is left-wing and has an agenda. The Communists call the people in the universities and the ones who scream at the cameras about apartheid useful idiots."

"The same ones who are marching against the war," I said.

"Yes. They say, 'Give South Africa back to the blacks!' Those people have never researched the facts. They just say what they are told to say. Here is the truth. You can look it up for yourself. This is no secret. The white people were here before the blacks!"

He slapped his hand on the table. "How can you reason with ignorance?" He took a long breath in frustration and continued. "And you can tell those people the facts — show them the proof, I tell you, and they continue on as if you were a slight interruption."

"When the Boer people, the whites, came to this land there were no blacks in the country. All the blacks were up north and slowly migrating south killing the blacks of other tribes as they came. We needed people to work the gold mines and the farms, so we hired blacks from north to work. They were not slaves but hired for wages. They would work and go back home. They were never meant to be citizens; they came for wages."

"We had schools for our people and such, but we could not take care of everyone. So, we told the black people, you must take care of your own people and we will take care of ours. That is where we get the word apartheid. It means separate development.

"Do you have that? Now let me tell you why your press tries to make that sound so bad."

Mrs. Johnson brought lemonade with the cubes clinking against the glass.

"The Communists in China and Russia want Africa. There are as many resources in this continent as the rest of the world combined. Either of those countries could just walk in and take the whole continent and nothing could stop them. Except for one thing: South Africa. We are the most advanced nation on the continent, as advanced as America. For them to take Africa, the Communists must do away with South Africa. Somehow, they must isolate or destroy us. Enter apartheid."

He stopped and poured us lemonade.

"So, Dale, all we hear is that we are a prejudiced, hateful people and must be isolated like a pariah until we submit. They will not trade with us or help us in any way. There is a boycott on all our goods. The attacks are already starting. They want to drive all white people out of Africa. The Communists and Cubans are already in Southwest Africa."

Mrs. Johnson added, "They are trying to get the blacks in this country to rise up and slaughter us from inside too."

"The fifth column. I know about that. I am ignorant but if they came just to work why are there so many of them now to be a threat?"

She placed both her hands around her glass and slowly said. "Until a generation ago, the black population of Africa was not larger than the land could nurture. The continent experienced ubiquitous tribal warfare. The tribes massacred each other, wiping out entire villages or hauling them off to slavery. That and disease kept the population small. Then the British made strict laws against tribal war and completely put it down. They also brought in medicine and ended many of the diseases that killed so many of them. The populations have multiplied, and the land cannot support them, and they are coming to the cities and hearing the propaganda the left puts out."

Mrs. Johnson tapped the glass with her fingernails, and she looked upward and stopped speaking.

I said goodbye in the driveway. Mrs. Johnson daubed her eyes with her apron, and I hugged her like a second mother. "I packed you some things for your travels and a few things to remember us by. Mr. Johnson's hand was large and strong, and his eyes drank in my image, and I knew that he would remember me as I went.

"I will consider your offer, sir. I have your address and I will see what happens in my war." As I pulled from their drive I saw them in my mirror, standing side by side and waving.

I stayed at an inn at the side of the road and slept soundly without dreaming. I woke only when the sun shone through the slats, and I smelled the heat on the brown grass. I heard animal sounds and a dove in the trees. They made a hearty breakfast and there was meat and fried potatoes and oatmeal. They said the animal sounds that I heard were hyenas. Their neighbor had cows in the barn that were calving, and the hyenas would be there to devour the calf before it was even licked clean. The hyena was a hated creature among the farmers.

I bought sandwiches and soft drinks and hot coffee for my thermos and left with directions for Rorke's Drift. I stopped along the way at a lion's kill and watched a half dozen huge birds with beautiful red necks feeding on the carcass. As I watched, they dipped their necks deep into the stomach cavity and retrieved that which was choice. Then I discovered that these were vultures that dipped their heads and neck full into the stomach, and the red that I saw was blood that soaked their feathers and left them blinking to clear their eyes. I stopped at a field and watched a warthog strut about, and I sat on the hood of the car to watch for the wildlife of the day. A troop of baboons with their blue noses came out of the foliage. They looked at me then moved at lightning speed and stopped and grunted at me. I slipped my sandwich into my pocket and slowly got into the car. Their anger was clear. They shrieked and grunted and false charged, then defecated into their hands and threw it at the car.

I had been eager to visit Rorke's Drift as I had always admired heroism. It was located beside the Buffalo River at a mission station of the Church of Sweden. One hundred fifty British soldiers fought four thousand Zulu warriors to a standstill. It is said that the Zulu saluted the bravery of the soldiers and finally left the battlefield. This at that time marked the southern migration of the blacks from northern Africa.

I stopped at a gas station restaurant and met a man slightly older than my father. He reminded me of Mr. Johnson. He had greying hair and was dressed in khaki and broad hat like Mr. Johnson. His movements were quick, someone used to getting things done. Somehow, we fell to talking and he sized me up as American and military and I told him I was on convalescent leave from the Vietnam War. In short, he adopted me at least for the day or more. "You need ale," he said. "It is what we have here at noon."

"I'm afraid, I don't drink alcohol."

"We don't think of this as a drink. It is full of calories and health. You can take it dark or light."

"Dark," I said.

"You will miss a lot of what you pass through. Just follow me in your car and when I stop, you stop, and I will tell you what you are seeing."

"What do you do for a living?"

He lowered his voice. "I was a cabinet minister in Botswana the next country up. The blacks came in and kicked out most of the white people. I came here to South Africa to live. My best friend is still there and oversees the game management for the country. He called me and said elephants are overpopulated now and are destroying the crops — could I come down and help thin the herd. Dale, why don't you come with me on safari and shoot some elephants?"

I did not know what to say. A safari would fulfill my dreams of Africa.

We traveled toward Botswana. A few miles down a narrow, tarred road he pulled over and got out. We found a place where we could see for miles. Long horned cattle roamed in the confines. "See all of that? I do not know how many square miles that farm is. All of that belongs to your actor, John Wayne."

We traveled miles more and he stopped. "See all those fields? That is tobacco growing there. That belongs to Gary Player, the golfer."

He stopped again and pulled to the side of the road. A black boy was selling watermelon. My guide spoke in rapid Bantu to the boy and gave him the money for the melon. Then the cabinet minister and I sat in the sandy ditch and ate watermelon, cutting it with our pocketknives.

"What language was that?"

"That was Bantu, but I get along with the Kikuyu and of course Swahili is the main one for the interior."

"Your knife," he said looking at mine, "Has only one blade. Is that practical?"

"Yes, for what I need. It is one of my weapons. I have one that Mr. Buck made and this is a Gerber. I must have only one blade in it so I can open it with one hand. Watch." I clicked my fingers a few times so he could see the movement, then inserted my knife between the fingers as I clicked them. "I've done that thousands of times. I practice getting it from my pocket into my hands and open for use in less than a second." I reached the small of my back and showed him my nunchaku. "My other weapon. I have these wherever I go. The Okinawans put piano wire between the sticks instead of chord. They could throw them and take a sentry's head off twenty feet away."

We came to the border of Botswana and I had to decide. This offer could be my only chance to experience this dream. I had no desire to shoot an elephant. More so, I had a fondness for them and considered the boss of the herd an old gentleman. Nor, for that matter, did I ever wish to shoot a hippo or rhino or a lion. I would, however, enjoy hunting an eland, kudo, cape buffalo, or one of the horned animals one would regularly eat. I would love to find myself sitting before a hardwood fire with the Commissioner eating roasted franklin fowl shot from a flock that rose earlier from the tall grass. I imagined talking with the old hunters, sharing adventures, the sounds of animals pacing outside the fire glow, a hyena's laugh, a trumpet of an elephant, the low growl of a prowling lion. "Ya know, Capstick told me this very place, this very campsite by the river that…" and one of them would tell the yarn. Another of them would say, "My father met David Livingston, the missionary, up north a ways in Zambia — that was before the lion maimed him and broke his jaw."

I thought, "I am getting close to using up all my convalescent leave. I could be AWOL for a week or ten days and come up with an excuse. I could probably get away with it."

I faced my new friend at the crossing, "I better not go. I will regret this, but I need to get back with my unit. I appreciate your offer more than you will ever know." We parted with a deep friendship and the moment that I said, "Goodbye," I regretted my decision.

As it happened, I found myself alone in 7,500 square miles of African wilderness. It was the vast animal-filled sanctuary called Kruger Park and unbeknownst to me, it was closed to the public for the season. I had made a very early start and met little traffic on the main road and when I left the blacktop and drove on the smooth dirt road to the gate, no one was at the park entrance. There were no rangers or ticket booths or even any signs that I could see, just the entrance greeting of "Welcome to Kruger National Park." It did not occur to me that there was a season at the park so I passed through the arches and monitored my speed, for the signs cautioned that I might encounter animals on the road. I was not aware of it, but I was the only person in the park.

For at least a hundred miles, wildlife was everywhere. Grant's Gazelle, Thomson's gazelle and various antelope effortlessly leaped across the road, landed on thin legs and glided through the foliage as though weightless. I rounded a bend in the road to find an impala gazing at me from the edge of the veld with its graceful horns curling outward, staring with its large dark eyes. It twitched its tail twice and bounded off.

A greater kudu stood in a stand of thin trees with pale bark in a background of dark shrubs. The kudu was grey-brown with pale vertical stripes along its flank and blended in so well that it was only noticed when it flicked one large ear. Its huge horns were majestic twisting two and a half turns to the end.

At a place, there was a large plane, a grassy savanna with herds of wildebeest and zebra and in the distance the grey forms of elephants moved at grazing speed. At the edge of the plains, were gold shapes of dozing lions, sleeping in the open in plain view of the herd. I never saw a view empty of an African animal.

At a curve in the dirt road, I found myself in the middle of a large herd of feeding elephants. Before I could stop the car, I was in their midst and had the attention of a large bull. He trumpeted and flared his ears out and advanced toward me. An elephant does not need to move fast to be a threat. I slammed the car into reverse and floored it back down the road and the beyond the curve. I waited for several minutes, then got out of the vehicle and crept to the edge of the field. The herd was grazing away, meandering into the trees and when I deemed it safe, I proceeded on my way.

Midafternoon the engine began to heat up. The temperature gauge was red lined. I was at a bridge and a small tributary of the Zambezi River. I sat there and let it cool down and slid down the bank to collect water. Filling the containers, I looked up to see the twin bumps of crocodile eyes at the waterline edging closer to me. I kept filling the radiator with water and driving as far as I dared before the engine froze altogether. I had not encountered a single vehicle and it seemed pointless to stay in the disabled car, so I decided to walk for help. Perhaps there was something along the way.

I had rounded a corner to find giraffe only a few dozen feet from me. They were feeding in the tree leaves and their movements were stately and graceful. I continued past them and soon heard lions. Clearly, they were lion sounds, but I could not pinpoint their location or interpret the meaning of the sounds. I decided to find a point of safety before me that I could run to, perhaps a tree to climb. I had my two weapons — my knife and my nunchaku. I had a confidence that my "chucks" could break the skull of most animals and perhaps knock them out. They were mahogany and strong but could splinter and break at the first blow. I could only hope that first blow would deliver me. As I walked I held my nunchaku ready to strike but noticed that its swinging end looked like an animal tail, so I cocked my elbow with the loose end over my elbow. And so, I walked tree to tree until I sensed the immediate danger had passed. About two hours later a truck drove alongside and stopped. Two rangers were in the front and several workers rode in the bed.

"Park's closed," said the man riding shotgun.

"Did not know that. There were no signs."

"That your car back there?"

I nodded. "The engine froze."

"We can give you a ride. You can call for help from our outpost."

I hopped in back and stood, holding the rail as the workers did.

At the outpost I was able to call the rental agency and they said they would have a replacement car to me the next day. The park rangers gave me a bungalow to stay in — a modern version of the native hut with a solid, snake-proof floor. A fan cooled the room under the thatched roof. They brought me a hearty meal and were courteous but disinclined to visit with this interloper of their park station.

The rental people had the vehicle to me by mid-morning, having driven all night or started very early. I was able to see Victoria Falls by afternoon. She was the largest waterfall in the world by volume of water. The splash of the water that cascaded to the bottom rose nearly a mile into the air rendering the area around the falls a perpetual rain forest. I climbed the sides of the cliffs and had to take care when I reached for hand holds for scorpions resided in all the water catches in the clefts of the rocks. Often creatures are caught in the current of the Zambezi River and pulled over the top. At the bottom, crocodiles gather in the pools to devour antelope, an occasional hippo, and even a hapless human. At the top again and soaking wet, I regretted only that there was no person nearby with whom I could share my amazement — a waterfall twice as tall as Niagara Falls and nearly two and a half times its width.

Wanke, in Southern Rhodesia, now called Zimbabwe, was the next place of my exploration. In the old days it was called the Wanke Game Preserve, an area approaching six thousand square miles of wildlife habitat. The preserve is now called Hwange National Park and is robust with animals. There are large areas of grassland and woodlands and the trees become sparser as you go south toward the Kalahari Desert. The abundance of birds and animal species left me wordless throughout the day. In the afternoon I ate at an inn set on a tall bluff, and had my meal outside on a huge covered deck. On each table next to the salt and pepper was a pair of binoculars to watch the passing herds. The soil was dry, dusty and red, and long lines of elephants passed one behind the other, all dusted red. Zebra passed, the spaces between their black stripes dusted Rhodesian red.

I gassed up in a small town in Southern Rhodesia (Zimbabwe). It was a pleasant place among the trees. A young man in his twenties came out to fill my tank, but when he looked at my plates noticed that the plate number ended in an even number. "Sorry mister, but I can't sell you gas until tomorrow — you know even numbered license plates can gas on even numbered days."

"I am sorry, but I did not know that. This is a rental car from South Africa, and I have to get back."

"Ah, no worries then. I'll gas you."

"Is there a shortage?"

"You did not know? The lefties in the U.S. and that whole lot say we are prejudice like South Africa so they will not sell us anything, and they will not buy anything from Rhodesia. It is a boycott on us to make us cave in. We don't treat our blacks poorly here."

"Is it working?"

"Well so far, we have made everything ourselves. Self-sufficient is what it has made us."

We got to talking about my reason for being in Africa and how I felt about Communism and how the "Reds" wanted to take over Africa.

We were inside and I was buying soft drinks and something to eat for the drive. "Let me tell you the insanity of the whole mess. Your bleeding-heart liberals in the U.S. of A hate the white man in Africa — who have done nothing to them — more than the Communists who want to destroy them. You probably did not know this, but Rhodesia produces more than two thirds of the world's chromium. Chromium is necessary and valuable. The only other place in the world that you can find it is in Russia. The United States is boycotting Rhodesia, a free country, and refusing to buy our chromium. Instead, they are buying it now from your enemy, Russia. And they are charging you four times as much as Rhodesia charges."

At the gas pumps I thanked the young man whose family had lived for generations in that land and wondered at his future. He would be in a battle against world opinion and forces that tried to starve him into submission whereas in a few days, I would be in a place where bullets spoke without disguise.

I flew commercially to Nairobi, Kenya. On the plane I had an immense toothache. It had been coming on for a couple of days but had abscessed and my jaw and tooth were swollen, and the ache throbbed with the beating of my heart. It got so bad I did not want to wait for a dentist, so I went to the bathroom and lanced my jaw with my pocketknife. There was immediate relief. The pressure lifted and I no longer felt the throbbing of my heart. A dentist would be my priority.

When the jet landed and I went to the terminal for my bag, it did not arrive. A black man at the counter looked at me with contempt and hatred. "We don' get bag for white mon. You get yo'self." He pointed to the jet on the apron. I went back to the plane. A black man pointed at the belly of the plane. There was no stoop to help me get into the cargo hold so I pulled myself up and rummaged inside until I found my bag.

With the bag, I walked across the tarmac toward at least twenty idling taxis. It had not occurred to me until then that there were no white people on the flight. "Taxi to Nairobi," I said.

The drivers sauntered about the cabs, some leaning against their fenders and sneered. "We don' give ride to white folk no mo."

At one end of the line of cabs was one set apart a few feet. "Here, Buddy," the voice said. "I'll take you."

"What's up with that?" I asked him.

He waited until we were inside the cab and underway before he answered. "Kenya, the jewel of Africa, has declared its independence. Jomo Kenyatta is the new dictator, and they are trying to drive out all the whites who have lived here for generations. Where are you going by the way?"

"Norfolk Hotel."

"Can't take you there. I have to take you to the Jamba Hotel. It is owned by Kenyatta himself and he gets his kickback.

"Kenyatta was one of the Mau Mau uprisings that massacred the white farmers. He was a big anti-colonial activist, and he went to Moscow. He went to, 'Communist University of the Toilers of the East.'" He pulled to a stop outside the Jamba Hotel.

"Thank you for being at the airport. I would be still there if it were not for you." I thanked him.

He dropped his hand in an "it's nothing" gesture. "I am truly sorry

I have to leave you here."

I paid at the desk with a black man who did not speak to me. "What is the room number?" I asked.

He just nodded in the direction of the open door and left me to carry the bag and find my way. I had forgotten and turned to him and asked, "The key?"

He sneered at my ignorance. "No key."

Indeed. No key was needed. It was configured as a barracks with army cots lined up in two rows. A common toilet was at the end of the hall. I picked out a place where I had a wall to my back and could see anyone who entered. I put my bag at the foot of the bed and placed my feet over the hump. I would not take off my clothes. If I had to use the toilet, I decided I would take my bag into the stall. So far there were no other guests and I wondered if the place would fill up after the bars closed and the winos and homeless would stagger in.

My tooth was starting to throb again. By hook or crook, I would get to the Norfolk and find a dentist.

The Norfolk was the gathering place of the Kenyan farmers who came for market and doctors and every other need a Kenyan might have. Early explorers and famous hunters based out of there. I ate at the open-air terrace of the Norfolk, perhaps at the very same tables where Ruark or Hemingway or Theodore Roosevelt or other names of literature may have dined. Perhaps Bror Von Blixen-Finecke scratched poems on paper napkins at this table.

By afternoon, I found my dentist and celebrated with a dinner on the veranda entirely of local fare.

Full of dreams lived, and my head filled with images of Africa and friends had made, I boarded a plane to Saigon, hopped a C-130 to Nha Trang, and signed in with 5th Special Forces. It was two days before a flight was scheduled for Kontum; it was an Air America plane with racks of live chickens and cages of pigs and stacks of boxes. Across from me was a recon team made up of one American and six tribesmen. The American was blond, about my age and dressed "sterile." A Swedish K leaned across his pack on the deck. I tried to place the tribesmen by the shape of their faces and guessed the plane would finish the day somewhere in Laos.

As we landed at Kontum and the door opened to let in the bright sunlight I squinted to see. Were the buildings that I remembered still standing? Were there incoming rounds falling on the city? As I walked onto the tarmac, I took in a deep breath and smelled the air. It was not the fresh fog smell of London, nor the odor of the marble of Greece, nor the heavy musty odor of the catacombs. Nor was it the scent of dry grass passing at the speed of grazing elephants on the plains of Africa. As I walked off the plane, I smelled Vietnam — the sandalwood and jungle and rice paddies and sweaty water buffalo and the silty Dak Bla River and *nuoc mam*. I was back.

Michael Buckland with Montagnards from RT Maine.

Author on a training group mission.

Author new in-country.

NORMAN A. DONEY `D-665`

CSM (R) Norm Doney, 84, passed away after a long illness on 20 February, 2013. Norm quit high school to join the Navy in 1946. He served aboard the USS Valley Forge and was discharged a Seaman 1st Class in 1947. He returned to finish school and after some time at the University of Oregon, he joined the Army in 1953. He served as a Combat Engineer in the 101st Abn Div, the 1st Cav (Korea) and the 82d Abn Div. He volunteered for Special Forces in 1961.He was assigned to the 7th SFG and participated in Operation White Star in Laos. In 1962 he was assigned to the 8th SFG n Panama and later as an instructor at Training Group. In 1966 he was reassigned to the 5th SFG in Vietnam and served with Detachment B-52, Delta Project. After a short tour with the 6th SFG at Ft. Bragg he returned to Vietnam and Delta Project as the Recon NCOIC. After another brief rotation to the 6th SFG, Norm returned to MACV-SOG, CCC in 1969. During this tour he published a series of articles entitled "Tips of the Trade/Lessons Learned." His "tips" were later published by Paladin Press in 1989 as the pamphlet "Project Delta, Special Forces Vietnam Recon Manual." His "tips" have been used by generations of Green Berets. After a tour with the 8th SFG in Panama he returned to Vietnam in 1971 with an assignment to the Special Mission Advisory Group (SMAG) and was the Team Sergeant of the last "A" Team in Vietnam. He left with the 5th SFG when the colors came down. In 1972 he was assigned to the 10th SFG at Ft. Devens, MA, retiring six month later. Among CSM Doney's numerous awards and decorations are the Silver Star, Bronze Star w/V (six awards), Purple Heart, CIB, Master Parachutist Badge, HALO Wings, the Presidential Unit Citation and the Special Forces Tab.

Norm retired to the Oregon Coast in the Astoria area. He has worked tirelessly on MIA/POW issues speaking and publishing newsletters. He returned to Vietnam one last time in 1989 in search of any information or remains. Norm has been recognized by the American Legion with numerous awards for his actions. He has earned performance awards from the VFW, the State of Oregon Highway Division and the American Red cross for chairing their blood drives. Norm was a member of the Special Operations Association; the Special Forces Association, Chapter 47, Military Order of the Purple Heart, DAV, VFW and many others.

He is survived by his wife, Patti, his family and many friends.

HAVE YARD WILL TRAVEL   CASUAL HERO
HERO OF THE OPPRESSED   WORLD TRAVELER

SSg DALE HANSON (Bushmaster)

SOA CCC

SPECIAL FORCES

AUTHOR, LECTURER TRAVELLER & BUM

FAREASTERN INDOCHINA SPECIAL FORCES AND JUNGLE FIGHTER'S ASSOCIATION, LTD.

WARS FOUGHT
REVOLUTIONS STARTED   BARS EMPTIED
ASSASSINATIONS PLOTTED   TIGER TAMED
UPRISINGS QUELLED   VIRGINS CONVERTED
GOVERNMENTS RUN   ORGIES ORGANIZED
ALLIGATORS CASTRATED   COMPUTERS VERIFIED

Dale Hanson's Business Card

Extraction of a Montagnard team on a hot LZ. Courtesy of Dale Hanson.

Extraction of a recon team by Doney ladder. Courtesy of John Plaster.

Extraction of a recon team by strings. Courtesy of Clarence Long.

Author on a Ford Drum mission in a Piper Cub.

Chapter Eighteen

BACK IN-COUNTRY — TWO MORE TOURS

The rubber tires of the Curtiss C-46 made a protesting "uurp" as it touched the hot runway, floated a dozen feet down the asphalt, and touched down again with a rumble. The captain taxied off the runway and maneuvered at speed toward the hangar. He was the same Air America pilot who showed me the massive gathering of sea snakes half a year before. I had only time to nod a good luck/farewell to the small silent recon team across the aisle and climb down to the tarmac before he revved the engines, made a turn, and fast-taxied back to the runway to takeoff. When out of the prop blast, I placed my left thumb behind the flash of my beret and placed it one inch above my left eye, leveled the beret across my brow and pressed down the right side. My cloth Combat Infantry Badge was sewn above the jump wings on my chest, and the red SOG patch was sewed on at the pocket. I was a veteran returning to the war. I felt valuable and capable. I had "sand." I had "grit." Despite the acute danger associated with C&C, I looked forward to the coming year.

A staff sergeant was there with the S-1 jeep and we exchanged news. He was as eager to hear the stateside news as I was to learn about the war situation. I looked for changes to the town as we drove to the FOB. The familiar landmarks were still there. The abandoned French buildings that were pockmarked by shellfire during Tet still stood at the edge of the road, safe in their uselessness. I looked for rocket damage and new scars of the war suffered while I was away. I noticed that people did not stroll but moved with purpose, their faces focused on some goal ahead. Passing White Mice headquarters, it happened that the same thin Vietnamese man in a white shirt leaned against the same column of the porch, smoking a cigarette — Salem, of course. His eyes narrowed as we drove by. "'Will you walk into my parlor?' said the spider to the fly." We passed the various shops with their doors open like mouths and I smelled their separate breaths: sandalwood, *nuoc mam*, Jade East aftershave and the sweet incense of India. Next to the sidewalk, under the shade of a tree, a toothless man panted as he waited on his pedicab.

We had to wait to cross the Dak Bla River. A span of the bridge was out, perhaps blown by sappers, and traffic was one way at a time across a pontoon bridge. We waited at the side of the road behind a line of deuce-and-a-half trucks. Haggard tribesmen with sunken eyes crossed on foot. They were hatless and wore tribal black clothing and carried their belongings in woven baskets strapped on their backs. A woman with drooping eyelids carried an infant held tight to her bare chest by wraps of cloth. The baby's head lolled side to side in rhythm with the mother's footsteps as it suckled at a shriveled breast. An old farmer urged his buffalo across, tapping its side with a thin prod. Facing us and crossing the river was a long column of trucks filled with soldiers. It was a Vietnamese unit, part of a division, moving west for a distant battle. Many of the soldiers stood in the back to feel the breeze as they traveled. They looked small under their steel helmets.

The column ahead of us at the bridge was American. Faded Fourth Infantry Division patches were on their shoulders. A piece symbol was drawn in marker on the cloth covering of one soldier's helmet. We backed a few feet out of the stench of diesel. The driver in front of us was impatient and revved his engine and black sooty exhaust belched from the stacks. Someone must have looked at the long oncoming line of trucks and realized it would be a long wait. One by one the drivers shut off their engines, and except when the oncoming trucks whined to make it up the slope of the pontoon bridge, it was quiet. The last sound of animal hooves on the planks echoed back to me. A GI in the truck ahead found AFVN, the armed forces radio station, and a song blared from his transistor:

> *Thought I heard a rumblin' calling to my name*
> *Two hundred million guns are loaded, Satan cries,*
> *'Take aim'*
>
> *Better run through the jungle*
> *Better run through the jungle*
> *Better....*

The Americans started their trucks, the engines' growl drowning out the rest of the lyrics. Black smoke rose and fell as soot on the hood of our jeep. We let them move ahead of us a space and proceeded toward the FOB.

We drove past the headquarters building and the two flagpoles and stopped at S-1 where I signed in and received instructions to go to Commo for my code name.

"You want to pick one yourself, Sarge?"

"Same one as last year," I said, thinking that one's code name lasted a lifetime.

"I suppose that Double-O-Seven is taken," I said as an afterthought. He smiled.

"Figures. Well, my code name was Bushmaster when I was in recon." The sergeant thought a moment. "They want all the code names to be five letters now. Makes it easier to encode and send messages."

I thought of the difficulty of trying to remember such things when under the pressure of a fire fight. My hair was blond, and I was Scandinavian. "Swede," I said. "It might be easier for the team to remember."

"Swede it is."

I had not sought out an assignment yet but assumed that I would just go back to recon. I had a twinge of nervousness as I thought of it. I crossed the compound, making my way to the Recon Company office, and looking for familiar faces.

"Dale!"

"Mike!"

"You made it." In the center of the parade field, we hugged and I looked at him. Mike Buckland had brown hair and eyes — almond shaped eyes that squinted day or night. He was the youngest of our group. We even played coy with his age to get him over here with the rest of the group, but he looked older now, seasoned with the war.

"Yes," I said, "It seems that I have been gone a long time. It was a wonderful time for the most part, but I felt guilty knowing what you guys must have been going through while I was gone. Sometimes when I was most happy and enjoying myself, that was when I felt most guilty for being home instead of with our guys. Anyway, I am back and ready to go back to the field."

"Well, you were missed. Doney missed you. I think he has hope of a future for you in the military. Your Vietnamese missed you too. 'Buckland, you talk Han-Son. Him come back?'"

I know that I smiled as I heard that. "Well, Mike, I am glad you are alive."

Mike's face became downcast, and his voice was low. "You and I are the only ones left that came here from our class. Randy Rhea was killed while you were gone."

I know that I stared with my mouth open. And then I wept. Another roommate, classmate and close friend. Randy was quiet and wholesome, an all-American boy.

I wept until I was finished. It did not matter that anyone saw. I wept.

"What happened?"

"He was at Dak Pek rushing to a helicopter when they mortared the place. When he went down, he collapsed in a heap. He did not move. There was no blood, and they could not find a wound at first. Then they found a tiny hole the size of a part of a wood matchstick. It pierced his heart and he died instantly."

Mike looked at me and added, "And you have been wounded. What they told us is true. We will all be dead or wounded before the tour is done."

He paused. "Where were you going now?"

"I was heading to Recon to see if they had a team that I could be on. I haven't been assigned anywhere yet, but I thought I would see what was available."

"Dale, I don't think you should go in the field just yet. Let's go to my hootch so we can talk first."

We crossed the compound as a half dozen helicopters passed over our camp and descended to the pad on the far side. From the firebase to the east, howitzers fired in volleys at an unseen target. Red-bereted Vietnamese paratroopers in their tailored uniforms strode between a beehive of buildings. The activity of common cause around me was something I had missed while I was away.

Mike Buckland's hootch was an oasis, a place of quiet and refuge from the war. Given time, most of us would build one like his. A thick, comfortable Air Force bunk and mattress invited rest from the far side of the room. Those beds were in high demand and could cost a captured SKS rifle in trade. A dresser with several drawers faced a bed and a small table and chairs. The hardwood dresser had been purchased from the camp carpenter in his shop in town. On it were books and the latest reel-to-reel tape deck with high quality speakers. His diamond possession was a small refrigerator purchased from the post exchange. On the fridge door Mike had painted the cartoon image of Snoopy, the Charles M. Schulz *Peanuts* character. It was rendered in full color and Snoopy wore a green beret complete with the 5th flash. Written in black letters in an arch above Snoopy's head were the letters "SOC ET TUUM," which at first glance appeared to be Latin.

"Coke?" he asked.

"Thanks."

"Don't go back to the field right away. It isn't the same anymore. It is not worth the risk right now. Maybe that will change."

A very loud crack of an artillery round passed overhead and broke the sound barrier. It halted our conversation until our brains processed that the boom was not incoming.

"Here is what is happening: They are sending our American troops home and expecting the South Vietnamese to take over. It is called Vietnamization."

"I know about that. It is a big deal in the States now."

Mike nodded. "The Fourth Infantry Division has been sent home and there are no Conventional forces near us anymore — only us Special Forces in the A camps and special ops."

"I thought I saw some Fourth Infantry people coming in."

"If you did, they might be the very last ones — someone to turn out the lights."

"That troop withdrawal has left the three provinces around us empty, and the North Vietnamese have taken them over. They have become sanctuaries and unmolested supply routes. The South Vietnamese have abandoned the area around us to the Communists. Doing a local mission now is almost as dangerous as going over the fence on our old operations."

He took a long drink from the can and continued. "The people are not the same either. A lot of our SF people have become casualties and the big shots have sent some 75th Rangers as replacements. It is not to knock their courage, but the fact is they are not Special Forces and it shows."

Mike looked at his feet as he slowly and quietly spoke. "Dale, you and I have talked about this before — we would risk death to win against Communism. But I am not so sure that anyone is trying to win anymore. The Viets run or get beat every time they go out there. And some of the new teams in the field hunker down and give Covey new coordinates every day just as if they were moving. They get picked up at the same LZ they went in on."

I was digesting what my friend said, my thumb picking up the old habit of sliding round and around the rim of the soda can. Big Norway rats infested the warehouses and we often found feces on the cans, so we always rubbed the tops clean before we opened them. I pondered as my thumb circled the rim.

"When I was home everything in the news was anti-Vietnam War.

The press does not report the news. It is left wing propaganda and they give aid and comfort to the enemy. Walter Cronkite is still calling the Tet Offensive the biggest defeat of American forces ever. Never mind that the Viet Cong attacked over a hundred targets in one night and lost every battle, and lost 35,000 soldiers, which all but destroyed the Viet Cong."

I was on a roll, venting. "I heard one announcer on TV sneer — I mean sneer — and say, 'So if the Viet Cong lost 35,000 soldiers and were all but destroyed, tell us, who is doing all the fighting?' His voice was mocking, an undisguised hatred for us fighting the war. It never occurred to him that the Viet Cong had been replaced by hardcore North Vietnamese regulars with modern equipment to include tanks and even MIGs and helicopters.

"We have a bunch of anti-war, pro-Communist senators such as Senators Church, Mansfield and Fulbright and others who take our top secret missions and at the end of the day's session, read them into the Congressional Record. That way they are not really giving the information directly to the enemy. They would say it is not their fault the Communists read the official document and got the message.

"Just before I left, the newspapers showed a picture of a crowd marching against the war in Washington D.C. The newspaper banner said that ten thousand people protested at the capitol. But Carl Macintyre in his magazine showed that the picture was cropped to make it look like a large crowd. He showed a picture of the same group from a distance. It was only a few hundred. But the press still clung to the heading that there were thousands, and that Americans were all against the war."

Mike let me talk until I was finished and got it all out of my system. "Don't get me wrong," he said, "SOG is still fulfilling its mission as it always has. They are still the most professional and skilled soldiers in the world. I just think it might be good to look around for a while before you go back to the ground."

This was not what I had anticipated when I hopped off the Air America airplane a couple of hours before. "You are probably right. Perhaps it would be wise after all to see our 'old hands' first and get their advice and get a feel for the teams."

That night I had a dream. It recalled an event that occurred in my childhood when life was new and I was impressed with common things. It was a thing forgotten but tucked away to be retrieved later, like something found again in an old attic. It had been a winter of snow and cold and wind in northern Minnesota where I lived. The snow fences along the country roads were buried, but here and there one or two slats still showed through like yellow teeth. Snow drifted in heaps on the Canada side of barns and covered the low windows and the snow from the roof merged with the drifts on the ground into a continuous grade. Black and white Holstein cows gathered on the lee side away from the wind and lay in groups, contented and chewing their cuds.

But when spring came that year it arrived in gentleness and unusual warmth. Crows cawed in the trees and water trickled under the crusts of snow as loudly as wind chimes. In places where the ditches were still frozen the melt gathered on the top and swirled in greyness and drifted to the lakes and rivers. Country roads became slush. In short weeks the fields lay bare and black and the rock piles in them were clear of snow and the willows produced the first buds of the year. Then the Roseau River began to flood. There was still two or three feet of ice on the river and the melted snow collected on top and crept over the banks and clawed its way into the fields and even into the streets of the town. In places, new streams found new beds on the country roads and rushed along their lengths, tearing channels as they went. We were going to our grandparents' house and my dad straddled the channels with the car.

In the dream, I remember that we arrived at a bridge that was nearly flooded over. Dad stopped the car and got out to check the safety of crossing. Mom was terrified to cross in the car so she got out and walked across on the planks and she shaded her eyes with one hand so she would not see the churning water. My brother and I got out to see. The current gathered mud along the banks and the water was grey and opaque and ran over the top of the crossing. The surge bore a large hole in the gravel at the shoulder of the road from below. My dad and we boys investigated the hole. The water was clear there and full of minnows. It was a natural minnow bucket kept fresh by the stream and hundreds of bait sized minnows swam in the confines. Dad mentioned a name and said, "I wonder if he is using this to keep his minnows,"

Dad made us boys cross on foot, then with the driver's door open so he could jump out, he drove our car across the bridge. Along the road were homesteads next to the river. The flood gathered at the sides of the fields, and we saw the advance of the encroaching flood. There were ripples where the flood pushed against the fields and lay the brown grass flat on the earth. In two or three places, small islands remained in the meadows where the farmer had piled rocks that were exposed by the plow when he cleared his land. Those piles were higher than the rest of the field. I watched the water as it crawled over the field seizing more and more of the earth. Nothing was there to stop the flood. My dad watched silently as the farmer lost his field to the flooding. Only the piles of rocks remained with the grass and scrub brush and willow trees. I watched as mice or voles scurried to the high ground. An owl eyed the mice and it seemed, in my memory, that the mice would sacrifice one or two of their own for the safety of the dry land.

I woke with my pillow wet with sweat and a soft sound in the room. Above my head in the layers of ceiling, thin claws scratched their way, barely scraping the wood. I imagined a mouse with thin, white, almost fragile claws on pink feet, and with light-grey fur, clean and dry. And I recalled in my dream the advancing flood waters driving everything before it. There seemed to be no end to the streams of Communist soldiers that invaded this land. Here and there was a rock pile in the center of the field — a Special Forces camp there to stop the enemy. We had companies of our tribesmen to attack them, and we could call in massive B-52 strikes where intelligence could pinpoint their location.

I smelled bacon and French toast and fried potatoes as I entered the mess hall and took a tray. The Viet cook looked at me with his brows raised in question. "Three over medium," I said, and he cracked the eggs on to the huge, flat stove top then looked to the next soldier in line. With my tray full of food, I slid my chair under a dining table and smiled — still propped upright on the plastic tablecloth between the salt and pepper shakers, was the small sign of months before that read, "Take two salt tablets and drive on." Ralph Rodd, Ted Wicorek and Mike Buckland were already seated and well into breakfast.

"Good morning to you guys," I said, and I closed my eyes in a simple silent prayer before the meal.

"'Bout time you got here. We were about to leave."

Someone put his hand on my shoulder and I looked up to see "Plastic Man" John Plaster.

"Hey, I'm glad to see you. You have lost weight," I said to him. John was slender with dark hair and mustache and seemed always ready for the next thing to do.

"That's recon, malaria and black water fever. I'm glad you are back, Dale. Say, I have your thirty-round magazine that you wanted. Remember, you put up fifty dollars for one?"

I did remember. I could have been the poster child used to urge a company to produce them. I had been shot changing the magazine in my CAR-15. There had been three NVA facing me, and I took two of them down, leaving me with an empty magazine. My adversary had ten more rounds in his rifle and shot me in the hand as I was reaching for my next magazine. At that time there was no large capacity magazine for the CAR-15 in existence. John drafted a letter requesting its production. Each of us in recon signed the letter and chipped in fifty dollars."

"It has only been five months. I'm surprised you have them already."

John laughed. "I didn't go through the government or Colt. I went to a private manufacturer. They designed, produced and mailed them to us in ten days."

I just smiled and shook my head.

"Come over to my hootch and I will give it to you."

John left to join his teammates at another table. "Guys," I said to the rest, "Since I have been gone for a while, fill me in. What has been coming down the 'trail'? What have our missions been like?"

"Well, I can tell you what has been coming down the trail. It is a highway, I can tell you." Ted's voice was loud in the room. He had one of those voices. Ted was solid and stocky around two-twenty. He had short blond hair and his mannerism showed him to be fully involved in the topic. "Intelligence says a hundred thousand troops are coming down the trail every year. They have ten thousand truckloads of supplies making the trip every year and that doesn't include those tens of thousands of bicycles they push with two hundred pounds of supplies on each either."

"Shush," Mike warned. Even though we were among our own we needed to be guarded when we spoke of intelligence.

In a lower voice Mike said, "They say that PAVN has ten thousand anti-aircraft guns strung out along the trail. Ten thousand! Some eighty thousand soldiers are tasked with guarding the trail, and that doesn't count the tens of thousands of soldiers who maintain the road and supply depots, truck stops and rest areas." Mike paused and tapped his spoon on the tablecloth three times and continued. "These are not country peasants stumbling down the trail. We are looking at a sophisticated logistics system out there. They have depots run like a city."

Ted spoke as softly as he could, but his voice still carried, "A couple of our teams have reported seeing helicopters in their AO. We checked. They were not ours. They were all black with no markings. The guess is that they are Russian, but of course Saigon discounted the sighting. And…" he said tapping the table with his fingers, "And, some of our pilots have encountered MIGs in our target areas."

Ralph Rodd listened to us talk without speaking, but in a pause in the conversation he quietly said, "You never know what you will find. You think there will be a handful of them out there and a battalion shows up." Ralph was an old hand for his years with at least twenty missions across the fence — most of them we would call "hairy." He, like us, was in his early twenties. With his average height and size and red-blond hair he would have gone unnoticed in a crowd. His features were square and somber. When Ralph spoke of any of his missions, he related facts as he would in an after-action report with the view that the details, no matter how harrowing they were, would be of help to the rest of us. He had a quiet courage in which he outthought the enemy and made calm decisions and survived when the odds said that he could not.

"Like that POW snatch you made," Mike prompted.

Ralph's voice was soft, and we leaned forward to better hear. "It was almost as if they knew we were coming because every time we moved toward the 'Trail,' they seemed to be waiting, cutting us off from the road. I had to do some maneuvering to get down there, but we found a good stretch of the road where we could set up a prisoner snatch — a straight stretch where I did not have to worry what would be just around the bend. We set up flank security on both ends and I set up the ambush between them. What I didn't have with lots of people, I made up for with Claymore mines. I had eight of them in my kill zone with a space in the middle where I hoped to get a prisoner — you know, pretty much the standard tactic. So, we sat there waiting along the road. We were close to the road, about forty or fifty feet, so I could run out and grab the prisoner and get off the road before they could react.

"We crouched there waiting with our hearts beating in our ears. It had to be around noon when I heard boots crunching in the gravel. There were lots of them because they were around the bend where we could not see, but we could hear them coming. There were so many footsteps that I could not hear individual steps. I heard voices in the group and one or two of them coughed. I did not have to whisper, 'Get ready,' because we all heard them coming long before we saw them. I had hoped to find three or four of them or at most a squad when we set up, but when the first of the column rounded the bend and started down the straight stretch, I knew there were way more than we could handle."

Ralph paused and looked up at us, for he had been speaking with his eyes cast down at his coffee cup. "I was afraid my people on the flank would panic and shoot them up, but I couldn't warn them off without the enemy seeing my slightest movement. Thankfully, I think my people were too petrified to do anything. The column kept coming. There were too many to engage for sure, but I could at least study them for intelligence. I counted them as they came and tried to notice how they moved and the equipment they carried. We scrunched into the grass and made ourselves as small as we could. I hoped they would just march through. I kept counting them and looking at their weapons and uniforms. One hundred, two hundred, three hundred soldiers with the officers and non-coms walked alongside. They filled the entire kill zone between both flanks. There is a terror to have that many enemies so close to you. You can smell their sweat. You can hear their breathing and the rubbing of the cloth in their sleeves. Enough electricity passed through my body that I wondered if I could function if I had to. Then, all hope that they would pass through disappeared. A sergeant blew a whistle, and an officer halted them right in front of us and called the battalion to order. They stacked arms and proceeded to eat their noon meal.

"I couldn't believe it. How long would it be until they saw us? We didn't dare move or even blink. There was a soldier right across from me in the road, He was sitting on his rucksack eating rice and faced directly toward me. I was afraid to look him in the eye lest he feel he was being watched. I gazed down to his chest instead and saw that he had a button missing. I stared at the buttonhole. I do not remember breathing. A sneeze and we would all be dead."

Ralph drank the last of his coffee.

"Then, one of the soldiers went to the side of the road to empty his bladder. He did — right on top of my interpreter. It was too much for my man. In shock and disbelief, he stood up in front of those three hundred enemy soldiers and stared at his wet front. And that was it — the show was on.

"I set off all eight of my Claymores. That is nearly six thousand steel balls flying at them. We emptied our rifles on the ones still standing, then threw grenades as fast as we could. I didn't wait to see the damage we inflicted on them, but I do not recall a single soldier left standing when we left. We all took off running away from the road. We expected all hell to fall on us, but as it was, we didn't hear a single return shot for more than five minutes and that was probably from a unit responding to the sounds of our ambush.

"We got scattered and our choppers picked us up one and two at a time. Except for all those soldiers dead or wounded on the road, the woods were alive with furious enemy. It was a wonder that we all got out of there and not even one of us was wounded."

Ted was remembering what he had said about the MIGs and black helicopters operating in our AO, far from their normal haunts farther north near Hanoi and Haiphong. He asked, "Can you imagine hearing the sound of choppers and one hovers directly over you through a break in the trees and tosses a rope down to you? We would probably think it was one of ours, snap in, and it would lift us out and bring us to a base camp where the 'friendly Cubans' would interrogate us."

We all stared at Ted. One of us shuddered. "How do you come up with these things? I don't even want to think of that."

"Well, it could happen," Ted said.

I met the CO of the S-2 shop as I crossed the parade field. "Sergeant Hanson," he said approaching me. I stopped to render a salute, but instead he reached out and shook my hand. "I am Major Potter in charge of the intelligence section of the FOB. I was just talking to S-1. The captain tells me you were offered a direct commission to captain in an airborne division and you turned them down. Why don't you come and work for me in the intel section? You are 11-F, so you are already trained in intelligence. I think it might be a good fit for you."

I fell in beside him as we walked. The major was slim, of average height with short white hair under his beret. He had piercing blue eyes which seemed full of wisdom and life. He struck me as someone who was very conscious of health and fitness — someone who ate raw carrots and celery. "It seems to me," he said, "that with the waves of enemy coming our way and the grave danger our teams have in the field, that we need to give them the best information we can get before we send them. You have been there and know what it is like. Would you like that assignment?"

I had about decided to take Mike's advice about working in the "Two Shop" when the Major asked that. "Yes sir," was all that I said.

"Good, because I already had them assign you to my shop. By the way, I see you have another stripe. S-1 said that you ranked two out of thirty-seven. Congratulations, Staff Sergeant."

I felt guilty that I did not go directly back to the field to fight, so I poured myself into my new assignment. I had been trained in 11-F school to operate in the shadow world of espionage and spies, cut-outs, blind drops, double agents, codes, silenced weapons, invisible inks and setting up spy networks. So, I was fitted for my work in the secure bowels of the intelligence shop to gather all available intelligence regarding a coming mission and present it to the teams in a meaningful manner. The shadow of missing teams, teams completely wiped out, and the casualties of my brothers on previous missions were a constant reminder that the life of a team might hinge on my faithfulness to fully give them all information relating to their mission. I prepared topographical maps of the recon team's target area — forty-nine square miles of enemy sanctuary. I gathered every thread of intelligence and information regarding a team's mission, briefed them before they were committed, and then debriefed them upon their return from the field. Like a nurse I hovered over the teams, not only in the top secret briefing room, but while they were in the field on their assigned missions. Our SOG people placed their lives on the line to complete their mission.

When I was on convalescent leave, I heard a reporter interview a general who was just given a new assignment. I was dumbstruck when I heard the general's response to a question for which any squad leader knew the answer. If his response was representative of other leaders, I considered at the time that we were in peril.

"General Smith, what is your chief purpose on your new duty station?"

Smith's answer was a political bromide. "My mission is the safety of my men."

I was astounded that one could rise to the highest echelons of leadership and miss completely what every basic soldier knows: The mission is first. Always.

Operations and Intelligence students at Fort Bragg are presented a dilemma to underscore the imperative to accomplish the mission. In my case, we arrived at the classroom located at the far side of the parade field. It was olive drab and the only identification on the old barracks building was the building number on the right side of the door. Nothing else. We entered and took our seats and the instructor did not speak until there was utter silence in the room, not even the sound of a boot sliding against the floor. He did not give a word of preamble to his talk and his voice was soft so we strained to hear him clearly.

"Your team is given a mission to capture or kill a high-ranking enemy agent and capture his satchel of information. Intelligence has learned that the agent makes his rounds between two base camps along a certain high-speed trail deep into enemy controlled territory. You are not told why the satchel is important, only that you must capture it. You set up an ambush along the trail and silently wait for his arrival. Hours pass. Something crawls under your headgear. Is it a Carib beetle or sweat rolling down your scalp? You desperately want to scratch but you do not. You dare not move and betray your position. You watch a leech flop end over end and disappear into your sleeve. You let it. Then you hear voices around the bend, from the direction you expect the agent to arrive. There is a muffled cry around the corner of the trail. Pain, dread and fear describe the crying, A squad of North Vietnamese soldiers has kidnapped a young girl from a nearby hamlet and are dragging her to a place of seclusion. The tops of her feet have no skin from being dragged down the gravel path. She has been dragged a long distance for not only is her skin worn away but much of the flesh, and you see the pink of bone on her flopping feet. Dirt and twigs stick to the place,"

"She cries out and one soldier fists her in the stomach, then places one hand on her lower jaw and the other under her nose and pries her mouth open," The instructor mimics the motion with his two hands in front of the class. Perhaps it is the light, but the instructor's eyes have become snake grey. "Another NVA stuffs her mouth with dirt," here the instructor mimicked handfuls of dirt being stuffed into her mouth, and he pushed his palm into the mouth of the imaginary victim. 'No one will hear you now. Go ahead, cry for mother,' one soldier mocks. "They have stopped directly in front of your ambush."

There was a pause in the instructor's talk to give us time to let the mental scene unfold in front of our ambush. "You hear the cloth rip as the soldiers tear away her skirt. It is the beaded garment that Montagnard virgins wear. The men leer and laugh. And you are ashamed that as you lay there in the tall grass moments before, you let a leech concern you as in front of you a squad of men proceeds to abuse and rape this young maiden. What do you do?"

The room was quiet. "What do you do?" He demands.

"Continue the mission." Was the expected and only answer he will accept. "You will let it happen. It runs contrary to the fiber of your being. Unlike many other cultures that would not be repulsed by our little drama, we were raised in America and the roots of our Judeo-Christian ethic are in our souls.

"Some of you might work your way down there and do away with those soldiers and pull their bloody bodies off the trail. And you might even get away with it. But gentlemen, your mission is first."

Here the instructor took a place in front of the lectern and stood slim and tall in his starched fatigues and looked at each of us seated before him. "We all have hearts. And if the story I have told you should ever happen to you and you do nothing — and you must do nothing — the image of that little girl will give you nightmares and you will be smothered in guilt and shame the rest of your life. But should you intervene, the slightest slip, one shot that the enemy gets off before you kill them all, the early arrival of the agent coming on the scene, or the little girl who runs back to her home screaming, 'American soldiers save me!' will be all it takes to roll up your mission."

One of the students had not lifted his eyes the whole lecture but had held his pencil at the sharpened end between his thumb and forefinger and rolled the eraser end back and forth, back and forth. The instructor stood directly in front of him. "Who knows but that the satchel contained the enemy's plans to destroy a dozen little hamlets in which dozens of precious little girls like the one on the trail reside? Gentlemen, the mission is first, last, and always."

That lecture seemed long ago as I prepared for an intelligence briefing for one of our teams. Our people could refuse to go on a mission. But they never did. They stepped aboard the waiting helicopter ready to die if it happened, trusting that it was all worth it. And I recalled that not only was a little innocent Montagnard girl expendable to the mission, but in the broad scheme of things, so was the team itself — at least to the strategic planners. After all, we went on our missions sterile, with nothing to identify us as American. If we were captured, the Government said they would deny any knowledge of us. But there was one certitude a team in the field could count on: They would never be expendable to the rest of us at the FOB, including me in the Two Shop. We would do everything to get our people back safely.

I recalled an incident during my first tour in recon. One of our teams was sent on a mission to secure a certain item. It took great courage and stealth, but they captured the object. The team maneuvered toward an LZ where they expected a pickup. The enemy was in hot pursuit. B-40 rockets were exploding in the trees when they made it to the LZ. But at the clearing they discovered there was no Covey or support aircraft; instead a single helicopter arrived and hovered above them. It was a CIA helicopter. The pilot radioed the team leader, "Put the item on the floor of the helicopter."

This was strange. "What?" was all the One Zero could say.

"I said place the item on the floor of the helicopter and back away."

Shards of B-40 rockets sliced the canopy of trees around them. The enemy was getting voice-close, but it was the voice of the door gunner he could not believe. He could not be hearing what he heard.

The chopper again instructed, "Place the item on the floor of the chopper and back away."

It was clear to the team that they were about to be abandoned to the enemy.

"That is a negative, chopper. If you want the item, you will have to take us on to get it."

"I said, place the item on the floor. That is an order."

"And that is a negative. You either take us all aboard or we will keep your object and take our chances with the enemy."

"You will be court martialed," the voice screamed.

"Up to you, chopper. I have no time to dicker with you with PAVN on my tail. Besides, my Montagnard people know what is going on and they would just as soon shoot you down.

The One Zero heard a sigh on the radio. "Get aboard then."

I knew that there would be missions in which the information was of more value than the messengers who brought it. Regardless of the attitude of the strategic analysts elsewhere, I would do all that I could from the Shop to help each team accomplish their mission and make it back home.

I met every team as it came in. They were always exhausted, bent over under their rucksacks, trudging as they walked, their clothing greased with sweat and mud. They smiled, but it was the weary smile of those who have narrowly escaped death. In their eyes you could see profound weariness. It took great effort for them to speak. We were all there at the helipad. We greeted them with cold drinks for their dry mouths and hugged them and told them how glad we were they made it safely back. The tribesmen of the team never ceased to look like warriors, and we greeted them with fondness and esteem. One by one we all drifted away and began to leave the chopper pad.

The One Zero then looked to his team of Montagnards. I saw his pant leg was torn and stained around the tear. It was a tense escape from the field, and I wondered if the team leader even realized that he had been wounded. He placed his hands on the shoulders of his people and he looked into their eyes and called them by name and said, "We did it. We accomplished our mission. Thank you." There was deep affection as he did so.

The One Zero looked for someone in our group. "Can we get a meal for them?"

"Give us a half hour," the mess sergeant said.

The One Zero returned to his team. One arm was over the shoulder of his Montagnard team leader. "Get a shower and we will get you something to eat, then I will see you after."

Then, at a time when the immediate concerns were through, I went to the One Zero and put my hand on his shoulder. "I know you are tired, but I need to debrief you on your mission while the information is fresh."

The "old hands" would always answer the same, "Of course. Do we have time to shower and eat and take care of the team?"

His question was rhetorical for his care of his team was first. "Of course," I said, "Three hours enough time? I can meet you at the S-2."

"We will be there."

The old SF guys knew the value of the information that they learned. They came prepared for two or three hours of detailed questioning regarding what might seem to them the most insignificant detail of what they learned. They were weary but came prepared with their folded maps and notebooks in one hand and something cold in the other. They had showered but there was still dirt under their fingernails and traces of green camouflage behind their ears. It would take multiple showers to remove it all. They were not put out that I asked if the trees were deciduous hard wood or if the creek had a stony bottom and would be dry in the off season.

I recall one mission when survival was dubious and afterwards laying on my back safely in bed, reliving the events of it all. I recalled King David in the Old Testament. He and his soldiers had been in battle and at the end of the day David rolled to his back and in his thirst (which every man in fierce combat has experienced), thought of the cool clean water in the deep well at the town of Bethlehem, the place he was born. He spoke to himself, "Oh I wish I had a cup of water from that well in Bethlehem."

David did not realize it, but he said the words aloud and some of his commandos heard it. There were three of them and they were in David's list of thirty-three famous heroes. The problem was Bethlehem was on the other side of the Philistine army. The three warriors loved David and without telling him, decided to get the water. They fought their way through the Philistine army and arrived at the outskirts of Bethlehem and lowered the bucket into the depths. With the precious water they fought their way back through the enemy lines and presented it to David. David was overwhelmed at the selfless act. The king glanced at the sparkling water and fully knew the cost of it. "Is this not the blood of the men who went in jeopardy of their lives?" The One-Zeros also knew the value of the information they had learned. They would not let what they learned at the risk of blood be for naught by letting it stale and sour on a shelf because they were too weary to be debriefed.

I debriefed several teams in those months and noticed that several teams led by the new non-Special Forces replacements were not that way. They were often put-out when asked to be debriefed so soon after being taken from the field. "Why not tomorrow?" There was often a measure of arrogance also when they were interviewed by someone who was "rear echelon." Further, they were not as careful to record details and coordinates of the mission.

I briefed our Hatchet Force missions also. They were larger, platoon and company size elements that went in to do reconnaissance in force, bomb damage assessment after the massive B-52 bombers dropped their loads, or they were sent in to attack a target. About the time I began briefing, Company B was sent in by helicopter to block the entire Ho Chi Minh Trail on a mission called Grand Slam II. They brought in machine guns and mortars and recoilless rifles, and thousands of sandbags. Within hours they filled the sandbags with gravel and created a base area on a rise just above the trail. When the first enemy truck convoys started past, they destroyed the first and last of the trucks and as there was no room for them to get past the destroyed vehicles on the one-lane road, B Company called in airstrikes and destroyed the convoy. For the next week all traffic was halted on the Ho Chi Minh Trail, the jugular that supplied the enemy with soldiers and supplies in the South. The Communists tried to dislodge B Company by frontal attack and mortar and artillery barrage. Trucks stacked up behind the ambush site with no place to go and jets pulverized the stalled convoys. Hundreds of enemies were killed, and large amounts of supplies were destroyed.

It was a day's work for the Hatchet Force.

Chapter Nineteen

SAPPER ATTACK

April 1, 1970. On the far side of our compound, the side opposite the well-lighted road, behind the motor pool in the darkest area of our camp, something moved near the wire. A soldier from the Security Company had stopped at the place to relieve himself against the building and heard the movement. He froze and peered into the shadows until his eyes watered as he sought the source of the sound. A problem for him as he looked for the suspect shadow was that in the darkest part of the FOB, night itself was an immense shadow, yet he remained, holding his breath as he slowly investigated the scene. He would not be able to describe what he heard in a simple word, but there was a rustle in the night that moved with the lightness of a bird among the deep shadows.

He focused, willing himself to define shape in the shadow. He heard it again and gazed at the area. This time he indeed saw a shadow pass the paleness of a layer of sandbags, moving right to left, then another followed behind. He slid his carbine from his shoulder taking care not to be heard. Then he heard a squeak as the two shadows moved in a flash toward him then clawed up the rough-sawed beams of the motor pool shed. The soldier by then had his rifle to his shoulder, and he heard at last the rats chasing in the rafters. He let out a sigh of relief and laughed quietly. He had been educated as a young man before the war, before it took him from being a scholar and made him a soldier, and before his wounds kept him from the field and made him a guard instead. He smiled to himself. "Issa, the famous poet of haiku should have been here tonight. What a poem he would have written about courtship among the rats in the rafters." He placed his rifle over his shoulder, turned and continued his patrol.

Perhaps it was only another hour when North Vietnamese sappers slid shadow-like into this same place. They were the enemy counterpart to Special Forces, courageous and trained for this mission. They slid into our camp in a sewage drain thought too small for a man. It was filled with raw sewage and was the home of rats and snakes. There were fifteen in the group, and they crawled through with their weapons and explosives and assembled at a place in the shadow of the motor pool. Their spy in our camp told them this was the place to assemble. All had their targets memorized. Their leader gave the signal and they disappeared like phantoms to their various targets. At a sign they would begin the attack.

I was deep in sleep when the explosions began, but even then, I knew that this was not incoming from the outside, but that we were under a full attack from within. I did not hear anything from the perimeter to indicate that we were engaging anyone from the wire. Numerous grenades were going off, many of them sounding muffled as if being thrown inside of buildings.

I scrambled into the fatigues I had set out on my chair before I went to bed. My web gear was buckle-out as always on the back of the chair, and I buckled it on. My rifle chambered, I ran to the door and cracked it open to ensure there was no waiting enemy on the other side. The building next to mine exploded outward with a "Wuumph!" Its shutters bowed outward and burst from the structure and landed on the sidewalk. Another explosion followed from inside and yellow flames raced up the studs and engulfed the building. There could be no living person inside, so my sense was to rush toward the conflict, however at the same time I wanted to find a place at the perimeter to fight off any attack, but I was not sure just where that was. I also did not want to be shot by our own people when I rushed into the dark. I wondered if I would be able to tell our own indig people from any enemy I might encounter.

In the end it seemed that most of the explosions were happening near the TOC, and I rushed in that direction. White explosions were going off in a dozen places. There was shouting in the darkness. People were rushing toward the dispensary, and I assumed that they were the medics or the wounded. Grenades and the more powerful satchel charges exploded at the Montagnard barracks and muffled cries came from inside. There was no small-arms fire to indicate that we were engaging our attackers. Massive explosions were going off at the TOC and I heard secondary explosions in other parts of the camp. White flashes arched into the sky above the explosions and in places, a steady red glow revealed the fires of ruined buildings. I joined with a group of our people and we began a search of the compound to find the enemy sappers. Although we searched the compound until red streaks of sunrise lightened the sky, we found none.

When daylight came, we organized a full, systematic search and discovered that the sappers after completing their mission, exfiltrated the camp through the sewage, the way they had come in. Not a single sapper was found. A reinforced recon team led by Franklin Miller tracked the enemy, losing the trail in the low mountains that surround Kontum. Many of our buildings were destroyed and ten of our Montagnard fighters died when the sappers threw explosives into the barracks. The camp commander's quarters were demolished, and the TOC had been gutted and smoldered. Shredded, grey smoke shouldered its way from under the eaves and escaped into the air, moving slowly like a wounded thing.

It was still early morning, and it was uncertain whether there were any more enemy in our compound. I saw our colonel sitting down on the flag stand. He had been assigned to us by General Abrams and was not held in high regard by any of us. We called him "Brows," as he had huge black caterpillar eyebrows. He sat there bent over, clearly not engaged in the situation. He appeared to be in shock with his head between his fists, his elbows propped on his knees. He sat alone not involved with the status of his compound. None approached him to await orders. I wanted to bring him to reality — get him in charge of things.

"Colonel, what would you like me to do?"

"Huh?" he said.

I said, "There are things to do, and I am free now. What can I do for you?"

"Huh," he said again, and he looked up at me — this person who stood before him. I was certain that he did not have a clue what we had to prioritize. Then, as he raised his eyes to look at me as I spoke, he could see the burning Tactical Operations Center in front of his eyes.

"Huh. Clear the TOC," and he let his head drop back down to the place between his knees. The words were not an order from a leader — more of a wistful suggestion. He seemed unaware of anything around him. I watched him a moment, then stepped backward from him, and faced the TOC.

I looked at the building. It was our headquarters, huge, two stories and still on fire in places. As far as I knew, no one had been in the building since the attack began. Perhaps the enemy were inside rifling files for intelligence as I looked. It really needed several of us to clear the structure properly. "Okay," I thought, "I asked him, and this is what he ordered."

I stepped into the building with my rifle at the ready and peered down the hall. There was no electricity, and it was mostly dark except where flames or embers shed just enough light to maneuver. Smoke filled the upper third of the hall and the smell was strong and acrid and hurt my nostrils. Debris was everywhere and pieces of charred material crunched under my feet. The sound of every step traveled before me down the halls. There was no way that I would be able to surprise anyone. I walked slowly, looking carefully for anything, listening for movement ahead of me. Steam sizzled as moisture escaped out of burning wooden studs, and here and there burning things sputtered and crackled. I moved down the hall, "Crunch, crunch, crunch," and would get to a doorway and charge in at a crouch, ready to engage whoever lurked in the darkness.

Down the hallway. First the room at the left, then the one on the right. Further down the hall — left door, right door. Everything had a red glow in the embers. Halfway down the hall. I was about to charge into a room on the left when I clearly heard popping as if someone were in the room on the right, stepping on coals. I changed direction and spun to the right and dashed into the room ready to shoot the sapper inside. The guy was good. I never heard him behind me and before I knew it, a noose was around my neck and tightening. I had been garroted. I immediately swung my rifle back behind me in a butt-stroke. Nothing. I spun to the right trying to do the same thing with the barrel of my rifle. I swung and stroked hard enough to pierce him through with the barrel. Again nothing. The noose was getting tighter. I spun left and butt-stroked again. I couldn't seem to hit him. Then to the right with the barrel. Again nothing. The noose was ever tighter. I heard ringing in my ears and I was getting dizzy. Reflex took over and I lurched backward to make contact with his body and throw him with a judo throw — tai-otoshi would be a good one.

I slid back to get into position for the throw, and I felt nothing behind me, but the noose had slackened. I turned my head to the side and grabbed the noose with one hand and jerked it away from my neck. I turned toward my assailant. There was nobody there! I looked around and felt foolish, I laughed aloud. I had charged into the room where an electrical wire had fallen from the ceiling in a loop and wrapped around my neck. The sound was the popping of embers that watched me with evil red eyes. I had been garroting myself. I would not be telling anyone about my phantom assailant.

By mid-morning the compound appeared to be clear of enemy, but with an uncertainty of what waited outside of the wire, we began to rebuild in earnest. As it was with Nehemiah in the Old Testament, "Everyone with one of his hands wrought in the work and with the other hand, held a weapon." SOG's mission would continue. We had teams in the field to support. Elsewhere that first night of April, the Communists made thirteen ground assaults and shelled more than a hundred locations across the country. The night brought the most casualties of the year in Vietnam and was the start of the Spring–Summer offensive. The enemy began the siege of the Special Forces camps at Dak Pek and Dak Seang. The Pathet Lao began to drive across Laos crushing any anti-Communist resistance. Some believe that April 1st was the beginning of the Communist Khmer Rouge civil war to conquer Cambodia, which ultimately produced the killing fields. Anyone without calluses on their hands, anyone who owned a book or ever went to school, or wore glasses, or wore shoes, were tortured and murdered. In time the killing fields could hold no more millions of corpses and the Mekong River became a dumping place. Tens of thousands of decomposed, bloated bodies and parts of bodies floated with the current past the villages that lined the banks. Like a newspaper for those who could not read, the river told of the horrors of went on across the river.

Major Potter commandeered space in a nearby building for the Two Shop and by early afternoon we had a sense of order in the three rooms. We could say that we were operational. Although many of our file cabinets were charred and the surface was now ash or blistered paint, the contents survived remarkably well. Because they were airtight, the contents did not combust, but top secret pages took on the look of Egyptian papyrus or the parchment our founding fathers may have used. Metal desks still held their contents and after some cleaning would be used until replaced.

Major Potter stood before us as we finished.

He looked around the room and said, "Well, gentlemen, it just needs some curtains, and we are set, I think."

He sat on the edge of a desk and said, "Thank you for all your work. Obviously, because of the sensitivity of what we do we cannot hire anything out. We are the ones who need to do everything. If you can, give me a list of anything that we need to be fully functional."

He stood and noticed that his hands were black from the desk and glanced back at his pants. "We will get some cleaner and take care of those things. I will help with that too." The captain, his XO (executive officer) looked at the major not quite believing that he, an officer, would be doing housecleaning.

"What obligations do we have outstanding that we need to prioritize?"

"I was supposed to brief a recon team tomorrow," I said. "All of our support is based outside of this FOB so that is covered. I will check with commo to see if they will be up and ready. I can check with Operations to make sure it is still a go."

Mike added, "I am scheduled with a photo recon flight tomorrow. All our assets are based off-post so there is no reason that it should not happen."

He nodded. "Okay. The lieutenant and I will see if we can scrounge some file cabinets and desks so we don't have to clean all of these. Sergeant Wicorek, see what we can do about securing this building. That's all."

Most of the Two Shop left to do their assignments. Mike Buckland and I remained to work toward our missions. Sergeant First Class Armstrong was at his desk. It had been in a corner and was the least burned of our furnishings. His lamp of a hula girl with the weighted stand so it would not tip was still there with his dog tags hanging from her upraised hand. The bulb was broken, and his dog tags swayed as he stood.

He walked over to Mike, his boots loud on the floor. "I'm taking that flight," he said.

"That's okay. I'll do it. I am on the schedule."

"No. I am taking that flight. I wear more stripes and I decide."

"Sergeant. That is a very dangerous target. We always get shot at when we go. This is not the kind of target you go on for your first mission of Ford Drum."

"I don't need your advice. That is all there is to it."

Mike sighed. I could hear it across the room. "Then let me give you some advice anyway. Do not make a second pass over a suspect area — no matter how big a find you think you have. That is a very dangerous target."

It appeared that SFC Armstrong was going to say something

further, but thought twice, turned and left the room.

Mike looked at me with resignation and said, "Dale, that target is incredibly dangerous. This is not the one to fly your first mission. Any mistake is fatal. I hope the pilot can keep him safe."

Most of the FOB were unaware of the extremely hazardous missions the Two Shop routinely flew. The highly classified missions went by the whispered name of Ford Drum, and they involved the enlisted men of the S-2 intelligence and a select company of pilots who volunteered to fly for us. They were called SPAF pilots which stood for "Sneaky Pete Air Force." We flew in pairs, two Piper Cub airplanes with the pilot in the front seat and a Special Forces soldier in the seat behind. We flew miles into enemy territory, directly over their sanctuaries and base camps. At times we would pass over an opening in the jungle and pass over a column of enemy soldiers at so low an altitude that when they looked up in surprise, we could see the expressions of their faces. Had we known them we would recognize them. Our cameras would click and record their uniforms and weapons, their alertness and surprise, then we were gone before they could raise their rifles to their shoulders. Should we ever pass that group twice in the same flight, they would not be caught in surprise. Every rifle or anti-aircraft gun would be ready to shoot us down.

Thursday, April 2, 1970, most of us were in the S-2 working on various projects. The major found a few file cabinets and one desk, and we were transferring files into the new ones. Ted Wicorek was working on some photos he had taken on a photo mission. As we worked, SFC Armstrong trudged into the shop as if his boots were leaden and he had just awakened. His fatigue clothes were rumpled and baggy. Wordlessly he came in, went to his desk, and picked up a loose sheet of paper from the top. A 12.7 shell was its paperweight — a reminder of what he could expect on each mission. He silently read the words — notes he had gleaned about the flight. There he was that Thursday morning in his sterile fatigues — nothing to identify him as American. He dug into his desk drawers and his dog tags which always hung from the lamp jostled as he searched. Files were not in the same order after the attack and he bent over drawers as he scurried mouse-like from place to place in the shop, never taking the time to fully stand upright between stops. Finding what he needed, he looped his compass string through a buttonhole, stuffed a map in his upper pocket, grabbed his web gear, rifle and camera and headed for the door. He never uttered a word as he left.

A few hours later I was preparing for a briefing when the major came in. He paused at the doorway, then drifted to Armstrong's desk and lifted the dog tags from the lamp where they hung without moving. He brushed his thumb over the embossed letters with the gentleness of closing a soldier's eyes in death. The tag read, "Armstrong, Donald G." The major cupped the tags in the palm of one hand and rolled them to the other, back and forth until the chain sifted between his fingers. His voice was quiet and somber. "Gentlemen, I have bad news to tell you. Sergeant Armstrong was just killed. Anti-aircraft fire got him through the window of his airplane. I am sorry."

The major let it sink in and gave us time to reflect and grieve as we were inclined, then went to his office. Through the opening in the doorway, I could see the major as he looked down at that metal symbol of a soldier's life on his desk. I knocked at the door and entered. "Major, I will take his place."

So, I became a part of the highly classified photo reconnaissance missions behind "enemy lines," of which few people ever heard. We were the annoying mosquitos that appeared suddenly and sucked intelligence from the supply artery of PAVN, then escaped before its massive fist could swat us out of the sky.

Chapter Twenty

FORD DRUM—MONTHS
AMONG THE HEADHUNTERS

Black smoke, thin as beach grass, still rose from the ashes of buildings in our compound when we drove to the gate. Here and there some structures remained corpse-like with wall studs standing like ribs, with tendons of red cables and wiring dangling from them into their cavities. I drove at funeral speed as I passed a dozen tribesmen who were grimly raking through the burned rubble of the 'Yard barracks. They moved with reverence, never looking up from their work, their rakes gently rolling over each layer of debris. They sought for clues — a burned Seiko watch, the metal shank from a combat boot, the purple bones of a half-closed fist reaching from the ashes. One more soldier was still missing. A line of Vietnamese workers who had not learned of the attack waited along the side of the road and were being dismissed to come back another day. A convoy of trucks crept past our compound as the drivers sensed the heightened activity. They gazed at our bombed buildings and smelled the odor of the charred ruins, even over that of their diesels.

We turned right after the gate and drove beyond the city to the far side of the Kontum airport, to a small compound that housed the 219th Aviation Company. From the outside, seeing just a few Cessna "Bird Dog" airplanes near the revetments with no weaponry or "spook stuff" aboard, a newsman might think the section not worthy of notice, that the blood of the war would be found elsewhere. But just as "Universal Exports" was the innocuous cover for the James Bond movies, so too was the 219th Aviation Company; although a real military unit, it masked the top secret missions they flew for the Special Forces of SOG. The project was known as "Ford Drum" in top secret intelligence circles, but to those of us who flew them, we just called them photo recon missions. We were amused that we had our own "Sneaky Pete Air Force" and had a possessive fondness for our SPAF pilots who called themselves "The Headhunters."

Two airplanes were out of their revetments facing the runway, side by side. The planes sweltered in the heat, and you knew not to touch their metal skins. It was hot for so early in the day. The dark surface of the asphalt was melted, and heat waves rose and carried the odor of melted tar. A glance down the runway revealed it as a pool of shimmering water and sky reflected on its surface. Just beyond the two Bird Dogs, a short distance away, was a third. Its form was crumpled, and the airplane was canted to one side. A portion of the tail was torn away and hung to one side dangling by a cord.

The pilots expected us and were waiting under the shade of their airplane wings. They stepped from the relative coolness and waved as we drove up. They were young and clean-cut in their green flight suits. The pride they had in their aircraft and mission was apparent. They did not fly cobra gunships, or fighter jets, nor the massive B-52 bombers. Instead, they piloted these small, unarmed observation planes mere feet above the enemy. They did not receive the applause of others in their secret war. Only the headhunters themselves knew the controlled terror of those adrenaline-packed flights over enemy territory and the grave importance of the intelligence they gathered. Often, the intelligence they learned made it unnecessary to send a recon team into the field.

There were two lieutenants and a captain, and they smiled as they greeted us. Although I did not know the officers yet, I sensed a tension behind their smiles.

"Mike, Ted," they said in greeting as they extended their hands.

"Hello," Mike said. "This is Sergeant Hanson. He will be flying back seat with us."

"Call me Bill," said a brown-haired lieutenant.

"I'm Dale," I said, taking the cue and shaking his hand.

They introduced themselves. The captain was the older of the pilots, mid-thirties with dark brown hair and moustache. Rows of wrinkles extended from the corners of his eyes. "And you are recon, I can tell."

"How did you know that?"

"Your web gear." I glanced down at my belt as he continued. "There is no soldier in all of Vietnam that wears his web gear like that. Ammunition and grenades in canteen covers, signal and survival gear, and even an extraction rig on the harness. That is a mark of a SOG recon man."

I hadn't considered having my field gear any other way.

"That is just what we want," he said. "If we ever go down out there, you are in command of everything. We count on you to defend us at the crash site, and if we have to walk out to friendlies, we take our orders from you. We just fly these things," he said patting his .45 on his belt to show how few weapons he carried.

A lieutenant with red hair and freckles rested his hand on my shoulder. "Welcome to the headhunters. We always feel better when we have you recon men in the back seat," he said nodding his head toward a very damaged Bird Dog a few steps away.

Without realizing it we all migrated to the damaged plane.

Ted Wicorek stopped beside the shot-up airplane and marveled as he surveyed the wreckage. "How could this even fly?" he asked in his loud voice. "I cannot believe you were able to make it back."

The captain spoke. "It was very close I assure you. Sergeant Armstrong was there when he was shot," he said, pointing to the observer's window. A line of large 12.7 bullet holes stitched from the lower left of the fuselage to the upper right, ending just above the window. "You can see by the angle that the gunner led us, and our flight path carried us through his pattern. Half my ailerons were gone and as you can see, nearly all my tail too. We had a slight cross wind on the strip, so I had to shove the door open and use it as a rudder to compensate for the side drift and keep us on the runway."

The captain ran his hand along the aileron, and I could see that his hands were still shaky from his ordeal. He let out a long sigh and faced us. "I am not sure what we will be doing with this Bird Dog. They could get a crew here to rebuild this one — I am familiar with all its quirks — or if they might send us a new one. My guess is that we will get a new one."

Sweat was running down his forehead and he wiped it with his sleeve. "We have been talking among ourselves. Next time it could be one of us headhunters to get hit. Either dead or wounded, we need to try to get back to friendlies with the airplane." He paused a moment for this to sink in. "We want you Green Berets to be able to fly the plane from the back seat and get us home. It is dangerous out there. Sergeant Armstrong might be just the first. What do you think, gentlemen?"

I looked at the wounded airplane beside me. The front seat was just wide enough for the pilot. There was only one door and the observer had to slide in from the pilot's door and squeeze in behind him. That space was even more narrow than the front seat. The back of my web gear was clear of anything on it, but I was not sure my seat was wide enough to wear it in the plane. The airplane itself looked flimsy compared to the solid looking Kingbee choppers that could take numerous bullets before being shot from the sky. "What a terror," I thought, "to be in the back seat and have the pilot collapsed in the cockpit."

I was new and deferred to the others.

"Do you think your commander would let you guys take time for some lessons? To be honest, we haven't flown from the backseat ourselves," the captain said, looking at his two subordinates, "Maybe we pilots should take a few trips with one of us in the backseat and then give the controls to the pilot in the back just to learn the problems."

"Yes, sir," they both said, using rank for the first time in our conversation.

"I think our major would definitely be for that once he understands the problem. The only variable would be when SOG assigns us a mission. Two of our A camps are under siege and they might want us to see what is happening on the other side of the fence," I said.

"We are free now. We are not scheduled for any flights today," Mike said.

The captain glanced at each of us. "Then let us make the best use of the time we have now. We only have two planes to work with. You two lieutenants take Dale and Mike and do what you can, then work with Ted later."

I got the sandy-haired lieutenant to train me. His name was Arnold, and he was from the South. "Let's you and me go inside by the air conditioner and talk about why airplanes fly. You see, airplanes don't stay up there against natural law, ready to topple down. It is because the laws of flight make the plane want to fly. Let's you and me go over all of that on paper first. Then we will study what parts of an airplane make it do what we want the plane to do. Then we will go outside and see those parts on the Cessna. After all that we will learn what controls we have, to make it do what we want. Y'all follow that?"

"Yes sir," I said.

"Arnold," he said.

We found a long table near the air conditioner. "How about here?" Arnold asked as he rummaged for paper. Not finding any, he turned to a poster on the wall and gazed at it a moment. The poster depicted a red sky with a saffron sun near the top. The colors matched those on the Vietnamese flag. A squadron of Huey helicopters passed through the circle of sun and below them were the words APOCALYPSE NOW. Arnold carefully removed the poster from the wall and flipped it over to the back side for his lesson. We sat side by side so he would not have to write and draw upside down. With a pencil he drew a simple shape. "This here is a wing. We just took a slice of it like a slice of bread from a loaf. This is a side profile of a wing. This right here is the reason things can fly. Birds are like this. Sails on a boat are like it. You see here, the bottom of the wing is flat. The front edge is called the leading edge and it is shaped like a bump. The top edge of the slice of wing is curved and narrows almost to a point at the back. That is called…" and he waited a minute to see if I would supply the word.

"The trailing edge," I offered.

"Right. If the front end is the leading edge, then the other end is the trailing edge. Now notice, the surface of the top of the wing is curved and it is called 'camber.'"

I nodded, for I was following his explanation.

"Now pretend that this wing is going through the air. The leading edge of the wing goes through the air first. That is the wider, curved part of the wing. Then the trailing edge goes through last. Y'all follow?"

"Yes."

"Now pretend we have a chunk of air at the front of the wing. You can't see it so let's pretend it is a chunk of Jell-O. Let's pretend that our leading-edge splits that Jell-O right in two, half goes over the top half and half under the bottom."

Tom looked at me to be sure I was following him.

"Now this is important. This is what makes things fly. As our wing goes through the Jell-O, both halves, the top and the bottom, arrive at the trailing edge at the same time. Can you see that?"

"Yes."

"Now notice: Since the top half of the wing is curved and the bottom half is in a straight line, the Jell-O on the top half of the wing had to travel farther than the bottom half to get to the end. If the Jell-O on the top half had a brain it would have spent all its attention trying to get to the back at the same time as his friend on the bottom half, instead of maintaining pressure on the sides."

I waited for him to bring it all together.

"In short, that creates low pressure on the top of the wing and that is called 'lift.' It wants to make the wing fly."

I was following it to an extent.

"Hey, looka here." Tom ran to the toilet and came back with a short strip of toilet paper. He held it by an edge and blew across the top and I watched as the low pressure above it lifted the paper into the air. "There is a name for that, called Bernoulli's Principle, but we don't need any of that now. Now you can see how the big wing is like that but so are all the control surfaces, the cross piece of the tail, even the propellor blades."

For the next two hours we studied the various control surfaces of the Bird Dog on paper and how all the various movements of an airplane are accomplished. We went over them several times. The lieutenant walked over to the window and looked at his Bird Dog. "It's a sauna out there. Let's you and me open up them doors and windows of our airplane and have lunch. Maybe it might cool off some."

It was still roasting hot when we went out after we ate but we continued our lesson for we did not know when we would get another block of free time. Arnold stopped at each part of the fuselage, and we repeated its use and what it contributed for flight. With the main door open, Arnold operated the flight controls, and we could see what occurred on the exterior of the aircraft. "Now you get in. Sit in my seat. When I tell you what I want the plane to do, you operate the right controls to make it happen."

This we did over and over with sweat rolling down my forehead and into my eyes. "Don't be discouraged. We will do this every flight. We want you to be able to fly us out when… I mean, if, one of us headhunters are hit."

"Inevitable?" I asked.

"Y'all believe in God?" He asked. "Well, it is 'by the grace of God,' as my mother would say, that we haven't been all shot out of the sky already. We were up with Ted Wicorek over there and we dipped in and out of small openings and we were shot at continuously for forty-five minutes and did not get hit one time. All their rounds, you could see the green tracers, passed behind us, which meant they weren't ready for us. But any leak of secrecy that would have them expect us could be the end of us. Going over the same opening twice, or a large opening in the jungle could be all it takes. It is heating up over the fence and it is just a matter of time… well, let's not talk about that. Let's get you into the back seat."

He opened the pilot's door and slid the seat forward for me and I crawled in. It was cramped with just a canvas seat and no controls that I could see to fly the plane. Visibility was good as there were not only windows on the whole circumference of the airplane, but the roof was windowed as well. The Bird Dog was high winged which meant that we hung below the wings and there was nothing to obstruct the view. With my web gear on I was nearly immobile in the seat. I would have to figure out how to get positioned in the window to take pictures. Our cameras could be set on a repeat setting to automatically shoot pictures one after another by clicking only one time. "You strap in here and this is your helmet and headset. To talk to me just press this button. To talk with the other plane on the mission use this button. This one is to talk with other aircraft."

Sitting in the back and strapped in, it was obvious to me that the pilot filled the whole of the front seat and there would be no going over him or around him to get to the controls. If the pilot were dead or wounded and slumped to the side, it would be a challenge to get the door open if we were alive after surviving a crash.

"Watch me, Dale. See my controls for the wings. They raise and lower the nose and bank the plane. That yoke goes into this pipe, see it? That pipe goes along the floor, under my seat and along your floor. See it? Now if I get shot you must fly this thing. Look on the floor by your feet. There is a hole in the pipe. Off to your side there is a curved pipe. You will probably have that pipe laying on the floor beside you so you can move about in the back seat. You must find and pick up that pipe and stick it into the tube, and then you will have a yoke. If I am dead and slumped over the yoke you will need to yank me away from the controls. You will have to hurry because if I am heading for the trees you will have to be very fast to get the pipe in and lift us out."

I learned how to access other controls. Attached to the left side and forward of my seat was a throttle "Listen, Dale. Not to panic. Once you have any sort of control, the other plane will be there to guide you and talk you into what to do. He will probably head you east and guide you into the closest airstrip. For now, if you can just take control of the airplane, we can talk you through the rest.

"How do you feel, Dale? Let's go for a flight and I will do the flying and I will just have you do some straight and level flying and maybe a few gentle turns and come back. It has been a full day."

Over the next weeks as we flew the photo recon missions, we

integrated flying from the back seat. It was crucial, that in the stress of having to take control of a pilotless airplane while under fire, our response would be reflexive and correct.

We were en route to a mission to find the enemy artillery that was bombarding Dak Pek from west of the Vietnamese Border. We were passing over the mountainous region of the Central Highlands when the high plane radioed to us in an excited voice, "Hey look down there. I think those are tanks."

"Where?" I asked. I couldn't see anything that looked like tanks.

"There, just inside the tree line."

"Y'all guide us, and we'll take a look down there," said Arnold in his slow Southern drawl. He descended rapidly and leveled off at about a thousand feet. I stared out of my window. My eyes sought for anything in the maze and tangle of brush and trees that might be a tank, straight lines, curved features, any solid square of color, but I could not see any tanks.

"Hey," shouted the high plane. "There is an anti-aircraft battery next to that bamboo grove. Watch yourselves."

High plane came back, "You are taking heavy fire from the tree line. Watch it. Watch it!"

Arnold's voice came back high pitched and full of dread. "Ya, I got tracers coming at me and… Ahhh! I'm hit! I'm hit!"

Arnold slumped forward with his chest against the yoke. The nose of the plane pitched forward, and we began to dive.

Electricity shot through me. The ground and the side of the mountain was fast approaching. "Hey Arnold, Arnold," I shouted as I slapped him on the back. His head lolled to one side and his arms hung limp. I looked again and saw the ground continue to close with the plane and realization hit me, "The pilot is dead."

It took only a moment for it to sink in that Arnold was leaning against the yoke and putting us into a dive. With both of my hands I grabbed his collar and yanked him to the side. I glanced through the window. The ground was closing with a blur. I grabbed the pipe and tried to jam it into the tube on the floor. My hands were shaking, and the bar bounced all around the tube and I could not fit it in. "Control yourself!" I shouted in my head and willed the pipe into the tube. My eyes wanted to tear when I felt the pipe fit into place. I glanced through the window. Individual branches of the trees appeared. I pulled back on the stick and let out a long breath of air as the Cessna came out of the dive and we leveled. I gave it throttle, raised the nose and gained altitude. My heart slammed against my chest as trees shrank to shrubs below us. Adrenaline pumped through me. My heart pounded in my ears, but I felt I was in control for the moment — enough time for the high plane to guide us back.

"Nice job," a voice said over the headset. "Nice job, now wake up Arnold. Tap him on the shoulder."

I stared at the handset.

Someone was shouting. I looked up. Arnold was looking back at me, unwounded and quite alive. "Nice job Yankee. Well, I guess we would have survived that one." He smiled and winked.

"Welcome to the Headhunters," he said.

A Communist Spring Offensive was indeed underway. Across South Vietnam, PAVN and the remnants of the Viet Cong struck everything from military bases to sleepy hamlets. In neighboring Laos, the Pathet Lao overran the CIA's version of Special Forces camps, took district capitals, and placed great swaths of territory under their control. Near us in Kontum, the Special Forces camps of Dak Seang and Dak Pek were under siege. They were attacked the same night sappers hit us at CCC and for two weeks the fighting continued unabated. Although those two A camps received their support from the B team at Pleiku and not directly from us in SOG, their welfare was of great concern to us.

We were familiar with the dozen Green Berets at Dak Pek. Their camp was a staging base for some of our deep penetrations into southern Laos. It was at their airstrip our battered chase-medic choppers limped in, and our wounded were helped from those bloody metal floors. They would catch the swinging ropes that hung under the helicopter and free us from our strings when we had been snatched from a hot LZ and dangled for an hour in the air. And it was from that airstrip our silent, stoic Montagnard wounded were rushed to the dispensary for life-saving care.

As we followed the events of the siege, I visualized it as if it were played out on a map before me — seven small hills enclosed inside the perimeter. Sappers took out some of the bunkers and under the cover of a heavy artillery barrage, several battalions attacked and in time overcame the first strong points. As hill after hill and each strong point was taken over the days of siege, I imagined a replay of the French against the Viet Minh at Dien Bien Phu. It also was built on small hills made into strong points. One by one they fell: Huguette, Dominique, Claudine, and Eliane. It appeared that Dak Pek was similarly dying, hill by hill. And even now thirty-seven loyal Montagnard tribesmen who fought to the death and did not listen to the propaganda speakers that urged, "Kill the Americans and we will let you go," were zipped into body bags and lay along the dispensary wall.

It was not our mission to support those two camps but when CCC's recon teams and our Ford Drum recon missions infiltrated the enemy sanctuaries and mapped out enemy staging areas and logistics sites, we hoped we gave relief to the pressure on the camps.

It was early one day when Mike Buckland and I left the FOB for the airfield, long before the highway had been cleared of mines, and the buses and convoys and pedicabs felt it safe to travel the main roads. It had rained during the night, but the morning was cloudless, and the moist pavement reflected the sun and watered my eyes. Our tires hissed on the wet asphalt as we drove, and a water buffalo lifted its head as we passed. Its horns were still wet from the night and glistened. The powerful beast seemed weary as it pulled itself from the ditch and carried the sun on its wet back.

"This will be good weather for finding the enemy," Mike was saying. "We might find a truck park. The reflection of the sun on their windshields shows through the camouflage like it does on water."

I didn't say anything. I wondered if the sun would also be shining on the wet barrels of all the anti-aircraft guns we would be flying over.

Nearly in answer to my thought he said, "We will be coming in from the east and the sun will be in their eyes."

"I am for that."

Mike and Ted Wicorek had flown several more missions than I and when I joined them on those first flights over the fence, I felt somewhat worthless. On some of my early missions we were under machine gun fire from suspected base areas, and we made some very violent evasive maneuvers while flying the "low bird." I held my Olympus "PEN double E" camera out of the window with one hand and my rifle out with the other hand. When the pilot made a full roll, then tilted the wings and slid vertically between two trees, righted itself, then made a hard turn in the other direction, my vision blurred and I felt that whatever was in my stomach was on its way to my mouth.

"Did you get a picture of that?" said an excited voice.

I did not say anything.

Many flights involved such maneuvers and it seemed that the only difference in each flight was the variation of the aerobatics. Half of my time I had been airsick. I learned that you cannot puke out of the back window of a birddog as the airflow throws it all back inside the airplane. Nor could you throw a full puke bag out of the window for the same reason. On my third or fourth flight I had a nearly full bag in one hand with my other hand under the bag to support the weight until I could tie it off and set it on the floor. We banked for a photo and several green tracers entered my window inches from my face and the bullets exited the other window. I flinched and squeezed the bag and was back to square one. In time, I mastered the malady, but still, I often did not eat breakfast when our missions involved a particularly "hot target."

Our pilots had already completed their pre-flight and were waiting for us when we met them at the airfield. It was clear that they were anxious to begin before the noon sun shortened any shadows that pointed to targets of opportunity. We grouped around a map.

"Last time, you remember, we found a new road spur leading off the main road into a grove of trees. We thought it might be a truck park or staging area, Saigon would like some more pictures," Mike said. "Also, they would like us to do a BDA in this area," he said with his finger on the map. They did a B-52 strike on the 'trail' and also on that place we thought could be a staging area for the attack on Dak Pek."

The pilot glanced at the sun and nodded his head. "Perfect conditions, I would think. Let's do it."

Mike and his pilot would fly high plane about four or five thousand feet to locate and direct us in the low plane to the target. My pilot and I would fly at treetop, perhaps fifty feet above the ground. I would have to be ready with the camera when Mike directed us to a suspect area.

We taxied to the active runway and accelerated down the asphalt, our shadows racing before us until we lifted off and left them behind. We flew west, side by side, wingtip to wingtip, able to see each other as we talked over the radio. Below us, under the canopy of trees and camouflage, were the staging and movements of war which would have been portrayed by red and blue arrows and symbols of battalions and regiments on paper, paper that was free of grime, sweat or blood. In another war, on a huge polished table, someone would have been moving symbols here and there with long polished sticks. And generals perhaps, with their chins propped on their fists, elbows anchored to their side, just above their wide leather belts would say, "Hmmm, move the Fourth over there." The words would be uttered simply and without effort, but hundreds of soldiers would slog and slip over mud and strain up steep jungle hills, and cross nearly unfordable streams.

"Let's do the BDA first," said the captain in his new airplane. "We fly over that area first anyway."

From the air the Ho Chi Minh Trail resembled the moon along its length. Weeks of airstrikes had left it cratered and treeless, and the shattered hardwoods, trunk to limb, had been hauled away to build bunkers, buildings and bridges. Many of the craters were from old bomb strikes and were water filled from the rains. Days-old bomb craters were sun-dried and bleached tan in color. Anything new was fresh turned and moist and brick-red. As we passed over, many craters on the trail were red and recently filled. Impressions made by heavy truck tires embossed the surface of the red soil of last night's Arc Light strike. It was a line of print that said in brail for those of us who would not see, "You did not stop us, and we continue to our war of liberation."

Half a mile farther west where the road had been cut through a hillside, the Air Force had bombed the slope and created a slide that buried it. Feverish work was underway by slaves and prisoners to clear the debris. We made a low pass, my camera clicking away, and found signs of a detour around the slide. It segued to the left into a stand of hardwood trees where it disappeared. The forest was expansive, and we looked for clues to trace the road under the canopy. Several times the high plane steered us to small breaks in the trees to nearly invisible segments of road.

"There, just at your ten o'clock in that break in the trees," Mike quietly said into the radio.

I readied the camera and peered out of the window. It was a small opening in the foliage, but what I saw was unmistakable — a stretch of red soil, free of any vegetation. I snapped the photo. It was a segment of newly formed road. Three times we found such hyphens of construction. The captain marked the coordinates and connected the dots we had found and traced the new road on the map. A mile or two farther on, a small river bounded the area. The new segment of road would have to cross it somewhere. There had to be a bridge. If we could find that crossing, we could call in "fast movers" and knock it out and stop traffic for days. Twice we passed over the area but found nothing.

"Hey! There," I shouted and pointed to a place just ahead of us and below.

"Yes, I see it too," Arnold shouted back.

With the sun just right at a place where the banks were brick red, its rays pierced the shallow water to a yellow gravel bottom. It was an underwater bridge, invisible from the air. With the clarity of the moment, I even saw where a thin cloud of silt drifted downstream from the crossing — a truck had just passed over and stirred up the bottom. We found it.

We moved off to the side and were making precise coordinates of the crossing when Mike noticed reflections through the hardwood trees, like something reflecting on water, but we were not near standing water or the river.

"Hey," he said. "I see shining like sun on metal or glass, and they are all in a row. I think we have found our truck park or supply depot."

Arnold made a low pass over the site banking the plane so I could take a better photo out of the window. Although I expected to, we drew no fire.

"I think that Charlie doesn't want to fire us up and confirm that he is there," Arnold said into my headset. "But we know that he is there and if we got too nosey, he will let us have it."

The captain confirmed the coordinates and inscribed them in his pad.

We had another BDA to check just over the border slightly to the west of Dak Pek. It was a target found by one of our recon teams, set deeply into the trees. A nearly hidden spur road linked the site to the main Ho Chi Minh Trail. The recon team stated that the site was highly fortified and there was the presence of artillery in the area. They couldn't learn more as they got into contact and barely made it out. The cost of that information was one KIA and two WIA.

We found the area and flew low along the path of the Arc Light strike. None of us spoke. We studied the churned-up ground below us. We knew that we were probably not the first to visit the site of this bombing run. Very angry enemy, furious beyond speaking, would also be below us assessing the damage, often finding parts of their comrades' bodies in the trees. They could at this moment be waiting for our arrival to shoot us down in seething revenge, hoping we would be still alive when they found us in the wreckage. Our five-hundred-pound bombs removed every tree, every shrub, even the grass from the camouflaged complex. Not a building, or truck, or artillery piece, or anything above ground remained. Only that which had been below ground held its shape. Under the slanting rays of the morning sun, the zipper shaped trenches which had surrounded the base area were in deep shadow and were etched in the dirt as clearly as a lead pencil would have drawn them on parchment. Every fifty feet or so, a large square of shadow showed where a bunker had been. Numerous interconnecting trenches led to a second line of defense and large rectangles of shadow showed where two days before, warehouses, barracks buildings, or administration sites had been. The bombs had removed the mask and revealed the red death that had been hidden under the triple canopy.

We made a low pass, and I took pictures. Our boys in the photo lab would study the frames with magnifying glasses and find a boot or rifle, a body lodged in the fork of the one remaining tree snag, an axle of a truck with one wheel buried in the ground. Our boys would also lay out the photographs in three dimension and would find what was invisible to us — a group of soldiers crouched in the border of the frame with branches stuck in their helmets and backpacks. Like us, those soldiers came to appraise the damage of the huge bombers. On the opposite edge of the picture frame, also camouflaged, was one very large weapon on a tripod — soldiers who heard the engines of our headhunter planes and froze in place with downcast eyes, but for one who looked up at the plane and would remember the sound of our engines. When our boys would blow up the photo to near-grainy size, they would see (or was it their imagination?) one soldier looking up at the plane with a sneer of malevolent hatred.

"We need to watch our fuel," the captain said as he banked to the east. "We can pass over Dak Pek as we go."

The land sloped down as we flew east toward the harried camp, but the tall hills of the highlands still marked the land. There was no mistaking the location of the scene of the battle. Black smoke rose from several locations within the shrinking perimeter. Numerous white and yellow explosions flashed without and inside the camp. Larger flashes revealed where rockets found their mark. We changed our frequency to listen to the traffic between the ground and the supporting aircraft. Mike remained at altitude, but Arnold took us down to eight hundred or a thousand feet keeping us out of the way of our fast movers and the artillery fire that supported the camp.

Over the last two weeks the Communists dug trenches that crawled ever closer to the last remaining strongpoint of the defenders. I watched a mass of moving specks on the ground. They were advancing enemy that were close enough for us to see. Flashes belched from their mortar tubes and rifles.

A Special Forces sergeant was on the radio. I do not remember the call signs, but the pilot of an F-4 Phantom jet said, "Okay Dak Pek. I have a load of NAPE on board and am ready to dump. Where would you like it?"

The sergeant answered as calmly as a waiter taking an order. "They are just outside my wire. Put it fifty meters out, along my west perimeter."

"Roger. Get your heads down."

Below me, I watched the bombing run of that jet as it passed south to north along the wire. A gigantic ball of igniting white phosphorus rose along the entire west side of the American stronghold. A long column of grey smoke billowed above the strike.

"Right on target, Phantom. You got about a hundred of them that time." His voice was calm, and gravel dry.

"Roger. Copy. What can I do for you next?"

"Copy Phantom. Your next target is…"

We watched the battle below us as the sergeant maneuvered his assets and the frantic effort of the enemy battalions to conquer the camp while they had the resources. The defenders fought on. As I watched in fascination above the fray, dry-mouthed men below us held their position and counted their remaining cartridges and grenades with grimed and bloody fingers. Their weary eyes were blurry with fatigue, and they blinked to focus on their sights as they made each bullet count.

"Fuel," the captain reminded us, and reluctantly, out of necessity, we banked toward Kontum.

Back at CCC I showered and felt guilty as I ate dinner at a clean mess hall table. I drank a Coca-Cola with frost along the side of the can and enjoyed the brain freeze from its coldness, and I watched the condensation gather where my hand had been and slide down the can. In my comfort, I was aware that short miles away my brothers in the outposts were fighting for their lives.

Just as it grew dark and bats circled around the yard light at the gate, I had a charge of adrenaline. From the sounds and scrambling activity around me, we were being attacked from inside the camp. Several bursts of automatic rifle fire ripped from the far side of the compound. I grabbed my rifle and gear but by the time I ran halfway to the site, some of our people met me shouting, "It's okay. False alarm.

Not to worry." They held up their hands like a traffic cop to stop me. "False alarm!"

"What do you mean?"

"Well, little fella," the voice said in his best John Wayne drawl, "It seems that the Duke and his blue coats were in a firefight with a pile of Comanches. Well just about the time John Wayne was saying, 'Wait, wait. Hold your fire. Steady, steady,' our tribesmen watching the show, were getting into the thing. You remember don't cha, Dale, that the Yards identify with the Indians as they sorta look alike. Just as he starts to say, 'Now!' a half dozen of our little people opened up full auto with their rifles at John Wayne and his men. They shot the screen up good."

A stillness descended over both Dak Seang and Dak Pek. Not even a breeze infiltrated through the remaining brown grass. The last rocket landed a dozen meters from the commo bunker at Dak Pek. It was a dud. It was impaled in the dirt at an angle, the tail pointing toward the shooter who was no longer there. Anxious tribesmen noted thin smoke seeping from the ground around its edges and kept their distance. Incoming fire of all kinds ceased, and an eerie silence fell on the camp. Soldiers, when it was first noticed, stopped mid-stride and gazed upward, puzzled at the strangeness of it all. There were no more enemy in any of the trenches. Even the dead were gone. At least, most of them. It was only in the perimeter wire where the dead remained, burned crispy black and prone to break apart when pulled from the barbs.

Cautious patrols maneuvered just outside the wire at first, then extended their search well into the jungle. They found no enemy. The NVA policed the jungle where they had been, taking every scrap that proved that they had been there at all. Every bullet casing and every kernel of rice vanished. Pools of blood, all in neat rows, that marked where a hospital had been, were hidden under small mounds of moist earth. Even the bamboo and thatch of the roof had been hauled away. Only the trails remained where the wounded had been carried to sanctuaries in Laos. PAVN simply slipped away.

Chapter Twenty-One

HATCHET FORCE

It had been on my mind for some time to go back to the field. I do not know why I had this moth-to-flame draw to return to peril when every indication was that our involvement in the war was slowly dying down. I know the attacks on our A camps supplied some of that narcotic. I wanted to be a closer to — no, in that battle itself. I did not want to cheer them on; I wanted to be with them. I wanted to be sliding mortar rounds down the tube as fast as they could tear off the extra charges. I wanted to steady my rifle against the leaking sandbags of the perimeter as I engaged the attackers, close enough to the soldier next to me with the machine gun that the empty shell cases would pile up near my neck and burn my skin. I even longed for the smell of the adrenaline of fear that clung to my clothing after the fight. That odor eloquently said, "You are alive." As one of the famous lines in Special Forces reads, "You have never lived until you have almost died. For those who fight for it, life has a flavor the protected will never know."

I remember an extended fight when I held an AK-47, and the heat of the firing pushed the oil from inside the weapon to the barrel and the oil slid across the metal like melting butter, boiling as it slid — and I heard the sizzle of the gasses next to the rear sight, and I smelled the hotness of it in the fight. I wanted to call in a Phantom air strike again when nervousness was so pent up in me that my words poured out like a cartoon voice on high speed. Despite the fear and tension of jungle fighting, and the fact that we were accomplishing so much in those Ford Drum missions, I had to be closer to the fight than I was. I looked for a way to return to hands-on combat.

The answer was before me in the long barracks buildings next to our Two Shop. A hundred and twenty Montagnard soldiers slept in long rows of cots in those single-story structures. They were the courageous, loyal and battle tested men of A Company, one of the two Hatchet Forces of CCC. They were sent where severe combat was expected, and they fought with courage and distinction. If a recon team was in grave peril, it was the Hatchet Force that was often sent in to engage the enemy and rescue the team. When intelligence suspected a lucrative target, they were sent in to confirm and destroy it. They did reconnaissance in force deep into enemy controlled territory. Hatchet Forces, also referred to as Mike Forces or Reaction Forces, often relieved remote Special Forces camps by finding and engaging the enemy units that attacked them. The two Hatchet Force companies were the biceps of CCC.

It was the "little people" who resided in that barracks who were on Linebacker Two. They dropped in on a rise of land along the Ho Chi Minh Trail and halted all traffic for days. Every attempt to dislodge them was repulsed. They called in airstrikes and destroyed long truck convoys and formations of attackers. Their presence along that road said in unambiguous terms, "We are here, and no one passes this point until we say so." And the Communist effort to bring war material to the south was utterly stopped for two weeks.

These were also the commandos of Operation Tailwind, the legendary mission deep inside the enemy bastions and command center of southern Laos. It was one of the most significant intelligence hauls of the war, which included hundreds of pounds of top secret documents — entire footlockers full of battle plans, logistics routes, staging areas, storage facilities, codes and operational orders. Hundred-foot-long warehouses filled with rockets, mortar rounds and other munitions were destroyed.

Tailwind occurred at the request of the CIA, whose mercenary army was being overrun by the Pathet Lao in the Bolovens Plateau. "Could SOG make such a significant diversionary attack forty miles from the center of the battle, that the enemy would be compelled to draw units from its fight with the CIA?" CCC did so by committing the B Company Hatchet Force. The sixteen Americans and one hundred and ten Montagnards were airlifted into the heart of a Communist sanctuary where they fought for four days and nights continuously. Fighter aircraft lent nearly constant close-air support. Many hundreds of enemies were killed by American firepower. Fighting was so intense as the last platoon was lifted out of the LZ, that seventy-two-fighter aircraft expended half a million tons of explosives, napalm and rockets to cover the withdrawal. At the end of that successful mission those quiet Montagnards returned to their Spartan quarters in the barracks, their few possessions and their cots.

I had a certain fondness for our Reaction Force because I gave the intelligence briefing for them as they prepared for Tailwind. Along with most of us on our compound, I followed the course of the running battle. Many of my friends were in the force. One Medal of Honor was earned on the mission. All sixteen Americans had been wounded at least once, several twice. We at CCC had an immense pride and great relief when at the end we greeted them back at the airfield. Although all were wounded and weary, none shuffled down the ramp. They strode with the pride of Spartans.

On a Wednesday morning I reported for duty with the SOG Hatchet Force. My fatigues were "STRAC," clean and pressed, and I paid a maid to give my jungle boots an extra shine. I was not sure what I expected. Certainly, there would be a dozen or more Special Forces assigned to the three platoons and the weapons sections of the company. I walked up the three or four wooden steps to the office, my footsteps resembling the slow rap of heavy knuckles on a door. I knocked and stepped inside. Coming from the bright day, my eyes needed to adjust to the dim room. Other than one overhead light, only a single small window next to the door let in daylight. On one wall, which I barely noticed, was the company manning table with its boxes and connecting lines to indicate the platoons, sections and chain of command. A training schedule and calendar were tacked to the facing wall. At one time the office had been a modest sized room but had been divided into two much smaller rooms, each about twice the width of a desk. These were not the offices of those who spent much time in them. The outer office belonged to the First Sergeant and the inner office was the sanctum of the company commander. The First Sergeant sat behind a large grey, metal desk with a sheaf of papers in his hands and slowly looked up as I approached.

"First Sergeant, I am Sergeant Hanson. I have been assigned to your company."

He slowly stood and looked at me showing no emotion, his face indifferent to my arrival, as if he would decide in due time whether to be pleased or not. His last name was Roberts, but his features were that of a Greek or Italian. He was five ten or more and powerfully built — large boned and heavy of solid flesh. His hair tended to curly, and I could tell that he wore a bandana in the field and not a flop hat for the hair at the top of his head was bleached light brown with a band of darker brown just below. The flesh around his face tended to sag, especially around his eyes. In those moments I tried to take his measure, for I would be following him into combat. Without any evidence to do so, I concluded that the sergeant was someone who had seen it all and nothing now would surprise or excite him. Robert's uniform, while not entirely rumpled, bore no resemblance to the pressed quality of men in garrison, but rather was that of a soldier whose priorities were in the field. He, by choice and inclination, was assuredly not a "garret trooper."

I have very strong hands, but my hand disappeared into his as he shook it. "I am First Sergeant Roberts. Good that you are with us. We were hoping for a third person to round out the company."

I was not sure that I understood him correctly. Did he mean that I was one of three soldiers newly assigned or that there were only three in the company?

"Third?"

"Third," he said, indicating that I had heard him correctly. "With you, there are three of us in the company. That is all that we need. Three."

The captain marched from his office and stood before me. If First Sergeant Roberts was "yin," then the captain was "yang." The captain was slim but athletic, shorter than I — about five six. His uniform was pressed and newly cleaned, his hair was short and blond, and his demeanor was formal, crisp, military, almost Prussian. Nothing about him was relaxed. Even his beret did not sag down on the right side but was stiffly straight out to the side at attention. He faced me with his heels together.

"I am Captain Roasch. Three of us is all that ve need. My company is a vell-oiled machine and ve are professionals. Our people are vell trained and haff goot discipline. The Colonel tells me that you are a goot leader and a professional soldier or he vood not haf sent you to me."

He looked at me with his blue eyes, then pausing before doing so, offered me his hand.

"Ve haf three platoons in dis company and ve haf three special forces. I, the captain, vill take one platoon, the first sergeant vill take the second platoon, and you, sergeant Hanson vill be in charge of the third platoon."

By way of dismissal he said, "Sergeant Roberts vill brief you," and he turned and strode into his office.

Roberts gave the officer time to seat himself at his desk on the other side of the wall, then pointed to the door with his jaw, a simple gesture which said, "We can talk more freely outside."

We passed a small metal Conex on the way to the barracks and he said, "That is our stockade when we have punishment like drunkenness and fighting. It is just an empty metal box with no chair or bed. It can be 140 degrees inside it during the day. If the little people are angry at the prisoner, they sometimes throw rocks at the box. It could break an eardrum."

"The captain is okay," he said. "Actually, he is a good officer. He just takes getting used to. He was in the German army — the West German side. He represented Germany in the Olympics in the biathlon. He immigrated to the United States, joined Special Forces, and is our captain. He is German "old school" and doesn't fraternize with the men. He tries, but the old ways are difficult for him to leave behind. I saw that he shook your hand. He probably thought he would never do so with a subordinate."

We were nearing the barracks, so he stopped in the middle of the field to finish what he wanted to say. "The captain said we only need three of us. That is because he sees this company as so disciplined and well-trained that we are a machine like some of the very elite German units of the last world war. He would expect our little people to charge the enemy machine guns without hesitation if he were to order them. What the captain does not know is that our little people are so loyal and trusting toward Special Forces they would do it anyway."

Roberts hard shell softened, and he spoke as to another sergeant who was a part of the team. "It will surprise you to learn that I think this company can function well with just a few of us leading it too, but for different reasons."

He looked at me with his drooping eyes. "Sarge, I have been fighting in Southeast Asia for eleven years now. Eleven tours. Some of them were before anyone knew there were any Americans here. I was in the black pajama days when a mission was six months long. Just a handful of us were dropped into Indian country and we created our own army. We hired and trained them — Lao tribesmen, Moi, Yards, even stranded Chinese. We set up our drop zones and Air America would drop us ammo and supplies. See, I am used to having just a few Special Forces around to wage war. Twice I was the only American for six months at a time. So, I agree with the captain that we can wage war with just the three of us."

I did not respond to Robert's assessment. What he had just told me was what we learned in training group regarding operating behind enemy lines for extended missions. I imagined him with a group of Lao tribesmen in their black pajama uniforms turning the crank of the KY-38 as he tapped in the Morse code to a secret place on the other side of the world. I imagined an ambush with Montagnard tribesmen in loincloths and black, filed teeth taking out an enemy patrol with booby traps, crossbows, rifles from the last war and Montagnard swords. They would turn and look back from the carnage at the face of a younger Sergeant Roberts. With utter clarity I saw them in my mind, smiling in satisfaction and waiting for his approval.

We left the outside freshness and entered the close air and dim interior of the first barracks. A soldier closest to the door called "Attention!" and Roberts gave them ease. I met the men of A Company and my own platoon in particular. Over the coming days and weeks, I learned the strengths of my people and their indigenous chain of command and how to train them to operate as a unit. Who could I rely on in crisis? Who had a natural proclivity to see the need of the hour and fill it? I studied my men as I would the parts of my rifle.

The captain, with his martial bearing and formality, was the force which made our people want to click their heels together and snap to the task at hand and obey without question. The First Sergeant, with his experience of years in the field, was never surprised, and every occasion, no matter how stressful, was routine to him. He knew what to do, and he acted with confidence, and they gave him their trust. It was my experience in recon and the very close relationship I had with my people there, that contributed to my leadership with these tribesmen. After hours, when the other two Americans departed the company area, I spent time with them in the barracks. I learned about their home villages, their families, their taboos and moors, battles they had fought and the lessons they had learned after them, how to make a crossbow, what is held in value in their cultures, Montagnard and American games, and principles of freedom.

One night the oldest man in our group brought us fresh rats that he had killed, and we ran long slivers of bamboo through the mouths and out of the anuses and roasted them over a fire of C-4. Squatting there between the rows of cots, we tore strings of flesh from them and ate, and we spoke as we did so of rice fields and growing crops in the mountains, survival in the jungle, and Christianity. They learned that I came to their country to rid the land of the Communists and they learned from me they were not expendable pawns in a chess game. I cared for them, and I felt a warmth and loyalty in return. When we were in the field, there were several firefights with the enemy in which there would be a pause in the fighting — the enemy were dead or had retreated into the thickness of the jungle. I would look around to assess the situation and the welfare of my people and would discover several of my people had made a protective circle around me during the engagement. Like my Chinese, who said, "Han Son — Never Die," my tribesmen guarded me with their lives.

One of my people stands out in my memory. His name was Bieh, and as a typical American thing, everyone called him Beer. He was shorter than many of the Yards and was disfigured in war. Napalm had burned off his upper lip exposing his teeth. It gave him the aspect of a perpetual snarl, a thing that would frighten children in another place, but in a country with decades of war, scars from wounds were commonplace. But the appearance of a snarl did not correctly describe his character. Bieh had a wonderful sense of humor and loved to be with people. He was intelligent and spoke good English and was one of my shadows on a mission. Bieh understood the nuance of a thing and would explain it to the rest of the men.

Over the months we were committed to the field on several occasions. They were short in duration, and none were given a formal name to mark their importance. I was on a very fast learning curve. There were only the three of us in the company so I functioned both as an officer and as a platoon sergeant. The quirks of the other Americans in the company added to the necessity of learning quickly. When a mission was concluded and we stood in formation before the barracks, the captain yielded command to the first sergeant. They would salute, the captain would do a left-face and "March!" to the officer's club. The routine aspects of caring for a company were apparently for the enlisted to perform. But then as our officer removed himself from the company area, First Sergeant Roberts would turn to me, salute with his large hand, and say, "Sergeant Hanson, take charge." He would do a left-face and shuffle from the formation en route to the bar of the Huckleberry Inn. He would remain there in the second stool from the left until they turned out the lights for the evening. If I had to relay information to him, he would still be in the grimy uniform that he wore in the field. He would not be showered and would drink with his head down.

Roberts never seemed to get drunk. He was a soldier who functioned well in the field but hated the routine in camp. He would be there in that stool, unspeaking, pensive, with his black bandanna slid from his forehead to his neck, his compass and maps still strung and hanging from his pockets. When the lights went out in the bar after last call, Roberts would walk steadily in the dark to his billet, drop fully clothed on top of the blanket of his bunk and be instantly asleep. If he was awake for breakfast he would be seated at the table, still in his camouflage paint and muddy fatigues. Assuming that I had taken care of the routine aspects of running a company, he would wait for the club to open, seat himself on the second stool from the left and begin the day with a drink — one with orange juice in it. I was de facto tasked with every aspect of caring for a company of mercenaries. And I loved it.

A Company was tasked for a reconnaissance-in-force of a suspected base area in which heavy contact with the enemy was expected. Monsoons were approaching and aircover could not be counted on to support a smaller recon team if it got into trouble. A larger force that could better fend for itself was a better option. Two more sergeants were assigned to our company to augment us for the mission. Both were buck sergeants. One of them was assigned to the captain's platoon and the other, Dean Hendricks — code named Spanky — was attached to the First Sergeant's platoon. We trained together as a company and did a couple short local field exercises before being committed to the mission SOG had in mind.

The first auspicious break in the weather found us at the Dak To launch site ready for immediate insertion. Our day began in Kontum while it was still dark, long before camp workers lined up before the gate and any VC sympathizers among them could report our activity. We arranged a hot breakfast for the Montagnards, made an equipment inspection in front of the barracks airlifted to our staging area, and it was still early when we arrived. The day was cloudless. The sun had cleared the hills in the east and fingers of shadow crawled across the tarmac and touched the edge of our formation. I spaced my platoon a short distance from others, still on the assembly area, but in the back side of a building where the enemy on the hillside could not count our numbers or be tempted to send rockets. Roberts approached me, walking like a powerful bear, the loose end of his bandanna drooping down the side of his face. "They have a recon team in trouble just to the west of our area and all the assets are committed to them. We will go when they get them out."

Roberts shuffled back toward his platoon, resting his forearms on his ammo pouches. Part way there, he stopped and walked back to me, more quickly this time. He stood close, one hand on my shoulder, his head down, his voice low. "On the other hand, if they need serious help on the ground, we are here and all ready for bear. They just might call on us to be a Bright Light to rescue the team. We should be ready. I better go and make sure the captain has thought of that."

A charge of electricity shot through my nerves — the same one that was there when I stood in the door of an airplane in my chute and waited to jump. I glanced at my platoon. There was nothing that needed to be done to make them more ready. They waited without speaking, their thoughts turned inward. Most were seated on their rucksacks in their separate squads. Bieh was asleep, his head on his rucksack. Laying there unmoving, with his closed eyes and his lipless mouth gaped open baring his broken teeth, he had the appearance of a corpse. I looked away.

I heard choppers in the west, the "whup" of the rotor blades sounded hurried, and in moments a helicopter sloped down to a stop in front of us. The One Zero of the recon team hopped off the struts about the same time they touched earth. Blood ran down from inside his boonie hat and streamed along one eye. "Hey! You guys have a medic here?" He turned and helped the first tribesman out of the interior. Two medics arrived at a run even as he shouted. The other American on the team and two of his people hopped from the other door and lifted out a wounded soldier. The SOG man held him under his armpits and shuffled backward with him as the tribesmen carried him by his legs. One arm dangled limply below him. His forearm was bandaged and blood ran down his wrist into his cupped hand, cupped as if to prevent its escape. But it filled his clinched fist and escaped between his fingers and streamed down his little finger. His hand quivered and blood splattered on the group from the fingertip.

A medic slid another Montagnard soldier across the blood-slippery helicopter floor. He was on his back and they pulled him by his harness to the door where at the edge his head hung straight down. The medic examined the stricken man and looked back at the One Zero. Sadly, he shook his head and slid him back inside.

I glanced over to my platoon. They were standing, watching, searching the faces of the wounded. One of my people turned to the other and said, "I think him name be Y Bah."

The captain, Roberts, and I looked for an appropriate moment to talk with the One Zero, for he came out of an area close to our target. "You got a wound yourself, Sarge," I said.

"Oh, yes. I forgot."

"I know that you have things to do and this is not a good time, but we might be going in near where you guys were. We could sure use your insight.," I said.

The captain unfolded his map. "Can you show us vare you vere on this?"

The One Zero unfolded his own map. "I am not sure. The area covered on my map is much smaller than yours. Our mission was only ten klicks on a side."

He held his map next to ours and we looked for any clue to connect the two. "I don't have that big field on mine."

We moved the small map side to side and up and down above ours but could not find where his ended and ours began.

"How about there?" Roberts asked, placing his finger on a large stream on the map and tapping a stream on our own.

We moved his map over the top of our own until, like a camera flash, all the contour lines matched. The captain used a finger and thumb to measure the distance from the recon team's fire fight to our own LZ. "Seven klicks. About four miles. You drew a black line on your map. Vat is that?"

"We found a new road that is not on the map so I drew it in. Very high speed. Wide enough for a truck. Hard clay. There is no vegetation on it and the trees are tied across so it cannot be seen from the air. I see it is headed your way, Captain."

He glanced back at the waiting helicopter. "I really need to get back to my men. I need my map for debriefing but I will see if my One will give you his."

We watched as the One Zero climbed aboard and leaned back next to the opening of the Huey. He held a wounded man in his lap — the one with the quivering hand — and smoothed the soldier's hair with one hand, and with his other held the shaking limb in the air, elevated above the man's heart. Captain Roasch stood at attention and saluted. We waved, and the One Zero having no free hand, nodded his farewell. We shielded our eyes from the debris of the prop blast as they lifted off and watched until the dust settled and the engine noise diminished until we could hear again.

The captain held his map with one hand as we gathered around him. "Vell, they haff got the recon team out now. They vere close to our target — about five or ten klicks so their information is important to us." He glanced to the fuel pumps in irritation. "Ve haf to vait for them to refuel. Dat vill mess vit my var plans."

He opened the map and pointed with his finger. "Ve haff time. Ve might as vell go over this again."

His fingertip rested on an area of pale yellow indicating a treeless field. The field was shaped like an artist's paint palette. The map was solid green surrounding the pale yellow, showing thick vegetation which extended between the two fingers of the palette shape.

"Vell, as I haff told you, the first and second platoons, led by me and the First Sergeant, vill insert in this larger finger of the LZ in two lifts. The LZ vill be prepped by fire as ve go in. Ve vill secure the LZ and come on line on this side of it. At my command we vill move on line to the east. This vooded strip of land is about a thousand meters wide and ends at the other part of the LZ. It is believed that the enemy may haff concentrated in this area between the two fingers. Ve vill search and destroy as we find them and ve vill drive them across the peninsula to the other side vere Sergeant Hanson is set up to ambush them — hammer and anvil."

The captain, as he said this, looked about him to be sure that everyone understood. He had an overbite, and now his jaw was thrust even more forward and his teeth were clamped firmly shut.

"Sergeant Hanson, your people must be ready to jump off the helicopters when they glide in as soon as you are low enough. I do not vant them to hover and let the enemy know that you are landing — let them think that it is just a low pass to draw fire. Questions? "

The crew chief of the closest Huey signaled that they were ready.

The captain and his platoon moved briskly to the waiting helicopters and boarded. Captain Roasch seated himself in the doorway with his thrust-out chin and his boonie hat cinched under his jaw by its cord lest the wind take it away. The fleet arose as one and banked to the west, the helicopters getting smaller and smaller on the horizon, finally merging into one dot, then disappeared.

Roberts strolled slowly back and forth in front of his people. His green bandanna was dark with sweat. He stopped to say something to one of his soldiers, then continued his pacing on the ramp. Thirty minutes later someone shouted from the tower, "Coming in. You can see them through the cut between the two ridges." Roberts did not look toward the western ridge line but made one more pass before his people, again with an image of disinterest, almost boredom. He glanced at his people one more time and his lack of anxiety calmed them just as the rumble of engines filled the launch area.

Roberts spoke into his handpiece, "Good on the LZ?"

"Roger, good to go," was the reply.

He signaled his people to rise and pointed to each "stick" of men in turn and pointed to the helicopter that they should board. He turned and waved to me, gave the thumbs up to the pilot and seated himself in the door and let the wind squint his eyes and tug on his bandanna.

It was mid-morning, ten o'clock, clear skies to work air assets, and plenty of time to maneuver before darkness gathered color into her basket and greyed all uniforms the same, both ours and theirs. Dust raised during the liftoff settled back to the runway. Conex containers ticked as their metal sides stretched from the sun. I put my boonie hat in my leg pocket so it would not blow away in the flight.

I positioned my people — seven rows of six soldiers each, a line of men for each chopper, and waited.

"Coming in!" shouted the man in the tower.

"Company okay?" I asked the voice.

"As far as I know."

The Hueys hummed in the distance and in moments they were on the tarmac. The pilot of the nearest one gave me a thumbs up and I nodded in reply. I pointed to Bieh and shouted, "That one is yours," and I slapped him on the back as he and his group hustled by. When the last Montagnard was seated, I gave the pilot the thumbs up, took my place in the door and the fleet lifted off, heading toward a finger-shaped field in Laos.

Rivers and grey-blue mountains passed under us. Below some of the steep slopes, a few valleys were still filled with long snakes of night fog and writhed as the sun ate away their sides. We were flying at altitude, above small arms fire. Twice the squadron changed direction to mask our destination. I glanced about me and saw the rest of our formation. My Montagnard platoon sergeant was in the doorway of his Huey seated next to the American gunner, close enough that he returned my wave. Richard Wagner's *Ride of the Valkyries* could not be heard over any loudspeaker but the triumphal feeling was.

We descended toward our landing zone. I searched the ground ahead and made out the area in the distance. I half stood and glanced at it over the pilot's shoulder and saw that the mark did not move up or down in the window. We were on a straight glide-slope to the site.

The fleet slowed and with seconds to go, I gave a "get ready" signal to my people. The tops of yellow reeds and grass slapped the skids and struck my boots. A glance at the crew chief confirmed the time and I stepped off the skid. I anticipated jumping as we moved at speed but not the height. The grass was tall, nearly chest high. I landed on the ground with a hard jolt. My breath was knocked from my lungs and I heard a "Hummph" leave my mouth. I glanced to the side. One of my people landed toe to chin, and I worried for his neck. One tribesman crumpled and disappeared in the tall weeds and I watched until he reappeared unhurt. My interpreter summersaulted in the air, his backpack flying, but he scrambled to his feet, his rifle clutched in his hand. I thought I heard bullets passing above us. I glanced among the trees, looking for muzzle flashes and tracers.

We rushed abreast to the edge of the underbrush and by the time the Hueys veered off and the engine noise with them, we were out of sight under the canopy. My people in place, I sent out short patrols ahead for signs of enemy.

"No VC. No ambush. Many small trails but not big," was the report.

I reconned the area along the field. PAVN could just as well be set up on my side of the strip of jungle as the captain's side. I looked for and found a good ambush position. It was a slight ridge-shaped rise of land that paralleled the field. It lent good control and fields of fire. I set up a small observation post to my rear and flank, set out machine guns to the ends and center of my force, and briefed my squad leaders. We waited.

I had my handset next to my ear with the volume down. Jungle and deep forest can swallow the sounds of battle even a few hundred meters away. The radio would be the only way to know when the drive across began. In the silence, the earth gave up her smaller sounds — a swift rustle of a bug and a lizard under a dry leaf, a flutter in the trees, a drip from a leaf. A swarm of black ants attacked a large lime-green caterpillar. Its belly was the color of pale skin and tender as baby fat and quivered where the jaws took hold.

The radio squelched. I felt the vibration rather than heard sound for the volume was nearly off. I put the handpiece to my ear and whispered my call sign.

"In position?"

"Affirm."

"Starting. Nothing yet."

"Copy. Waiting."

I crawled down the line with my interpreter. Most of my people had propped their rucksacks for shields and rested their weapons on them as they looked to the front. Small shrubs and leaves camouflaged their positions. I touched their backs as I passed and nodded my confidence in them. I whispered to one or two of them. "Papasan, you ready fini VC? You have grenades?"

He smiled sheepishly and patted a bulging canteen cover on his belt.

"Have," he said.

Papasan was not his real name. He had earned it in combat when he was still a boy. He charged an enemy position, throwing grenade after grenade, throwing his last one as the last enemy in the complex was destroyed. In reality he was a baby-san, a young boy, too young in fact to be one of the SCU. But with his heroism they called him a man — papa — and added the title of respect — san. He was thereafter, Papasan.

"I do not know when VC come. Maybe soon. Maybe two hours."

He nodded his understanding.

"Maybe they do not come at all if they hear that Papasan is here," I said.

In my location near the center of my people I heard nothing to indicate what was happening with the rest of the company. No crump of distant grenades or mortar fire penetrated the thick underbrush no matter how hard I listened. Thick grass could muffle the exchange of small arms fire if it had occurred. I listened for voices and breaking twigs. There was nothing. I looked to the side. My Montagnards heard the jungle far better than I, but they seemed unconcerned. At a point, I heard a hum. I looked to my interpreter and cupped my ear. He signed to me that they were bugs singing.

I felt my handset vibrate.

"Swede," I whispered.

"We are two to four hundred meters from you. Signs of enemy, but no contact so far. Maybe coming your way."

"Copy."

I looked to either side and tapped my eye — "Be ready." My people were already cautioned to be sure to fire on the NVA and be sure it was not our own people coming through.

I watched, hardly breathing. I listened for the most subtle sound of movement and searched for the smallest twitch of vegetation.

Twenty minutes. Nothing. I moved only my eyes. There was a nothingness, like the vacuum before the actual explosion.

Definite movement to the front. A few twigs — small moist ones, parted. Tall grass rubbed together with the passing of something.

I did not move. I sensed the men beside me tensing behind their weapons. Then a shape appeared. It stopped its movement for a few seconds and moved again. Another shape emerged from the patch of brush and joined the other. It froze in place and I made out the shapes. They were two deer. They did not look in our direction. Their interest was in something deeper in the thicket. One turned its head and watched the backtrail. The pair moved like phantoms eluding a danger behind them. The larger of the two deer barked — like a dog. There were two barks of alarm and the pair made up their mind and moved more quickly to the side. They made a single bound. Their hooves landed silently on the ground and they were gone.

But the danger that drove them was not gone. I slowly turned my head to the tribesman next to me. He nodded and smiled, for the deer told us of the danger.

Fifteen minutes later we heard the movement of many people to the front. Twigs broke. Larger pieces of debris gave noisily under heavy boots. Tall bushes swayed to the front. Reeds and ferns were swept aside in haste but I still did not give word to fire. I would be sure that it was not our company coming through. They were approaching the kill zone of my Claymore mines. Then, at the place the deer emerged from the forest, soldiers in mustard yellow uniforms appeared. I fired my Claymores. My people opened up with their weapons. There were shouts and cries of pain. The pop of AK-47s returned our fire on full-automatic, but it was a desultory response. We tossed grenades and continued to fire until we received no more incoming.

"Move it!" I shouted. We assaulted the enemy firing single shot and short bursts where we could not see through the brush. Several enemies lay in postures that only death could produce. One soldier lay across the chest of another — his eyes and mouth open in surprise, his skin the pallor of a caterpillar's belly. There were no wounded. Near the ambush site was a well-used trail and the surface was churned up perhaps by the boots of escaping enemy. My interpreter pointed to waist high leaves slick with fresh blood. They had wounded with them.

My radio vibrated and I turned up the volume.

"SITREP," said the captain.

"Several enemy KIA. Some escaped via well-used trail. I have no casualties. How far out are you so my people do not fire you up?"

"By the sounds of your rifle fire, a hundred meters."

"Copy. We will not shoot."

I called to my Montagnard platoon sergeant, "Go down the line. Tell them no shoot. Company come."

I pulled my people back to our ambush site and waited. Fifteen minutes. The undergrowth parted and a Montagnard appeared. My platoon sergeant whistled softly and the approaching Yard answered. Our elements joined.

"Twelve," Roberts said.

"Twelve?"

"Twelve. You got twelve. Did you go through their things for intel yet?"

"Negative. Waited for you. Didn't want to fire you up."

"We will do it."

"They look like NVA regulars," I said as he turned to go. "All in uniforms with patches. AK rifles. Full ammo pouches. They are ready for something."

Captain Roasch appeared holding a handful of bloody papers. A bullet hole pierced one corner. "This one vas a *Dai uy* — a captain. He had orders," he said, holding up the papers. "You said that they had vounded that escaped?"

"Yes. At least one, based on blood on the trail. The trail is churned up like there were others running down the trail. I can show it to you."

"Goot. Ve vill follow it."

"I have a small observation post that I need to collect before we go."

He nodded.

I spoke to one of my squad leaders. "Get two or three men and have them retrieve our people."

The company assembled, and with Robert's platoon in the lead, followed the path.

Our pace was brisker than I was used to, coming from recon. On the recon teams we moved shadow-like at the speed set by a sun dial. But I think the captain, knowing there were wounded among the enemy, wanted to close with them. A few hundred meters into the highland's undergrowth, the trail became faint.

We received small arms fire there. It was not well aimed and was of short duration. Only two or three of them perhaps. They were probably a rear guard sent to slow us down. Our people returned fire and assaulted the ambush site, but the enemy had fled. There were no signs of blood. The path disappeared, having fragmented into tiny rivulets. There was no sign that anyone had ever passed this way. Our Montagnards searched like bloodhounds ranging left and right before us. I wondered if at some point along the way we had passed a hidden entrance to a subterranean complex.

"Captain," I said. "Is there any possibility that they went underground. I cannot imagine them proceeding with wounded and not leaving a trail of some kind."

He listened with his jaw extended. He all but snorted at my words.

"Or," I continued, "We may have followed a wrong fork in the trail."

"Yes," he finally said. "Ve vill stop in place and send a patrol to the beginning of the blood. Sergeant Hanson, you are at the rear of the column. Take a squad of your tribesmen. See vat happened."

I took ten of my men and backtracked to where the blood painted the leaves and branches. This time as we followed, we moved recon style. My people let nothing pass unexamined. Every twig or scuffmark was examined on the ground. Brush and low limbs were examined. A hair on a twig was not missed. Twenty ears listened for any out-of-place sound. They smelled the air — the iodine of blood, the sweat of fear, fresh soil that could reveal the entrance of an opening in the ground. We moved quietly, weapons ready — perhaps we would catch someone coming out of a hole.

The NVA seemed to have vanished in the air. "Hep," I whispered to my point man. "We have sign that VC were here," I said pointing to the last sign of trail. "After this, there is no more trail. VC stop here. If VC have tunnel it must start here."

Hep was a former VC who had turned and joined our ranks. He knew the way of the enemy. He gravely nodded as he looked about him. "Yes. Think VC close by."

Without me telling them to, my people sensed the nearness and dropped to their knees and faced outward. Hep and two others moved like ferrets, searching, testing the ground, listening, smelling.

Hep came to me with a puzzled look on his face. "I know VC here. I know," he said emphasizing 'know.' "But no can find. Hide number one."

My people hunkered without moving, expecting a fight at any moment.

"Never see before. But I know VC here. Maybe VC watch us now. Hide number one, never see before."

We could not find the opening. I considered that we could set up an ambush and wait for someone to come out — a wait that could be days. I did not think the captain would be up for that.

"Hep, lead us to the company. Go slow so we do not get ambushed. And go slow for our tail gunners."

I pointed to three of my men. "You will watch our back trail. You will walk backwards and watch for enemy."

I gave my report to the captain. He seemed irritated that I spent so long in my search and was not impressed when I told him that the hair on my head stood up where the trail ended.

"Ve vill continue on and find the high-speed trail that recon team found. Ve vill stop at the first good RON site."

By late afternoon we found a rise of land where the shrubs thinned and lent good fields of fire and set up an RON. We positioned around the military crest of the rise, my platoon occupying the north end. I positioned my people with machine gunners at good locations with fields of fire. "We will dig your foxhole," one of my people shouted to me.

I studied the area in front of me. If I were the enemy commander, what would be my best avenues of attack? I placed Claymore mines there. I only had a few of them left, having used some on my ambush. Some of my people were making cooking fires with C-4. Hunched over so I had a low profile, I was nearly back to my foxhole when the Communists hit my end of the perimeter. I began with B-40 rockets and a few mortar rounds, followed by an infantry charge directly at me.

I dove into my foxhole and discovered that it was only knee deep. I had forgotten that Montagnards squat with their butts on the backs of their heels. My tribesmen sprang to their assigned places on the line. Meals, nearly cooked, spilled on the ground. We returned fire and in a few minutes it was over. Incoming fire ceased. I wondered if they were just probing our lines.

"Third platoon, every other person, move out," I shouted. Half of us moved at a fast walk down the rise. They did not shout, but solemnly finished business, shooting only where they could not see through the thicket, stopping where we found enemy soldiers who died in the probe of our lines. There were three of them in mustard-yellow uniforms. Two died on their stomachs and I wondered if the momentum of their charge carried them forward when they died. The third was thrust backward by our bullets where he remained half upright, entangled by the underbrush, but dead. But as his body did not fall, he was shot twice more in our charge. Two of them held AK rifles and the third had an SKS with a small scope that was missing most of the bluing.

We settled on that rise. I examined my portion of the perimeter. I paired my men at each location so one would always be awake, and I was comfortable with their fields of fire and concealment. As twilight set in, I examined the Claymores to be sure that the enemy had not slipped in and turned them around toward us should they come again. I placed a small dab of luminous tape on the back of each mine. As long as we saw the faint glow, they still faced the enemy. Last, I set out an observation post for the night and settled in.

It sprinkled during the night, enough to send shivers up our spines but not enough that our people would not be alert. Although the day promised sun, it began as a grey, sullen overcast. Our people were stiff and sore when they woke. Most of them slept on the bare ground beside their foxholes. The soil was stony and hard and none of them slept soundly. They were cooking when the Communists hit us again. This time they did not charge or probe our perimeter. They fired B-40 rockets — one after another over the length of the hill. "Kawunph, kawumph," over and over. They fired them into the trees so the fragments would rain down on us. Thousands of pieces of metal. Then it abruptly stopped. We knew they were close by. They knew our position exactly. They would be waiting when we left the RON.

Robert's people led us out that morning. Although PAVN knew our location, they did not know the direction we would leave. I was apprehensive that with the abundance of confidence both Roberts and the captain had, they would drive headlong into a probable ambush, believing in their invincibility. After all, finding and engaging the enemy was what this was about. I was relieved then, when they chose to follow some higher terrain that would be of help to us in a fight. Roberts also had a small point element a short distance ahead to give us early warning. The element would scout a distance ahead and wait as the company caught up with them, then move ahead again.

Our slow movement irritated the captain. I might go forward for something only to find him standing, looking about and fidgeting as the men rested around him. He was anxious for the column to move and proceed with slogging it out in World War fashion — finding and fixing the foe, then overpowering him.

I think I understood the workings of his mind. He had been influenced by one of the greatest commandos of World War Two.

One afternoon several months before, I picked up the company mail and while trying to decipher the name on the envelope, was surprised at the handwriting. It was in the German hand, like my Grandmother Hecker's. Without trying to do so, I discovered I held a handwritten letter from Otto Skorzeny to Captain Roasch. It was the first of several I would bring. I knew the name. Skorzeny was perhaps the most famous commando of the Second World War, some said the most famous commando that ever lived. During the war, newspapers said he was the most dangerous man in Europe. Accounts referred to him as the Third Reich's Scarlet Pimpernel. He was the head of Germany's Special Forces. Skorzeny considered his specialty to be commando raids and Guerrilla warfare — just like our American Special Forces Green Berets. I was convinced that the German legend was the paradigm of my captain and that he was mentored by him.

I had studied Skorzeny. I read his book and studied his missions. I did so for my own learning and what I knew of Skorzeny revealed much about my captain.

Skorzeny was six four with a deep livid scar that ran down his entire left cheek to the tip of his chin. He received it in a saber duel when he was a young man — one of more than fifteen in which he fought. He fought with courage in conventional war, earning the Iron Cross twice and the Knight's Cross. He parachuted into Holland and fought there, then France, and after that he fought on the Eastern Front until wounds sidelined him for a time.

It was this legendary soldier who rescued Benito Mussolini where he was jailed in an impregnable fortress on the top of Gran Sasso Mountain. He and his team went in by glider, landing on a tiny lawn at the gates, sprung him and escaped in a single engine airplane.

Another time he was on a mission to assassinate the big three — Roosevelt, Churchill and Stalin — while they were together at a conference, but only a leak in intelligence alerted the allies and the mission was scrubbed. He did succeed at another time however, to assassinate "Winston Churchill" but they later discovered that he had made a clean kill on Churchill's double.

In October 1944, Hungary was considering leaving the axis powers. Skorzeny was sent in to kidnap the regent of the country. He did so, wrapping him in a carpet and made it to German controlled territory. The mission ensured that the regent's father would keep Hungary in the war on the side of Germany.

Skorzeny was in command of Operation Greif in which a few hundred German commandos were dropped behind the lines during the Ardennes Offensive. They were English speaking Germans in

American uniforms and equipment. They captured key bridges and turned road signs around, putting the allies into confusion. Fake orders were left in opportune places. Word came out that the commandos had infiltrated. Confusion and paranoia ensued. GIs grilled each other to be sure that were actually talking to other Americans. (Heaven help the soldier who did not know who won the last World Series.) Generals were detained at checkpoints. In his arrogance, Field Marshall Bernard Montgomery refused to show his ID and his car tires were shot out and he was dragged into a barn until his identity was confirmed.

Skorzeny, capitalizing on the fear of the day, spread the rumor that General Eisenhower was the actual target of the deception. "Ike" was placed in protective custody, nearly a house arrest, unable to perform many of his duties as his double made all of his appearances.

At the end of the war, Skorzeny was held in Dermstadt Prison. He escaped. It was believed that his escape was aided by the OSS (later called the CIA) in return for certain services. He went to Ireland where he began a business that was actually a front for getting certain Germans out of Germany to Argentina. (ODESSA) He later went himself and became the bodyguard of Eva Peron.

He went to Spain and was approached by two Israeli Mossad agents. Skorzeny thought at first that they were a hit team.

"No, we do not want to kill you. We want to hire you. Nassar of Egypt has a team of scientists who are developing missiles to destroy Israel. We want you to take them out."

"I don't need money. But if you can get Simon Wiesenthal to take me off his most wanted list, I will do it."

In the next few months Skorzeny eliminated all the scientists.

It is nearly certain that Skorzeny advised American Special Forces in techniques of his raids and guerilla warfare. One of them was perhaps my Popeye-jawed Captain Heinz Roasch.

I thought of these things and I would smile and give Captain Roasch his letters. When we were in the field, I always considered that the mentoring of Skorzeny was also there. I expected Skorzeny bravado on our missions in enemy controlled territory.

We had a small firefight a hundred meters from our RON. It was overcome with small arms alone. Robert's people suppressed the fire and the lead squads came on line and moved through the ambush and halted. Roberts considered the enemy was trying to draw us into a larger fight. Our company inched closer to the black grease pencil line on the sergeant's map. We contoured the side of a ridgeline, always moving in that direction. Twice more we received fire. One of those times it was directed at my own platoon, the last in the line of march. They had let the bulk of the company through. But they had fired on my flank and we had the most fire power to the side. Two of the enemy dropped. Crashing brush traced the route of terrified, escaping enemy. I examined the patches on the bodies. They were of the same unit that we hit on the LZ. My people were getting loaded with captured weapons. I cut the patches from the sleeves, left my Montagnard commander in charge for a few minutes and went forward to show the captain. We moved on.

It was late in the day when we found the high-speed trail. On it, two elephants laden with supplies could march abreast. The bare hard-packed surface indicated heavy activity. The North Vietnamese Army could move troops and crew-served weapons quickly. There were no twigs to snap on the path. If any vehicles used this jungle highway, the smooth hardness of the surface did not tell.

Roasch took the lead with his platoon, with Roberts taking the tail. Roasch put two of his machine gunners closer to the front and had Hendricks with his 60mm mortar slightly forward of center. A squad of men moved ahead on point.

We followed the road half a mile expecting to find bunkers or sideroads leading to supply or staging areas but the area was eerily quiet. As the road contoured a hillside, one side was above us and I considered that if PAVN ambushed us there, he could simply roll his grenades down on us. I could not discern enemy among the ferns and brush. I looked for clues of alarm in the faces of my people.

At the front of the column, one of the men at point rushed back. "VC come! VC come down trail!" Our people trained for this. The captain signed for his people to move off the trail for a hasty ambush.

Movement on the hard pack rendered so little noise, that at nearly the same time they heard the swish of clothing, or a scrape on metal, they met the enemy head-on on the road. Our people were expectant and ready. The enemy, thought safe in their own backyard, were not. Six or eight North Vietnamese were hit with the volley of our fire, many with their rifles still slung. But the Communists behind their lead group assaulted like a reflex. Our soldiers in the front were nearly overpowered until our platoon rushed into the fight and turned the tide with machine-gun and rifle fire. Our mortars sent round after round down the road. The "thump, thump, thump" of rounds leaving the tubes was muffled by the trees, but on landing they exploded with a loud "crump" sending shards of shrapnel through the air.

The enemy broke contact and retreated down the road, but we knew they would scramble to set up a hasty defense. The next fight would not be as easy.

"Third platoon move out," the captain yelled.

"Hep! Move out" I shouted to my own people. "I want two machine guns forward."

I knew, as did the captain, our best course of action required an immediate assault before they had a chance to fortify.

We assaulted at a fast walk, nearly a run, our backpacks shoving the air from our lungs with each footfall. Equipment jostled noisily. Straps and buckles scraped and clacked in time with each trudging step. Contact occurred less than fifty meters down the road. We were nearly out of breath and our rifles swayed with labored breathing. We caught the enemy as they were scrambling to create a defense. A small unit of NVA were blocking the road to buy time for the rest to set up. We dropped the blocking force and ran over the bodies in the road. Seeing we were on them, the balance of the force fled down the road, some of them firing their rifles over their shoulders without looking back. My two M-60 machine guns joined at the front as the last enemy soldier escaped around a bend in the road.

I sent a squad of my people a distance down the road and waited as the captain and Roberts joined me. Robert's bandanna was black with sweat and it dripped down his cheek. He came forward without speaking and waited with his weapon across the crook of one arm. The captain was animated, his movements quick. He glanced about him, not focusing on any particular thing. He caught his breath. "Vell, ve can keep chasing them and catch them again, but PAVN knows ve are coming. After the next contact they vill be ready and ve vill not be so lucky. The next fight vill be just to hold us up until they are ready farther on."

The captain's blue eyes sparkled and he thrust his jaw forward and waited for us to see the situation as he did. I nodded. Roberts seemed to slowly unfold like a just-waking thing. "We have only about two or three hours of light left," he offered.

"I vill contact FOB and see vat air support is available if we get into trouble. Ve vill proceed down this road much slower. If ve do not haff air support ve vill find a suitable place to RON."

We were advised by FOB to avoid contact if possible until the following day. We followed the road another hundred meters and discovered a second high-speed trail joined the first at right angles. The junction presented a problem not to be solved in the last hours of the day. "We know they will be waiting for us," I offered. "If we continue down this road, they can bring forces from the other high speed and take us from both sides. The only place for us to put up for the night is to climb this ridge above the road."

The captain listened quietly for he had not determined a course of action.

Roberts seemed to wake. "We can do this, sir." Roberts appeared to have the wisdom of phrasing a solution in which the commander thought it was his own idea. "One time in Laos when I was in the black pajamas, I had a company and we just stopped on the highway and dared them to take us off. Stopped all traffic."

The captain nearly smiled, at least his jaw loosened and there was a hint of amusement about his mouth. He thought a moment, then stood stiffly erect. "Ve vill do that now. Ve vill RON right here on this road." He looked about him at the junction. "Both roads! Ve vill stop all traffic down this road."

We set up at the junction with platoons along the three axes. We set out claymores and machine guns. We had a few trip flares that we set out for early warning. Tribesmen lined the road and used trees for cover.

"We just slept right on the top of the road," Roberts had said, recalling his days with the Lao.

As it occurred, the very place I rolled up in my poncho liner for the night was exactly where the two roads met — the junction of two supply routes. As I lay there, I considered the possibility of being squashed by an elephant carrying supplies on its back, or by an army truck, full to the brim with troops or ammunition. But that was just a thought.

I woke as the sky was just greying, not yet surrendering color to the morning. My people slept well I think, for the Montagnard knows how to gauge his slumber. But because it was possible to move without sound on the hard clay surface, and the enemy could silently be upon us, my sleep was light. My ears strained for any anomaly. Even normal night noises had to be evaluated and dismissed. But I must have been asleep on two occasions. I recall springing upright when a troop of spider monkeys swung by in the trees. At another time I was not alone in my alarm. The trip flare, which we had set at a distance across the road with its nearly invisible string had been tripped with a hiss. A faint glow showed around the bend. Our people at that end of our night defense would have certainly stood-to. No claymores were used and there was no small arms fire. The enemy had fled the scene and backed off for another option.

Our people groaned as they woke and stretched. They began to light cooking fires with pieces of C-4 explosives. Soon the air was filled with the odors of cooking food. A luxury of being in a company is that you can cook. I opened a C ration can of ham and eggs that had been packed during the Korean War. I was looking forward to the can of peaches that I had brought when the captain approached me.

"I vant everyone avake and ready to go. You can haf half of them eat at a time vile the rest vatches. I vant to be off this road before they drop mortars on us or haf time to move on us. My platoon vill lead.

Roberts vill take the last."

"Yes sir."

I walked the length of my perimeter telling each squad leader to pack up before they ate. I glanced at the shallow valley that was bounded by the two roads. A blue-grey fog covered the lowest portion, filtering up between the trees and hovered above like a canopy. I stood there with peaches in my mouth, and it occurred to me that night fog should be white or light grey, not blue. As the realization hit me, I smelled wood smoke. I looked around to be sure it did not originate with my own people. It came from the valley. About then I heard faint, muffled camp sounds. PAVN was encamped below us.

I ate the last bite and stomped the can into the ground and shoved dirt over it with my foot.

"You are in charge," I told my Montagnard platoon leader, and I went to the captain with my findings. He was back with me in minutes.

"Ve vill attack."

Roberts joined us.

"The fork in the road leads us right to them," I said. "But they will certainly have a listening post or ambush set up."

"Ve could bypass the road and go through the voods."

"Yes," I said, "but I do not think we could move quietly enough. Anyone on the road would hear us and be ready. Also, our mortars could not support us through that canopy."

Captain Roasch did not look at me but stared at the smoke coming from the valley as he thought. "Vat do you think Sergeant Roberts?"

"Hit 'em fast down the middle of the road. Do it right now with maximum fire power to the front. Run right over the top of them. Have Sergeant Hendricks set up with his mortars at the first open space in the road."

Roasch was still staring into the valley. "Ve go now. Sergeant Hanson, give me one of your machine gunners. I vill brief Hendricks. Ten minutes and ve start."

We sent a point element a few dozen meters ahead to warn us of waiting ambush — we would assault, not stumble into them. We found no enemy along the way and wondered what waited for us in the valley. Was it possible they were unaware of us?

The road leveled. It was an idyllic hamlet site, needing only a small fast-moving stream turning a small, white, water wheel and bamboo chimes. Trees were spaced with grass below. Sunbeams found paths through the leaves. It was a place suitable for gardens and parks and homes and schools. But families — fathers and aged ones and laughing children did not live there today. This was an encampment of Communist soldiers. Around several cooking fires, uniformed soldiers prepared the first meal of the day. Steam from huge fire-black pots joined woodsmoke and rose into the sky. At the far side of the clearing, were several long barracks-type buildings. Separate from them, under the shade of a dozen trees, were bungalows for officers on bamboo stilts. A middle-aged man shuffled to the deck of one of them and washed himself. Finished, he leaned over the rail and threw a basin of grey water over the side. Yawning, he scratched his belly with the fingernails of one hand, turned without looking in our direction, and went inside.

"Ve vill move quickly until ve are noticed. Then ve vill begin our assault. Hendricks, then you engage vith your mortars."

We advanced rapidly down the road. I was concerned that the noise of our equipment would give us away, but we made it to level ground and got on line and off the path. Although we saw enemy soldiers, we did not engage them and were within fifty yards before we were noticed. It was a hatless man in a faded sleeveless T-shirt at the cooking fire who first saw us. He held a large wood stir-stick with both hands and stirred in large slow circles, scraping the bottom of the caldron so the rice would not stick. He was humming and happened to look up in our direction. The stirring stopped. At first, he did not know who we were. He stared for several seconds. His mouth gaped open as the realization came to him. The forgotten spoon dropped into the rice and he shouted and reached for a rifle next to the fire. Our point man shot once. The cook fell against the caldron knocking it into the fire. A cloud of sparks rose from the ashes. We charged, our advance taking us through the kitchen and to the bunkers. Hendricks' mortars crashed into the bamboo structures knocking some of them from their stilts.

A building sagged to one side, spilling soldiers. First platoon swept through the barracks area. They were on low stilts and I saw the legs of running men below them as they broke through the back and ran into the forest. Only the soldiers we first encountered shot at us. Many enemies, not being near their weapons when we attacked, bolted into the woods.

My people's target was a fortified encampment near the barracks. Bunkers with connecting trenches protected a sandbagged command center. We threw grenades through the apertures of the fighting positions and buildings as we stormed down the trench system. Had the position been fully occupied and ready when we struck, it could have held off a force much larger than ours. We overran and secured the fortification, searched for documents and collected weapons.

The captain called for helicopters to take out captured weapons and intelligence while I made a perimeter around the site. Roasch looked around at the ridges. I too was concerned with the high ground. Although the area was idyllic, we were exposed in the open. I wondered when those PAVN soldiers would halt their headlong retreat, regain control, and rocket or attack us with ground forces.

"We have a ready-made bunker complex that the enemy built for us 'if we need to get out of the rain,'" I said, pointing with my thumb at the complex my people had just secured. The captain was not one for irony nor was he aware of the expression that I used, but he nodded and looked toward the protection of the bunkers I indicated.

"Most of them ran in that direction," he said pointing toward the road above. "Ven the chopper comes and takes the veapons, Sergeant Hanson, I vant you to set up an ambush here, just like ve did on the LZ. You know what to do. The rest of us vill go back along the road vere ve spent the night and find the enemy. Ve vill eliminate them there or drive them down to you. Hammer and anvil, like before."

"Yes sir."

Some of our people walked to the fire and scooped up rice and *nuoc mam* with their cups and returned to their positions. It was sticky rice and they ate it with their fingers as they looked into the forest.

Roasch noticed it, became instantly angry at their perceived lack of discipline. He was about to shout at their indiscretion.

"Sir," I said, "I think they are putting *nuoc mam* on their breath so the enemy will smell them coming and think they are friendlies."

Roasch's head snapped in my direction. He thought a moment. Then he nodded his head and almost smiled — almost.

First and second platoons trudged back uphill on the same road from which we mounted our assault. The hard clay yielded no sound of their heavy, equipment-laden steps. Even the passing of their cloth sleeves over their sides sounded only like a whisper of breeze. Spilled food from the nearby cooking pots dripped and spattered into the fires and recalled me to my own duty. I wanted my people to be positioned and concealed before the larger unit left the area so any watchers would conclude that all of us had left. I glanced about and was satisfied. Although I knew their individual positions, my eyes had to penetrate the camouflage to locate them. They were silent and unmoving along the fortification. I was concerned that survivors of our assault on the camp might return and I placed a few listening posts to our rear. I considered that we could have significant contact with an angry, returning and reinforced enemy. The captain said that it would take an hour or two for him to get in place. We settled in to wait.

The firefight along the road above us began suddenly, loudly and in fury. The clash of small arms fire was such that individual rounds could not be heard. The continuous burst was more a tearing of cloth in which the individual threads were lost in the ripping of the whole. Explosions followed. Two or three per second. The explosions began as grenades were thrown in rage. Then came the crunch of explosions from our three mortars, the ordnance sent as quickly as the soldiers could drop rounds down the tubes. The Communists answered with their own mortars, then with B-40 rockets. Even from where we waited, I heard shrapnel shredding branches as rockets exploded in the trees. The furious sounds of the American M-16s mixed with the "pop" of AK-47 rifles filtered across. There was no sound of abatement of either side. I heard shouting or screaming on the other side of the dense vegetation. Surely, I thought, they were too far away for me to hear voices.

We waited. The outcome of the fight was in question. Perhaps it would be our Company that would be defeated by the North Vietnamese this day. The fury continued. I glanced at my people. Tribesmen lay on their stomachs, rifles forward, their eyes piercing the undergrowth. For now, it appeared that the fight in its entirety would be fought at the upper road and that there would be no enemy pushed toward the anvil of third platoon. I slowly turned my head and looked to the rear to be sure it was clear of stalking enemy, an enemy who might have moved in stealth and cut the throats of my listening post and was creeping nearby. I fully expected to be involved in a firefight of my own.

The exchange of fire above continued with neither side being dominant. It had been twenty minutes. The volume lessened. I no longer heard the rocket propelled grenades explode in the trees, nor exploding grenades or bursts of RPD machine guns. Men shouted from the road. I did not have to tell my people to be vigilant. I was listening so intently for movement of escaping enemy in the dense undergrowth in front of me, that I did not notice that the fighting at the road reached a new crescendo.

Brush crashed to my front. People were running headlong in my direction. Someone groaned in the thicket. Vegetation swayed. The enemy was being driven my way. In one or two minutes I would initiate the fight. They were close, completely unaware that we would soon destroy them. They continued on. My soldiers did not move, barely breathed.

Someone shouted! Someone very close to me was shouting, talking very loudly. I could not believe it. I swung in that direction in fury. Two Vietnamese officers were shouting into a radio. Where did they come from?

"Shuush!" I said as loud as I dared and not ruin the ambush, and I waved my hand to get their attention.

They continued to shout loudly into the handset. I glanced to my front to see if the enemy had heard them and stopped coming in my direction.

"Shuuush!"

I threw a stick at them, then small rocks. "Shuuush!"

One of the two Vietnamese looked up at me. His look was one of dismissal and annoyance. He looked down at his radio and continued to talk as loudly as before into the mouthpiece.

I glanced again to the front. The movement in the bushes ceased.

I wanted to kill the two Lieutenants. "Stop!" I demanded. They ignored me. Their loud talking was certainly warning off the enemy. Hunched over, I ran to them and jerked the handpiece out of the speaker's hands and threw the radio set over the embankment. I know that they were convinced by the look in my face that they were close to being killed by me. It seemed clear that the two of them either did not want us to be involved in the fight or were warning off the North Vietnamese. I went to my nearest Montagnard and told him to keep his eyes on the two officers. I considered that when my back was turned, they would shoot me. The tribesman gravely nodded his head and swiveled his body to face them, pointing his rifle in their direction. There was no love lost between Montagnard and Vietnamese. He would gladly take them out.

I returned to my position and glanced back. My circle of protectors surrounded me.

I glanced to my front. Was my ambush ruined? Did they hear the Vietnamese officers?

Movement in the bushes had moved away from us and was deeper into the undergrowth and well to the flank, well out of my kill zone. Only by using my mortar and M-79 grenade launchers was there any chance of inflicting casualties on the enemy. They heard the loud talking of the Viets. I was so angry I could not speak. I did not know if they were traitors, cowards, or simply stupid. Where did these officers come from? I had not seen them the entire mission. How could they be here and not be noticed by me. I had to control my anger. Then it hit me. They must have come in on the helicopter that picked up the weapons. Captain Roasch dumped them on me. They were left in place with me so they "vood not mess vit his var plans."

I finally noticed the crescendo of fighting back at the road had increased. I felt the vibration of my radio — I did not have the volume up lest I ruin the ambush. I answered my call sign.

"Sergeant Hanson, ve are in heavy contact. Outcome in question. Get here ASAP." Roasch's voice was breathless and full of tension.

"Yes sir, on the way."

I stood and shouted to my people, "On your feet!"

I pointed to three of the nearest tribesmen. "Bring the soldiers in from the three listening posts. Run, run! Bring them back now. We are leaving."

I picked six to be point ahead of the platoon. "We go fast, very fast — force march to rescue company. Go very fast but watch for VC. Remember, VC like to ambush force when we come rescue," I said in pigeon.

"Yes, Han-Son," and they turned and moved out. It was uphill on the road and our rucksacks slammed down with every step. I considered ditching the rucks until the battle was over, but mortar rounds, rifle ammunition and Claymores were inside them.

My outposts jogged in, their packs slapping their backs as they ran. I briefed my leaders in one or two sentences, and we followed our point trudging up the slope as fast as we could move without it being a run. Our legs became rubber. We panted and sweat rolled down our faces. My bare forearms were slimy with sweat. I glanced at my people. Their mouths were wide open as they gasped for air. Their eyes glazed and they were exhausted. I did not let them stop. I rushed to the front of my column.

"*Di, di mau*. Keep going, go fast."

Sounds of desperate fighting was still another mile away. I cupped my ear so the tribesmen would remember why I would not let them stop.

Behind me, one of my men was on hands and knees in the center of the road puking. It first seemed to be a pile of steaming maggots but was white rice that he ate from the cooking fire in the valley. A tribesman nearby pulled his canteen and gulped water and poured some over his face. I patted his shoulder in understanding. One or two of my men slumped to the ground. I walked over and lifted them up by their arms. "I know. Just a little farther and we stop." I pointed in the direction that the company continued its desperate fight. I pointed toward the sound. "Soon."

The road leveled but our legs were still rubber. Sounds of the firefight were more pronounced. This time there was no mistaking the shouting above the rifle fire. A few hundred yards to go. We could hardly lift our feet.

"*Xin loi,*" I said, "*Xin loi* — I am sorry." My people were in agony of weariness and I felt with them. "Soon, soon."

Another hundred yards. We were getting close to the fighting. The rifle fire was loud and crisp, not muffled by distance and vegetation. People were shouting in Vietnamese perhaps only a hundred yards away and around the bend of the road. My interpreter stood and pulled at my sleeve. "Voice them, VC, *Bac* Vietnam,"

"Do you know what they are saying?"

"Voice VC say, 'Kill American, kill Montagnard.'"

"Well, that is not very nice. That is number ten," I said, trying to encourage him with lightness and humor, over the situation.

My interpreter looked up at me in total exhaustion but managed a weary smile. "Hanson, me think you *dinky dao.*" (Crazy.)

I looked at my people. They were collapsing in the road. We had covered in twenty or thirty minutes what took the rest of the company two hours to accomplish. Gasping sounded like it sourced from empty drain pipes.

We were taking mortar fire, dozens of rounds exploded in the trees around us and two or three in the road nearby.

My people were in no condition to fight. They could barely stand. I had to rest them before we joined the company. I was at the front and I turned to them. "Fini. Fini. Rest," I said and I signed with both hands pushing downward in the universal sign. There was a loud collective moan as they slumped to the bare road. We were under indirect fire but it could not be helped. We would rest even as mortars fell among us.

"Spanky," I shouted into the radio. I discovered that I was breathing heavily. "We are at your flank just about to come up on you. Tell your people not to fire on us."

"Roger."

"I am under mortar fire. Is that you? Call them off!"

"Negative. Not ours."

"I am under enemy fire then."

The captain's voice came on the radio. Amazement marked his voice. "You are here already?"

"Yes sir."

"I did not expect you to get here so soon. Join us and I think ve vill prevail."

"Yes sir."

Two more mortar rounds crunched down in our area but they fell deeper in the trees and I hoped that they were traversing and were not sure our exact location.

I took stock of my people. Some of them lay on their backs, their arms splayed out to their sides. Chests still heaved. If I gave them leave, my whole platoon would be instantly asleep. They panted for air. A couple of my men were massaging their legs to relieve them of cramps. Their eyes were glazed. Enemy mortar fire lessened with most of the rounds landing in the trees. A Montagnard was puking over the shoulder of the road. I would give them needed rest before I joined the company.

I walked down the column. "Ten minutes, ten minutes." And I watched the impact of the mortars. If they got any closer, we would move out immediately.

"On your feet! *Di*. We go fini VC." I went down the column and helped some of my people to their feet. I nodded to three of my men on point and pointed down the road. Although weary, they moved as disciplined soldiers, rifles ready, eyes searching. Minutes later we joined the company at the end of the column. The incoming fire diminished.

Roberts was out of breath and there was a tremor in his hands when he made his way over to me. He was a wet wash-rag. His clothes were black with sweat and pasted to his skin. His skin dripped and reflected the daylight. His soaked headband kept sliding down his forehead as he talked. "Captain wants for all of us to use maximum fire power on the enemy for one minute. After we suppress their fire, he wants you to attack them from your flank and take the position while we support you."

"Got it."

"He will give the signal to start one minute on full auto to get their heads down. When you hear us stop full auto it is time for you to go."

"Got it."

I briefed my people and the command was given. For a solid minute the roar of our weapons crashed into the jungle below us. My people that manned my 60mm mortar dropped round after round down the tube. I was certain that the Communists sensed our additional firepower in the fight.

"Move out!"

We assaulted on line through the brush, moving as fast as we could to overrun them before they emerged from cover. We fired into every place that could conceal a soldier. Next to my ear my M-79 man fired round after round — "thump, thump, thump" — out of the barrel, the rounds crashing into enemy cover. Return fire was uncertain and sporadic. My people shouted, "Kill VC!"

Return fire stopped altogether. Brush crashed ahead of us as the NVA ran headlong into the jungle. We came across blood spatters. Their backpacks lay in the paths of their retreat. Then it was their web gear. I found an RPD machine gun at the edge of a soldier's spider hole, left as he fled. When we found their discarded rifles, we knew the enemy in mustard-yellow were in full panic and retreat.

"Vat do you find?"

I told him. "We will not be able to catch them now. Most of them have left anything that will slow them down. We can stop now and let you catch up with us. There is a lot of abandoned equipment we can pick up."

There was satisfaction in the captain's voice. "Gather vat you can and join us at the road."

We struggled up the slope. My "little people" were weary with our forced march and the captured weapons we carried. Montagnards from the other platoons offered their hands and helped us up the bank. Even my strongest people sighed loudly and sat, not even having the strength to slide the extra weapons from their shoulders.

I saw the two Vietnamese shouting to Captain Roasch and pointing at me. They had not come with us on our rush to rescue the company but appeared now that the fighting was over. My anger was renewed upon seeing them. I slid the captured RPD machine gun from my shoulder and stood to confront the lieutenants with the captain.

Roberts noticed and put his hand on my shoulder and guided me to the side of the road.

"No! I see what is about to happen. Listen to me."

We stopped at the edge of the road, but I could not take my eyes from the two men. I was a Bantam rooster about to scrap.

"Listen to me. Those two men are officers and the captain will not take your side in front of the men. I do not know what happened down there but you cannot win up here."

"They warned off the enemy. They shouted on the radio so they would hear. I threw their radio over the embankment."

Surprise marked Robert's face. His eyebrows raised. "Let me give you some advice."

I was not eager to hear it.

"Listen to me. I am going to give it to you straight. Those two lieutenants could get you transferred from CCC. It is called Vietnamization. Remember? It is the government's plan that the Vietnamese take over the war. When we get back to camp those two officers will take credit for this whole operation. The record will show their great courage and leadership it took to destroy this place. And our people, including our captain, will affirm that this is so."

I looked at Roberts, then at the Vietnamese, then back at Roberts. He was right. If the mission was Vietnamization, then the report must affirm that it was working. America was accomplishing its own mission. It galled me.

"Time for me to grow up on this one," I thought.

"There will be diplomacy when we get back," Roberts said. "The lieutenants will see a glowing report of their leadership on this mission, and the eyewitness statement of Sergeant Hanson attesting to the fact. Oh, you did not know that you will write one? Our people will do that for you. That should save your bacon."

I did not look back at the two officers in their clean uniforms — uniforms without a trace of the grime of combat.

We spent the night along the ridge that shouldered the road, on the military crest, low enough that our profile would not be etched against the sky, yet close enough to the road that we could halt traffic with our weapons. I was not entirely sure if we were in ambush, waiting for traffic, or were making our presence known to the enemy, telling them that road business was closed for the night. It was perhaps neither. Our soldiers were spent. Ammunition was low after that last battle, and we were not anxious for a sustained fight again. I hoped that the captain would let us slip into our RON quietly to lessen the chance we would be mortared and hit by rocket fire before morning. The three of us — Roasch, Roberts and I — went over the map looking for an LZ for extraction. Nothing seemed suitable except for the enemy camp in the valley that we had overrun.

"They could drop indirect fire on us from the ridges, but they do not know we are leaving so would not have any reason to set up. Going back there will also give us time to see if the enemy has revisited the camp."

Captain Roasch, who did not normally solicit advice, listened as I spoke, then turned to the First Sergeant. "Sergeant Roberts?'

"Sounds good to me." He took the map from the captain with his sausage fingers and looked down at it and spoke as if he were reading the words from the document. "If we could leave here early and time it so the first lift arrives about the same time that we do, they will not have time to bring up fire. We will not be exposed so long on the LZ."

Roasch's Popeye chin was thrust out. He had decided. "I vill call FOB and have the first lift arrive in the valley at precisely 10:00 a.m. Ve vill leave this RON at 8:00 a.m. exactly. Ve vill arrive and secure the LZ and set up around it. Sergeant Roberts, your platoon vill be on the first lift. My platoon vill be the last one to leave." He looked up. "I have vork to do."

At dusk, Sergeant Hendricks brought me coffee. "First chance to talk with you this trip," he said. "I gotta tell you, I've never seen anyone as calm as you in a fight. I don't know how you do it." I wondered at that — how my outside masked my pounding heart.

"How are you holding out, Dean?"

He ran his hands through his black hair. "I think I have been too busy to get scared. We are getting low on mortar rounds. At least that makes our backpacks lighter."

I liked Dean. His heart was transparent and had an excitement and energy for the mission. Dean had also a genuine love for our little people.

"I am low too. I only have one Claymore left and I need to open that one to be sure that my Yards haven't taken the C-4 out of it to cook with. I do not think my M-79 people have a dozen grenades among them. But tomorrow the sky should be filled with firepower."

The night passed without incident on the road although we saw the glow of headlights on the far side of a low ridge. It brightened the sky as the moon does just before it crests. But the night was quiet. I heard snoring twice and someone talked in sleep until a buddy woke the offender. I considered that the enemy was not sure where we were and did not want to risk an encounter.

We left our RON early, just after tree bats settled in with their brown foliage. Our pace was steady with security on all sides, timed to arrive just before the Hueys did for the first lift. My people secured the area. Charlie had picked up their dead and removed all signs that they had ever been there, but a few white birds pecked rice in the grass and waddled about where men had fallen.

Robert's platoon was first to go. The Vietnamese, although I did not see them, left on the first chopper with many of the war trophies. I guessed as much when Roberts' little people slung the tradable SKS rifles over their shoulders along with their own.

My people went out next, and the captain and his people left on the last lift. We arrived at noon. The steel helipad seemed to evaporate in the heat waves. Anyone watching could see the weariness of the men by the effort it took to climb into the beds of the waiting deuce-and-a-half trucks. We formed in platoons in front of the barracks.

Captain Roasch called the company to attention and turned it over to Roberts and saluted. Roberts turned the company over to me and said, "Sergeant Hanson, take charge." We saluted. The captain then marched stiffly in the direction of the officer's club. Roberts turned and moseyed in the direction of the Huckleberry Inn, the second stool from the left.

I looked after my people. They were bone-tired but stood at attention. I was proud of them. I used my interpreter to tell them so. I told them how good they were, that they were the finest soldiers on Earth. "Put up your gear. We will clean everything… tomorrow. Take a shower. Rest. And I will see what they have in the mess hall for you." I smiled at them and saluted.

"Company, attention! Dismissed!"

It was Sunday. Tonight was steak night.

I had been visiting my wounded in the camp dispensary. We had few casualties on this mission and none of them were serious, but two or three were in beds, their skin dark-brown against the white sheets. Patches of red seeped through gauze strips that covered their wounds. I was gratified that I did not have to zipper any of my Montagnard people into heavy olive-drab body bags, slide them into the bed of a three-quarter-ton truck and escort them to their home villages.

I think my Yards especially appreciated my time with them at their bedside. The French called them "*Moi*" or savages. But to Special Forces, these loyal, courageous men were respected and beloved.

I was leaving the steps of the dispensary when the master sergeant from S-3 walked up to me.

"Oh, there you are. Been looking for you." He glanced around to be sure we were out of earshot and led me from the door. "I have a warning order for your captain. You know that place we just pulled you out of? Well, Saigon thought it was such a fruitful area, they want you to go back in."

"When?"

"Day after tomorrow."

I had that tingle of electricity. "When is the warning order?"

"Sixteen hundred today."

"I will find them and let them know."

He gave me a slip of paper and walked back to his office. I turned and went back into the dispensary and found the medic in charge.

"*Bac Si*," I said. "We just got back from a mission. According to my own log of events, seventeen times that we had some kind of contact with the enemy. We have no medic in our company. We are supposed to go back in. If we needed a medic, is it possible for you to supply one?"

"No medic?"

"None, and we are going back into the same area."

"Unbelievable."

"Just a minute," he said as he went back inside and consulted his roster. "You have it. I can shake *Bac Si* Brown from other duty."

"I have to clear it with the captain first. I would think he would want one."

The officer's club was around the corner of the mess hall at a secluded, not traveled part of the compound. Captain Roasch seemed irritated that an enlisted soldier would intrude into their sanctum. I motioned him out so I would not violate security.

I handed him the slip of paper which I had not opened. "They want us to go back into the same area we just came out of — day after tomorrow. Briefing is at sixteen hundred. I can let Sergeant Roberts know and we can attend if you want."

He read the paper as if I were not there and did not answer.

"That is all," he said in dismissal, and I turned to leave.

"Oh," I said turning back to him. "I stopped by the dispensary. We had so many contacts on that last mission, I checked to see if they had a medic that we could take on this one. They do."

The captain faced me, thrust out his jaw and stood at attention.

"Sergeant Hanson, you are messing vit my var machine!"

Sadly, Captain Heinz Roasch was killed September fourteenth, nineteen seventy-one.

403

Chapter Twenty-Two

DEROS

Leaving the front gate of the FOB in Kontum was one of the most difficult events of my life. It is said that our Special Forces operations were the watershed of life — every event thereafter would be judged against the template of that experience. Danger, courage, loyalty, sacrifice, accomplishments — name any of them, even simple mundane things — were bonds that made us brothers. We drank of the same cup of life. I recalled a story of three prisoners of war in the infamous Japanese camp at Cabanatuan. Like the rest of the emaciated skeletons imprisoned there who went through extreme hardship, these three shared a special challenge. None of the three prisoners had teeth, but one of them had a pair of dentures taken from someone who had passed on. They shared those teeth. One would use them as he ate his meager meal and, finished, he would swish the teeth in his cup of water, then pass them to the next prisoner. That simple act of intimacy and brotherly love repeated day after day was a bond that knit them forever. The bond not only is seen in the simple act of everyday life, but in the act of certain death — as one of our Medal of Honor winners, who, though wounded, gave up his last chance to be pulled out on strings so another soldier could leave on the chopper.

For the last three tours I would nod my farewell to warrior friends as they boarded a helicopter for a mission, etching the last view of their faces, not on the retinas of my eyes, but on the table of my heart, never knowing if we would ever meet again. So also it was that morning at the gate of the camp as I bid goodbye. If we never saw each other again in person, we undoubtedly would when we considered our own personal St. Crispin's Day. We would then roll up our sleeves and show the scars and say in our spirit, "This, I received on a high-speed trail in Laos, and this I received from a sniper in Cambodia, and this was when we rescued a recon team in North Vietnam, and last, this I received dragging a wounded comrade across an LZ to a waiting Huey."

Shortly I would pass through the portal of the compound and hop on a C-130 for Nha Trang to sign out. Norman Doney, my mentor, team leader and friend, would be there, probably at the airplane. He was now the Command Sergeant Major of 5th Special Forces Group. He would hug me as a son but would be formal in the presence of others.

"Sergeant Hanson, today you will dine at my table and we will have steak. We will then go to a movie — they have a new one on base. Then you and I will go and have ice cream. Real ice cream! We will go to the club and you will tell me about your tour and your future and then you will promise to visit me in Oregon when I retire."

But I was still in Kontum. I was at the main gate about to leave the most incredible experience of my life. I waved to the slender Chinese guard in the blue and white helmet liner — the same man who greeted me nearly three years before. About to cross, I heard someone shouting my name.

"Han-Son, Han-Son, Han-Son."

There were several who called — all in unison, "Han-Son." I stopped and looked back. A five-ton idled near the gate, waiting. "Han-Son."

A platoon of fully armed Montagnard tribesmen sat on the flatbed and waved me over. This was my platoon. These were my people!

"Han-Son. We come talk you goodbye."

They became silent, overcome with an emotion these good people rarely expressed. They perhaps thought they would give me a joyous sendoff never realizing that it would be an event of sorrow. They sadly looked at me, drinking my image, never to forget me. Would this moment be forever? Bieh stared with his wounded mouth open. His eyes misted over. I felt like weeping. These were my people. These were my children!

"I will miss you greatly. I will not forget you. I will pray for you."

One of my people who rarely talked said, "Han-Son, stay with us. You be Montagnard."

Bieh swallowed and gathered his emotions. "Han-Son, we give you Montagnard bracelet. We did not carve the tribal markings on it. We from Sedang, Bahnar and Jarai tribes, markings not same."

I slid it on. "I will never take it off." (For more than forty years it was there until the brass wore so thin it simply dropped away.)

My Montagnard team sergeant cleared his throat to speak and the others became silent. He was older than the rest, an elder in his tribe. His arms bore numerous scars of war and his ears had enormous holes in the lobes from earrings he wore in another life. "Han-Son, you are Montagnard!" He tapped his knee with an open hand in emphasis. "You friend Montagnard. You are Montagnard forever."

The men on the flatbed shouted their approval.

I, left to my own proclivity, would have wept openly then and there, but was saved when the driver pressed the pedal and black soot rose from the stack. The huge truck began to move toward the gate. I watched them go and I read sorrow in their faces. They turned right at the gate and I stepped into the street and my eyes never left them. Their faces were all turned toward me. Halfway to the Dak Bla bridge, when individual faces gave way to a whole, I waved one last time. The men on the back of the five-ton waved once more and they disappeared into the haze of the day, and the haze of memory.

I was standing there in the middle of the road caught up in this last farewell. I do not know how long I stood there — like someone at a deathbed refusing to leave until the last breath was gone. And I heard a soft voice next to me.

"Time to go, Sergeant."

Chapter Twenty-Three

FERNANDO

"You know what yer life is?" She said to me. Anger and bitterness and a challenge marked her voice. Her skin was as white as the bed sheets and was as wrinkled also as the sheets from her tossing in her bed. She would not wear her teeth just to please everybody and so it was that her nose nearly touched her chin as she waited for me to answer her challenge. She reminded me of what I thought Babba Yabba, the witch in the Russian fairy tales, would look like.

"Well, do ya?" And she smirked and cackled at me and lowered herself back into the nursing home bed. "Yah, you wouldn't know anything about life."

I stood there beside the bed thinking what to say, for as a Christian I had much to say about life. But she sprang up in bed again as someone who is afraid of the dark does when they hear scratching outside the window. She glared at me with her cloudy grey eyes. The whites around them, I saw, were pale yellow. She grabbed the bed rail with her white hands. Blue veins coursed just under the skin.

"Do ya?"

"Yes, I do Mrs. Olsen. I am a Christian and I know what life is about."

She snorted at me and wiped her nose on her sleeve.

"Nah," she spat and she looked away from me. I was relieved not to look into her eyes. She had a pink mole on her chin with white hairs on it. It quivered before she spoke again.

"Nah! You ask me what your life is? I'll tell ye."

She pointed at the window with her crooked finger. She often thought she was back on the homestead and that the well was just outside. "You take that tin cup offen the pump spout and fill it up and then you put your finger in it. That finger is your life and the water is the world.

I suppose that she waited in her talk to be sure that my mental finger was fully immersed in the cup. She paused and collected herself. The old lady became quiet, almost sad. She looked at me square in the face and said, "Yer life is like when you take yer finger out of that water and you look back into the cup and nobody knows that you were ever there."

She sighed deeply and laid back on the bed. "That's all that I want to say today." And her mouth clamped shut. Her nose would have touched her chin, were it not for her pink mole.

Some of what the old lady said was true. Certainly, what we did was known to God if no human being ever took notice. I know of several SOG heroes who without any fanfare returned to their home town and quietly raised families. They found work as janitors in the local school and pushed a dust mop along the halls, cleaned slop off dining tables, and after hours set up the chairs around the stage for school functions. The lights never shined on them. They never took a bow. No newspaper ever mentioned their names. They would retire, grow old, and die — their finger finally leaving the tin cup at the well. And only then when the town read the obituary, would they discover the sacrifice and heroism of the quiet janitor they barely noticed as he swept the hall.

Some of our guys needed the quiet after our war and they found a spot along a river in a remote place in Alaska, or the Olympic Forest, or on an island in northern Minnesota. They built a cabin, owned a dog named "Shep," and were the uncle the family knew little about.

Some of us were accomplished. One buck sergeant who ran recon became a four-star general. One of us was an owner of Walmart — John Walton. Others were elected to office. Some were accomplished in other ways. Many performed the important duty of raising families — a cornerstone of society.

For many of us, there was a need to see each other at least once a year. We joined the Special Forces Association, and the Special Operations Association and we went to the reunions. We told the old stories and relived the watershed that we shared. We caught up on things; our families, the concern for our country, those who did not make it to reunion that year and would not again, our health. We would find each other and take a seat at those round tables in the convention hall and gaze across at that old man who was so young when it all happened so many decades ago.

A group of us were sitting at the tables in the hospitality room and talking. From a few feet away the voices of the group sounded like a soft murmur. We were reminiscing when someone from the edge of the group played a song from his machine. The words were written by ABBA and the first notes of the instruments hushed the area. Most of us are half deaf from the war but every syllable of the words was heard.

> *Can you hear the drums, Fernando?*
> *I remember long ago another starry night like this*
> *In the firelight, Fernando*
> *You were humming to yourself and softly strumming on your guitar*
> *I could hear the distant drums*
> *And sounds of bugle calls were coming from afar*
>
> *They were closer now, Fernando*
> *Every hour, every minute, seemed to last eternally*
> *I was so afraid, Fernando*
> *We were young and full of life and none of us prepared to die*

And I'm not ashamed to say
The roar of guns and cannons almost made me cry

There was something in the air that night
The stars were bright Fernando
They were shining there for you and me
For liberty, Fernando

Though we never thought that we could lose
There's no regret
If I had to do the same again
I would, my friend, Fernando
If I had to do the same again
I would, my friend, Fernando

I looked up without moving my head — only my eyes looked up and looked across the table. The others were listening to those transformational words too — old men now, men who had done it and slept under those same bright stars.

Now we're old and grey, Fernando
Since many years, I haven't seen a rifle in your hand
Can you hear the drums, Fernando
Do you still recall the fateful night we crossed the Rio
Grande
I can see it in your eyes
How proud you were to fight for freedom in this land

There was something in the air that night
The stars were bright, Fernando
They were shining there for you and me
For liberty Fernando

Though we never thought that we could lose
There's no regret
If I had to do the same again
I would, my friend, Fernando...

We were quiet and perhaps a little embarrassed that we let our emotions go for a time. I heard a sniff in the room but did not look to see who it was, for that old man simply expressed my own heart. Most of us had to clear our throats before we talked again. And I recalled what old Mrs. Olsen cackled in that metal bed in the old folks' home. "Yah, ya wouldn't know anything about life."

My mind made the synapse from the two young privates in the song to *Lonesome Dove*.

"Do you guys remember," I said, "how Augustus McCrae was dying in that bed from gangrene? Sepsis from the Indian arrows had taken one of his legs and he wouldn't let them take the other. His lifetime friend, Woodrow Call was at the bedside and Gus was getting weaker and weaker. What a life they had lived! Gus goes more deeply into sleep and softly closes his eyes. Call thinks that he is gone and he strokes his brow and cheek and in utter sorrow whispers, 'Augustus.'

"Gus' eyes flutter and slowly open. He looks at Woodrow. Perhaps he has been dreaming of one of their adventures. A weary smile appears and he says, 'Woodrow, it's been quite a party, ain't it!'

"He closes his eyes one last time."

One of the guys at the table had lost weight since the last year and had an oxygen tube under his nose. He slowly gestured with his arm, his hand scribing a circle around us. His breath came in puffs but he tried to fill his chest for what he had to say "Yes fellers. It has been quite a show."

About the Author

Photo courtesy of Rafe Hanson

Dale Hanson is an accomplished sculptor who has led a life of adventure and enjoyed numerous accomplishments. He is a black belt martial artist, an author, a pilot of fixed wing and glider airplanes, has flown aerobatics and is a Special Forces underwater diver. He is a disabled veteran and a member of MENSA.

During the Vietnam War, Dale was a highly decorated Green Beret who served three years as a commando in the famous SOG program, whose mission involved extremely dangerous raids far behind enemy lines. This unit received more decorations and suffered higher rates of casualties than any American unit since the American Civil War. On one of these raids, Dale earned the first of several purple hearts as his right hand was mangled by a burst of machine gun fire. It is ironic that he became a sculptor, a field in which one's hands are so critical.

Printed in the USA
CPSIA information can be obtained
at www.ICGtesting.com
LVHW091040011023
759814LV00023B/1311/J